2018 SUPPLEMENT TO FOURTEENTH EDITIONS
MODERN CRIMINAL PROCEDURE
BASIC CRIMINAL PROCEDURE
AND
ADVANCED CRIMINAL PROCEDURE

■ ■ ■

Yale Kamisar
Clarence Darrow Distinguished University Professor Emeritus of Law,
University of Michigan
Distinguished Professor Emeritus of Law, University of San Diego

Wayne R. LaFave
David C. Baum Professor Emeritus of Law
and Center for Advanced Study Professor Emeritus,
University of Illinois

Jerold H. Israel
Alene and Allan F. Smith Professor Emeritus of Law,
University of Michigan
Emeritus Ed Rood Eminent Scholar in Trial Advocacy and Procedure,
University of Florida, Fredric G. Levin College of Law

Nancy J. King
Lee S. & Charles A. Speir Professor of Law,
Vanderbilt University Law School

Orin S. Kerr
Frances R. & John J. Duggan Distinguished Professor
University of Southern California Gould School of Law

Eve Brensike Primus
Professor of Law,
University of Michigan

AMERICAN CASEBOOK SERIES®

WEST
ACADEMIC
PUBLISHING

The publisher is not engaged in rendering legal or other professional advice, and this publication is not a substitute for the advice of an attorney. If you require legal or other expert advice, you should seek the services of a competent attorney or other professional.

American Casebook Series is a trademark registered in the U.S. Patent and Trademark Office.

© 2015–2017 LEG, Inc. d/b/a West Academic
© 2018 LEG, Inc. d/b/a West Academic
    444 Cedar Street, Suite 700
    St. Paul, MN 55101
    1-877-888-1330

West, West Academic Publishing, and West Academic are trademarks of West Publishing Corporation, used under license.

Printed in the United States of America

ISBN: 978-1-64242-024-1

PREFACE

This Supplement to the fourteenth editions of *Modern Criminal Procedure*, *Basic Criminal Procedure* and *Advanced Criminal Procedure* contains all significant cases decided by the United States Supreme Court since publication of those fourteenth editions. It also includes a number of lower court cases and citations to, or extracts from, recent academic commentary. This volume also contains Appendices A through D, containing selected provisions from the U.S. Constitution and U.S. Code, and current and pending provisions of the Federal Rules of Criminal Procedure.

YALE KAMISAR
WAYNE R. LAFAVE
JEROLD H. ISRAEL
NANCY J. KING
ORIN S. KERR
EVE BRENSIKE PRIMUS

July 2018

TABLE OF CONTENTS

PREFACE III

TABLE OF CASES XI

PART 1. INTRODUCTION

Chapter 1. On Studying the Legal Regulation of the Criminal Justice Process 3
§ 2.   The Steps in the Process 3
     B.   Steps in the Process 3

Chapter 2. Sources of Criminal Procedure Law 5
§ 2.   The Problem of Bodily Extractions: Another Look at the "Due Process" and
     "Selective Incorporation" Approaches 5
     Jerold Israel, *Free-Standing Due Process and Criminal Procedure* 5

**Chapter 3. Some General Reflections on the Constitutionalization of Criminal
     Procedure** 7
Justice Stephen Breyer—Dissenting in **GLOSSIP V. GROSS** 7
Justice Antonin Scalia—Concurring in **GLOSSIP V. GROSS**................................8
Justice Clarence Thomas—Concurring in **GLOSSIP V. GROSS** 9
Justice Sonia Sotomayor—Dissenting in **UTAH V. STRIEFF**..............................11
Rachel A. Harmon, *Legal Remedies for Police Misconduct*, in Academy for Justice,
     A Report on Scholarship and Criminal Justice Reform (Erik Luna, ed. 2017)..............12
U.S. Dept. of Justice, Bureau of Justice Statistics, Local Police Departments, 2013:
     Personnel, Policies, and Practices 17
U.S. Dept. of Justice, Bureau of Justice Statistics Special Report: State and Local Law
     Enforcement Training Academies, 2006 (Revised 4/14/2009) 18

Chapter 4. The Right to Counsel 21
§ 1.   The Right to Appointed Counsel and Related Problems..............................21
     A.   The Right to Appointed Counsel in Criminal Proceedings.....................21
     B.   The "Beginnings" of the Right to Counsel: "Criminal Prosecutions" and
        "Critical Stages" 22
§ 5.   The Right to "Counsel of Choice"...23
     CAPLIN & DRYSDALE, CHARTERED v. UNITED STATES 23
     LUIS v. UNITED STATES...23

Chapter 5. The Performance of Counsel 25
§ 2.   The *Strickland* Standards..25
     WEAVER V. MASSACHUSETTS 25
§ 4.   The *Cronic* Exceptions and Other Possible Per Se Violations.....................32
§ 6.   Client Control...33
     MCCOY V. LOUISIANA 34

PART 2. POLICE PRACTICES

Chapter 6. Arrest, Search and Seizure.. **45**
§ 1.   The Exclusionary Rule 45
§ 2.   Protected Areas and Interests 45
       CARPENTER V. UNITED STATES...45
       COLLINS v. VIRGINIA 51
§ 3.   "Probable Cause" 52
§ 4.   Search Warrants...54
       C.   Special Problems: Computer Searches 54
§ 5.   Warrantless Arrests and Searches of the Person 56
       BIRCHFIELD v. NORTH DAKOTA 57
§ 7.   Warrantless Seizures and Searches of Vehicles and Containers 59
§ 8.   Stop and Frisk..59
       A.   Police Action Short of a Seizure 59
       B.   Grounds for Temporary Seizure for Investigation.........................59
       C.   Permissible Extent and Scope of Temporary Seizure.....................61
            RODRIGUEZ v. UNITED STATES...61
       E.   Protective Search 64
§ 9.   Administrative Inspections and Regulatory Searches: More on Balancing the Need
       Against the Invasion of Privacy..66
§ 10. Consent Searches...69
       A.   The Nature of "Consent" 69
            BIRCHFIELD v. NORTH DAKOTA..69
       B.   Third Party Consent 71

Chapter 8. Network Surveillance.. **73**
§ 1.   The Fourth Amendment...73
       B.   Rights in Non-Content Information...73
§ 2.   Statutory Privacy Laws..79
       C.   The Pen Register Statute..79
       D.   The Stored Communications Act..79

Chapter 9. Police Interrogation and Confessions **81**
§ 2.   The *Miranda* "Revolution" 81
§ 3.   *Miranda*, the Privilege Against Compelled Self-Incrimination and Fourteenth
       Amendment Due Process: When Does a Violation of These Safeguards Occur?..........86
§ 4.   The *Patane* and *Seibert* Cases: Is Physical Evidence or a "Second Confession"
       Derived From a Failure to Comply with the *Miranda* Rules Admissible? The
       Court's Answers Shed Light on *Dickerson* 87
§ 6.   The "Due Process"—"Voluntariness" Test Revisited......................................88
       A.   *Miller v. Fenton*: What Kinds of Trickery or Deception, if Any, May the Police
            Employ After a Suspect Has Waived His Rights? 88
       B.   *Colorado v. Connelly*: Did the Court Decline to Expand the "Voluntariness"
            Test or Did It Revise the Test Significantly? 88
            Richard A. Leo, *Police Interrogation and American Justice* 90
            Causes of False Confessions..90
            Proposed Reforms 93

Lawrence Rosenthal, *Against Orthodoxy: Miranda is Not Prophylactic and the Constitution is Not Perfect*...94

§ 7.   *Massiah* Revisited; *Massiah* and *Miranda* Compared and Contrasted.....................96

   A.   The Revivification of *Massiah* 96

Chapter 10. Lineups, Showups and Other Pre-Trial Identification Procedures.... 99

§ 1.   *Wade* and *Gilbert*: Constitutional Concern About the Dangers Involved in Eyewitness Identifications 99

§ 4.   Social Science Research on Identification Procedures and the Need for Reform.........99

Chapter 11. Grand Jury Investigations 103

§ 3.   Other Objections to the Investigation 103

§ 5.   Self-Incrimination and the Compelled Production of Documents 103

   B.   The Act-of-Production Doctrine... 103

Chapter 12. The Scope of the Exclusionary Rules 105

§ 1.   "Standing" to Object to the Admission of Evidence.. 105

   A.   The Fourth Amendment 105

       BYRD v. UNITED STATES 105

§ 2.   The "Fruit of the Poisonous Tree"... 107

   A.   Fourth Amendment Violations... 107

       UTAH v. STRIEFF 107

   D.   Sixth Amendment Violations 109

PART 3. THE COMMENCEMENT OF FORMAL PROCEEDINGS

Chapter 13. Pretrial Release.. 113

§ 1.   The Right to Bail; Pretrial Release Procedures.. 113

Chapter 14. The Decision Whether to Prosecute... 115

§ 2.   Some Views on Discretion in the Criminal Process and the Prosecutor's Discretion in Particular.. 115

       A.B.A. Standards for Criminal Justice: Prosecution Function.......................... 115

§ 3.   Challenging the Prosecutor's Discretion 116

   B.   The Decision to Prosecute.. 116

       UNITED STATES v. DAVIS 116

   C.   The Diversion Decision 117

Chapter 15. The Preliminary Hearing.. 119

§ 4.   Preliminary Hearing Procedures... 119

   A.   Application of the Rules of Evidence.. 119

       CITY OF HAYS, KANSAS v. VOGT.. 119

Chapter 16. Grand Jury Review 125

§ 3.   Challenges to the Evidence Before the Grand Jury 125

Chapter 19. Joinder and Severance... 127

§ 2.   Failure to Join Related Offenses 127

       CURRIER v. VIRGINIA.. 127

Chapter 20. Speedy Trial and Other Speedy Disposition.......................... 129
§ 2.   Other Speedy Disposition.. 129
        BETTERMAN v. MONTANA 129

PART 4. THE ADVERSARY SYSTEM AND THE DETERMINATION OF GUILT OR INNOCENCE

Chapter 22. Guilty Pleas 133
§ 1.   Some Views of Negotiated Pleas... 133
     C.   Accurate and Fair Results 133
§ 2.   Rejected, Kept and Broken Bargains; Unrealized Expectations 133
        HUGHES v. UNITED STATES 136
§ 3.   The Role and Responsibility of Defense Counsel.................... 138
        LEE v. UNITED STATES 139
§ 6.   The Effect of a Guilty Plea 140
        CLASS V. UNITED STATES 140

Chapter 23. Trial by Jury 147
§ 1.   Right to Jury Trial.. 147
§ 2.   Jury Selection 147
     B.   Selecting the Jury from the Venire: Voir Dire 147
        PEÑA-RODRIGUEZ v. COLORADO 147

Chapter 25. The Criminal Trial.. 151
§ 2.   Confrontation and Testimonial Hearsay................................ 151
§ 3.   Rights to Remain Silent and to Testify 153
§ 5.   The Right to a Public Trial.. 154
        PRESLEY V. GEORGIA.. 154

Chapter 26. Reprosecution and Double Jeopardy 159
§ 1.   Reprosecution After Mistrial 159
     B.   Defense Consent to Mistrial 159
§ 4.   Reprosecution by a Different Sovereign................................ 159
        PUERTO RICO V. SANCHEZ VALLE ET AL. 159

Chapter 27. Sentencing 163
§ 1.   Introduction to Sentencing.. 163
     A.   Purposes of Punishment 163
     B.   Types of Sentences 163
     C.   Who Sets the Sentence? 165
§ 2.   Allocating and Controlling Sentencing Discretion 165
     A.   Mandatory Minimum Sentences 165
     B.   Sentencing Guidelines 165
§ 3.   Constitutional Limits on Sentencing Procedure.................... 166
     A.   Information Considered in Setting the Sentence........ 166
     D.   Jury Trial and Burden of Proof 166

PART 5. APPEALS, POST-CONVICTION REVIEW

Chapter 28. Appeals **169**
§ 1.   The Defendant's Right to Appeal 169
§ 4.   Review for Claims Not Raised on Time 169
§ 5.   The Harmless Error Rule 171
    B.   Constitutional Error 171

Chapter 29. Post-Conviction Review: Federal Habeas Corpus **173**
§ 2.   Issues Cognizable 173
§ 4.   Claims Foreclosed by Procedural Default 173
§ 5.   Retroactivity—Which Law Applies? 173
§ 6.   Standards for Reviewing State Court Interpretations and Applications of Federal
    Law 174
    A.   Contrary Decisions and Unreasonable Applications 174

Appendix A. Selected Provisions of the United States Constitution **175**

Appendix B. Selected Federal Statutory Provisions **179**
Wire and Electronic Communications Interception and Interception of Oral
    Communications 179
Stored Wire and Electronic Communications and Transactional Records Access 197
Searches and Seizures 204
Bail Reform Act of 1984 205
Speedy Trial Act of 1974 (As Amended) 215
Jencks Act 220
Litigation Concerning Sources of Evidence 221
Criminal Appeals Act of 1970 (As Amended) 222
Crime Victims' Rights 222
Jury Selection and Service Act of 1968 (As Amended) 225
Habeas Corpus 230
Privacy Protection Act of 1980 241
Guidelines 245
Foreign Intelligence Surveillance Act 247

**Appendix C. Federal Rules of Criminal Procedure for the United States
District Courts** **257**

**Appendix D. Pending Amendments to the Federal Rules of Criminal
Procedure** **319**

TABLE OF CASES

The principal cases are in bold type.

Abbate v. United States, 161
Adams v. Williams, 11
Aleman v. Village of Hanover Park, 88
Alston, State v., 85
Are, United States v., 83
Arizona v. Fulminante, 26, 38
Atkins v. Virginia, 174
Atwater v. Lago Vista, 11
Atwood, State v., 53
Auld, State v., 166
Bain, United States v., 50, 107
Banks-Harvey, State v., 59
Bartkus v. Illinois, 161
Bastaldo, Commonwealth v., 100
Belleau v. Wall, 45
Betterman v. Montana, 129
Bevel, State v., 86
Birchfield v. North Dakota, 57, 69
Black, United States v., 60
Blackledge v. Perry, 140
Bonilla, United States v., 84
Brathwaite, United States v., 83
Bridgers v. Dretke, 81
Brignoni-Ponce, United States v., 11
Broce, United States v., 141, 143
Broussard, Ex parte, 146
Brown v. Illinois, 107
Brumfield v. Cain, 174
Bryant, United States v., 22
Buck v. Davis, 166
Burgett v. Texas, 22
Byrd v. United States, 105
Cain v. City of New Orleans, 164
Calandra, United States v., 126
California Bankers Assn. v. Shultz, 48
Camara v. Municipal Court, 68
Capers, United States v., 87
Caplin & Drysdale, Chartered v. United States, 23
Carillo, United States v., 83
Carloss, United States v., 52
Carpenter v. United States, 45, 73
Carpenter, United States v., 73
Carter v. People, 81
Carter, State v., 36
Chrisicos, State v., 83
Class v. United States, 140, 169
Cleverly, State v., 63
Collins v. Virginia, 51
Colon v. State, 83
Colondres, Commonwealth v., 52
Cooke v. State, 35
Cremer, State v., 120
Cruz, State v., 82
Cummings, People v., 63
Currier v. Virginia, 127

Daniels, United States v., 84
Darryl P., In re, 97
Davila v. Davis, 173
Davis v. Ayala, 149
Davis, People v., 83
Davis, United States v., 116
Demesme, State v., 85
Devenpeck v. Alford, 11
Dickson, State v., 99
Dionisio, United States v., 48
District of Columbia v. Wesby, 53
Doe, United States v., 136
Donovan v. Dewey, 67
Donovan v. Lone Steer, Inc., 48, 68, 77
Dorelas, Commonwealth v., 55
Dowling v. United States, 5
Drury v. State, 82
Elizalde, People v., 82
Farfan-Galvan, State v., 138
Fisher, People v., 136
Fleming v. Metrish, 84
Flick v. Meko, 84
Florence v. Board of Chosen Freeholders of County of Burlington, 12
Flores, People v., 85
Florida v. Bostick, 11
Florida v. Harris, 53
Florida v. Nixon, 34
Foster v. Chatman, 149
Fried, In re, 126
Garcia, United States v., 84
Genao, United States v., 82
Gilkeson, United States v., 87
Globe Newspaper Co v. Superior Court, 156
Glossip v. Gross, 7, 8, 9
Gonzalez v. United States, 34, 36
Grady v. North Carolina, 45
Grice, People v., 97
Grice, State v., 50
H.V., In re, 87
Haak, United States v., 88
Hale v. Henkel, 48
Haring v. Prosise, 141
Harris v. New York, 41
Harris, State v., 81
Haynes v. United States, 140
Hays, Kansas, City of v. Vogt, 119
Heath v. Alabama, 160
Heien v. North Carolina, 11
Heron, United States v., 87
Higazy v. Templeton, 121
Hill v. United States, 82, 96
Hoey, State v., 85
Holt, United States v., 62
Horton, United States v., 54
Hubbard, State v., 81

Hughes v. United States, 136
Hurst v. Florida, 166
Hyde, People v., 71
Illinois v. Cummings, 64
Illinois v. Wardlow, 11
Jackson, Ex parte, 77
Jenkins, United States v., 85
Johnson v. United States, 53, 137
Jones v. Barnes, 33, 36
Jones v. United States, 59
Jones, State v., 52
Jones, United States v., 83
Keysor v. Kentucky, 86
Knapp, State v., 87
Kolsuz, United States v., 69
Koons v. United States, 137
Kuren v. Luzerne County, 32
Lawson, State v., 86
Lee v. United States, 139
Lee, United States v., 85
Liulama, State v., 97
Los Angeles, City of v. Lyons, 14
Los Angeles, City of v. Patel, 66
Luce v. United States, 154
Luis v. United States, 23
Luker, United States v., 83
Mable, Ex parte, 146
Manuel v. City of Joliet, Ill., 56
Marks v. United States, 87
Martin, Commonwealth v., 87
Martinez, Commonwealth v., 54
Maryland v. King, 12
Mateo-Medina, United States v., 10
Mathews v. Eldridge, 5
Mathews, People v., 81
McCoy v. Louisiana, 34
McPhaul v. United States, 48
Medina v. California, 5
Menna v. New York, 140
Miller, United States v., 48
Mitchell v. United States, 122
Molina-Isidoro, United States v., 69
Molina-Martinez v. United States, 169
Monell v. Dep't of Soc. Servs., 13
Monsanto, United States v., 23
Montgomery v. Louisiana, 173
Moore v. Madigan, 64
Morales Diaz v. State, 139
Morrison, United States v., 84
Morton Salt Co., United States v., 48
Murchison, In re, 149
Nelson v. Colorado, 5
Nesbeth, United States v., 165
New York v. Hill, 41
Newton, Town of v. Rummery, 133
Nix v. Whiteside, 37
Northrup v. City of Toledo Police Department,
  60
Ohio v. Clark, 152
Oklahoma Press Publishing Co. v. Walling, 48,
  77
Oliver, In re, 156

Olmstead v. United States, 48
Oquendo-Rivas, United States v., 84
Overmyer, Commonwealth v., 53
Paetsch, United States v., 60
Palmberg, Ex parte, 146
Payne, United States v., 82
Peña-Rodriguez v. Colorado, 147
Perry, State v., 53
Perry, United States v., 157
Peterson, State v., 87
Powell, United States v., 48
Presley v. Georgia, 154
Press-Enterprise Co. v. Superior Court of
  California, Riverside County, 155
Price v. U.S. Department of Justice Attorney
  Office, 133
Provost, State v., 83
Puerto Rico v. Sanchez Valle et al., 159
Reid, People v., 58
Reyes, United States v., 82
Rhode Island v. Innis, 96
Rippo v. Baker, 149
Risk, State v., 85
Ritchison, United States v., 137
Robinson v. State, 53
Robinson, United States v., 64
Rodriguez v. United States, 61
Rodriguez, United States v., 45, 59
Romano, State v., 71
Rommy, United States v., 96
Rosales-Mireles v. United States, 170
Salinas v. Texas, 85
Sanchez, State v., 97
Sanchez-Gomez, United States v., 151
Sanney, State v., 136
Sawyer, State v., 82
Scarpa, United States v., 97
Schlingloff, United States v., 54
Schmidt v. State, 145
Sears v. Maryland, 85
See v. City of Seattle, 48, 68
Seppala, United States v., 85
Shinaul, People v., 138
Smith, Commonwealth v., 63
Smith, State v., 82
Sokolow, United States v., 11
Sornberger v. City of Knoxville, Illinois, 121
Stoot v. City of Everett, 121
Suggs, United States v., 82
Sullivan v. Louisiana, 28
Talkington, State v., 107
Teeter, State v., 120
Thomas v. Eighth Judicial Dist. Court, 159
Thompson, State v., 58
Timberlake, State v., 59
Tollett v. Henderson, 140, 142
Trapp, United States v., 84
Trop v. Dulles, 9
Tucker, United States v., 22
Tumey v. Ohio, 28
Turner v. United States, 22, 138
Utah v. Strieff, 11, 107

Vallar, United States v., 82
Vanhollenbeke, State v., 71
Virgen-Moreno, United States v., 82
Vogt v. City of Hays, Kansas, 87, 119, 120, 121
Waller v. Florida, 161
Waller v. Georgia, 155
Warren, Commonwealth v., 10
Warren, United States v., 81
Warshak, United States v., 77
Washington, United States v., 82
Weaver v. Massachusetts, 25, 156, 169, 171
Welch v. United States, 173
Wheeler, United States v., 159
Whren v. United States, 11
Williams v. Pennsylvania, 149, 171
Williams, United States v., 82
Wisconsin v. Knapp, 87
Wood v. Ercole, 85
Yates v. Evatt, 39
Young v. State, 101
Ziglar v. Abbasi, 45

2018 SUPPLEMENT TO
FOURTEENTH EDITIONS
MODERN CRIMINAL PROCEDURE
BASIC CRIMINAL PROCEDURE
AND
ADVANCED CRIMINAL PROCEDURE

PART 1

INTRODUCTION

■ ■ ■

CHAPTER 1

ON STUDYING THE LEGAL REGULATION OF THE CRIMINAL JUSTICE PROCESS

■ ■ ■

§ 2.   THE STEPS IN THE PROCESS

B.   STEPS IN THE PROCESS

14th ed., p. 16; substitute for the last sentence in the Note on Step 17:

As for the outcomes on defense appeals as a matter of right, see Supp. p. 169.

CHAPTER 2

SOURCES OF CRIMINAL PROCEDURE LAW

■ ■ ■

§ 2. THE PROBLEM OF BODILY EXTRACTIONS: ANOTHER LOOK AT THE "DUE PROCESS" AND "SELECTIVE INCORPORATION" APPROACHES

14th ed., p. 31; replace Note 4 with the following:

4. ***"Free-standing" procedural due process claims.*** Whereas *County of Sacramento* addresses the continued vitality of free-standing *substantive* due process claims (and asks whether the state's behavior was "conscience-shocking"), the tests for addressing free-standing *procedural* due process claims are different. The traditional test for addressing questions of procedural due process comes from *Mathews v. Eldridge*, 424 U.S. 319 (1976). Under the *Mathews* balancing test, a court evaluates (a) the private interest affected; (b) the risk of erroneous deprivation of that interest through the procedures used; and (c) the governmental interest at stake in order to determine if the procedures in question are constitutionally sufficient. In *Medina v. California*, 505 U.S. 427 (1992), however, the Supreme Court adopted a different procedural due process test for "assessing the validity of state procedural rules [that] are part of the criminal process." In cases involving challenges to procedural rules about the burden of proof, the admissibility of evidence, or other aspects of state criminal process, *Medina* asks whether the state practice "offends some principle of justice so rooted in the traditions and conscience of our people to be ranked as fundamental."

For a recent case that raises questions about whether *Mathews* or *Medina* provides the right framework, see *Nelson v. Colorado*, 137 S.Ct. 1249 (2017) (holding that a state is obligated to refund fees, court costs, and restitution taken from a defendant after that defendant's criminal conviction is invalidated by a reviewing court and no retrial occurs). Justice Ginsburg, writing for the majority, used the *Mathews* balancing approach to strike down Colorado's procedural scheme for violating defendants' due process rights. The majority believed that this was a case about the continuing deprivation of the defendants' property rather than a case involving state criminal procedures. In contrast, Justice Alito, concurring, would have reached a similar result using the *Medina* standard. He believed that the presumption of innocence was at issue—a core feature of criminal procedure law that necessitated application of the *Medina* standard.

5. ***Continued application of "free-standing" due process.*** Jerold Israel, *Free-Standing Due Process and Criminal Procedure: The Supreme Court's Search for Interpretive Guidelines*, 45 St. Louis U.L.J. 303 (2001), reviewed the Court's application of the *Medina* standard in the post-incorporation decades. The article concludes that while the Court has set forth various guidelines for determining the independent content of due process, it has not been consistent in applying those guidelines. The Court has noted that "beyond the specific guarantees enumerated in the Bill of Rights, the Due Process Clause has limited operation" and will be "construed very narrowly." *Dowling v. United States*, 493 U.S. 342 (1990). This position rests on the ground that, since the "Bill of Rights speaks in explicit terms to many aspects of criminal procedure," the expansion of constitutional regulation under the "open-ended rubric of the Due Process Clause * * * invite[s] undue interference with both considered legislative judgments and the careful balance that the constitution strikes between liberty and order." *Medina v. California*, supra.

5

Notwithstanding such statements, free-standing due process has emerged as: (1) the dominant source of constitutional regulation of the pre-trial and post-trial stages of the process (most notable as to guilty pleas and sentencing); (2) a major source of constitutional regulation of the trial; (3) a lesser, but still significant source of regulation of police practices (see e.g., ch. 10, § 3). So too, while the Court has repeatedly stressed that the historical acceptance of a practice is a strong indicator that the practice does not offend fundamental fairness, it has on various occasions relied on deductive reasoning (often tied to the character of a "fair hearing") to hold unconstitutional practices that were entirely consistent with the common law (typically without discussing historical acceptance). Most often, the Court has described free-standing due process as looking to the circumstances of the particular case and resting, at least in part, on fact-sensitive determinations (particularly as to a likelihood of prejudicial impact), but in several areas, the Court has relied on free-standing due process to formulate per se prohibitions and automatically presume prejudice. The Court at times has advance a procedural due process counterpart of *Graham v. Connor*, but at other times has turned to free-standing due process without first considering the possible application of a specific guarantee (indeed, even announcing a preference for relying on free-standing due process in *Pennsylvania v. Ritchie*, 14th ed., p. 1178).

CHAPTER 3

SOME GENERAL REFLECTIONS ON THE CONSTITUTIONALIZATION OF CRIMINAL PROCEDURE

■ ■ ■

14th ed., p. 51; after extract from Justice Scalia's concurring opinion in Kansas v. Marsh, add:

JUSTICE STEPHEN BREYER—DISSENTING IN GLOSSIP V. GROSS
135 S.Ct. 2726 (2016).

[Oklahoma death-row inmates maintained that the use of midazolam in administering capital punishment violated the Eighth Amendment. The U.S. Supreme Court disagreed, concluding, inter alia, that the death-row inmates had failed to establish that any risk of harm was substantial when compared to a known and available alternatives method of execution. Justice Alito delivered the opinion of the Court, in which Chief Justice Roberts and Justices Scalia, Kennedy and Thomas joined. Justice Scalia filed a concurring opinion, in which Justice Thomas joined. Justice Thomas filed a concurring opinion, in which Justice Scalia joined. Justice Sotomayor filed a dissenting opinion, in which Justices Ginsburg, Breyer and Kagan joined. Justice Breyer wrote a dissenting opinion, in which Justice Ginsburg joined.]

Dissenting Justice Breyer, joined by Ginsburg, J., called for a "full briefing" on "whether the death penalty violates the Constitution." According to Justice Breyer, "[t]oday's administration of the death penalty involves three fundamental constitutional defects: (1) serious unreliability (2) arbitrariness in application, and (3) unconscionably long delays that undermine the death penalty's penological purposes. Perhaps as a result, (4) most places within the United States have abandoned its use."

Justice Breyer went on to describe "each of these considerations, emphasizing changes that have occurred during the past four decades." "[I]t is those changes, taken together with my own 20 years of experience on this Court, that lead me to believe that the death penalty, in and of itself, now likely constitutes a legally prohibited 'cruel and unusual punishmen[t].' U.S. Const., Amdt. 8."

Breyer noted that one of the constitutional difficulties "resulting from lengthy delays is that those delays undermine the death penalty's penological rationale, perhaps irreparably so. The rationale for capital punishment, as for any punishment, classically rests upon society's need to secure deterrence, incapacitation, retribution, or rehabilitation. Capital punishment by definition does not rehabilitate. It does, of course, incapacitate the offender. But the major alternative to capital punishment—namely, life in prison without the possibility of parole—also incapacitates."

Recently, noted Breyer, the National Research Council "reviewed 30 years of empirical evidence and concluded that it was insufficient to establish a deterrent effect and thus should 'not be used to inform' discussion about the deterrent value of the death penalty."

To put it another way, "an offender who is sentenced to death is two or three times more likely to find his sentence overturned or commuted than to be executed; and he has a good chance of dying from natural causes before any execution (or exoneration) can take place. In a word, executions are *rare*. And an individual contemplating a crime but evaluating the potential punishment would know that, in any event, he faces a potential punishment of life without parole."

Breyer recognized that "[r]etribution is a valid penological goal." But he maintained that "[t]he relevant question here * * * is whether a 'community's sense of retribution' can often find vindication in 'a death that comes,' if at all, 'only several decades after the crime was committed.' "

According to Breyer, "the fact of lengthy delays undermines any effort to justify the death penalty in terms of its prevalence when the Founders wrote the Eighth Amendment. When the Founders wrote the Constitution, there were no 20- or 30-year delays. Executions took place soon after sentencing."

"Why can't Congress or the States deal directly with the delay problem? The answer is that shortening delay is much more difficult than one might think. * * * For one thing, delays have helped to make application of the death penalty more reliable. * * * [I]t is difficult for judges, as it would be difficult for anyone, *not* to apply legal requirements punctiliously when the consequences of failing to do so my well be death, particularly the death of an innocent person. * * * "

JUSTICE ANTONIN SCALIA—CONCURRING IN GLOSSIP V. GROSS
135 S.Ct. 2726 (2016).

I join the opinion of the Court, and write to respond to Justice Breyer's plea for judicial abolition of the death penalty.

Welcome to Groundhog Day. The scene is familiar: Petitioners, sentenced to die for the crimes they committed (including, in the case of one petitioner since put to death, raping and murdering an 11-month-old baby), come before this Court asking us to nullify their sentences as "cruel and unusual" under the Eighth Amendment. They rely on this provision because it is the only provision they can rely on. They were charged by a sovereign State with murder. They were afforded counsel and tried before a jury of their peers—tried twice, once to determine whether they were guilty and once to determine whether death was the appropriate sentence. They were duly convicted and sentenced. * * *

Even accepting Justice Breyer's rewriting of the Eighth Amendment, his argument is full of internal contradictions and (it must be said) gobbledy-gook. He says that the death penalty is cruel because it is unreliable; but it is *convictions*, not *punishments*, that are unreliable. Moreover, the "pressure on police, prosecutors, and jurors to secure a conviction," which he claims increases the risk of wrongful convictions in capital cases, flows from the nature of the crime, not the punishment that follows its commission.

* * * If [Justice Breyer] thinks the death penalty not much more harsh (and hence not much more retributive), why is he so keen to get rid of it? With all due respect, whether the death penalty and life imprisonment constitute more or-less equivalent retribution is a question far above the judiciary's pay grade. Perhaps Justice Breyer is more forgiving—or more enlightened—than those who, like Kant, believe that death is the only just punishment for taking a life. I would not presume to tell parents whose life has been forever altered by the brutal murder of a child that life imprisonment is punishment enough.

And finally, Justice Breyer speculates that it does not "seem likely" that the death penalty has a "significant" deterrent effect. It seems very likely to me, and there are statistical studies that say so [citing many studies]. [We] federal judges live in a world apart from the vast majority of Americans. After work, we retire to homes in placid suburbia or to high-rise co-ops with guards at the door. We are not confronted with the threat of violence that is ever present in many Americans' everyday lives. The suggestion that the incremental deterrent effect of capital punishment does not seem "significant" reflects, it seems to me, a let-them-eat cake obliviousness to the needs of others. Let the People decide how much incremental deterrence is appropriate.

Of course, this delay is a problem of the Court's own making. As Justice Breyer concedes, for more than 160 years, capital sentences were carried out in an average of two years or less. But by 2014, he tells us, it took an average of 18 years to carry out a death sentence. What happened in the intervening years? Nothing other than the proliferation of labyrinthine restrictions on capital punishment, promulgated by this Court under an interpretation of the Eighth Amendment that empowered it to divine "the evolving standards of decency that mark the progress of a maturing society," *Trop v. Dulles*, 356 U.S. 86, 101 (1958) (plurality opinion)—a task for which we are eminently ill suited. Indeed, for the past two decades, Justice Breyer has been the Drum Major in this parade. * * *

Capital punishment presents moral questions that philosophers, theologians, and statesmen have grappled with for millennia. The Framers of our Constitution disagreed bitterly [about capital punishment]. For that reason, they handled it the same way they handled many other controversial issues: they left it to the People to decide. By arrogating to himself the power to overturn that decision, Justice Breyer does not just reject the death penalty, he rejects the Enlightenment.

JUSTICE CLARENCE THOMAS—CONCURRING IN GLOSSIP V. GROSS
135 S.Ct. 2726 (2016).

There is a reason the choice between life and death, within legal limits, is left to the jurors and judges who sit through the trial, and not to legal elites (or law students). That reason is memorialized not once, but twice, in our Constitution: Article III guarantees that "[t]he Trial of all Crimes, except in cases of Impeachment, shall be by Jury" and that "such Trial shall be held in the State where the said Crimes shall have been committed." Art. III, § 2, cl. 3. And the Sixth Amendment promises that "[i]n all criminal prosecutions, the accused shall enjoy the right to a . . . trial, by an impartial jury of the State and district wherein the crime shall have been committed." Those provisions ensure that capital defendants are given the option to be sentenced by a jury of their peers who, collectively, are better situated to make the moral judgment between life and death than are the products of contemporary American law schools.

It should come as no surprise, then, that the primary explanation a regression analysis revealed for the gap between the egregiousness scores and the actual sentences was not the race or sex of the offender or victim, but the locality in which the crime was committed. What is more surprising is that Justice Breyer considers this factor to be evidence of arbitrariness. The constitutional provisions just quoted, which place such decisions in the hands of jurors and trial courts located where "the crime shall have been committed," seem deliberately designed to introduce that factor.

* * * It is bad enough to tell a mother that her child's murder is not "worthy" of society's ultimate expression of moral condemnation. But to do so based on cardboard stereotypes or cold mathematical calculations is beyond my comprehension. In my decades on the Court, I have not seen a capital crime that could not be considered sufficiently "blameworthy" to merit a death sentence (even when genuine constitutional errors justified a vacatur of that sentence). * * * Whatever one's views on the permissibility or wisdom of the death penalty, I doubt anyone would disagree that each of these crimes was egregious enough to merit the severest condemnation that society has to offer. The only *constitutional* problem with the fact that these criminals were spared that condemnation, while others were not, is that their amnesty came in the form of unfounded claims. Arbitrariness has nothing to do with it. To the extent that we are ill at ease with these

disparate outcomes, it seems to me that the best solution is for the Court to stop making up Eighth Amendment claims in its ceaseless quest to end the death penalty through undemocratic means.

14th ed., p. 56; remove footnote i and add the following after the Maclin excerpt:

NOTES AND QUESTIONS

1.   *Considering race in a reasonable suspicion analysis.* A few courts have taken Professor Maclin's suggestion and now consider race in reasonable suspicion analyses. For a recent example, consider the Supreme Judicial Court of Massachusetts's statements about flight in *Commonwealth v. Warren*, 58 N.E.3d 333 (Mass. 2016): "[W]here the suspect is a black male stopped by the police on the streets of Boston, the analysis of flight as a factor in the reasonable suspicion calculus cannot be divorced from the findings in a recent Boston Police Department (department) report documenting a pattern of racial profiling of black males in the city of Boston * * * . We do not eliminate flight as a factor in the reasonable suspicion analysis whenever a black male is the subject of an investigatory stop. However, in such circumstances, flight is not necessarily probative of a suspect's state of mind or consciousness of guilt. * * * Such an individual, when approached by the police, might just as easily be motivated by the desire to avoid the recurring indignity of being racially profiled as by the desire to hide criminal activity. Given this reality for black males in the city of Boston, a judge should, in appropriate cases, consider the report's findings in weighing flight as a factor in the reasonable suspicion calculus."

2.   *Implicit bias.* In *United States v. Mateo-Medina*, 845 F.3d 546 (3d Cir. 2017), the Third Circuit held that a federal district court had erred in considering the defendant's bare record of prior arrests that did not lead to conviction when imposing a sentence. Chief Judge McKee, writing for the court, noted:

"In 2013, The Sentencing Project released a shadow report to the United Nations Human Rights Committee, *Regarding Racial Disparities in the United States Criminal Justice System* (Sentencing Project Report).[31] The Sentencing Project Report pointed to a wide body of scholarship indicating that socioeconomic factors influenced disparities in arrest rates.

"The Sentencing Project Report also remarked on recent research indicating that police are more likely to stop, and arrest, people of color due to implicit bias. Implicit bias, or stereotyping, consists of the unconscious assumptions that humans make about individuals, particularly in situations that require rapid decision-making, such as police encounters. 'Extensive research has shown that in such situations the vast majority of Americans of all races implicitly associate black Americans with adjectives such as "dangerous," "aggressive," "violent," and "criminal." '

"In addition, a recent empirical study analyzed thirteen years' worth of data on race, socioeconomic factors, drug use, and drug arrests.[35] The study found that African-Americans, Hispanics, and whites used drugs in roughly the same percentages, and in roughly the same ways. The study controlled for variables such as whether the participant lived in high-crime, gang-controlled areas. Despite those controls, the study concluded that 'in early adulthood, race disparities in drug arrest[s] grew substantially; as early as age 22, African-Americans had 83% greater odds of a drug arrest than whites and at age 27 this disparity was 235%.' With respect to

---

[31]   The Sentencing Project, Report of The Sentencing Project to the United Nations Human Rights Committee Regarding Racial Disparities in the United States Criminal Justice System (August 2013), available at http://sentencingproject.org/wp-content/uploads/2015/12/Race-and-Justice-Shadow-Report-ICCPR.pdf   (hereinafter Sentencing Project Report).

[35]   Ojmarrh Mitchell & Michael S. Caudy, *Examining Racial Disparities in Drug Arrests*, JUSTICE QUARTERLY (Jan. 2013), *available at* http://dx.doi.org/10.1080/07418825.2012.761721.

Hispanics, the study found that socioeconomic factors such as residing in an inner-city neighborhood accounted for much of the disparity in drug arrest rates."

14th ed., p. 59; after The Justice Department's Policy Guidance, add:

JUSTICE SONIA SOTOMAYOR—DISSENTING IN UTAH V. STRIEFF
136 S.Ct. 2056 (2016).

[Edward Joseph Strieff, Jr. was stopped by a Utah police officer without reasonable suspicion to justify the stop. As part of that illegal stop, the officer discovered an outstanding traffic warrant and arrested Strieff, finding methamphetamine incident to that arrest. The question presented was whether the Fourth Amendment's exclusionary rule required suppression of the evidence, because it was obtained as a result of an unconstitutional seizure or whether the discovery of the outstanding warrant was a sufficient intervening circumstance to break the causal chain between the unlawful stop and the subsequent arrest/search and render the discovery of the evidence sufficiently attenuated from the initial illegality to permit its use in a subsequent criminal trial. A 5–3 majority of the Supreme Court held that the evidence was admissible. Justices Ginsburg, Sotomayor, and Kagan dissented. Extracts from Justice Sotomayor's separate dissent are below.]

* * * Writing only for myself, and drawing on my professional experiences, I would add that unlawful "stops" have severe consequences much greater than the inconvenience suggested by the name. This Court has given officers an array of instruments to probe and examine you. When we condone officers' use of these devices without adequate cause, we give them reason to target pedestrians in an arbitrary manner. We also risk treating members of our communities as second-class citizens.

Although many Americans have been stopped for speeding or jaywalking, few may realize how degrading a stop can be when the officer is looking for more. This Court has allowed an officer to stop you for whatever reason he wants—so long as he can point to a pretextual justification after the fact. *Whren v. United States*, 517 U.S. 806, 813 (1996). That justification must provide specific reasons why the officer suspected you were breaking the law, *Terry*, 392 U.S., at 21, but it may factor in your ethnicity, *United States v. Brignoni-Ponce*, 422 U.S. 873, 886–887 (1975), where you live, *Adams v. Williams*, 407 U.S. 143, 147 (1972), what you were wearing, *United States v. Sokolow*, 490 U.S. 1, 4–5 (1989), and how you behaved, *Illinois v. Wardlow*, 528 U.S. 119, 124–125 (2000). The officer does not even need to know which law you might have broken so long as he can later point to any possible infraction—even one that is minor, unrelated, or ambiguous. *Devenpeck v. Alford*, 543 U.S. 146, 154–155 (2004); *Heien v. North Carolina*, 574 U.S. ___ (2014).

The indignity of the stop is not limited to an officer telling you that you look like a criminal. The officer may next ask for your "consent" to inspect your bag or purse without telling you that you can decline. See *Florida v. Bostick*, 501 U.S. 429, 438 (1991). Regardless of your answer, he may order you to stand "helpless, perhaps facing a wall with [your] hands raised." *Terry*, 392 U.S., at 17. If the officer thinks you might be dangerous, he may then "frisk" you for weapons. This involves more than just a pat down. As onlookers pass by, the officer may " 'feel with sensitive fingers every portion of [your] body. A thorough search [may] be made of [your] arms and armpits, waistline and back, the groin and area about the testicles, and entire surface of the legs down to the feet.' " *Id.*, at 17, n. 13.

The officer's control over you does not end with the stop. If the officer chooses, he may handcuff you and take you to jail for doing nothing more than speeding, jaywalking, or "driving [your] pickup truck . . . with [your] 3-year-old son and 5-year-old daughter . . . without [your] seatbelt fastened." *Atwater v. Lago Vista*, 532 U.S. 318, 323–324 (2001). At the jail, he can fingerprint you, swab DNA from the inside of your mouth, and force you to "shower with a delousing agent" while you "lift [your] tongue, hold out [your] arms, turn around, and lift [your] genitals." *Florence v. Board of Chosen Freeholders of County of Burlington*, 566 U.S. ___, ___–___ (2012) (slip op., at 2–3); *Maryland v. King*, 569 U.S. ___, ___ (2013) (slip op., at 28). Even if you are innocent, you will now join the 65 million Americans with an arrest record and experience the "civil death" of discrimination by employers, landlords, and whoever else conducts a background check. Chin, The New Civil Death, 160 U. Pa. L. Rev. 1789, 1805 (2012). And, of course, if you fail to pay bail or appear for court, a judge will issue a warrant to render you "arrestable on sight" in the future.

This case involves a *suspicionless* stop, one in which the officer initiated this chain of events without justification. As the Justice Department notes, many innocent people are subjected to the humiliations of these unconstitutional searches. The white defendant in this case shows that anyone's dignity can be violated in this manner. But it is no secret that people of color are disproportionate victims of this type of scrutiny. See M. Alexander, The New Jim Crow 95–136 (2010). For generations, black and brown parents have given their children "the talk"—instructing them never to run down the street; always keep your hands where they can be seen; do not even think of talking back to a stranger—all out of fear of how an officer with a gun will react to them. See, e.g., W. E. B. Du Bois, The Souls of Black Folk (1903); J. Baldwin, The Fire Next Time (1963); T. Coates, Between the World and Me (2015).

By legitimizing the conduct that produces this double consciousness, this case tells everyone, white and black, guilty and innocent, that an officer can verify your legal status at any time. It says that your body is subject to invasion while courts excuse the violation of your rights. It implies that you are not a citizen of a democracy but the subject of a carceral state, just waiting to be cataloged. We must not pretend that the countless people who are routinely targeted by police are "isolated." They are the canaries in the coal mine whose deaths, civil and literal, warn us that no one can breathe in this atmosphere. See L. Guinier & G. Torres, The Miner's Canary 274–283 (2002). They are the ones who recognize that unlawful police stops corrode all our civil liberties and threaten all our lives. Until their voices matter too, our justice system will continue to be anything but.

RACHEL A. HARMON, *LEGAL REMEDIES FOR POLICE MISCONDUCT*, IN ACADEMY FOR JUSTICE, A REPORT ON SCHOLARSHIP AND CRIMINAL JUSTICE REFORM (ERIK LUNA, ED. 2017)

* * * A variety of legal remedies for constitutional violations by police officers, including the exclusionary rule, civil suits for damages or reform, and criminal prosecution, exist to ensure that officers follow the law and to provide redress when they do not. In recent years, commentators have increasingly complained that police officers violate the law with impunity because these legal means for controlling their behavior are too weak. Over several decades, federal courts have left legal remedies for constitutional violations in place, but cut away at them so that, although they are frequently invoked, they are often not effective at remedying or deterring constitutional violations. The consequence is that policing has a lot of law and little remedy. Police officers are surrounded by potential legal review for every act, even legitimate ones, making them feel constantly scrutinized and overregulated. And yet, the law only infrequently holds officers and departments accountable for constitutional violations, leaving victims of police misconduct and their communities deeply dissatisfied. Both police and citizens feel wronged by the present system. * * *

II.   Civil Suits for Damages

The Civil Rights Act of 1871—codified at 42 U.S.C. § 1983 and often known simply as Section 1983—provides a statutory basis for civil suits against police conduct that violates the U.S.

Constitution or federal law as a means to deter unconstitutional conduct, vindicate constitutional rights, and provide compensation for victims of constitutional violations. This long-standing statute gained new traction in the late 1970s after the Supreme Court clarified the circumstances in which the suits were available to plaintiffs and Congress passed 42 U.S.C. § 1988, which permitted prevailing parties in Section 1983 cases to recover reasonable attorney's fees.

Although Section 1983 suits are far less common than motions to suppress evidence under the exclusionary rule, Section 1983 authorizes a remedy in circumstances in which the exclusionary rule does not. [For example, damages actions provide a remedy for] violations the exclusionary rule does not address, such as constitutionally excessive force—which produces no evidence—and Fourth Amendment violations against those who are never charged with a crime.

Despite the potential scope of Section 1983, plaintiffs face many practical barriers to bringing lawsuits. There may not be independent witnesses to an event, making misconduct difficult to prove. Victims of police misconduct often have criminal records or other qualities that may make them unappealing to juries, who are, in any case, reluctant to second-guess police decision-making, given the risks officers face on the street. In addition, because of uncertain outcomes and legal obstacles to recovery, potential plaintiffs cannot always find willing, effective, and experienced attorneys to represent them.

Beyond these practical hurdles, there are often overwhelming legal obstacles to Section 1983 actions. Most importantly, according to the Supreme Court's interpretation of the statute, individual officers are entitled to "qualified immunity" from civil damages for violating a person's constitutional rights unless the right at issue was "clearly established" at the time of the alleged conduct. In recent years, the Supreme Court has required increasingly specific and robust precedent to establish a constitutional right clearly, noting that "existing precedent must have placed the statutory or constitutional question beyond debate," with the result that qualified immunity protects all but the "plainly incompetent" officer.

* * * A city (or its department) is only liable under Section 1983 for constitutional violations that it causes through its policies or customs. To establish liability against a city, a plaintiff must show that there was a constitutional violation, that the city caused the violation, and that the violation is attributable to a city policy, formal or informal.[21] Usually, proving these elements requires evidence that city actors knew of and permitted a pattern of similar constitutional violations, as well as evidence that the constitutional violation was actually caused by and was closely related to the policy deficiency. In many cases, proving municipal liability is therefore not only difficult, but requires extensive, expensive discovery.

Even when plaintiffs win civil suits for damages or settle them favorably against individuals or departments, damages actions may not influence police conduct going forward. Individual officers are almost always indemnified by their departments for judgments against them. This means that judgments against individuals are paid for by departments and cities rather than by individual officers. In theory, paying out money should lead departments and cities to seek to prevent constitutional violations by officers to avoid future payments. But in practice, cities sometimes use financial arrangements to pay settlements and judgments that do not penalize police departments, and therefore do not create strong incentives to avoid additional violations. As a consequence, though Section 1983 damages actions can result in considerable costs to cities, they often do little to deter misconduct.

III. Civil Suits for Equitable Relief by Private Actors

Under federal law, when compensatory damages are an inadequate remedy for a constitutional violation, especially a future harm, private plaintiffs, individually or in aggregate,

---

[21]   *See* Monell v. Dep't of Soc. Servs., 436 U.S. 658, 690–92 (1978).

may seek alternative remedies, known as "equitable relief." This relief usually takes the form of a court's declaration of the rights of the parties or an injunction—a court order requiring or prohibiting certain actions. Equitable relief can be simple and prohibitory or can involve complex mandates for changing government behavior, and private plaintiffs sometimes sue municipalities seeking an order requiring government agencies to engage in substantial departmental reforms. These reforms do not act—like damages or the exclusionary rule—to deter constitutional violations indirectly. Instead, they are intended to cure the systemic conditions that cause constitutional violations.

Lawsuits for complex reforms, often known as structural reform litigation, developed in the 1950s and expanded through the mid-1970s. This litigation was not then and is not now limited to police departments. In fact, structural reform litigation has been more often and more famously used for other purposes, such as to desegregate schools, to improve prison conditions, and to fight housing discrimination by local and state agencies. Nevertheless, both simple and complex forms of equitable relief are often sought in suits against police departments.

Scholars and commentators have long been divided over the value and legitimacy of suits for equitable relief. By the mid-1970s, the U.S. Supreme Court sided with skeptics and imposed some significant limits on private efforts to obtain declaratory relief and injunctions. For plaintiffs challenging policing practices, the most important of these limits is the Court's application of constitutional standing requirements. In *City of Los Angeles v. Lyons*, the Court held that the plaintiff, Lyons, who had been choked to unconsciousness by police officers during a traffic stop, had not demonstrated a "real and immediate" threat of future injury sufficient to establish Article III standing for injunctive relief.[26] Even if the Los Angeles Police Department used illegal chokeholds, as Lyons alleged, the Court held that "it is no more than speculation to assert either that Lyons himself will again be involved in one of those unfortunate instances or that he will be arrested in the future and provoke the use of a chokehold by resisting arrest, attempting to escape, or threatening deadly force or serious bodily injury."[27] Therefore, he could not sue for injunctive relief. * * *

[C]ourts are more likely to find standing and allow equitable challenges under *Lyons* when a policy targets relatively innocent or common conduct, when the department engages in the challenged conduct frequently, when some plaintiffs have suffered harm more than once, and when the department directs the challenged conduct against a visible subpopulation of which the plaintiff is part. Each of these conditions raises the probability that a particular plaintiff will experience future constitutional injury. Some police practices are far more likely than others to meet these conditions. For example, plaintiffs challenging racial profiling, or the illegal, widespread use of enforcement strategies such as stops, frisks, and arrests against minor conduct, will more easily satisfy the requirements of *Lyons* than plaintiffs attempting to change strip-search practices at jails or uses of excessive force. In this way, and others, court-imposed limits on suits for equitable relief have made such suits a powerful but infrequent tool for challenging and changing unconstitutional conduct by law enforcement.

IV. Civil Suits for Equitable Relief by Public Actors

* * * In 1994, Congress gave the Department of Justice the power to bring suits for equitable relief against police departments in the Violent Crime Control and Law Enforcement Act.[30] Using this authority, the Department of Justice has developed a program of investigating and suing police departments engaged in a "pattern or practice" of constitutional violations and negotiating settlements that impose significant changes on those departments. As of the beginning of 2017,

---

[26]   461 U.S. 95, 105 (1983).

[27]   *Id.* at 108.

[30]   42 U.S.C. § 14141.

the Department of Justice had engaged in substantial investigations of 69 departments and had entered into 40 reform agreements.

* * * [P]attern or practice investigations and litigation by the Department of Justice has varied in volume and aggressiveness during the three presidential administrations that have had the power to enforce the law. Despite this variation, there are some notable constants in pattern-and-practice suits brought by the Department of Justice so far. First, the investigations and suits have focused heavily on the use of excessive force; illegal stops, searches, and arrests; and discriminatory policing by departments. Second, in most cases, when the Department of Justice has found a pattern or practice of constitutional violations by a police department, it has entered into an enforceable agreement with the municipality in which the city agrees to make substantial and specific reforms to the police department. Most of these agreements have been in the form of court-enforceable consent decrees. Third, implementation of the consent decrees has been monitored by independent teams who report to the federal courts supervising the decrees. Finally, although the reforms sought by the Civil Rights Division have evolved over time, they have consistently emphasized reducing discrimination, clarifying the policies that officers follow, improving training and supervision, strengthening data collection and transparency, and reforming citizen complaint and internal accountability systems within police departments.

Legal scholars and other commentators have long viewed pattern-and practice suits as a powerful tool for improving policing, and the program is largely considered successful in reforming departments that have substantial ongoing problems. Still, these suits raise some concerns. Pattern-and-practice suits are resource intensive for both the federal government and the cities that are sued, and they can represent a substantial federal intrusion in local government. In addition, the limited empirical research studying the effects of pattern-and-practice suits so far has found that, though reforms adopted seemed to improve internal processes and reduce unconstitutional policing, they also tended to alienate line officers. Finally, reforms imposed by consent decree may not be self-sustaining once ongoing monitoring by the Department of Justice and the federal court ends.

In recent years, the Department of Justice has sought to refine its pattern-and-practice program to address some of these concerns. It has also supplemented this program with an alternative: voluntary technical assistance for departments struggling to prevent constitutional violations through the COPS Collaborative Reform program. * * *

V.   Criminal Prosecution

Police officers may be prosecuted for constitutional violations under both federal and state law. Under federal law, 18 U.S.C. § 242 makes it a crime to willfully deprive any person of his or her constitutional rights. * * * Criminally prosecuting police officers is harder than suing them civilly. As in all criminal cases, prosecutors are required to prove elements of a crime beyond a reasonable doubt, and Section 242 has elements that can be especially difficult to prove. A federal prosecutor must establish not only that the officer violated the Constitution, but also that the officer did so "willfully," that is, that the officer had the specific intent to do what the law forbids. * * * Not surprisingly, fewer than 100 federal prosecutions are brought against law enforcement officials for constitutional violations each year. * * *

Criminal prosecutions against police officers are likely to be inevitably too rare to deter much misconduct. Nevertheless, they remain of substantial symbolic and normative importance. No other form of remedy so clearly expresses the government's condemnation of specific police violations of law, and none shows as much respect for the victims of police misconduct, especially with respect to police violence.

VI. State Decertification

* * * In most states, the commissions that provide for the training and certification of officers, or other state boards, also have the power to deprive an officer of his license or certification to punish serious misconduct. While the threat of decertification may discourage bad acts, decertification also has a more direct effect: It prevents future violations of the public trust by stopping officers who have committed serious misconduct from continuing to serve as sworn officers in the state. Decertifying officers can also help reassure the public about the state's commitment to law-abiding law enforcement and demonstrate law enforcement's commitment to professional norms. Presently, decertification is inconsistently used, and police departments do not have reliable access to information about decertifications in other states. More systematic use of this tool and an improved system for communicating decertification actions between states, could improve its capacity to reduce police misconduct. * * *

VII. Departmental and Municipal Remedies

Some of the most effective means of preventing police misconduct are within the control of police departments and municipalities. There is wide agreement that hiring well-qualified officers, providing them with extensive and ongoing training, setting forth specific and realistic policies to guide their work, and supervising them well are all critical to ensuring that officers comply with the law. In addition to these management practices, however, departments and municipalities also respond to specific incidents of misconduct in ways that can affect future officer behavior. Most importantly, departments and cities receive citizen complaints about officer conduct, and they investigate and impose discipline for violations of law and departmental policies. This process is important both for deterring misconduct and for communicating a commitment to lawful policing. Since disciplinary mechanisms can be used for misconduct that violates departmental policies as well as law, these mechanisms have far greater potential impact on policing than legal remedies that merely enforce constitutional law.

In most cities, citizen complaints about officer misconduct are investigated and resolved by units of the police department itself, often know as internal affairs units, and discipline, if appropriate, is imposed by command staff. Like legal remedies, internal affairs units often impose scrutiny and burdens that officers resent, and yet rarely vindicate the interests of individuals who feel mistreated by the police. Scholars and other commentators widely criticize internal complaint, investigation, and disciplinary systems in police departments for their ineffectiveness, bias, and lack of transparency. The Department of Justice has leveled similar criticisms in its pattern-and-practice investigations. In many cities, communities distrust the police in part because they believe that internal disciplinary mechanisms do not work. * * *

VIII.   Looking Beyond Constitutional Remedies

* * * Although constitutional rights provide an important floor below which police action cannot go, they do a poor job of balancing competing interests when the police enforce the law and individuals are harmed. Because rights are held by individuals, they often do not limit policing practices that impose substantial aggregate harm to communities. Because they are defined categorically and in advance, they must be more permissive toward law enforcement than a careful weighing of the interests at stake would warrant in order to permit discretion in extreme cases. And because they are defined and applied in the context of court rulings, they are formulated based on considerations, such as the ease of judicial administration, that have nothing to do with whether the police practices in question are overly harmful. * * *

This is not to say that constitutional and other legal remedies for policing are no longer important. As the above descriptions suggest, constitutional remedies serve functions other than shaping police action. Criminal prosecutions of officers remain a principal way to declare conduct culpable and to show societal respect for victims. Civil damages compensate injured plaintiffs. And structural reform litigation mitigates systemic problems in policing. Thus, reformers may want to push to strengthen these remedies in the courts; to support pattern-and-practice suits and criminal prosecutions by the Department of Justice; and to promote stronger state tort remedies and criminal prosecutions. Nevertheless, those interested in reform would be wise to look beyond expanding constitutional and statutory remedies to consider alternative means of spurring changes in departments.

U.S. DEPT. OF JUSTICE, BUREAU OF JUSTICE STATISTICS, LOCAL POLICE DEPARTMENTS, 2013: PERSONNEL, POLICIES, AND PRACTICES

By Brian A. Reaves, Ph.D., BJS Statistician
(*available at* http://www.bjs.gov/content/pub/pdf/lpd13ppp.pdf).

As of January 1, 2013, more than 12,000 local police departments in the United States employed an estimated 605,000 persons on a full-time basis. This total included about 477,000 sworn officers (those with general arrest powers) and about 128,000 nonsworn employees.

Highlights

• About half (48%) of departments employed fewer than 10 officers.

• More than half (54%) of local police officers were employed in jurisdictions with 100,000 or more residents.

• About 1 in 8 local police officers were female, including about 1 in 10 first-line supervisors.

• About 27% of local police officers were members of a racial or ethnic minority, compared to 15% in 1987.

The overall average starting salary for entry-level local police officers in 2013 was $44,400. * * * In 2013, the average base starting salary for entry-level local police officers was at least $45,000 in all population categories of 25,000 or more. The average starting salary was highest in jurisdictions with 100,000 to 249,999 residents ($50,700) and lowest in jurisdictions with fewer than 2,500 residents ($30,900).

In 2013, about 23% of officers were employed by a department that required new entry-level officers to have a 2-year degree, compared to 7% in 2003. In 2013, all local police departments serving a population of 100,000 or more, and nearly all departments in smaller jurisdictions, had a minimum education requirement for new officers. The most common requirement (84% of departments) was a high school diploma. An estimated 15% of departments had some type of college requirement, including 10% that required a 2-year degree and 1% that required a 4-year degree. An estimated 54% of departments with a degree requirement considered military service as an alternative. Departments serving a population of 1 million or more (29%) were most likely to require a degree. In smaller population categories, the percentage of departments with a degree requirement ranged from 9% in jurisdictions with fewer than 2,500 residents to 20% in jurisdictions with 25,000 to 49,999 residents.

U.S. DEPT. OF JUSTICE, BUREAU OF JUSTICE STATISTICS SPECIAL REPORT: STATE AND LOCAL LAW ENFORCEMENT TRAINING ACADEMIES, 2006 (REVISED 4/14/2009)

By Brian A. Reaves, Ph.D., BJS Statistician
(*available at* http://www.bjs.gov/content/pub/pdf/slleta06.pdf).

Overall, an estimated 57,000 recruits entered basic training programs during 2005. On average, these programs included 761 hours of classroom training. A third of academies had an additional mandatory field training component with an average length of 453 hours. * * *

Just over two-thirds (68%) of training academies required their full-time instructors to have a minimum number of years of law enforcement experience. Among academies with a minimum experience requirement, the average was about 4 years. * * *

Overall, 19% of the academies required their full-time instructors to have a college degree. Slightly more academies required a 4-year degree (11%) than required a 2-year degree (8%).* * *

Eighty-nine percent of academies required full-time trainers to have a state-level certification, and 62% required certification as a subject-matter expert. A less common requirement was certification by the academy (25%). * * *

Basic training included a median 60 hours of firearms instruction and 51 hours of self-defense instruction. Recruits spent the most time learning firearms skills (median instruction time of 60 hours) and self-defense skills (51 hours). The next highest median was for health and fitness training (46 hours). Nearly all academies also trained recruits in procedures related to patrol, investigations, and emergency vehicle operations with a median instruction time of 40 hours each.

Basic first aid (24 hours) and report writing (20 hours) were also included in the basic training program of nearly all academies. Recruits also received a median of 8 hours training on the use of computers and information systems, although such training was limited to 58% of academies.

Legal training was included in all basic training programs with a median of 36 hours of instruction in criminal law and 12 hours in constitutional law. Nearly all academies provided instruction on cultural diversity (a median of 11 hours), community policing strategies (8 hours), and mediation skills/conflict management (8 hours). Special topics covered by basic training programs included domestic violence (a median of 14 hours), juveniles (8 hours), domestic preparedness (8 hours), and hate crimes (4 hours). * * *

[L]ess than half of academies in 2006 provided community policing training on assessing the effectiveness of problem-solving responses (45%), creating problem-solving teams (43%), analyzing crime/calls for service data (38%), using crime mapping to analyze community problems (36%), or applying research methods to study crime and disorder (35%).* * *

A majority of recruits were trained in academies more oriented toward a stress-based military model than a non-stress academic model. The more traditional stress-based model of training is based on the military model and typically includes paramilitary drills, intensive physical demands, public disciplinary measures, immediate reaction to infractions, daily inspections, value inculcation, and withholding of privileges. Proponents of this approach believe it promotes self-discipline in recruits resulting in a commitment to follow departmental policies, better time management, and completion of duties even when undesirable.

The non-stress model emphasizes academic achievement, physical training, administrative disciplinary procedures, and an instructor-trainee relationship that is more relaxed and supportive. Proponents of this approach believe it produces officers better able to interact in a cooperative manner with citizens and community organizations, and therefore more suited to the problem-solving approaches of community-oriented policing. * * *

By type of academy, 43% of state police academies reported their training environment was predominantly stress-based. The next highest percentages were for academies operated by county police (26%) or sheriffs' offices (25%). More than three-fifths of academies operated by county police (89%), state police (75%), sheriffs' offices (71%), or municipal police (66%) had training environments they described as either predominantly stress or more stress than non-stress. * * *

State POST (16%) and college and university academies (13%) were most likely to report using a predominantly non-stress training environment. A majority of state POST (64%) and college and university (60%) academies had training environments that were more non-stress than stress or predominantly non-stress compared to less than half of other academies. * * *

In academies with a training environment described as predominantly non-stress, female and male recruits both had a completion rate of 89%, but as the stress orientation of the training environment increased, completion rates dropped more for female recruits than for male recruits.

In academies with a training environment that was more stress-oriented than non-stress, completion rates for female recruits dropped to 79% compared to 88% for male recruits. In academies with a training environment that was predominantly stress, the difference in completion rates between female (68%) and male (81%) recruits was even greater.

CHAPTER 4

THE RIGHT TO COUNSEL

■ ■ ■

§ 1.   THE RIGHT TO APPOINTED COUNSEL AND RELATED PROBLEMS

A.   THE RIGHT TO APPOINTED COUNSEL IN CRIMINAL PROCEEDINGS

14th ed., p. 67; replace footnote d with the following:

    ^d As of 2013, 28 states and the District of Columbia had state-administered indigent defense programs. See Suzanne M. Strong, U.S. Dep't of Justice Bureau of Justice Statistics, NCJ 250249, State-Administered Indigent Defense Systems (May, 2017). However, only 23 states completely fund their indigent-defense systems at the state level. In 19 states, counties shoulder the burden for more than half of the funding. See Eve Brensike Primus, *Defense Counsel and Public Defense, in* Academy for Justice, A Report on Scholarship and Criminal Justice Reform (Erik Luna ed., 2017).

14th ed., p. 68; in Note 3, replace the citation to the Thomas H. Cohen article with the following citation:

Thomas H. Cohen, *Who is Better at Defending Criminals? Does Type of Defense Attorney Matter in Terms of Producing Favorable Case Outcomes*, 25 Crim. Just. Pol'y Rev. 29 (2014).

14th ed., p. 68; replace Note 4 with the following:

    4.   *Counsel of choice.* One county in Texas permits indigent defendants to choose their own attorneys from a list of qualified attorneys. Data collected after the first year of this program suggests that the client-choice program participants pled guilty to lesser charges or proceeded to trial more often than their peers. See M. Elaine Nugent-Borakove & Franklin Cruz, *The Power of Choice: The Implications of a System Where Indigent Defendants Choose Their Own Counsel*, p. iii (March 2017), *available at* http://www.tidc.texas.gov/media/55476/the-power-of-choice.pdf. For a discussion of the pilot project, see Adam Liptak, *Need-Blind Justice*, N.Y. Times (Jan. 4, 2014). For a discussion of the theory behind the program, see Stephen J. Schulhofer, *Client Choice for Indigent Criminal Defendants: Theory and Implementation*, 12 Ohio St. J. Crim. L. 505 (2015).

14th ed., p. 69; end of Note 5, add:

For a discussion of the current problems with indigent defense delivery systems and a canvassing of proposed solutions, see Eve Brensike Primus, *Defense Counsel and Public Defense, in* Academy for Justice, A Report on Scholarship and Criminal Justice Reform (Erik Luna ed., 2017).

14th ed., p. 69; after Note 5, add:

    5A. *Data collection and the possibility of evidence-based standards for indigent defense delivery systems.* Many scholars have called for more data collection about public defender practices and have advocated for the development of evidence-based standards (based on a combination of expert opinion, empirical research/data, and client/defender input) for indigent defense delivery systems. *See, e.g.,* Pamela Metzger & Andrew Guthrie Ferguson, *Defending Data,*

88 S. Cal. L. Rev. 1057 (2015). Others caution that quality data about best practices in public defender offices is difficult to collect and involves normative judgments about what is good public defender work; that a focus on data collection might divert limited resources away from skills training for public defenders; and that there is a risk that the data collected could cause perverse or unintended effects either because it is insufficiently granular and therefore fails to validate worthy indigent defense programs or because it may demonstrate that increased funding will lead to marginal benefits in outcomes. *See, e.g.*, Jennifer E. Laurin, Gideon *by the Numbers: The Emergence of Evidence-Based Practice in Indigent Defense*, 12 Ohio St. J. Crim. L. 325 (2015).

14th ed., p. 73; end of Note 6, add:

For an interesting argument that equal protection and due process principles should be interpreted to guarantee indigent misdemeanants a right to counsel even when the Sixth Amendment does not, see Brandon Buskey & Lauren Sudeall Lucas, *Keeping* Gideon*'s Promise: Using Equal Protection to Address the Denial of Counsel in Misdemeanor Cases*, 85 Fordham L. Rev. 2299 (2017).

14th ed., p. 74; end of Note 7, add:

Compare *Nichols* with *United States v. Tucker*, 404 U.S. 443, 448 (1972) (holding that prior invalid uncounseled felony convictions cannot be relied upon at sentencing to impose a longer term of imprisonment for a subsequent conviction, because "(t)o permit a conviction obtained in violation of Gideon v. Wainwright to be used against a person either to support guilt or enhance punishment for another offense . . . is to erode the principle of that case" (quoting *Burgett v. Texas*, 389 U.S. 109 (1967)). For an interesting discussion of the line between *Scott* and *Nichols* on the one hand and *Tucker* and *Burgett* on the other, see *United States v. Bryant*, 136 S.Ct. 1954 (2016) (holding that uncounseled tribal court convictions for domestic violence could be used as predicate offenses for a federal habitual domestic violence offender statute, because "the Sixth Amendment does not apply to tribal-court proceedings" and the Indian Civil Rights Act of 1968, which governs criminal proceedings in tribal courts, did not require appointed counsel for the prior convictions, thus making the prior tribal-court convictions like the uncounseled misdemeanor conviction at issue in *Nichols*).

B.   THE "BEGINNINGS" OF THE RIGHT TO COUNSEL: "CRIMINAL PROSECUTIONS" AND "CRITICAL STAGES"

14th ed., p. 82; after Note 6, add:

7.   *Pre-indictment plea bargaining.* Is a criminal suspect who has been offered a plea agreement that requires pre-indictment acceptance an "accused" who is entitled to the assistance of counsel under the Sixth Amendment? Most lower courts say "no," citing the Supreme Court's language in *Gouveia* that the right does not attach until "the initiation of adversary judicial criminal proceedings—whether by way of formal charge, preliminary hearing, indictment, information, or arraignment." *See, e.g.*, *Turner v. United States*, 885 F.3d 949, 952 (6th Cir. 2018) (en banc). Some judges disagree, noting that, under *Rothgery*, the Supreme Court's attachment rule is not "a mechanical, indictment-based rule." *Id.* at 980 (Stranch, J., dissenting). Rather, courts should scrutinize any confrontation, "evaluating both the relationship of the state to the accused and the potential consequences for the accused." *See id.*; *see also id.* at 955 (Bush, J., concurring *dubitante*) (arguing that the original public meaning of the Sixth Amendment supports earlier attachment of the right).

§ 5. THE RIGHT TO "COUNSEL OF CHOICE"

14th ed., p. 117; end of Note 3, add:

For an interesting argument that indigent defendants have a constitutional right to counsel of choice, see Janet Moore, *The Antidemocratic Sixth Amendment*, 91 Wash. L. Rev. 1705 (2016).

14th ed., p. 117; replace Note 5 with:

5. ***Forfeiture statutes and the right to counsel of choice.*** In CAPLIN & DRYSDALE, CHARTERED v. UNITED STATES, 491 U.S. 617 (1989), a law firm sued the United States government to recover legal fees that it did not receive after defending Charles Reckmeyer on charges of running an illegal drug operation. The law firm had not received its fees, because the government had seized Reckmeyer's funds in accordance with a federal statute providing that a person convicted of specified drug violations forfeits all property "constituting or derived from" the proceeds of those violations. This federal statute, the law firm argued, effectively denies defendants convicted of the qualifying drug offenses of their Sixth Amendment rights to counsel of choice. The Supreme Court, in a 5–4 decision written by Justice White, disagreed, noting that a "defendant has no Sixth Amendment right to spend another person's money for services rendered by an attorney, even if those funds are the only way that defendant will be able to retain the counsel of his choice." The majority also noted that "there is a strong governmental interest in obtaining full recovery of all forfeitable assets, an interest that overrides any Sixth Amendment interest in permitting criminals to use assets adjudged forfeitable to pay for their defense." That governmental interest, according to Justice White, includes (1) an interest in "recovering all forfeitable assets, for such assets are deposited in a Fund that supports law-enforcement efforts in a variety of important and useful ways;" (2) an interest in "returning property, in full, to those wrongfully deprived or defrauded of it;" and (3) an interest in "lessen[ing] the economic power of organized crime and drug enterprises."

In a companion case, *United States v. Monsanto*, 491 U.S. 600 (1989), the Supreme Court extended its holding in *Caplin & Drysdale* to permit statutorily-authorized *pre-trial* seizure of assets accumulated as a result of alleged narcotics trafficking. Justice White again wrote for the 5–4 majority: "[I]f the Government may, post-trial, forbid the use of forfeited assets to pay an attorney, then surely no constitutional violation occurs when, after probable cause is adequately established, the Government obtains an order barring a defendant from frustrating that end by dissipating his assets prior to trial."

The Supreme Court limited the scope of *Caplin & Drysdale* and *Monsanto* in LUIS v. UNITED STATES, 136 S.Ct. 1083 (2016), when it drew a sharp distinction between, on the one hand, assets obtained as a result of the crime or property that is traceable to the crime and, on the other hand, property that is untainted by the defendant's alleged criminal activities. According to five members of the Court, "the pretrial restraint of legitimate, untainted assets needed to retain counsel of choice violates the Sixth Amendment." Justice Breyer, writing for a plurality, distinguished *Caplin & Drysdale* and *Monsanto*, noting that, in those cases, the property was " 'tainted,' and that title to the property therefore had passed from the defendant to the Government before the court issued its order freezing (or otherwise disposing of) the assets." When the property is untainted, however, it remains the property of the defendant and the Government has no "equivalent governmental interest in that property." The plurality then balanced the government's interest in restraining defendant's use of her property against her Sixth Amendment right to retain counsel, and noted that "a Sixth Amendment right to assistance of counsel . . . is a fundamental constituent of due process of law," whereas the Government's contingent interest in securing criminal forfeiture and the victims' interest in securing restitution "would seem to lie somewhat further from the heart of a fair, effective criminal justice system." Justice Thomas disagreed with this balancing approach, but agreed that a pretrial freeze of untainted assets violates the Sixth Amendment right to counsel of choice, because "history" and "the common law drew a clear line between tainted and untainted assets."

Justice Kennedy, writing for himself and Justice Alito, dissented noting that the majority's decision is inconsistent with precedent and "rewards criminals who hurry to spend, conceal, or launder stolen property by assuring them that they may use their own funds to pay for an attorney after they have dissipated the proceeds of their crime." Justice Kagan wrote a separate dissent questioning the wisdom of the Court's decision in *Monsanto*, but noting that the result in this case should be dictated by that precedent. Do you agree with the majority or the dissent? Do you think drawing a line between tainted and untainted assets is workable?

CHAPTER 5

THE PERFORMANCE OF COUNSEL

■ ■ ■

§ 2. THE *STRICKLAND* STANDARDS

14th ed., p. 143; after Note 9, add:

WEAVER V. MASSACHUSETTS
___ U.S. ___, 137 S.Ct. 1899, 198 L.Ed.2d 420 (2017).

JUSTICE KENNEDY delivered the opinion of the Court. * * *

I

In 2003, a 15-year-old boy was shot and killed in Boston. A witness saw a young man fleeing the scene of the crime and saw him pull out a pistol. A baseball hat fell off of his head. The police recovered the hat, which featured a distinctive airbrushed Detroit Tigers logo on either side. The hat's distinctive markings linked it to 16-year-old Kentel Weaver. He is the petitioner here. DNA obtained from the hat matched petitioner's DNA. * * * Petitioner was [later] indicted in Massachusetts state court for first-degree murder and the unlicensed possession of a handgun. He pleaded not guilty and proceeded to trial.

The pool of potential jury members was large, some 60 to 100 people. The assigned courtroom could accommodate only 50 or 60 in the courtroom seating. As a result, the trial judge brought all potential jurors into the courtroom so that he could introduce the case and ask certain preliminary questions of the entire venire panel. Many of the potential jurors did not have seats and had to stand in the courtroom. After the preliminary questions, the potential jurors who had been standing were moved outside the courtroom to wait during the individual questioning of the other potential jurors. * * * As all of the seats in the courtroom were occupied by the venire panel, an officer of the court excluded from the courtroom any member of the public who was not a potential juror. So when petitioner's mother and her minister came to the courtroom to observe the two days of jury selection, they were turned away.

All this occurred before the Court's [2012] decision in *Presley v. Georgia* [Supp. p. 154] made it clear that the public-trial right extends to jury selection as well as to other portions of the trial. Before *Presley,* Massachusetts courts would often close courtrooms to the public during jury selection, in particular during murder trials. * * * In this case petitioner's mother told defense counsel about the closure at some point during jury selection. But counsel "believed that a courtroom closure for [jury selection] was constitutional." As a result, he "did not discuss the matter" with petitioner, or tell him "that his right to a public trial included the [jury *voir dire*]," or object to the closure.

During the ensuing trial, the government presented strong evidence of petitioner's guilt. Its case consisted of the incriminating details outlined above, including petitioner's confession to the police. The jury convicted petitioner on both counts. The court sentenced him to life in prison on the murder charge. * * * Five years later, petitioner filed a motion for a new trial in Massachusetts state court. As relevant here, he argued that his attorney had provided ineffective assistance by failing to object to the courtroom closure. After an evidentiary hearing, the trial court recognized a violation of the right to a public trial based on the following findings: The courtroom had been closed; the closure was neither *de minimis* nor trivial; the closure was unjustified; and the closure was full rather than partial (meaning that all members of the public, rather than only some of them, had been excluded from the courtroom). The trial court further determined that defense counsel failed to object because of "serious incompetency, inefficiency, or inattention." On the other hand, petitioner had not "offered any evidence or legal argument establishing prejudice." For that reason, the court held that petitioner was not entitled to relief.

Petitioner appealed the denial of the motion for a new trial to the Massachusetts Supreme Judicial Court. The court consolidated that appeal with petitioner's direct appeal. As noted, there had been no objection to the closure at trial; and the issue was not raised in the direct appeal. The Supreme Judicial Court then affirmed in relevant part. Although it recognized that "[a] violation of the Sixth Amendment right to a public trial constitutes structural error," the court stated that petitioner had "failed to show that trial counsel's conduct caused prejudice warranting a new trial." * * * There is disagreement among the Federal Courts of Appeals and some state courts of last resort about whether a defendant must demonstrate prejudice in a case like this one—in which a structural error is neither preserved nor raised on direct review but is raised later via a claim alleging ineffective assistance of counsel. * * * This Court granted certiorari to resolve that disagreement. The Court does so specifically and only in the context of trial counsel's failure to object to the closure of the courtroom during jury selection.

II

This case requires a discussion, and the proper application, of two doctrines: structural error and ineffective assistance of counsel. The two doctrines are intertwined; for the reasons an error is deemed structural may influence the proper standard used to evaluate an ineffective-assistance claim premised on the failure to object to that error.

The concept of structural error can be discussed first. In *Chapman v. California* [14th ed., p. 1451], this Court "adopted the general rule that a constitutional error does not automatically require reversal of a conviction." If the government can show "beyond a reasonable doubt that the error complained of did not contribute to the verdict obtained," the Court held, then the error is deemed harmless and the defendant is not entitled to reversal. The Court recognized, however, that some errors should not be deemed harmless beyond a reasonable doubt. These errors came to be known as structural errors. The purpose of the structural error doctrine is to ensure insistence on certain basic, constitutional guarantees that should define the framework of any criminal trial. Thus, the defining feature of a structural error is that it "affect[s] the framework within which the trial proceeds," rather than being "simply an error in the trial process itself." For the same reason, a structural error "def[ies] analysis by harmless error standards." *Arizona v. Fulminante*, 499 U.S. 279 (1991). The precise reason why a particular error is not amenable to that kind of analysis— and thus the precise reason why the Court has deemed it structural—varies in a significant way from error to error. There appear to be at least three broad rationales.

First, an error has been deemed structural in some instances if the right at issue is not designed to protect the defendant from erroneous conviction but instead protects some other interest. This is true of the defendant's right to conduct his own defense, which, when exercised, "usually increases the likelihood of a trial outcome unfavorable to the defendant." *McKaskle v. Wiggins,* [14th ed., Note 4, p. 100]. That right is based on the fundamental legal principle that a defendant must be allowed to make his own choices about the proper way to protect his own liberty. See *Faretta v. California,* [14th ed., p. 96]. Because harm is irrelevant to the basis underlying the right, the Court has deemed a violation of that right structural error. See *United States v. Gonzalez-Lopez* [14th ed., p. 109].

Second, an error has been deemed structural if the effects of the error are simply too hard to measure. For example, when a defendant is denied the right to select his or her own attorney, the precise "effect of the violation cannot be ascertained." *Gonzalez-Lopez*, supra. Because the government will, as a result, find it almost impossible to show that the error was "harmless beyond a reasonable doubt," *Chapman*, the efficiency costs of letting the government try to make the showing are unjustified.

Third, an error has been deemed structural if the error always results in fundamental unfairness. For example, if an indigent defendant is denied an attorney or if the judge fails to give a reasonable-doubt instruction, the resulting trial is always a fundamentally unfair one. * * * It therefore would be futile for the government to try to show harmlessness.

These categories are not rigid. In a particular case, more than one of these rationales may be part of the explanation for why an error is deemed to be structural. For these purposes, however, one point is critical: An error can count as structural even if the error does not lead to fundamental unfairness in every case. See *Gonzalez-Lopez,* supra at n.4 (rejecting as "inconsistent with the reasoning of our precedents" the idea that structural errors "always or necessarily render a trial fundamentally unfair and unreliable").

As noted above, a violation of the right to a public trial is a structural error. It is relevant to determine why that is so. In particular, the question is whether a public-trial violation counts as structural because it always leads to fundamental unfairness or for some other reason. * * * [*Waller v. Georgia* [14th ed., Note 2, p. 1330] and *Pressley*, supra, address the scope of the public trial guarantee.] These opinions teach that courtroom closure is to be avoided, but that there are some circumstances when it is justified. The problems that may be encountered by trial courts in deciding whether some closures are necessary, or even in deciding which members of the public should be admitted when seats are scarce, are difficult ones. For example, there are often preliminary instructions that a judge may want to give to the venire as a whole, rather than repeating those instructions (perhaps with unintentional differences) to several groups of potential jurors. On the other hand, various constituencies of the public—the family of the accused, the family of the victim, members of the press, and other persons—all have their own interests in observing the selection of jurors. How best to manage these problems is not a topic discussed at length in any decision or commentary the Court has found.

So although the public-trial right is structural, it is subject to exceptions. * * * Though these cases [of justified closure] should be rare, a judge may deprive a defendant of his right to an open courtroom by making proper factual findings in support of the decision to do so. The fact that the public-trial right is subject to these exceptions suggests that not every public-trial violation results in fundamental unfairness.

A public-trial violation can occur, moreover, as it did in *Presley,* simply because the trial court omits to make the proper findings before closing the courtroom, even if those findings might have been fully supported by the evidence. It would be unconvincing to deem a trial fundamentally unfair just because a judge omitted to announce factual findings before making an otherwise valid decision to order the courtroom temporarily closed. As a result, it would be likewise unconvincing if the Court had said that a public-trial violation always leads to a fundamentally unfair trial. Indeed * * * in the two cases in which the Court has discussed the reasons for classifying a public-trial violation as structural error, the Court has said that a public-trial violation is structural for a different reason: because of the "difficulty of assessing the effect of the error." *Gonzalez-Lopez,* supra at n. 4; see also *Waller,* supra at n. 9.

The public-trial right also protects some interests that do not belong to the defendant. After all, the right to an open courtroom protects the rights of the public at large, and the press, as well as the rights of the accused. * * * *Press-Enterprise II* [14th ed., Note 5, p. 1330]. So one other factor leading to the classification of structural error is that the public-trial right furthers interests other than protecting the defendant against unjust conviction. These precepts confirm the conclusion the Court now reaches that, while the public-trial right is important for fundamental reasons, in some cases an unlawful closure might take place and yet the trial still will be fundamentally fair from the defendant's standpoint.

III

The Court now turns to the proper remedy for addressing the violation of a structural right, and in particular the right to a public trial. Despite its name, the term "structural error" carries with it no talismanic significance as a doctrinal matter. It means only that the government is not entitled to deprive the defendant of a new trial by showing that the error was "harmless beyond a reasonable doubt." *Chapman*. Thus, in the case of a structural error where there is an objection at trial and the issue is raised on direct appeal, the defendant generally is entitled to "automatic reversal" regardless of the error's actual "effect on the outcome." *Neder v. United States* [14th ed., p. 1455]. * * * The question then becomes what showing is necessary when the defendant does not preserve a structural error on direct review but raises it later in the context of an ineffective-assistance-of-counsel claim. To obtain relief on the basis of ineffective assistance of counsel, the defendant as a general rule bears the burden to meet two standards: * * * deficient performance * * * [and] prejudice. *Strickland*.

The prejudice showing is in most cases a necessary part of a *Strickland* claim. * * * That said, the concept of prejudice is defined in different ways depending on the context in which it appears. In the ordinary *Strickland* case, prejudice means "a reasonable probability that, but for counsel's unprofessional errors, the result of the proceeding would have been different." But the *Strickland* Court cautioned that the prejudice inquiry is not meant to be applied in a "mechanical" fashion. *Strickland* at [14th ed., p. 130, last ¶] For when a court is evaluating an ineffective-assistance claim, the ultimate inquiry must concentrate on "the fundamental fairness of the proceeding." Ibid. Petitioner therefore argues that under a proper interpretation of *Strickland,* even if there is no showing of a reasonable probability of a different outcome, relief still must be granted if the convicted person shows that attorney errors rendered the trial fundamentally unfair. For the analytical purposes of this case, the Court will assume that petitioner's interpretation of *Strickland* is the correct one. In light of the Court's ultimate holding, however, the Court need not decide that question here.

As explained above, not every public-trial violation will in fact lead to a fundamentally unfair trial. Nor can it be said that the failure to object to a public-trial violation always deprives the defendant of a reasonable probability of a different outcome. Thus, when a defendant raises a public-trial violation via an ineffective-assistance-of-counsel claim, *Strickland* prejudice is not shown automatically. Instead, the burden is on the defendant to show either a reasonable probability of a different outcome in his or her case or, as the Court has assumed for these purposes, to show that the particular public-trial violation was so serious as to render his or her trial fundamentally unfair.

Neither the reasoning nor the holding here calls into question the Court's precedents determining that certain errors are deemed structural and require reversal because they cause fundamental unfairness, either to the defendant in the specific case or by pervasive undermining of the systemic requirements of a fair and open judicial process. See Murray, A Contextual Approach to Harmless Error Review, 130 Harv. L. Rev. 1791, 1813, 1822 (2017) (noting that the "eclectic normative objectives of criminal procedure" go beyond protecting a defendant from erroneous conviction and include ensuring " 'that the administration of justice should reasonably appear to be disinterested' "). Those precedents include *Sullivan v. Louisiana*, 508 U.S. 275 (1993) (failure to give a reasonable-doubt instruction); *Tumey v. Ohio,* 273 U.S. 510 (1927) (biased judge); and *Vasquez v. Hillery* [14th ed., Note 8, p. 986] (exclusion of grand jurors on the basis of race). This Court, in addition, has granted automatic relief to defendants who prevailed on claims alleging race or gender discrimination in the selection of the petit jury, see *Batson v. Kentucky*

[14th ed., p. 1283], * * * though the Court has yet to label those errors structural in express terms. * * * The errors in those cases necessitated automatic reversal after they were preserved and then raised on direct appeal. And this opinion does not address whether the result should be any different if the errors were raised instead in an ineffective-assistance claim on collateral review.

The reason for placing the burden on the petitioner in this case, however, derives both from the nature of the error and the difference between a public-trial violation preserved and then raised on direct review and a public-trial violation raised as an ineffective-assistance-of-counsel claim. As explained above, when a defendant objects to a courtroom closure, the trial court can either order the courtroom opened or explain the reasons for keeping it closed. When a defendant first raises the closure in an ineffective-assistance claim, however, the trial court is deprived of the chance to cure the violation either by opening the courtroom or by explaining the reasons for closure.

Furthermore, when state or federal courts adjudicate errors objected to during trial and then raised on direct review, the systemic costs of remedying the error are diminished to some extent. That is because, if a new trial is ordered on direct review, there may be a reasonable chance that not too much time will have elapsed for witness memories still to be accurate and physical evidence not to be lost. There are also advantages of direct judicial supervision. Reviewing courts, in the regular course of the appellate process, can give instruction to the trial courts in a familiar context that allows for elaboration of the relevant principles based on review of an adequate record. For instance, in this case, the factors and circumstances that might justify a temporary closure are best considered in the regular appellate process and not in the context of a later proceeding, with its added time delays.

When an ineffective-assistance-of-counsel claim is raised in postconviction proceedings, the costs and uncertainties of a new trial are greater because more time will have elapsed in most cases. The finality interest is more at risk, see *Strickland* (noting the "profound importance of finality in criminal proceedings"), and direct review often has given at least one opportunity for an appellate review of trial proceedings. These differences justify a different standard for evaluating a structural error depending on whether it is raised on direct review or raised instead in a claim alleging ineffective assistance of counsel. * * * In sum, "[a]n ineffective-assistance claim can function as a way to escape rules of waiver and forfeiture and raise issues not presented at trial," thus undermining the finality of jury verdicts. *Harrington v. Richter* [14th ed., p. 148, 2nd ¶]. For this reason, the rules governing ineffective assistance claims "must be applied with scrupulous care."

IV

The final inquiry concerns the ineffective-assistance claim in this case. Although the case comes on the assumption that petitioner has shown deficient performance by counsel, he has not shown prejudice in the ordinary sense, *i.e.,* a reasonable probability that the jury would not have convicted him if his attorney had objected to the closure. * * * It is of course possible that potential jurors might have behaved differently if petitioner's family had been present. And it is true that the presence of the public might have had some bearing on juror reaction. But here petitioner offered no "evidence or legal argument establishing prejudice" in the sense of a reasonable probability of a different outcome but for counsel's failure to object. * * * In other circumstances a different result might obtain. If, for instance, defense counsel errs in failing to object when the government's main witness testifies in secret, then the defendant might be able to show prejudice with little more detail. Even in those circumstances, however, the burden would remain on the defendant to make the prejudice showing, because a public-trial violation does not always lead to a fundamentally unfair trial.

In light of the above assumption that prejudice can be shown by a demonstration of fundamental unfairness, the remaining question is whether petitioner has shown that counsel's failure to object rendered the trial fundamentally unfair. The Court concludes that petitioner has not made the showing. Although petitioner's mother and her minister were indeed excluded from the courtroom for two days during jury selection, petitioner's trial was not conducted in secret or in a remote place. * * * The closure was limited to the jury *voir dire*; the courtroom remained open during the evidentiary phase of the trial; the closure decision apparently was made by court officers rather than the judge; there were many members of the venire who did not become jurors but who did observe the proceedings; and there was a record made of the proceedings that does not indicate any basis for concern, other than the closure itself.

There has been no showing, furthermore, that the potential harms flowing from a courtroom closure came to pass in this case. For example, there is no suggestion that any juror lied during *voir dire*; no suggestion of misbehavior by the prosecutor, judge, or any other party; and no suggestion that any of the participants failed to approach their duties with the neutrality and serious purpose that our system demands.

* * *

In the criminal justice system, the constant, indeed unending, duty of the judiciary is to seek and to find the proper balance between the necessity for fair and just trials and the importance of finality of judgments. When a structural error is preserved and raised on direct review, the balance is in the defendant's favor, and a new trial generally will be granted as a matter of right. When a structural error is raised in the context of an ineffective-assistance claim, however, finality concerns are far more pronounced. For this reason, and in light of the other circumstances present in this case, petitioner must show prejudice in order to obtain a new trial.

JUSTICE THOMAS, with whom JUSTICE GORSUCH joins, concurring.

I write separately with two observations about the scope of the Court's holding. First, this case comes to us on the parties' "assumption[s]" that the closure of the courtroom during jury selection "was a Sixth Amendment violation" and that "defense counsel provided ineffective assistance" by "failing to object" to it. The Court previously held in a *per curiam* opinion—issued without the benefit of merits briefing or argument—that the Sixth Amendment right to a public trial extends to jury selection. See *Presley v. Georgia,* (Thomas, J., dissenting). I have some doubts about whether that holding is consistent with the original understanding of the right to a public trial, and I would be open to reconsidering it in a case in which we are asked to do so.

Second, the Court "assume[s]," for the "analytical purposes of this case," that a defendant may establish prejudice under *Strickland* by demonstrating that his attorney's error led to a fundamentally unfair trial. * * * *Strickland* did not hold, as the Court assumes, that a defendant may establish prejudice by showing that his counsel's errors "rendered the trial fundamentally unfair." Because the Court concludes that the closure during petitioner's jury selection did not lead to fundamental unfairness in any event, no part of the discussion about fundamental unfairness is necessary to its result.

In light of these observations, I do not read the opinion of the Court to preclude the approach set forth in Justice Alito's opinion, which correctly applies our precedents.

JUSTICE ALITO, with whom JUSTICE GORSUCH joins, concurring in the judgment.

This case calls for a straightforward application of the familiar standard for evaluating ineffective assistance of counsel claims. *Strickland v. Washington.* * * * The [*Strickland*] prejudice requirement—which is the one at issue in this case—"arises from the very nature" of the right to effective representation: Counsel simply "cannot be 'ineffective' unless his mistakes have harmed the defense (or, at least, unless it is reasonably likely that they have)," *Gonzalez-Lopez* [14th ed.,

p. 111, 1st ¶]. In other words, "a violation of the Sixth Amendment right to *effective* representation is not 'complete' until the defendant is prejudiced." Ibid. * * *

Weaver makes much of the *Strickland* Court's statement that "the ultimate focus of inquiry must be on the fundamental fairness of the proceeding." *Strickland* [14th ed., p. 130, last ¶]. But the very next sentence clarifies what the Court had in mind, namely, the reliability of the proceeding. In that sentence, the Court explains that the proper concern—"[i]n every case"—is "whether, despite the strong presumption of reliability, the result of the particular proceeding is unreliable." Ibid. In other words, the focus on reliability is consistent throughout the *Strickland* opinion. * * * [T]here are two ways of meeting the *Strickland* prejudice requirement. A defendant must demonstrate either that the error at issue was prejudicial or that it belongs to the narrow class of attorney errors that are tantamount to a denial of counsel, for which an individualized showing of prejudice is unnecessary [*Cronic,* 14th ed., Note 2, p. 161].

Weaver attempts to escape this framework by stressing that the deprivation of the right to a public trial has been described as a "structural" error, but this is irrelevant under *Strickland*. The concept of "structural error" comes into play when it is established that an error occurred at the trial level and it must be decided whether the error was harmless. * * * The prejudice prong of *Strickland* is entirely different. It does not ask whether an error was harmless but whether there was an error at all, for unless counsel's deficient performance prejudiced the defense, there was no Sixth Amendment violation in the first place. See *Gonzalez-Lopez* (even where an attorney's deficient performance "pervades the entire trial," "we do not allow reversal of a conviction for that reason without a showing of prejudice" because "the requirement of showing prejudice in ineffectiveness claims stems from the very definition of the right at issue") [14th ed., p. 112, 1st ¶]. Weaver's theory conflicts with *Strickland* because it implies that an attorney's error can be prejudicial even if it "had no effect," or only "some conceivable effect," on the outcome of his trial. That is precisely what *Strickland* rules out. * * *

JUSTICE BREYER, with whom JUSTICE KAGAN joins, dissenting.

The Court notes that *Strickland*'s "prejudice inquiry is not meant to be applied in a 'mechanical' fashion," and I agree. But, in my view, it follows from this principle that a defendant who shows that his attorney's constitutionally deficient performance produced a structural error should not face the additional—and often insurmountable—*Strickland* hurdle of demonstrating that the error changed the outcome of his proceeding. * * *

The Court has recognized that structural errors' distinctive attributes make them "defy analysis by 'harmless-error' standards." It has therefore *categorically* exempted structural errors from the case-by-case harmlessness review to which trial errors are subjected. Our precedent does not try to parse which structural errors are the truly egregious ones. It simply views *all* structural errors as "intrinsically harmful" and holds that *any* structural error warrants "automatic reversal" on direct appeal "without regard to [its] effect on the outcome" of a trial. *Neder v. United States* [14th ed., p. 1455].

The majority here does not take this approach. It assumes that *some* structural errors—those that "lead to fundamental unfairness"—but not others, can warrant relief without a showing of actual prejudice under *Strickland*. While I agree that a showing of fundamental unfairness is sufficient to satisfy *Strickland*, I would not try to draw this distinction. * * * Even if some structural errors do not create fundamental unfairness, *all* structural errors nonetheless have features that make them "defy analysis by 'harmless-error' standards." *Fulminante* [14th ed., p. 1455]. This is why *all* structural errors—not just the "fundamental unfairness" ones—are exempt from harmlessness inquiry and warrant automatic reversal on direct review. Those same features mean that *all* structural errors defy an actual-prejudice analysis under *Strickland*.

For instance, the majority concludes that some errors—such as the public-trial error at issue in this case—have been labeled "structural" because they have effects that "are simply too hard to measure." * * * But how could any error whose effects are inherently indeterminate prove susceptible to actual-prejudice analysis under *Strickland*? Just as the "difficulty of assessing the effect" of such an error would turn harmless-error analysis into "a speculative inquiry into what might have occurred in an alternate universe," *Gonzalez-Lopez*, so too would it undermine a defendant's ability to make an actual-prejudice showing to establish an ineffective-assistance claim.

The problem is evident with regard to public-trial violations. This Court has recognized that "the benefits of a public trial are frequently intangible, difficult to prove, or a matter of chance." *Waller v. Georgia*. As a result, "a requirement that prejudice be shown 'would in most cases deprive [the defendant] of the [public-trial] guarantee, for it would be difficult to envisage a case in which he would have evidence available of specific injury.'" Ibid. In order to establish actual prejudice from an attorney's failure to object to a public-trial violation, a defendant would face the nearly impossible burden of establishing how his trial might have gone differently had it been open to the public.

I do not see how we can read *Strickland* as requiring defendants to prove what this Court has held cannot be proved. If courts do not presume prejudice when counsel's deficient performance leads to a structural error, then defendants may well be unable to obtain relief for incompetence that deprived them "of basic protections without which a criminal trial cannot reliably serve its function as a vehicle for determination n of guilt or innocence." *Neder*. This would be precisely the sort of "mechanical" application that *Strickland* tells us to avoid. * * *

§ 4. THE *CRONIC* EXCEPTIONS AND OTHER POSSIBLE PER SE VIOLATIONS

14th ed., p. 169; after Note 1, add:

1A. Consider also *Kuren* v. *Luzerne County*, 146 A.3d 715 (Pa. 2016). Finding "the majorities' reasoning in * * * *Duncan* and *Hurrel-Harring* to be persuasive, and, indeed compelling," the Pennsylvania Supreme Court concluded that the Sixth Amendment provides the grounding for a "[civil] cause of action * * * entitling a class of indigent criminal defendants to allege prospective, systemic violations of the right to counsel due to underfunding, and to seek and obtain an injunction forcing a county to provide adequate funding to a county public defender's office." *Gideon*, the court noted, was not satisfied by the "mere existence of a public defender's office and the assignment of attorneys by that office," without regard to the level of performance of those attorneys, as "it is the defense, not the lawyers as such, that animates *Gideon*'s mandate." However, to gain the requested injunction, the plaintiffs would have to meet the traditional requirements for such relief—"demonstrating [1] the likelihood of a substantial and immediate irreparable injury, and [2] the inadequacy of remedies at law."

As for the evidence establishing the first element, a standard proposed by the Department of Justice [in its amicus brief supporting the plaintiffs] "offers a workable, if non-exhausting, paradigm for weighing such [Sixth Amendment] claims." In "setting forth [the] cause of action," and establishing "the 'likelihood of substantial and immediate irreparable injury,' the plaintiff should focus upon the following factors: (1) * * * on a system-wide basis, the traditional markers of representation—such as timely and confidential consultation with clients, appropriate investigation, and meaningful adversarial testing of the prosecution's case—are absent or significantly compromised; and (2) * * * substantial structural limitations—such as a severe lack of resources, unreasonably high workloads, or critical understaffing of public defender offices—cause that absence or limitation on representation."

Here, the plaintiffs' allegations met that standard. In count I, for example, they had alleged that, due to resource limitations, Luzerne County OPD attorneys frequently were: "(a) unable to interview or meet with clients prior to preliminary hearings; (b) unable to contact their clients between court appearances; (c) unable to conduct significant investigation or discovery; (d) unable to engage in significant motion practice; (e) unable to gather information needed for effective plea negotiations; (f) unable to engage in sufficient trial preparation; and (g) unable to [ ] litigate appeals because of a lack of appellate experience." These allegations supported "[plaintiffs'] argument * * * that inadequate funding created a system in Luzerne County where the OPD [lawyers], even when assigned and appearing in court, are so handicapped in the time and resources that they can dedicate to each defendant that their presence amounts to a mere formality," with the OPD "systematically incapable of providing constitutionally adequate representation."

The proof of such systemic failures also would meet the second injunction prerequisite—establishing the inadequacies of remedies at law (i.e., the postconviction review of counsel's performance under *Strickland* and *Cronic*). As *Duncan* noted, " 'the right to counsel' must mean more than just the right to an outcome!" A "person seeking to vindicate" the right to counsel need not "wait until he or she has been convicted and sentenced. To so hold would undermine the essentiality of the right during the pretrial process. It would render irrelevant all deprivations of the right at the earliest stage so long as they do not clearly affect the substantive outcome of the trial."

§ 6.　CLIENT CONTROL

14th ed., p. 190; replace all the notes in this section except notes 6 and 10:

1.　*Self-representation vs. attorney control.* In *Faretta v. California,* in the course of recognizing a constitutional right to self-representation, the Court noted that only self-representation gives the defendant absolute control over his defense. For "when a defendant chooses to have a lawyer manage and present his case," he assumes some relinquishment of control, as "law and tradition may allocate to the counsel the power to make binding decisions of trial strategy in many areas" (14th ed., p. 96, 4th paragraph). *Jones v. Barnes*, 463 U.S. 745 (1983), was the first post-*Faretta* ruling to further explore the range of control relinquished by a defendant's choice to be represented by counsel. *Jones v. Barnes* concluded that the range of "strategic" decisions within counsel's ultimate control was not limited to decisions during trial (in *Jones*, appellate counsel had ultimate authority as to what contentions to include in an appeal) and was not limited to settings in which timing considerations precluded consultation with the defendant.[a] The Court also noted, however, that certain decisions were within the "ultimate authority" of the accused. Here, counsel had to consult and follow the direction of the accused. These decisions came to be characterized as "personal" or "fundamental rights" decisions (in contrast, to the category of "strategic" decisions, where counsel has ultimate authority). Personal decisions were not limited to waivers that required the personal, on-the-record participation of the defendant, such as the entry of a guilty plea or the waiver of a jury trial. Accordingly, whether a particular decision fell within defendant's control was an issue often presented through a post-conviction challenge, with the defendant claiming that he had never been informed that the

---

[a]　In dissent, Justice Brennan, joined by Justice Marshall, rejected extending the attorney's control to decisions that were not subject to these limitations. The dissent noted: "A constitutional rule that encourages lawyers to disregard their clients wishes without compelling need can only exacerbate the clients' suspicion of their lawyers. * * * [U]ntil his conviction becomes final and he has had an opportunity to appeal, any restrictions on individual autonomy and dignity should be limited to the minimum necessary to vindicate the State's interest in speedy, effective prosecution. The role of the defense lawyer should be above all to function as the instrument and defender of the client's autonomy and dignity in all phases of the criminal process."

decision was his to make and that he would have objected had he been so informed.[b] Post-*Jones*, in a series of rulings, primarily involving this procedural setting, the Court has addressed the proper characterization (within defendant's control or counsel's control) of a lengthy list of defense decisions. The latest in this line of rulings, *McCoy v. Louisiana*, both summarizes those earlier characterizations and addresses an area of decisionmaking that arguably reveals ambiguities in the analysis that controls the characterization.

McCOY V. LOUISIANA
___ U.S. ___, 138 S.Ct. 1500, ___ L.Ed.2d ___ (2018).

JUSTICE GINSBURG delivered the opinion of the Court.

In *Florida* v. *Nixon*, 543 U.S. 175 (2004), this Court considered whether the Constitution bars defense counsel from conceding a capital defendant's guilt at trial "when [the] defendant, informed by counsel, neither consents nor objects." * * * We held that when counsel confers with the defendant and the defendant remains silent, neither approving nor protesting counsel's proposed concession strategy, "[no] blanket rule demand[s] the defendant's explicit consent" to implementation of that strategy.

In the case now before us, in contrast to *Nixon*, the defendant vociferously insisted that he did not engage in the charged acts and adamantly objected to any admission of guilt. App. 286–287, 505–506. Yet the trial court permitted counsel, at the guilt phase of a capital trial, to tell the jury the defendant "committed three murders. . . . [H]e's guilty." We hold that a defendant has the right to insist that counsel refrain from admitting guilt, even when counsel's experienced-based view is that confessing guilt offers the defendant the best chance to avoid the death penalty. Guaranteeing a defendant the right "to have the *Assistance* of Counsel for *his* defence," the Sixth Amendment so demands. With individual liberty—and, in capital cases, life—at stake, it is the defendant's prerogative, not counsel's, to decide on the objective of his defense: to admit guilt in the hope of gaining mercy at the sentencing stage, or to maintain his innocence, leaving it to the State to prove his guilt beyond a reasonable doubt. * * *

On May 5, 2008, Christine and Willie Young and Gregory Colston were shot and killed in the Youngs' home in Bossier City, Louisiana. The three victims were the mother, stepfather, and son of Robert McCoy's estranged wife, Yolanda. Several days later, police arrested McCoy in Idaho. Extradited to Louisiana, McCoy was appointed counsel from the public defender's office. A Bossier Parish grand jury indicted McCoy on three counts of first-degree murder, and the prosecutor gave notice of intent to seek the death penalty. McCoy pleaded not guilty. Throughout the proceedings, he insistently maintained he was out of State at the time of the killings and that corrupt police killed the victims when a drug deal went wrong. At defense counsel's request, a court-appointed sanity commission examined McCoy and found him competent to stand trial.

---

[b]   Concurring in Gonzalez v. United States, 553 U.S. 242 (2008), Justice Scalia urged the Court to abandon distinguishing between "fundamental" and "strategic" decisions in this context—where there had been no objection by the client when the counsel implemented the decision (typically a waiver by failing to object). In that setting, the Court should adopt "the rule that, as a constitutional matter, all waivable rights (except, of course, the right to counsel) can be waived by counsel". The "tactical-vs.-fundamental approach" was described as "vague and derived from nothing more substantial than this Court's say so." "Waiving *any* right can be a tactical decision" and "any right guaranteed by the Constitution would be fundamental." The "very notion of representative litigation [with counsel acting as the defendant's representative] suggests that the Constitution draws no distinction" between one constitutional right (e.g., the right of confrontation, deemed "tactical" and within counsel's control) and another (e.g., the right to a jury trial, deemed "fundamental" and controlled only by the defendant). While distinctions might be drawn under procedural rules, absent a protest by defendant withdrawing counsel's authority, there is "no basis for saying that the *Constitution* automatically invalidated *any* action not taken by the defendant personally, though taken by authorized counsel."

In December 2009 and January 2010, McCoy told the court his relationship with assigned counsel had broken down irretrievably. He sought and gained leave to represent himself until his parents engaged new counsel for him. In March 2010, Larry English, engaged by McCoy's parents, enrolled as McCoy's counsel. English eventually concluded that the evidence against McCoy was over-whelming and that, absent a concession at the guilt stage that McCoy was the killer, a death sentence would be impossible to avoid at the penalty phase.[1] McCoy, English reported, was "furious" when told, two weeks before trial was scheduled to begin, that English would concede McCoy's commission of the triple murders.[2] McCoy told English "not to make that concession," and English knew of McCoy's "complet[e] oppos[ition] to [English] telling the jury that [McCoy] was guilty of killing the three victims"; instead of any concession, McCoy pressed English to pursue acquittal.

At a July 26, 2011 hearing, McCoy sought to terminate English's representation, and English asked to be relieved if McCoy secured other counsel. With trial set to start two days later, the court refused to relieve English and directed that he remain as counsel of record. "[Y]ou are the attorney," the court told English when he expressed disagreement with McCoy's wish to put on a defense case, and "you have to make the trial decision of what you're going to proceed with."

At the beginning of his opening statement at the guilt phase of the trial, English told the jury there was "no way reasonably possible" that they could hear the prosecution's evidence and reach "any other conclusion than Robert McCoy was the cause of these individuals' death." . McCoy protested; out of earshot of the jury, McCoy told the court that English was "selling [him] out" by maintaining that McCoy "murdered [his] family." The trial court reiterated that English was "representing" McCoy and told McCoy that the court would not permit "any other outbursts." Continuing his opening statement, English told the jury the evidence is "unambiguous," "my client committed three murders." McCoy testified in his own defense, maintaining his innocence and pressing an alibi difficult to fathom. In his closing argument, English reiterated that McCoy was the killer. On that issue, English told the jury that he "took [the] burden off of [the prosecutor]." The jury then returned a unanimous verdict of guilty of first-degree murder on all three counts. At the penalty phase, English again conceded "Robert McCoy committed these crimes," but urged mercy in view of McCoy's "serious mental and emotional issues." The jury returned three death verdicts.

Represented by new counsel, McCoy unsuccessfully moved for a new trial, arguing that the trial court violated his constitutional rights by allowing English to concede McCoy "committed three murders," over McCoy's objection. The Louisiana Supreme Court affirmed the trial court's ruling that defense counsel had authority so to concede guilt, despite the defendant's opposition to any admission of guilt. The concession was permissible, the court concluded, because counsel reasonably believed that admitting guilt afforded McCoy the best chance to avoid a death sentence.

We granted certiorari in view of a division of opinion among state courts of last resort on the question whether it is unconstitutional to allow defense counsel to concede guilt over the defendant's intransigent and unambiguous objection. Compare with the instant case, *e.g., Cooke v. State*, 977 A. 2d 803, 842–846 (Del. 2009) (counsel's pursuit of a "guilty but mentally ill" verdict

---

[1]   Part of English's strategy was to concede that McCoy committed the murders and to argue that he should be convicted only of second-degree murder, because his "mental incapacity prevented him from forming the requisite specific intent to commit first degree murder." But the second-degree strategy would have encountered a shoal, for Louisiana does not permit introduction of evidence of a defendant's diminished capacity absent the entry of a plea of not guilty by reason of insanity.

[2]   The dissent states that English told McCoy his proposed trial strategy eight months before trial. English did encourage McCoy, "[a] couple of months before the trial," to plead guilty rather than proceed to trial. But English declared under oath that "the first time [he] told [McCoy] that [he] intended to concede to the jury that [McCoy] was the killer" was July 12, 2011, two weeks before trial commenced. App. at 286. Encouraging a guilty plea pretrial, of course, is not equivalent to imparting to a defendant counsel's strategic determination to concede guilt should trial occur.

over defendant's "vociferous and repeated protestations" of innocence violated defendant's "constitutional right to make the fundamental decisions regarding his case"); *State* v. *Carter*, 270 Kan. 426, 440, 14 P. 3d 1138, 1148 (2000) (counsel's admission of client's involvement in murder when client adamantly maintained his innocence contravened Sixth Amendment right to counsel and due process right to a fair trial). * * *

The Sixth Amendment guarantees to each criminal defendant "the Assistance of Counsel for his defence." At common law, self-representation was the norm. * * * Even now, when most defendants choose to be represented by counsel, an accused may insist upon representing herself—however counterproductive that course may be, see *Faretta v. California*, [14th ed., p. 95]. As this Court explained, "[t]he right to defend is personal," and a defendant's choice in exercising that right "must be honored out of 'that respect for the individual which is the lifeblood of the law.'" *Ibid* [14th ed., p. 97].

The choice is not all or nothing: To gain assistance, a defendant need not surrender control entirely to counsel. For the Sixth Amendment, in "grant[ing] to the accused personally the right to make his defense," "speaks of the 'assistance' of counsel, and an assistant, however expert, is still an assistant." * * * Trial management is the lawyer's province: Counsel provides his or her assistance by making decisions such as "what arguments to pursue, what evidentiary objections to raise, and what agreements to conclude regarding the admission of evidence." *Gonzalez* v. *United States*, 553 U.S. 242, 248 (2008).[c] Some decisions, however, are reserved for the client—notably, whether to plead guilty, waive the right to a jury trial, testify in one's own behalf, and forgo an appeal. See *Jones v. Barnes*, 463 U.S. 745, 751 (1983).

Autonomy to decide that the objective of the defense is to assert innocence belongs in this latter category. Just as a defendant may steadfastly refuse to plead guilty in the face of overwhelming evidence against her, or reject the assistance of legal counsel despite the defendant's own inexperience and lack of professional qualifications, so may she insist on maintaining her innocence at the guilt phase of a capital trial. These are not strategic choices about how best to *achieve* a client's objectives; they are choices about what the client's objectives in fact *are*.

Counsel may reasonably assess a concession of guilt as best suited to avoiding the death penalty, as English did in this case. But the client may not share that objective. He may wish to avoid, above all else, the opprobrium that comes with admitting he killed family members. Or he may hold life in prison not worth living and prefer to risk death for any hope, however small, of exoneration. When a client expressly asserts that the objective of "*his* defence" is to maintain innocence of the charged criminal acts, his lawyer must abide by that objective and may not override it by conceding guilt. U. S. Const., Amdt. 6 (emphasis added); see ABA Model Rule of Professional Conduct 1.2(a) (2016) (a "lawyer shall abide by a client's decisions concerning the objectives of the representation"). * * *

Preserving for the defendant the ability to decide whether to maintain his innocence should not displace counsel's, or the court's, respective trial management roles. See *Gonzalez*

---

c   In *Gonzalez*, the Court offered the following explanation of the defense attorney's full authority to manage the conduct of the trial (including, in that case, the authority to consent—apparently without previous client consultation—to having a magistrate, rather than the trial judge, conduct voir dire and jury selections): "Numerous choices affecting conduct of the trial, including the objections to make, the witnesses to call, and the arguments to advance, depend not only upon what is permissible under the rules of evidence and procedure but also upon tactical considerations of the moment and the larger strategic plan for the trial. These matters can be difficult to explain to a layperson; and to require in all instances that they be approved by the client could risk compromising the efficiencies and fairness that the trial process is designed to promote. In exercising professional judgment, moreover, the attorney draws upon the expertise and experience that members of the bar should bring to the trial process. In most instances the attorney will have a better understanding of the procedural choices than the client; or at least the laws should so assume."

("[n]umerous choices affecting conduct of the trial" do not require client consent, including "the objections to make, the witnesses to call, and the arguments to advance"). * * * In this case, the court had determined that McCoy was competent to stand trial, *i.e.,* that McCoy had "sufficient present ability to consult with his lawyer with a reasonable degree of rational understanding." *Godinez* v. *Moran,* [14th ed., Note 5, p. 105].[3] If, after consultations with English concerning the management of the defense, McCoy disagreed with English's proposal to concede McCoy committed three murders, it was not open to English to override McCoy's objection. English could not interfere with McCoy's telling the jury "I was not the murderer," although counsel could, if consistent with providing effective assistance, focus his own collaboration on urging that McCoy's mental state weighed against conviction.

Florida v. *Nixon* is not to the contrary. Nixon's attorney did not negate Nixon's autonomy by overriding Nixon's desired defense objective, for Nixon never asserted any such objective. Nixon "was generally unresponsive" during discussions of trial strategy, and "never verbally approved or protested" counsel's proposed approach. Nixon complained about the admission of his guilt only after trial.[d] McCoy, in contrast, opposed English's assertion of his guilt at every opportunity, before and during trial, both in conference with his lawyer and in open court. If a client declines to participate in his defense, then an attorney may permissibly guide the defense pursuant to the strategy she believes to be in the defendant's best interest. Presented with express statements of the client's will to maintain innocence, however, counsel may not steer the ship the other way. * * *

The Louisiana Supreme Court concluded that English's refusal to maintain McCoy's innocence was necessitated by Louisiana Rule of Professional Conduct 1.2(d) (2017), which provides that "[a] lawyer shall not counsel a client to engage, or assist a client, in conduct that the lawyer knows is criminal or fraudulent." Presenting McCoy's alibi defense, the court said, would put English in an "ethical conundrum," implicating English in perjury. 218 So.3d, at 565 (citing *Nix* v. *Whiteside,* 475 U.S. 739 (1986)[e]). But McCoy's case does not resemble *Nix,* where the defendant told his lawyer that he intended to commit perjury. There was no such avowed perjury here. Cf. ABA Model Rule of Professional Conduct 3.3, Comment 8 ("The prohibition against offering false evidence only applies if the lawyer knows that the evidence is false."). English harbored no doubt that McCoy believed what he was saying; English simply disbelieved McCoy's account in view of the prosecution's evidence. English's express motivation for conceding guilt was not to avoid suborning perjury, but to try to build credibility with the jury, and thus obtain a

---

[3]   Several times, English did express his view that McCoy was not, in fact, competent to stand trial.

[d]   The *Nixon* Court rejected the contention that counsel's concession was tantamount to a guilty plea, which requires the defendant's participation. The lower court there had relied on *Brookhart v. Janis,* 384 U.S.1 (1966). The *Brookhart* Court held that counsel unilaterally took action tantamount to entering a guilty plea by entering into an agreement "that all the state had to prove was a prima facie case, that he would not contest it, and that there would be no cross-examination of witnesses." Distinguishing *Brookhart,* the *Nixon* Court noted that counsel here did not accept a "truncated proceeding, shorn of the need * * * [to establish] guilt beyond a reasonable doubt." While acknowledging in his opening statement that defendant committed the murder, defense counsel: (1) did not thereby relieve the state of its obligation to present admissible evidence meeting the reasonable doubt standard; (2) retained the authority to object to the admission of prejudicial evidence and to cross-examine witnesses; and (3) did not preclude raising on appeal any "errors in the trial or jury instructions."

[e]   In that case, Whiteside's counsel, upon learning that Whiteside intended to commit perjury, warned Whiteside that such action would (1) lead counsel to seek to withdraw, (2) require counsel to advise the trial court of the perjury, and (3) that counsel "probably would [then] be allowed to attempt to impeach that testimony." As a result of those warnings, Whiteside testified without perjuring himself. Rejecting a *Strickland* claim, five justices concluded that counsel's proposed response to his client's perjury was "wholly consistent with the Iowa standards of professional conduct and law, with the overwhelming majority of courts, and with codes of professional ethics [i.e., the Model Code of Professional Responsibility and the Model Rules of Professional Conduct]." Accordingly, they reasoned, "since there has been no breach of any recognized professional duty, it follows that there can be no deprivation of the right to assistance of counsel under the *Strickland* standard." Four Justices concurred only in the judgment, relying solely on defendant's failure to meet the prejudice prong of the *Strickland* standard. See Note 7, p. 139.

sentence lesser than death. Louisiana's ethical rules might have stopped English from presenting McCoy's alibi evidence if English knew perjury was involved. But Louisiana has identified no ethical rule requiring English to admit McCoy's guilt over McCoy's objection. See 3 W. LaFave, J. Israel, N. King, & O. Kerr, Criminal Procedure § 11.6(c), p. 935 (4th ed. 2015) ("A lawyer is not placed in a professionally embarrassing position when he is reluctantly required . . . to go to trial in a weak case, since that decision is clearly attributed to his client.").

The dissent describes the conflict between English and McCoy as "rare" and "unlikely to recur." Yet the Louisiana Supreme Court parted ways with three other State Supreme Courts that have addressed this conflict in the past twenty years. * * * In each of the three cases, as here, the defendant repeatedly and adamantly insisted on maintaining his factual innocence despite counsel's preferred course: concession of the defendant's commission of criminal acts and pursuit of diminished capacity, mental illness, or lack of premeditation defenses. * * * These were not strategic disputes about whether to concede an element of a charged offense; they were intractable disagreements about the fundamental objective of the defendant's representation. For McCoy, that objective was to maintain "I did not kill the members of my family." In this stark scenario, we agree with the majority of state courts of last resort that counsel may not admit her client's guilt of a charged crime over the client's intransigent objection to that admission.

Because a client's autonomy, not counsel's competence, is in issue, we do not apply our ineffective-assistance-of- counsel jurisprudence, *Strickland* v. *Washington*, or *United States v. Cronic*, to McCoy's claim. To gain redress for attorney error, a defendant ordinarily must show prejudice. See *Strickland*. Here, however, the violation of McCoy's protected autonomy right was complete when the court allowed counsel to usurp control of an issue within McCoy's sole prerogative.

Violation of a defendant's Sixth Amendment-secured autonomy ranks as error of the kind our decisions have called "structural"; when present, such an error is not subject to harmless-error review. See, *e.g., McKaskle* [14th ed., Note 2, p. 99] (harmless-error analysis is inapplicable to deprivations of the self-representation right, because "[t]he right is either respected or denied; its deprivation cannot be harmless"); *United States v. Gonzalez-Lopez* [14th ed., p. 109] (choice of counsel is structural); *Waller v. Georgia*, [14th ed., p. 1455] (public trial is structural). Structural error "affect[s] the framework within which the trial proceeds," as distinguished from a lapse or flaw that is "simply an error in the trial process itself." *Arizona v. Fulminante*, 499 U. S. 279, 310 (1991). An error may be ranked structural, we have explained, "if the right at issue is not designed to protect the defendant from erroneous conviction but instead protects some other interest," such as "the fundamental legal principle that a defendant must be allowed to make his own choices about the proper way to protect his own liberty." *Weaver v. Massachusetts* [Supp. p. 26]. An error might also count as structural when its effects are too hard to measure, as is true of the right to counsel of choice, or where the error will inevitably signal fundamental unfairness, as we have said of a judge's failure to tell the jury that it may not convict unless it finds the defendant's guilt beyond a reasonable doubt. *Weaver*.

Under at least the first two rationales, counsel's admission of a client's guilt over the client's express objection is error structural in kind. Such an admission blocks the defendant's right to make the fundamental choices about his own defense. And the effects of the admission would be immeasurable, because a jury would almost certainly be swayed by a lawyer's concession of his client's guilt. McCoy must therefore be accorded a new trial without any need first to show prejudice.[4] * * *

---

[4] The dissent suggests that a remand would be in order, so that the Louisiana Supreme Court, in the first instance, could consider the structural-error question. * * * "[W]e did not grant certiorari to review" that question. *Post* [p. 42]. But McCoy raised his structural-error argument in his opening brief, and Louisiana

JUSTICE ALITO, with whom JUSTICE THOMAS and JUSTICE GORSUCH join, dissenting.

The Constitution gives us the authority to decide real cases and controversies; we do not have the right to simplify or otherwise change the facts of a case in order to make our work easier or to achieve a desired result. But that is exactly what the Court does in this case. The Court overturns petitioner's convictions for three counts of first-degree murder by attributing to his trial attorney, Larry English, something that English never did. The Court holds that English violated petitioner's constitutional rights by "admit[ting] h[is] client's guilt of a charged crime over the client's intransigent objection." [p. 35].[1] But English did not admit that petitioner was guilty of first-degree murder. Instead, faced with overwhelming evidence that petitioner shot and killed the three victims, English admitted that petitioner committed one element of that offense, *i.e.*, that he killed the victims. But English strenuously argued that petitioner was not guilty of first-degree murder because he lacked the intent (the *mens rea*) required for the offense. So the Court's newly discovered fundamental right simply does not apply to the real facts of this case.

I

The real case is far more complex. Indeed, the real situation English faced at the beginning of petitioner's trial was the result of a freakish confluence of factors that is unlikely to recur. * * * Retained by petitioner's family, English found himself in a predicament as the trial date approached. The evidence against his client was truly "overwhelming," as the Louisiana Supreme Court aptly noted. Among other things, the evidence showed the following. Before the killings took place, petitioner had abused and threatened to kill his wife, and she was therefore under police protection. On the night of the killings, petitioner's mother-in-law made a 911 call and was heard screaming petitioner's first name. She yelled: " 'She ain't here, Robert . . . I don't know where she is. The detectives have her. Talk to the detectives. She ain't in there, Robert.' " Moments later, a gunshot was heard, and the 911 call was disconnected.

Officers were dispatched to the scene, and on arrival, they found three dead or dying victims—petitioner's mother- in-law, her husband, and the teenage son of petitioner's wife. The officers saw a man who fit petitioner's description fleeing in petitioner's car. They chased the suspect, but he abandoned the car along with critical evidence linking him to the crime: the cordless phone petitioner's mother-in-law had used to call 911 and a receipt for the type of ammunition used to kill the victims. Petitioner was eventually arrested while hitchhiking in Idaho, and a loaded gun found in his possession was identified as the one used to shoot the victims. In addition to all this, a witness testified that petitioner had asked to borrow money to purchase bullets shortly before the shootings, and surveillance footage showed petitioner purchasing the ammunition on the day of the killings. And two of petitioner's friends testified that he confessed to killing at least one person.

Despite all this evidence, petitioner, who had been found competent to stand trial and had refused to plead guilty by reason of insanity, insisted that he did not kill the victims. He claimed that the victims were killed by the local police and that he had been framed by a far flung conspiracy of state and federal officials, reaching from Louisiana to Idaho. Petitioner believed that

---

explicitly chose not to grapple with it. In any event, "we have the authority to make our own assessment of the harmlessness of a constitutional error in the first instance." *Yates* v. *Evatt*, 500 U. S. 391, 407 (1991).

[1]　　When the Court expressly states its holding, it refers to a concession of guilt. See *ante* [p. 34]. ("We hold that a defendant has the right to insist that counsel refrain from admitting guilt, even when counsel's experienced-based view is that confessing guilt offers the defendant the best chance to avoid the death penalty"); *ante* [p. 35] ("counsel may not admit her client's guilt of a charged crime over the client's intransigent objection to that admission"). The opinion also contains many other references to the confession or admission of guilt. * * * At a few points, however, the Court refers to the admission of criminal "acts." *Ante* [pgs. 34, 36, 38]. A rule that a defense attorney may not admit the *actus reus* of an offense (or perhaps even any element of the *actus reus*) would be very different from the rule that the Court expressly adopts. I discuss some of the implications of such a broad rule in Part III of this opinion.

even his attorney and the trial judge had joined the plot. * * * Unwilling to go along with this incredible and uncorroborated defense, English told petitioner "some eight months" before trial that the only viable strategy was to admit the killings and to concentrate on attempting to avoid a sentence of death. 218 So. 3d, at 558. At that point—aware of English's strong views—petitioner could have discharged English and sought new counsel willing to pursue his conspiracy defense; under the Sixth Amendment, that was his right. See *United States* v. *Gonzalez-Lopez*, [14th ed., fn. a, p. 899]. But petitioner stated "several different times" that he was "confident with Mr. English."

The weekend before trial, however, petitioner changed his mind. He asked the trial court to replace English, and English asked for permission to withdraw. Petitioner stated that he had secured substitute counsel, but he was unable to provide the name of this new counsel, and no new attorney ever appeared. The court refused these requests and also denied petitioner's last-minute request to represent himself. (Petitioner does not challenge these decisions here.) So petitioner and English were stuck with each other, and petitioner availed himself of his right to take the stand to tell his wild story. Under those circumstances, what was English supposed to do?

The Louisiana Supreme Court held that English could not have put on petitioner's desired defense without violating state ethics rules, but this Court effectively overrules the state court on this issue of state law. However, even if it is assumed that the Court is correct on this ethics issue, the result of mounting petitioner's conspiracy defense almost certainly would have been disastrous. That approach stood no chance of winning an acquittal and would have severely damaged English's credibility in the eyes of the jury, thus undermining his ability to argue effectively against the imposition of a death sentence at the penalty phase of the trial. * * * So, again, what was English supposed to do?

When pressed at oral argument before this Court, petitioner's current counsel eventually provided an answer: English was not required to take any affirmative steps to support petitioner's bizarre defense, but instead of conceding that petitioner shot the victims, English should have ignored that element entirely. Tr. of Oral Arg. 21–23. So the fundamental right supposedly violated in this case comes down to the difference between the two statements set out below.

> *Constitutional*: "First-degree murder requires proof both that the accused killed the victim and that he acted with the intent to kill. I submit to you that my client did not have the intent required for conviction for that offense."

> *Unconstitutional*: "First-degree murder requires proof both that the accused killed the victim and that he acted with the intent to kill. I admit that my client shot and killed the victims, but I submit to you that he did not have the intent required for conviction for that offense."

The practical difference between these two statements is negligible. If English had conspicuously refrained from endorsing petitioner's story and had based his defense solely on petitioner's dubious mental condition, the jury would surely have gotten the message that English was essentially conceding that petitioner killed the victims. But according to petitioner's current attorney, the difference is fundamental. The first formulation, he admits, is perfectly fine. The latter, on the other hand, is a violation so egregious that the defendant's conviction must be reversed even if there is no chance that the misstep caused any harm. It is no wonder that the Court declines to embrace this argument and instead turns to an issue that the case at hand does not actually present.

II

The constitutional right that the Court has now discovered—a criminal defendant's right to insist that his attorney contest his guilt with respect to all charged offenses—is like a rare plant that blooms every decade or so. Having made its first appearance today, the right is unlikely to figure in another case for many years to come. Why is this so?

First, it is hard to see how the right could come into play in any case other than a capital case in which the jury must decide both guilt and punishment. * * * Second, few rational defendants facing a possible death sentence are likely to insist on contesting guilt where there is no real chance of acquittal and where admitting guilt may improve the chances of avoiding execution. * * * Third, where a capital defendant and his retained attorney cannot agree on a basic trial strategy, the attorney and client will generally part ways unless, as in this case, the court is not apprised until the eve of trial. Fourth, if counsel is appointed, and unreasonably insists on admitting guilt over the defendant's objection, a capable trial judge will almost certainly grant a timely request to appoint substitute counsel. * * * Finally, even if all the above conditions are met, the right that the Court now discovers will not come into play unless the defendant expressly protests counsel's strategy of admitting guilt. Where the defendant is advised of the strategy and says nothing, or is equivocal, the right is deemed to have been waived. See *Nixon.* * * * In short, the right that the Court now discovers is likely to appear only rarely, and because the present case is so unique, it is hard to see how it meets our stated criteria for granting review. * * *

III

While the question that the Court decides is unlikely to make another appearance for quite some time, a related—and difficult—question may arise more frequently: When guilt is the sole issue for the jury, is it ever permissible for counsel to make the unilateral decision to concede an element of the offense charged? If today's decision were understood to address that question, it would have important implications.

Under current precedent, there are some decisions on which a criminal defendant has the final say. For example, a defendant cannot be forced to enter a plea against his wishes. See *Brookhart* v. *Janis*, [Supp., p. 37, fn. d]. Similarly, no matter what counsel thinks best, a defendant has the right to insist on a jury trial and to take the stand and testify in his own defense. See *Harris* v. *New York*, 401 U.S. 222, 225 (1971). And if, as in this case, a defendant and retained counsel do not see eye to eye, the client can always attempt to find another attorney who will accede to his wishes. See *Gonzalez-Lopez.* A defendant can also choose to dispense with counsel entirely and represent himself. *Faretta.*

While these fundamental decisions must be made by a criminal defendant, most of the decisions that arise in criminal cases are the prerogative of counsel. (Our adversarial system would break down if defense counsel were required to obtain the client's approval for every important move made during the course of the case.) Among the decisions that counsel is free to make unilaterally are the following: choosing the basic line of defense, moving to suppress evidence, delivering an opening statement and deciding what to say in the opening, objecting to the admission of evidence, cross-examining witnesses, offering evidence and calling defense witnesses, and deciding what to say in summation. See e.g., *New York* v. *Hill*, 528 U.S. 110 (2000) [listing such rulings and adding "scheduling matters," including deciding to waive the timing requirements of the Interstate Agreement on Detainees]. On which side of the line does conceding some but not all elements of the charged offense fall?

Some criminal offenses contain elements that the prosecution can easily prove beyond any shadow of a doubt. A prior felony conviction is a good example. Suppose that the prosecution is willing to stipulate that the defendant has a prior felony conviction but is prepared, if necessary, to offer certified judgments of conviction for multiple prior violent felonies. If the defendant insists on contesting the convictions on frivolous grounds, must counsel go along? Does the same rule apply to all elements? If there are elements that may not be admitted over the defendant's objection, must counsel go further and actually contest those elements? Or is it permissible if counsel refrains from expressly conceding those elements but essentially admits them by walking the fine line recommended at argument by petitioner's current attorney?

What about conceding that a defendant is guilty, not of the offense charged, but of a lesser included offense? That is what English did in this case. He admitted that petitioner was guilty of the noncapital offense of second-degree murder in an effort to prevent a death sentence.[4] Is admitting guilt of a lesser included offense over the defendant's objection always unconstitutional? Where the evidence strongly supports conviction for first- degree murder, is it unconstitutional for defense counsel to make the decision to admit guilt of any lesser included form of homicide—even manslaughter? What about simple assault?

These are not easy questions, and the fact that they have not come up in this Court for more than two centuries suggests that they will arise infrequently in the future. I would leave those questions for another day and limit our decision to the particular (and highly unusual) situation in the actual case before us. And given the situation in which English found himself when trial commenced, I would hold that he did not violate any fundamental right by expressly acknowledging that petitioner killed the victims instead of engaging in the barren exercise that petitioner's current counsel now recommends.

IV

Having discovered a new right not at issue in the real case before us, the Court compounds its error by summarily concluding that a violation of this right "ranks as error of the kind our decisions have called 'structural.' " * * * The Court concedes that the Louisiana Supreme Court did not decide the structural-error question and that we " 'did not grant certiorari to review' that question." *Ante*, n. 4 [p. 38]. We have stated time and again that we are "a court of review, not of first view" and, for that reason, have refused to decide issues not addressed below. * * * Under comparable circumstances, we have refrained from taking the lead on the question of structural error. * * * There is no good reason to take a different approach in this case. * * *

---

[4]   The Court asserts that, under Louisiana law, English's "second- degree strategy would have encountered a shoal" and necessarily failed. *Ante*, n. 1 [p. 35]. But the final arbiter of Louisiana law—the Louisiana Supreme Court—disagreed. It held that "[t]he jury was left with several choices" after English's second-degree concession, "including returning a responsive verdict of second degree murder" and "not returning the death penalty."

PART 2

POLICE PRACTICES

■ ■ ■

CHAPTER 6

ARREST, SEARCH AND SEIZURE

■ ■ ■

§ 1. THE EXCLUSIONARY RULE

14th ed., p. 222; end of fn. k, add:

Nearly 50 years after *Bivens*, in *Ziglar v. Abbasi*, 137 S.Ct. 1843 (2017), an action by illegal aliens seeking damages from various federal officials for their roundup, detention and purported mistreatment in the immediate aftermath of 9/11 (including claimed Fourth Amendment violations for punitive strip searches during their detention), the Supreme Court in a 4–2 decision (with 3 Justices not participating) declined to extend *Bivens* to the instant case. Though *Bivens* "approved of an implied damages remedy under the Constitution itself," the majority noted, the Court's later "expressed caution as to implied causes of action under congressional statutes led to similar caution with respect to actions in the *Bivens* context," so that now "expanding the *Bivens* remedy is a 'disfavored' judicial activity." The *Ziglar* majority then concluded there were sufficient "special factors counseling hesitation" in the instant case regarding the "detention policy claims," for they involve conditions "imposed on illegal aliens pursuant to a high-level executive policy created in the wake of a major terrorist attack on American soil" and thus require "inquiry into national-security issues" properly "the prerogative of Congress."

14th ed., p. 225; end of fn. l, add:

Regarding point (3), consider that in *United States v. Rodriguez*, 799 F.3d 1222 (8th Cir.2015), the court declined to afford relief to the defendant who prevailed in *Rodriguez v. United States*, p. 61 infra, because "Rodriguez's seizure was lawful under the then-binding precedent."

§ 2. PROTECTED AREAS AND INTERESTS

14th ed., p. 253; before Note 1, add:

0.1 *Tracking a person.* In *Grady v. North Carolina,* 135 S.Ct. 1368 (2015), a recidivist sex offender was ordered "to wear tracking devices at all times * * * for the rest of his life." His Fourth Amendment challenge was rejected by the lower court on the ground "that the State's system of noncriminal satellite-based monitoring does not entail a search within the meaning of the Fourth Amendment." A unanimous Court summarily reversed, concluding that, "it follows" from *Jones* "that a State also conducts a search when it attaches a device to a person's body, without consent, for the purpose of tracing that individual's movements." (As for the "ultimate question of the program's constitutionality," the Court declined to address that issue "in the first instance" and instead left it for the lower court on remand. Another federal court subsequently upheld such a requirement, *Belleau v. Wall*, 811 F.3d 929 (7th Cir.2016).)

14th ed., p. 254; before *Jardines* case, add:

CARPENTER V. UNITED STATES
___ U.S. ___, 138 S.Ct. 2206, ___ L.Ed.2d ___ (2018).

CHIEF JUSTICE ROBERTS delivered the opinion of the Court.

[After the FBI identified the cell phone numbers of several robbery suspects, prosecutors obtained the suspects' cell phone records via a court order under the Stored Communications Act, which requires information short of probable cause. 18 U.S.C.A. § 2703(d). Whenever a person places a cell phone call, the call is routed through local cell sites that are needed to transmit the call. Cell phone providers keep records for their own business purposes of which cell sites were used by particular phones to route particular calls, which enable them to know the rough location of the phone when a call was placed (called cell-cite location information, or CSLI). In Carpenter's case, the FBI obtained 12,898 locations points cataloging Carpenter's movements over 127 days—an average of 101 data points per day.[a] Carpenter unsuccessfully sought to suppress that data, which showed he was near four robbery locations at the time those robberies occurred, and the Sixth Circuit affirmed on the ground that Carpenter lacked a reasonable expectation of privacy in the information he shared with his wireless carriers. The Supreme Court opinion for the 5-Justice majority initially noted that "requests for cell-site records lie at the intersection of two lines of cases," the first of which "addresses a person's expectation of privacy in his physical location and movements" (considered below), and the second of which supports the so-called third-party doctrine, i.e., that "a person has no legitimate expectation of privacy in information he voluntarily turns over to third parties" (discussed in Note 2 at Supp. p. 73).]

    * * * The location information obtained from Carpenter's wireless carriers was the product of a search.[3] A person does not surrender all Fourth Amendment protection by venturing into the public sphere. To the contrary, "what [one] seeks to preserve as private, even in an area accessible to the public, may be constitutionally protected." *Katz.* A majority of this Court has already recognized that individuals have a reasonable expectation of privacy in the whole of their physical movements. *Jones.* Prior to the digital age, law enforcement might have pursued a suspect for a brief stretch, but doing so "for any extended period of time was difficult and costly and therefore rarely undertaken." For that reason, "society's expectation has been that law enforcement agents and others would not—and indeed, in the main, simply could not—secretly monitor and catalogue every single movement of an individual's car for a very long period."

    Allowing government access to cell-site records contravenes that expectation. Although such records are generated for commercial purposes, that distinction does not negate Carpenter's anticipation of privacy in his physical location. Mapping a cell phone's location over the course of 127 days provides an all-encompassing record of the holder's whereabouts. As with GPS information, the time-stamped data provides an intimate window into a person's life, revealing not only his particular movements, but through them his "familial, political, professional, religious, and sexual associations." These location records "hold for many Americans the 'privacies of life.'" And like GPS monitoring, cell phone tracking is remarkably easy, cheap, and efficient compared to traditional investigative tools. With just the click of a button, the Government can access each carrier's deep repository of historical location information at practically no expense.

    In fact, historical cell-site records present even greater privacy concerns than the GPS monitoring of a vehicle we considered in *Jones*. Unlike the bugged container in *Knotts* or the car in *Jones*, a cell phone—almost a "feature of human anatomy"—tracks nearly exactly the movements of its owner. While individuals regularly leave their vehicles, they compulsively carry cell phones with them all the time. A cell phone faithfully follows its owner beyond public

---

    [a] While, as the Court noted, "modern devices, such as smartphones, tap into the wireless network several times a minute whenever their signal is on," the court orders obtained only required the two carriers to disclose information for Carpenter's phone "at call origin and at call termination for incoming and outgoing calls" for the specified time periods.

    [3] The parties suggest as an alternative to their primary submissions that the acquisition of CSLI becomes a search only if it extends beyond a limited period. See Reply Brief 12 (proposing a 24-hour cutoff); Brief for United States 55–56 (suggesting a seven-day cutoff). As part of its argument, the Government treats the seven days of CSLI requested from Sprint as the pertinent period, even though Sprint produced only two days of records. Brief for United States 56. Contrary to Justice Kennedy's assertion, we need not decide whether there is a limited period for which the Government may obtain an individual's historical CSLI free from Fourth Amendment scrutiny, and if so, how long that period might be. It is sufficient for our purposes today to hold that accessing seven days of CSLI constitutes a Fourth Amendment search.

thoroughfares and into private residences, doctor's offices, political headquarters, and other potentially revealing locales. * * * Accordingly, when the Government tracks the location of a cell phone it achieves near perfect surveillance, as if it had attached an ankle monitor to the phone's user.

Moreover, the retrospective quality of the data here gives police access to a category of information otherwise unknowable. In the past, attempts to reconstruct a person's movements were limited by a dearth of records and the frailties of recollection. With access to CSLI, the Government can now travel back in time to retrace a person's whereabouts, subject only to the retention policies of the wireless carriers, which currently maintain records for up to five years. Critically, because location information is continually logged for all of the 400 million devices in the United States—not just those belonging to persons who might happen to come under investigation—this newfound tracking capacity runs against everyone. Unlike with the GPS device in *Jones*, police need not even know in advance whether they want to follow a particular individual, or when.

Whoever the suspect turns out to be, he has effectively been tailed every moment of every day for five years, and the police may—in the Government's view—call upon the results of that surveillance without regard to the constraints of the Fourth Amendment. Only the few without cell phones could escape this tireless and absolute surveillance.

The Government and Justice Kennedy contend, however, that the collection of CSLI should be permitted because the data is less precise than GPS information. Not to worry, they maintain, because the location records did "not on their own suffice to place [Carpenter] at the crime scene"; they placed him within a wedge-shaped sector ranging from one-eighth to four square miles. From the 127 days of location data it received, the Government could, in combination with other information, deduce a detailed log of Carpenter's movements, including when he was at the site of the robberies. And the Government thought the CSLI accurate enough to highlight it during the closing argument of his trial.

At any rate, the rule the Court adopts "must take account of more sophisticated systems that are already in use or in development." While the records in this case reflect the state of technology at the start of the decade, the accuracy of CSLI is rapidly approaching GPS-level precision. As the number of cell sites has proliferated, the geographic area covered by each cell sector has shrunk, particularly in urban areas. In addition, with new technology measuring the time and angle of signals hitting their towers, wireless carriers already have the capability to pinpoint a phone's location within 50 meters. * * *

Accordingly, when the Government accessed CSLI from the wireless carriers, it invaded Carpenter's reasonable expectation of privacy in the whole of his physical movements. * * *

Our decision today is a narrow one. We do not express a view on matters not before us: real-time CSLI or "tower dumps" (a download of information on all the devices that connected to a particular cell site during a particular interval). * * *

Having found that the acquisition of Carpenter's CSLI was a search, we also conclude that the Government must generally obtain a warrant supported by probable cause before acquiring such records. * * *

Justice Alito contends that the warrant requirement simply does not apply when the Government acquires records using compulsory process. Unlike an actual search, he says, subpoenas for documents do not involve the direct taking of evidence; they are at most a "constructive search" conducted by the target of the subpoena. Given this lesser intrusion on personal privacy, Justice Alito argues that the compulsory production of records is not held to the same probable cause standard. In his view, this Court's precedents set forth a categorical rule—

separate and distinct from the third-party doctrine—subjecting subpoenas to lenient scrutiny without regard to the suspect's expectation of privacy in the records.

But this Court has never held that the Government may subpoena third parties for records in which the suspect has a reasonable expectation of privacy. Almost all of the examples Justice Alito cites contemplated requests for evidence implicating diminished privacy interests or for a corporation's own books.[5] The lone exception, of course, is [*United States v. Miller*, 425 U.S. 435 (1976),] where the Court's analysis of the third-party subpoena merged with the application of the third-party doctrine (concluding that Miller lacked the necessary privacy interest to contest the issuance of a subpoena to his bank).

Justice Alito overlooks the critical issue. At some point, the dissent should recognize that CSLI is an entirely different species of business record—something that implicates basic Fourth Amendment concerns about arbitrary government power much more directly than corporate tax or payroll ledgers. * * *

Further, even though the Government will generally need a warrant to access CSLI, case-specific exceptions may support a warrantless search of an individual's cellsite records under certain circumstances. "One well recognized exception applies when ' "the exigencies of the situation" make the needs of law enforcement so compelling that [a] warrantless search is objectively reasonable under the Fourth Amendment.' " Such exigencies include the need to pursue a fleeing suspect, protect individuals who are threatened with imminent harm, or prevent the imminent destruction of evidence.

As a result, if law enforcement is confronted with an urgent situation, such fact-specific threats will likely justify the warrantless collection of CSLI. Lower courts, for instance, have approved warrantless searches related to bomb threats, active shootings, and child abductions. Our decision today does not call into doubt warrantless access to CSLI in such circumstances. While police must get a warrant when collecting CSLI to assist in the minerun criminal investigation, the rule we set forth does not limit their ability to respond to an ongoing emergency.

As Justice Brandeis explained in his famous dissent, the Court is obligated—as "[s]ubtler and more far-reaching means of invading privacy have become available to the Government"—to ensure that the "progress of science" does not erode Fourth Amendment protections. *Olmstead v. United States*, 277 U.S. 438, 473–74 (1928). Here the progress of science has afforded law enforcement a powerful new tool to carry out its important responsibilities. At the same time, this tool risks Government encroachment of the sort the Framers, "after consulting the lessons of history," drafted the Fourth Amendment to prevent.

We decline to grant the state unrestricted access to a wireless carrier's database of physical location information. In light of the deeply revealing nature of CSLI, its depth, breadth, and comprehensive reach, and the inescapable and automatic nature of its collection, the fact that such information is gathered by a third party does not make it any less deserving of Fourth Amendment protection. The Government's acquisition of the cell-site records here was a search under that Amendment.

JUSTICE KENNEDY, with whom JUSTICE THOMAS and JUSTICE ALITO join, dissenting. * * *

---

[5] See *United States v. Dionisio,* 410 U.S. 1 (1973) ("No person can have a reasonable expectation that others will not know the sound of his voice"); *Donovan v. Lone Steer, Inc.,* 464 U.S. 408 (1984) (payroll and sales records); *California Bankers Assn. v. Shultz,* 416 U.S. 21 (1974) (Bank Secrecy Act reporting requirements); *See v. City of Seattle,* 387 U.S. 541 (1967) (financial books and records); *United States v. Powell,* 379 U.S. 48 (1964) (corporate tax records); *McPhaul v. United States,* 364 U.S. 372 (1960) (books and records of an organization); *United States v. Morton Salt Co.,* 338 U.S. 632 (1950) (Federal Trade Commission reporting requirement); *Oklahoma Press Publishing Co. v. Walling,* 327 U.S. 186 (1946) (payroll records); *Hale v. Henkel,* 201 U.S. 43 (1906) (corporate books and papers).

The location information revealed by cell-site records is imprecise, because an individual cell-site sector usually covers a large geographic area. The FBI agent who offered expert testimony about the cell-site records at issue here testified that a cell site in a city reaches between a half mile and two miles in all directions. That means a 60-degree sector covers between approximately one-eighth and two square miles (and a 120-degree sector twice that area). To put that in perspective, in urban areas cell-site records often would reveal the location of a cell phone user within an area covering between around a dozen and several hundred city blocks. In rural areas cell-site records can be up to 40 times more imprecise. By contrast, a Global Positioning System (GPS) can reveal an individual's location within around 15 feet. * * *

The Court's reliance on *Jones* fares no better. In *Jones* the Government installed a GPS tracking device on the defendant's automobile. The Court held the Government searched the automobile because it "physically occupied private property [of the defendant] for the purpose of obtaining information." So in *Jones* it was "not necessary to inquire about the target's expectation of privacy in his vehicle's movements."

Despite that clear delineation of the Court's holding in *Jones*, the Court today declares that *Jones* applied the " 'different constitutional principles' " alluded to in *Knotts* to establish that an individual has an expectation of privacy in the sum of his whereabouts. For that proposition the majority relies on the two concurring opinions in *Jones*, one of which stated that "longer term GPS monitoring in investigations of most offenses impinges on expectations of privacy." But *Jones* involved direct governmental surveillance of a defendant's automobile without judicial authorization—specifically, GPS surveillance accurate within 50 to 100 feet. Even assuming that the different constitutional principles mentioned in *Knotts* would apply in a case like *Jones*—a proposition the Court was careful not to announce in *Jones*—those principles are inapplicable here[,] where the Government uses court-approved compulsory process to obtain records owned and controlled by a third party * * *.

* * * Still the Court errs, in my submission, when it concludes that cellsite records implicate greater privacy interests—and thus deserve greater Fourth Amendment protection—than financial records and telephone records.

Indeed, the opposite is true. A person's movements are not particularly private. As the Court recognized in *Knotts*, when the defendant there "traveled over the public streets he voluntarily conveyed to anyone who wanted to look the fact that he was traveling over particular roads in a particular direction, the fact of whatever stops he made, and the fact of his final destination." Today expectations of privacy in one's location are, if anything, even less reasonable than when the Court decided *Knotts* over 30 years ago. Millions of Americans choose to share their location on a daily basis, whether by using a variety of location-based services on their phones, or by sharing their location with friends and the public at large via social media.

And cell-site records, as already discussed, disclose a person's location only in a general area. The records at issue here, for example, revealed Carpenter's location within an area covering between around a dozen and several hundred city blocks. * * *

JUSTICE THOMAS, dissenting. * * *

The more fundamental problem with the Court's opinion, however, is its use of the "reasonable expectation of privacy" test * * *. The *Katz* test has no basis in the text or history of the Fourth Amendment. And, it invites courts to make judgments about policy, not law. * * *

JUSTICE ALITO, with whom JUSTICE THOMAS joins, dissenting.

* * * The Court's reasoning fractures two fundamental pillars of Fourth Amendment law, and in doing so, it guarantees a blizzard of litigation while threatening many legitimate and valuable investigative practices upon which law enforcement has rightfully come to rely.

First, the Court ignores the basic distinction between an actual search (dispatching law enforcement officers to enter private premises and root through private papers and effects) and an order merely requiring a party to look through its own records and produce specified documents. The former, which intrudes on personal privacy far more deeply, requires probable cause; the latter does not. * * *

Second, the Court allows a defendant to object to the search of a third party's property. This also is revolutionary. The Fourth Amendment protects "[t]he right of the people to be secure in *their* persons, houses, papers, and effects" (emphasis added), not the persons, houses, papers, and effects of others. * * *

JUSTICE GORSUCH, dissenting.

* * * Instead, I would look to a more traditional Fourth Amendment approach. Even if *Katz* may still supply one way to prove a Fourth Amendment interest, it has never been the only way. Neglecting more traditional approaches may mean failing to vindicate the full protections of the Fourth Amendment.

Our case offers a cautionary example. It seems to me entirely possible a person's cell-site data could qualify as his papers or effects under existing law. Yes, the telephone carrier holds the information. But 47 U. S. C. § 222 designates a customer's cell-site location information as "customer proprietary network information" (CPNI), § 222(h)(1)(A), and gives customers certain rights to control use of and access to CPNI about themselves. The statute generally forbids a carrier to "use, disclose, or permit access to individually identifiable" CPNI without the customer's consent, except as needed to provide the customer's telecommunications services. § 222(c)(1). It also requires the carrier to disclose CPNI "upon affirmative written request by the customer, to any person designated by the customer." § 222(c)(2). Congress even afforded customers a private cause of action for damages against carriers who violate the Act's terms. § 207. Plainly, customers have substantial legal interests in this information, including at least some right to include, exclude, and control its use. Those interests might even rise to the level of a property right.

The problem is that we do not know anything more. Before the district court and court of appeals, Mr. Carpenter pursued only a *Katz* "reasonable expectations" argument. He did not invoke the law of property or any analogies to the common law, either there or in his petition for certiorari. * * * In these circumstances, I cannot help but conclude—reluctantly—that Mr. Carpenter forfeited perhaps his most promising line of argument. * * *

14th ed., p. 259; end of Note 3, add:

What then of *United States v. Bain*, 874 F.3d 1 (1st Cir.2017), where a reliable informant indicated Bain was regularly selling drugs near 131 Laurel St., where he lived, so police arrested him on probable cause outside that address, which they then discovered contained four separate apartment units within, but by trying keys found in Bain's pocket at each door they connected him to unit D, for which a search warrant was then obtained?

14th ed., p. 259; end of Note 4, add:

What if police, while on a permissible route per *Jardines*, from that vantage point see contraband elsewhere within the curtilage, which they then seize? In *State v. Grice*, 767 S.E.2d 312 (N.C.2015), where police on that route saw marijuana plants in defendant's back yard and then seized those plants, the court concluded: "Whatever special protection the curtilage enjoys against warrantless seizures, that protection does not support the creation of a rule that law enforcement is automatically prohibited from crossing from one lawfully arrived at portion of the curtilage to another portion of the curtilage to retrieve inadvertently discovered contraband in plain view." The dissent relied upon a statement by the plurality in *Texas v. Brown*, 14th ed., p.

370, that "plain view" provides grounds for seizure of an item when the officer's access to an object has some prior justification under the Fourth Amendment."

14th ed., p. 260; replacing Note 6, add:

6. ***Vehicles on the curtilage.*** In COLLINS v. VIRGINIA , 138 S.Ct. 1663 (2018), an officer investigating traffic incidents involving an orange/black motorcycle learned it was likely stolen and in possession of Collins, and he discovered photos on Collins' Facebook profile of the cycle parked on the driveway of a house. He drove to that house, saw a cycle under a tarp on the driveway, and then entered the curtilage and lifted the tarp and thereby confirmed from running a check on the license plate and vehicle identification numbers that the cycle was in fact stolen. Collins, charged with receiving stolen property, sought suppression of the evidence obtained by that warrantless search of the cycle, relying on *Jardines*, but his motion was denied on the basis that the warrantless search was justified under the automobile exception (reaffirmed in *California v. Carney*, 14th ed., p. 358, in light of "the element of mobility" and that "the expectation of privacy with respect to one's automobile is significantly less than that relating to one's home or office"). The Supreme Court, per Sotomayor, J., reversed:

"When a law enforcement officer physically intrudes on the curtilage to gather evidence, a search within the meaning of the Fourth Amendment has occurred. *Jardines*. Such conduct thus is presumptively unreasonable absent a warrant. * * *

"In physically intruding on the curtilage of Collins' home to search the motorcycle, Officer Rhodes not only invaded Collins' Fourth Amendment interest in the item searched, i.e., the motorcycle, but also invaded Collins' Fourth Amendment interest in the curtilage of his home. The question before the Court is whether the automobile exception justifies the invasion of the curtilage. The answer is no.

"Applying the relevant legal principles to a slightly different factual scenario confirms that this is an easy case. Imagine a motorcycle parked inside the living room of a house, visible through a window to a passerby on the street. Imagine further that an officer has probable cause to believe that the motorcycle was involved in a traffic infraction. Can the officer, acting without a warrant, enter the house to search the motorcycle and confirm whether it is the right one? Surely not.

"The reason is that the scope of the automobile exception extends no further than the automobile itself. * * * Virginia asks the Court to expand the scope of the automobile exception to permit police to invade any space outside an automobile even if the Fourth Amendment protects that space. Nothing in our case law, however, suggests that the automobile exception gives an officer the right to enter a home or its curtilage to access a vehicle without a warrant. Expanding the scope of the automobile exception in this way would both undervalue the core Fourth Amendment protection afforded to the home and its curtilage and ' "untether" ' the automobile exception ' "from the justifications underlying" ' it.

"The Court already has declined to expand the scope of other exceptions to the warrant requirement to permit warrantless entry into the home. The reasoning behind those decisions applies equally well in this context. For instance, under the plain-view doctrine, "any valid warrantless seizure of incriminating evidence" requires that the officer "have a lawful right of access to the object itself." * * * A plain-view seizure thus cannot be justified if it is effectuated 'by unlawful trespass.' Had Officer Rhodes seen illegal drugs through the window of Collins' house, for example, assuming no other warrant exception applied, he could not have entered the house to seize them without first obtaining a warrant."

What then would be the proper application of *Jardines* if, instead, the cycle had not been covered with a tarp and thus the officer had immediately confirmed that the cycle was stolen and thereafter entered the curtilage solely to make a *seizure* of it?

14th ed., p. 260; after Note 6, add:

    6A. *Implicit license.* Can the "implicit license" referred to in *Jardines* be nullified by prior action of the homeowner? See https://fourthamendmentsecurity.com/lawn-signs/, where two law professors offer for sale a variety of lawn signs, e.g., one reading:

No Entry

No Trespassing

No Consent to Entry

I Assert My Fourth Amendment Rights

The two law professors, who find *Jardines* "an odd application of the Fourth Amendment," view the signs as "one-part joke, one-part serious," www.abajournal.com/magazine/article/4th_amendment_lawn_postings. Compare *United States v. Carloss*, 818 F.3d 988 (10th Cir.2016) (it *cannot* be concluded "that a resident can revoke the implied license to approach his home and knock on the front door simply by posting a 'No Trespassing' sign," as such signs "would not have conveyed to an objective officer, or member of the public, that he could not walk up to the porch and knock on the front door and attempt to contact the occupants").

14th ed., p. 264; after Note 9, add:

    10. *Long-term surveillance from outside the curtilage.* In *State v. Jones,* 903 N.W.2d 101 (S.D.2017), police acting without a warrant attached a pole camera on a nearby public street light to record activities occurring outside the defendant's residence. The camera, operated 24-hours a day for two months, sent a recording of those activities to a distant location, where it could be reviewed by the police at any time and as often as they wished. While the state argued that "the pole camera merely captured what any person standing on the street could observe with the naked eye" and thus was not a search, the court in *Jones* concluded this most definitely was *not* the case: "The information gathered through the use of targeted long-term video surveillance will necessarily include a mosaic of intimate details of the person's private life and associations. At a minimum, it could reveal who enters and exits the home, the time of their arrival and departure, the license plates of their cars, the activities of the occupant's children and friends entering the home, information gleaned from items brought into the home revealing where the occupant shops, how garbage is removed, what service providers are contracted, etc."

§ 3. "PROBABLE CAUSE"

14th ed., p. 278; end of Note 5, add:

    While anticipatory warrant cases commonly assert that the warrant may be executed *only* after the specified "triggering event" has occurred, an exception was recognized in *Commonwealth v. Colondres*, 27 N.E.3d 1272 (Mass.2015). Two controlled buys of drugs were made from one Carlos, who in each instance detoured to defendant's apartment before the sale elsewhere. Later, an anticipatory warrant was obtained on an informant's assertion Carlos would be going to defendant's apartment "to retrieve the cocaine" that would then be delivered "to the South End section of the city." Surveilling police saw Carlos stop briefly at defendant's apartment and then arrested him and found two bags of cocaine on his person. The subsequent execution of the warrant was challenged by defendant because the specified "triggering event," "a delivery to a customer" by Carlos, had not occurred. The court concluded "that the execution of a search is authorized by an anticipatory search warrant once there is equivalent compliance, albeit not strict compliance, with the triggering conditions in the affidavit. * * * Because the future rarely goes exactly according to plan, the benefits of an anticipatory warrant would too often be lost if we required that the triggering conditions be satisfied to the letter before the warrant takes effect." There was equivalent compliance here, the court then concluded, as finding the cocaine on Carlos' person, just as surely as the specified "triggering event," showed Carlos was currently using defendant's apartment as a "stash house."

14th ed., p. 280; after Note 7, add:

8. ***Burden of proof.*** In *State v. Atwood*, 180 A.3d 1119 (N.J.2018), (following the prevailing rule that the state has the burden of proving the validity of a warrantless search or seizure, while a search warrant is presumptively valid and thus the defendant must prove it is based upon insufficient probable cause), the court was confronted with the issue "whether a search warrant granted after police performed an investigatory automobile stop can retroactively validate the stop and insulate the State from bearing, in a suppression hearing, the burden of demonstrating reasonable and articulable suspicion for the initial seizure of the moving vehicle." The state argued "that by including in a later-developed search warrant affidavit for defendants' automobile the facts that led police to perform a warrantless automobile stop of defendant's moving vehicle, the judge's grant of the search warrant rendered the preceding automobile stop constitutional," so that "defendant must carry the burden of proof on the challenge to the investigatory stop in this case because the stop was subsumed into, and approved by, the search warrant." Not so, a unanimous court concluded: "Search warrants are prospective in nature—they authorize the taking of action. A later-obtained search warrant does not retroactively validate preceding warrantless conduct that is challenged through a suppression motion focused on the legitimacy of the seizure that gave rise to a later search. The State must bear the burden of proving the legitimacy of the seizure that led to a later warrant and search—in this case the stop."

14th ed., p. 284; after Note 5, add:

6. ***"Totality of the circumstances."*** In *District of Columbia v. Wesby,* 138 S.Ct. 577 (2018), D.C. police, responding to complaints of a loud, late-night party at a home, ultimately arrested the 21 partygoers for unlawful entry (requiring they knew or should have known they entered without the owner's permission). In the partygoers' civil suit claiming violation of their Fourth Amendment rights, the lower court held probable cause was lacking, given that each of the partygoers had "claimed that someone had invited them to the house." The Supreme Court, per Thomas, J., concluding otherwise, asserted the lower court had failed to follow the approach described in fn. 2 of *Pringle*. Assessing "the plausibility of the explanation itself" in light of "all the surrounding circumstances," the Supreme Court concluded there *was* probable cause, given "the condition of the house" (vacant for months with no sign of habitation), "the partygoers' conduct" (strip club in the living room, sexual intercourse in the bedroom), and the "partygoers' reaction to the officers" ("scattering and hiding," giving "vague and implausible responses").

14th ed., p. 285; after Note 2, add:

2A. ***Effect of decriminalization.*** At least since the decision in *Johnson v. United States,* 333 U.S. 10 (1948), holding that the "presence of odors" is "evidence of the most persuasive character" in establishing probable cause, courts have without hesitation held that the distinctive odor of marijuana establishes probable cause for a search. But in recent years several states have "decriminalized" possession of small amounts of marijuana, resulting in reconsideration of that probable cause issue with varying results. Consider: *Commonwealth v. Overmyer*, 11 N.E.3d 1054 (Mass.2013) (strong odor of unburnt marijuana emanating from defendant's vehicle, standing alone, did not provide probable cause for search); *Robinson v. State*, 152 A.3d 661 (Md.2013) (given assertion in *Florida v. Harris*, 568 U.S. 237 (2013), that there is probable cause when there a reasonable basis for concluding "that contraband or evidence of crime is present," and since decriminalization "is not the same as legalization," search authority not altered); *State v. Perry,*

874 N.W.2d 36 (Neb.2016) (still probable cause of evidence of crime, as "the presence of any amount logically suggests that there may be more").

§ 4. SEARCH WARRANTS

C. SPECIAL PROBLEMS: COMPUTER SEARCHES

14th ed., p. 300; end of Note 1, add:

In *Commonwealth v. Martinez*, 71 N.E.3d 105 (Mass.2017), police discovered that a computer using a particular IP address and displaying a username "datflypapi" was sharing suspected child porn via a file-sharing program. An administrative subpoena to Comcast provided the response that this IP address was assigned to one "Angel Martinez" at a specified apartment, which police learned was leased by Maria Avilez. They then obtained a search warrant for that apartment to search for computers and related items connected with child porn, executed the warrant and seized and searched two computers found to contain such files. Martinez advanced two arguments as to why probable cause was lacking: (1) As for his objection that the police were unable to verify that the named subscriber actually lived at the apartment searched, the court responded that the question before the magistrate was whether that apartment "contained evidence of crime-period," not whether it contained evidence of "criminal activity on the part of Angel Martinez." (2) As for his objection "that investigators did not determine whether the Internet connection at the apartment used a wireless router and, if so, whether the wireless network required a password," thus leaving "open the possibility that someone other than the subscriber, located at a different physical address, was 'joyriding' on an unsecure wireless network based out of the apartment," the court responded that "probable cause does not require investigators to 'establish to a certainty that the items to be seized will be found in the specified location.'" But the court then appended a "cautionary note," i.e., that "technologies that apparently were not at issue in this case may further erode the connection between an IP address and a physical address," as by "mask[ing] original IP addresses through use of one or more intermediary IP addresses," meaning that "certain cases may require police to disclose in a search warrant affidavit the possibility that one of these technologies is, or may be, in play based on facts known or reasonably knowable to investigators at the time."

14th ed., p. 301; end of Note 4, add:

Sometimes it is contended that a search warrant was not needed because the government's investigation re defendant's computer did not constitute a search. Consider:

(a) The FBI, using software called Network Investigation Technique, installed NIT on Playpen, a child porn website it had taken over. NIT attached itself to anything downloaded from Playpen, and caused hundreds of downloading computers to transmit back each computer's IP address, otherwise unavailable because Playpen users made contact via Tor, an encrypted online network that uses a series of relay computers to mask the identity of online users. In *United States v. Horton*, 863 F.3d 1041 (8th Cir.2017), distinguishing cases "in which an IP address is voluntarily provided to third parties," concluded this use of NIT *was* a search, for "[e]ven if a defendant has no reasonable expectation of privacy in his IP address, he has a reasonable expectation of privacy in the contents of his computer."

(b) In *United States v. Schlingloff*, 901 F.Supp.2d 1101 (C.D.Ill.2012), agents obtained a search warrant to search a particular residence for evidence of passport fraud and harboring an alien, based on an affidavit indicating computer devices on the premises would contain records related to those crimes. A laptop and external storage device belonging to defendant, who resided there, was seized and sent to a forensics lab for analysis. Using a computer software program known as Forensic Tool Kit to index/catalog all the files into viewable formats (including an "alert" function to flag files identifiable from a library of known files previously submitted by law enforcement, such as contraband or child porn), two child porn files were identified and opened. Note, 70 Stan.L.Rev. 691, 713, 718 (2018), (observing that Richard Salgado, *Reply, Fourth Amendment Searches and the Power of the Hash*, 119 Harv.L.Rev.F. 38, 45–46 (2006), suggests the Supreme Court's dog sniff cases appear to "allow for the routine use by government of hash-based contraband detection in any search of a digital storage device, regardless of the scope of the search authority"), responds that *Jardines*, 14th ed., p. 254, is the better analogy.

14th ed., p. 301; Note 6, within last line, add:

If the approximate date of the sought files' creation is specified, does that limit the search, given the readily available software facilitating change of the 'date created' entry for computer files, noted in Orin Kerr, *Executing Warrants for Digital Evidence: The Case for Use Restrictions on Nonresponsive Data*, 48 Texas Tech.L.Rev. 1, 16 (2015)?

14th ed., p. 302; after carryover paragraph, add:

Consider *Commonwealth v. Dorelas*, 43 N.E.3d 306 (Mass.2016), asserting that "in the virtual world, it is not enough to simply permit a search to extend anywhere the targeted electronic objects possibly could be found, as data possibly could be found anywhere within an electronic device." But, as to a search warrant for defendant's iPhone on probable cause it contained "evidence of communications relating to and linking the defendant to the crime," in that witnesses said defendant had been receiving threatening messages on his phone and was heard arguing with a person on the phone just prior to the shooting, the court then rejected defendant's objection that the warrant "included authorization to search for such evidence not only in the iPhone's call history and text message files, but also in its photograph files," thus leading to the discovery of a photo of defendant holding a gun and wearing a jacket like that described by witnesses to the shooting, explaining that "[c]ommunications can come in many forms including photographic."

14th ed., p. 302; after Note 7, add:

8. ***Government efforts to bypass encryption.*** After obtaining a search warrant authorizing a computer search, investigators may find that information stored on the computer is inaccessible because it has been encrypted. In some cases, encryption will block access to all of the data stored on the computer. In other cases, the government will access some files on the computer but will then encounter an encrypted drive, folder, or file. In all of these cases, technology blocks or limits the search that the warrant authorizes. Investigators have several strategies to try to bypass encryption and complete the execution of the warrant.

The first strategy is to hope that the suspect wrote down the password somewhere, told it to someone else, or made an unencrypted backup copy of the data. In that case, the police can try to recover the password or backup copy just as they would any other kind of evidence. If agents are searching a home for a computer, for example, they might also search for slips of paper or notebooks containing a list of passwords. If agents are searching for a computer used by a suspect who lives with his wife, they may ask the wife if she knows any passwords to access the husband's computers. And if a suspect has recently made an unencrypted backup copy of his smart phone, the government can obtain a search warrant and seize and search the backup copy rather than try to bypass the encrypted version. This strategy can work in some cases but will not work in every case.

A second strategy is to try to bypass the encryption directly, either through guessing the password repeatedly or through gaining access using forensic programs. Guessing the password can work if the computer allows repeated guessing. For example, a 2011 study found that 10% of iPhone users use one of ten codes to protect access to their phones; the most popular passcode was "1234." *See* Matt Brian, *1234 Is The Most Common iPhone Passcode, App Developer Reveals*, available at thenextweb.com/apple/2011/06/13/1234-is-the-most-common-iphone-passcode-app-developer-reveals/. Forensic equipment might also allow the government to access particular model phones using particular operating systems. Like the first strategy, this can work in some cases but will not work in other cases.

If a suspect has set up a biometric means of authentication to access his computer, a third strategy may be to obtain a court order compelling the suspect to use the biometric ID to unlock the computer. This commonly arises with new-model smart phones, which typically can be configured so that the user's fingerprint unlocks the phone. A suspect can be ordered to place his thumb on the phone's sensor to unlock it just like a suspect can be ordered to submit to fingerprinting to check for a match with fingerprints found at the crime scene. *See* 14th ed., pp. 410–411. This strategy only works if the computer's user is known, available, and has set up a biometric form of authentication to access the device.

A fourth strategy for bypassing encryption is for the government to obtain a court order compelling the user to either disclose the password or to produce the data in unencrypted form. When the government obtains a court order to produce decrypted data, the suspect typically will be brought to a room with the computer and will be given the opportunity to enter in the password. If the suspect refuses to enter in or disclose the password, the suspect can be held in contempt for violating the order. The suspect can then be placed in jail if the court concludes that the suspect knows the password and is willfully refusing to disclose it or use it. An important wrinkle with this strategy is that it raises complex issues under the Fifth Amendment's right against self-incrimination. Courts are still in the process of articulating the precise Fifth Amendment limits on compelled decryption and password disclosure, and a detailed discussion must await later materials on the right against self-incrimination. *See* 14th ed., p. 823, Note 5.

A final strategy may be to seek decryption assistance from the manufacturer of the storage device or software manufacturer. For example, following terrorist attacks in San Bernardino, California, in December 2015, the federal government obtained an order requiring Apple to assist in the decryption of an iPhone used by one of the attackers. Apple challenged the court order, arguing (among other things) that it was beyond the power of a federal court to order a company to create a program needed to help the government access the phone. The legal dispute between the government and Apple was not resolved, however, as the public attention brought to the case led private computer security researchers to approach the government with a technical solution instead. The researchers sold the FBI a previously unknown exploit that allowed the government to unlock the phone without Apple's assistance. *See* Ellen Nakashima, *FBI Paid Professional Hackers One-Time Fee To Crack San Bernardino iPhone*, Washington Post, April 12, 2016.

§ 5. WARRANTLESS ARRESTS AND SEARCHES OF THE PERSON

14th ed., p. 311; end of last paragraph after "seizure," add footnote:

[dd] This is not to suggest that such judicial review will inevitably terminate any Fourth Amendment violation. In *Manuel v. City of Joliet, Ill.*, 137 S.Ct. 911 (2017), involving a lawsuit for damages, the Court concluded: "The Fourth Amendment prohibits government officials from detaining a person in the absence of probable cause. That can happen when the police hold someone without any reason before the formal onset of a criminal proceeding. But it also can occur when legal process itself goes wrong—when, for example, a judge's probable-cause determination is predicated solely on a police officer's false statements. Then, too, a person is confined without constitutionally adequate justification. Legal process has gone forward, but it has done nothing to satisfy the Fourth Amendment's probable-cause requirement. And for that reason, it cannot extinguish the detainee's Fourth Amendment claim * * *."

14th ed., p. 330; before Note 4, add:

In BIRCHFIELD v. NORTH DAKOTA, 136 S.Ct. 2160 (2016), concerning DUI "implied consent" laws (discussed at Supp. p. 69), the Court, per Alito, J., found it necessary first to determine whether *either* blood *or* breath testing of DUI arrestees without a warrant to determine blood alcohol concentration was a valid search incident to arrest:

"We begin by considering the impact of breath and blood tests on individual privacy interests, and we will discuss each type of test in turn.

"Years ago we said that breath tests do not 'implicat[e] significant privacy concerns.' That remains so today.

"First, the physical intrusion is almost negligible. Breath tests 'do not require piercing the skin' and entail 'a minimum of inconvenience.' As Minnesota describes its version of the breath test, the process requires the arrestee to blow continuously for 4 to 15 seconds into a straw-like mouthpiece that is connected by a tube to the test machine. Independent sources describe other breath test devices in essentially the same terms. The effort is no more demanding than blowing up a party balloon.

"Petitioner Bernard argues, however, that the process is nevertheless a significant intrusion because the arrestee must insert the mouthpiece of the machine into his or her mouth. But there is nothing painful or strange about this requirement. The use of a straw to drink beverages is a common practice and one to which few object.

"Nor, contrary to Bernard, is the test a significant intrusion because it 'does not capture an ordinary exhalation of the kind that routinely is exposed to the public' but instead ' "requires a sample of 'alveolar' (deep lung) air." ' Humans have never been known to assert a possessory interest in or any emotional attachment to any of the air in their lungs. The air that humans exhale is not part of their bodies. Exhalation is a natural process—indeed, one that is necessary for life. Humans cannot hold their breath for more than a few minutes, and all the air that is breathed into a breath analyzing machine, including deep lung air, sooner or later would be exhaled even without the test.

"In prior cases, we have upheld warrantless searches involving physical intrusions that were at least as significant as that entailed in the administration of a breath test. Just recently we described the process of collecting a DNA sample by rubbing a swab on the inside of a person's cheek as a 'negligible' intrusion. *Maryland v. King*, [14th ed., p. 333]. We have also upheld scraping underneath a suspect's fingernails to find evidence of a crime, calling that a 'very limited intrusion.' *Cupp v. Murphy*, [14th ed., p. 332]. A breath test is no more intrusive than either of these procedures.

"Second, breath tests are capable of revealing only one bit of information, the amount of alcohol in the subject's breath. In this respect, they contrast sharply with the sample of cells collected by the swab in *Maryland v. King.* * * *

"Finally, participation in a breath test is not an experience that is likely to cause any great enhancement in the embarrassment that is inherent in any arrest. The act of blowing into a straw is not inherently embarrassing, nor are evidentiary breath tests administered in a manner that causes embarrassment. Again, such tests are normally administered in private at a police station, in a patrol car, or in a mobile testing facility, out of public view. Moreover, once placed under arrest, the individual's expectation of privacy is necessarily diminished. * * *

"Blood tests are a different matter. They 'require piercing the skin' and extract a part of the subject's body. And while humans exhale air from their lungs many times per minute, humans do not continually shed blood. It is true, of course, that people voluntarily submit to the taking of blood samples as part of a physical examination, and the process involves little pain or risk. Nevertheless, for many, the process is not one they relish. It is significantly more intrusive than blowing into a tube. * * *

"In addition, a blood test, unlike a breath test, places in the hands of law enforcement authorities a sample that can be preserved and from which it is possible to extract information beyond a simple BAC reading. Even if the law enforcement agency is precluded from testing the blood for any purpose other than to measure BAC, the potential remains and may result in anxiety for the person tested.

"Having assessed the impact of breath and blood testing on privacy interests, we now look to the States' asserted need to obtain BAC readings for persons arrested for drunk driving.

"The States and the Federal Government have a paramount interest . . . in preserving the safety of . . . public highways." * * *

"Alcohol consumption is a leading cause of traffic fatalities and injuries. During the past decade, annual fatalities in drunk-driving accidents ranged from 13,582 deaths in 2005 to 9,865 deaths in 2011. * * *

"Petitioners * * * contend that the States and the Federal Government could combat drunk driving in other ways that do not have the same impact on personal privacy. Their arguments are unconvincing.

"The chief argument on this score is that an officer making an arrest for drunk driving should not be allowed to administer a BAC test unless the officer procures a search warrant or could not do so in time to obtain usable test results. * * *

"This argument contravenes our decisions holding that the legality of a search incident to arrest must be judged on the basis of categorical rules. In *Robinson*, [14th ed., p. 314] for example, no one claimed that the object of the search, a package of cigarettes, presented any danger to the arresting officer or was at risk of being destroyed in the time that it would have taken to secure a search warrant. The Court nevertheless upheld the constitutionality of a warrantless search of the package, concluding that a categorical rule was needed to give police adequate guidance: 'A police officer's determination as to how and where to search the person of a suspect whom he has arrested is necessarily a quick ad hoc judgment which the Fourth Amendment does not require to be broken down in each instance into an analysis of each step in the search.' "[a]

Is a urine test for alcohol content best analogized to a breath test or, as concluded in *State v. Thompson*, 886 N.W.2d 224 (Minn.2016), to a blood test?

[a] Sotomayor, J., joined by Ginsburg, J., dissenting in part, argued that "*McNeely*'s holding that a categorical exigency exception is not necessary to accommodate the government interests associated with the dissipation of blood alcohol after drunk-driving arrests" should apply equally to the "search-incident-to-arrest rule for breath tests." Thomas, J., dissenting in part, argued that the "far simpler answer * * * is the one rejected in *Missouri v. McNeely*."

14th ed., p. 332; end of paragraph after "infra," add:

Considering both *Knowles* and *Rawlings*, what then of *People v. Reid*, 26 N.E.3d 237 (N.Y.2014), where after a valid traffic stop grounds developed to arrest the driver for driving under the influence, and the officer then frisked the driver, found a switchblade knife, and placed the driver under arrest, but at the suppression hearing the officer testified he had no intention of arresting until he found the switchblade for which the driver was now being prosecuted?

§ 7. WARRANTLESS SEIZURES AND SEARCHES OF VEHICLES AND CONTAINERS

14th ed., p. 370; end of Note 5, add:

In *State v. Banks-Harvey,* 96 N.E.3d 262 (Ohio 2018), a vehicle, stopped for a traffic violation, had three occupants: driver Jamie; her boyfriend and vehicle owner, Hall; and a third person. After Jamie acknowledged she did not have a driver's license, she was moved to the police cruiser during a warrant check, which established that both she and the third party (but not Hall) had outstanding arrest warrants for drug possession, so both were arrested. The officer then retrieved Jamie's purse from the car, searched it and found drugs, which the state subsequently contended was justified under the *Lafayette* inventory-search exception. The court disagreed, noting that "this is not a case in which personal items came into the custody of the police as an incident of lawful police conduct. In this case, the trooper retrieved a personal item belonging to an arrestee from a place that is protected under the Fourth Amendment (the car). [H]ad the trooper obtained the purse in a legal way, such as retrieving it from the car at appellant's request, we would have been compelled to reach a different result." * * * But a law-enforcement policy that an arrestee's personal effects go with them to jail, does not, by itself, authorize an officer to retrieve the arrestee's personal effects from a place that is protected under the Fourth Amendment." The dissent objected: "The trooper's testimony that he acted pursuant to standard procedure that a purse goes with an arrestee was not disputed. The policy makes sense. A purse could hold identification, money, medication, or other items needed at the jail. And taking and inventorying an arrestee's purse and its contents protects police from claims that the purse was left in an unsafe place and was stolen."

§ 8. STOP AND FRISK

A. POLICE ACTION SHORT OF A SEIZURE

14th ed., p. 389; end of Note 2, add:

What then of the conclusion in *Jones v. United States*, 154 A.3d 591 (D.C.2017), that a warrant check *without* holding the suspect's identification has "converted an otherwise consensual street encounter with police into a seizure"?

B. GROUNDS FOR TEMPORARY SEIZURE FOR INVESTIGATION

14th ed., p. 395; end of Note 4, add:

See *Commonwealth v. Warren*, Note 1, p. 10 supra.

14th ed., p. 397; after Note 6, add:

6A. *Potentially "licensed" activity.* If police observe certain activity that is criminal unless "licensed," may the officer stop the suspect to determine whether he can produce the requisite license, or is the apparent lack of a license a prerequisite to the stop? Compare *United States v. Rodriguez,* 739 F.3d 481 (10th Cir.2013) (reasonable suspicion defendant carrying concealed weapon without valid handgun license where officer saw gun concealed on defendant's person, without any inquiry regarding license, as existence of license is a statutory "exception," and officer "had no affirmative obligation" prior to defendant's seizure to inquire whether possession fell within a statutory exception); *State v. Timberlake,* 744 N.W.2d 390 (Minn.2008) (where identified private citizen provided information about seeing man in particular vehicle in possession of handgun, that reasonable suspicion; court rejects defendant's claim there also must be reasonable suspicion defendant lacks a permit to carry the gun, as "the 'without a permit' language creates an exception to criminal liability that places a burden on the defendant to come forward with some evidence of a permit," and thus "police * * * did not need to know whether Timberlake had a permit"); with *Northrup v. City of Toledo Police Department,* 785 F.3d 1128 (6th Cir.2015) (where plaintiff in this § 1983 action was stopped because officer, responding to 911 call that plaintiff was openly carrying a gun, saw plaintiff "was visibly carrying a gun in his holster," stop was unlawful, for "[n]ot only has the State made open carrying of a firearm legal, but it also does not require gun owners to produce or even carry their licenses for inquiring officers"; unless "a consensual encounter" established that plaintiff "appeared dangerous," the officer's "*hope* that Northrup 'was not about to start shooting' remains another word for the *trust* that Ohioans have placed in their State's approach to gun licensure and gun possession"); *United States v. Black,* 707 F.3d 531 (4th Cir.2013) ("where a state permits individuals to openly carry firearms, the exercise of this right, without more, cannot justify an investigatory detention," and government's argument "that because other laws prevent convicted felons from possessing guns," the officers entitled to seize the gun-toting suspect until "a records check" was run rejected, as "[b]eing a felon in possession of a firearm is not the default status'). Is the matter settled by *Delaware v. Prouse,* 14th ed., p. 414?

14th ed., p. 398; end of Note 7, add:

Though two concurring Justices sought to confine *Heien* in ways not expressly stated by the majority (asserting (i) that the government "cannot defend an officer's mistaken legal interpretation on the ground that the officer was unaware of or untrained in the law," (ii) that "an officer's reliance on 'an incorrect memo or training program from the police department' makes no difference to the analysis," and (iii) that the test is satisfied only when the law at issue is " 'so doubtful in construction' that a reasonable judge could agree with the officer's view"), SEARCHSZR § 3.2(b) suggests *Heien* loses some of its luster when the likely effect of its coexistence with *Whren v. United States,* 14th ed., p. 323, the pretext-stop-is-ok decision, is taken into account, given the frequency of pretextual traffic stops in current practice. Consider in this regard that in *Heien* itself police parked by the side of the highway for the purpose of "conducting criminal interdiction" made the initial decision to follow defendant's vehicle, apparently in the hope of observing a traffic-code violation providing an excuse for a stop, grounded *solely* in the fact that the driver (a Hispanic) manifested the characteristics of a cautious driver, "gripping the steering wheel at a 10 and 2 position, looking straight ahead."

8.   *Group seizure.* When, if ever, is the simultaneous seizure of a group of persons justifiable under *Terry* when seeking a single perpetrator? Consider this sequence of events in *United States v. Paetsch,* 782 F.3d 1162 (10th Cir.2015): *3:47 p.m.:* a single robber took stacks of money at gunpoint from the Wells Fargo Bank, unaware that a GPS tracking device was concealed therein. *4:01 p.m.:* a computer monitor that could locate the device to about a 60-ft. diameter reported that the tracker was stationary at a certain intersection, so an officer present there (soon assisted by other officers), barricaded the 20 cars, containing 29 persons, then present at that intersection, and then awaited the expected arrival in 20–30 minutes of a hand-held homing beacon that could more precisely locate the GPS device's location. *4:30 p.m.:* the beacon had not yet arrived, but police then removed occupants of two cars "behaving suspiciously" and handcuffed each of them and had them sit on the curb nearby; one of them was Paetsch. *4:55 p.m.:* the beacon finally arrived, but the officers were unable to operate it correctly, though they did "get a weak signal" from Paetsch's vehicle. *5:25 p.m.:* after ordering all occupants of all the cars out of their vehicles, police then looked through the windows of each car and saw a "money band," a slip of paper banks use to wrap stacks of money, in Paetsch's car, at which point an expert at using the beacon arrived and obtained a "very strong signal" from Paetsch's car, so he was arrested and his

car searched, revealing the fruits and evidence of the robbery. *5:38 p.m.*: the other detained motorists were allowed to return to their vehicles while investigators gathered information from them. *6:19 p.m.*: the innocent motorists were allowed to leave. What would be the correct Fourth Amendment analysis (i) upon Paetsch's motion to suppress the items found in search of his car; (ii) upon a § 1983 suit brought by one of the innocent motorists?

C. PERMISSIBLE EXTENT AND SCOPE OF TEMPORARY SEIZURE

14th ed., p. 403; in lieu of *Everett* case within Note 7, add:

In RODRIGUEZ v. UNITED STATES, 135 S.Ct. 1609 (2015), a Nebraska K-9 police officer saw a vehicle drive onto a highway shoulder, a violation of state law, so he pulled the vehicle over at 12:06 a.m. The officer questioned driver Rodriguez about his conduct; obtained Rodriguez's license, registration and proof of insurance; ran a records check on Rodriguez; asked passenger Pollman for his driver's license and questioned him about the nature and purpose of their travels; ran a records check on Pollman; prepared a written warning for Rodriguez; called for a second officer; explained the warning to Rodriguez and returned the documents to the two men; asked for but was refused permission to walk his dog around the vehicle; and, 7 or 8 minutes after the written warning was issued, at 12:33 a.m. (when the other officer arrived) led his dog around the vehicle. The dog alerted, the vehicle was searched, and a bag of methamphetamine was discovered. In the subsequent federal prosecution, Rodriguez' suppression motion was denied by reliance upon Eighth Circuit precedent that "dog sniffs that occur within a short time following the completion of a traffic stop are not constitutionally prohibited if they constitute only *de minimis* intrusions." The Supreme Court, per Ginsburg, J., reversed:

"A seizure for a traffic violation justifies a police investigation of that violation. '[A] relatively brief encounter,' a routine traffic stop is 'more analogous to a so-called "*Terry* stop" ... than to a formal arrest.' Like a *Terry* stop, the tolerable duration of police inquiries in the traffic-stop context is determined by the seizure's 'mission'—to address the traffic violation that warranted the stop, and attend to related safety concerns. Because addressing the infraction is the purpose of the stop, it may 'last no longer than is necessary to effectuate th[at] purpose.' Authority for the seizure thus ends when tasks tied to the traffic infraction are—or reasonably should have been—completed.

"Our decisions in *Caballes* and *Johnson* heed these constraints. In both cases, we concluded that the Fourth Amendment tolerated certain unrelated investigations that did not lengthen the roadside detention. * * * An officer, in other words, may conduct certain unrelated checks during an otherwise lawful traffic stop. But * * * he may not do so in a way that prolongs the stop, absent the reasonable suspicion ordinarily demanded to justify detaining an individual.

"Beyond determining whether to issue a traffic ticket, an officer's mission includes 'ordinary inquiries incident to [the traffic] stop.' Typically such inquiries involve checking the driver's license, determining whether there are outstanding warrants against the driver, and inspecting the automobile's registration and proof of insurance. These checks serve the same objective as enforcement of the traffic code: ensuring that vehicles on the road are operated safely and responsibly.

" * * * Lacking the same close connection to roadway safety as the ordinary inquiries, a dog sniff is not fairly characterized as part of the officer's traffic mission.

"In advancing its de minimis rule, the Eighth Circuit relied heavily on our decision in *Pennsylvania v. Mimms*, [14th ed., p. 331, n. 1]. In *Mimms*, we reasoned that the government's 'legitimate and weighty' interest in officer safety outweighs the 'de minimis' additional intrusion of requiring a driver, already lawfully stopped, to exit the vehicle. * * *

"Unlike a general interest in criminal enforcement, however, the government's officer safety interest stems from the mission of the stop itself. Traffic stops are 'especially fraught with danger to police officers,' so an officer may need to take certain negligibly burdensome precautions in order to complete his mission safely. Cf. *United States v. Holt*, 264 F.3d 1215, 1221–1222 (C.A.10 2001) (en banc) (recognizing officer safety justification for criminal record and outstanding warrant checks). On-scene investigation into other crimes, however, detours from that mission. So too do safety precautions taken in order to facilitate such detours. Thus, even assuming that the imposition here was no more intrusive than the exit order in *Mimms*, the dog sniff could not be justified on the same basis. * * *

"The Government argues that an officer may 'incremental[ly]' prolong a stop to conduct a dog sniff so long as the officer is reasonably diligent in pursuing the traffic-related purpose of the stop, and the overall duration of the stop remains reasonable in relation to the duration of other traffic stops involving similar circumstances. The Government's argument, in effect, is that by completing all traffic-related tasks expeditiously, an officer can earn bonus time to pursue an unrelated criminal investigation. The reasonableness of a seizure, however, depends on what the police in fact do. In this regard, the Government acknowledges that 'an officer always has to be reasonably diligent.' How could diligence be gauged other than by noting what the officer actually did and how he did it? If an officer can complete traffic-based inquiries expeditiously, then that is the amount of 'time reasonably required to complete [the stop's] mission.' As we said in *Caballes* and reiterate today, a traffic stop 'prolonged beyond' that point is 'unlawful.' The critical question, then, is not whether the dog sniff occurs before or after the officer issues a ticket, as Justice Alito supposes, but whether conducting the sniff 'prolongs'—i.e., adds time to—'the stop.' "

Thomas, J., dissenting, joined by Alito, J., and in part by Kennedy, J., noting that the 29 minutes that passed in the instant case was "hardly out of the ordinary for a traffic stop by a single officer of a vehicle containing multiple occupants even when no dog sniff is involved," emphasized these points: (1) "The majority's rule * * * imposes a one-way ratchet for constitutional protection linked to the characteristics of the individual officer conducting the stop: If a driver is stopped by a particularly efficient officer, then he will be entitled to be released from the traffic stop after a shorter period of time than a driver stopped by a less efficient officer. Similarly, if a driver is stopped by an officer with access to technology that can shorten a records check, then he will be entitled to be released from the stop after a shorter period of time than an individual stopped by an officer without access to such technology. * * * [This is contrary to our prior cases, where we] have repeatedly explained that the reasonableness inquiry must not hinge on the characteristics of the individual officer conducting the seizure. * * *

"The majority's logic would produce * * * arbitrary results. Under its reasoning, a traffic stop made by a rookie could be executed in a reasonable manner, whereas the same traffic stop made by a knowledgeable, veteran officer in precisely the same circumstances might not, if in fact his knowledge and experience made him capable of completing the stop faster. We have long rejected interpretations of the Fourth Amendment that would produce such haphazard results, and I see no reason to depart from our consistent practice today."

(2) "The majority's approach draws an artificial line between dog sniffs and other common police practices. The lower courts have routinely confirmed that warrant checks are a constitutionally permissible part of a traffic stop, and the majority confirms that it finds no fault in these measures. Yet its reasoning suggests the opposite. Such warrant checks look more like they are directed to 'detecting evidence of ordinary criminal wrongdoing' than to 'ensuring that vehicles on the road are operated safely and responsibly.' Perhaps one could argue that the existence of an outstanding warrant might make a driver less likely to operate his vehicle safely and responsibly on the road, but the same could be said about a driver in possession of contraband."

(3) "Traffic stops can be initiated based on probable cause or reasonable suspicion. * * * Although all traffic stops must be executed reasonably, our precedents make clear that traffic stops justified by reasonable suspicion are subject to additional limitations that those justified by probable cause are not. A * * * stop based on probable cause affords an officer considerably more leeway. In such seizures, an officer may engage in a warrantless arrest of the driver, a warrantless search incident to arrest of the driver, and a warrantless search incident to arrest of the vehicle if it is reasonable to believe evidence relevant to the crime of arrest might be found there.

"The majority casually tosses this distinction aside. It asserts that the traffic stop in this case, which was undisputedly initiated on the basis of probable cause, can last no longer than is in fact necessary to effectuate the mission of the stop. And, it assumes that the mission of the stop was merely to write a traffic ticket, rather than to consider making a custodial arrest."

(4) "Today's revision of our Fourth Amendment jurisprudence was also entirely unnecessary. Rodriguez suffered no Fourth Amendment violation here for an entirely independent reason: Officer Struble had reasonable suspicion to continue to hold him for investigative purposes." (Because the magistrate had ruled otherwise, the district court adopted that conclusion, and the court of appeals did not review that determination, the majority left that matter "for Eighth Circuit consideration on remand.")

Alito, J., also dissenting separately, stated in that part of his opinion referenced by the majority that the Court's decision "is unlikely to have any appreciable effect on the length of future traffic stops," as "[m]ost officers will learn the prescribed sequence of events."

In light of *Rodriguez*, what should the result be on the facts of *Commonwealth v. Smith,* 547 S.W.3d 276 (Ky.2018), where a detective surveilling Smith because of a tip he was selling cocaine, upon seeing him turn without signalling, contacted a nearby canine officer to make the traffic stop, and just minutes after the stop, before ticketing and other actions deemed part of the "mission" of a traffic stop could have been completed in any event, the officer let his dog circle the car, and the dog alerted and thereby provided probable cause for the productive search of the vehicle that followed.

In *State v. Cleverly,* 385 P.3d 512 (Kan. 2016), a pickup truck was stopped at 1:15 a.m. "based on the officer's observation that neither occupant of the pickup was wearing a seat belt." One officer dealt with passenger Cleverly; he ran a "warrants check," which was negative, and made no effort to issue him a traffic ticket. The other officer issued a ticket to the driver only "for no proof of insurance," and, seemingly viewed that as the end of the traffic stop, for he then obtained the driver's valid consent to answer "a couple more questions," ultimately resulting in the driver's valid consent to a search of the vehicle that "produced a glass pipe with scorch marks hidden in a pile of laundry between the driver and passenger seats." An officer then asked for Cleverly's consent to search cigarette packages he had earlier placed on the hood of the truck; Cleverly handed the packages to the officer, who found three small baggies of meth therein, resulting in Cleverly being arrested and subsequently prosecuted for possession of the meth. If Cleverly claims his otherwise valid consent was tainted by an illegal seizure of him, but the prosecution contends the contested search was incident to Cleverly's "theoretical arrest" (compare Notes 6 & 7, 14th ed., p. 331–32), what should the result be?

In *People v. Cummings*, 6 N.E.3d 725 (Ill.2014), an officer suspected a van's registration had expired, but a check revealed the registration was valid though the female owner had an outstanding warrant. Unable to determine the gender of the driver, the officer stopped the van, but upon approaching the vehicle saw that the driver was a male. The officer nonetheless continued the stop by asking the driver for his license and proof of insurance, leading to the driver's prosecution for felony driving while his license was suspended. Though the court held that "[r]equesting the defendant's license impermissibly prolonged the stop because it was unrelated to the reason for the stop," in *Illinois v. Cummings*, 135 S.Ct. 1892 (2015), the Court granted cert. and then remanded the case for further consideration in light of *Rodriguez*. On remand, the state court held that though "reasonable suspicion the driver was subject to arrest vanished upon seeing defendant, * * * [t]he interest in officer safety [still] permits a driver's license request of a driver lawfully stopped," 46 N.E.3d 248 (Ill.2016).

14th ed., p. 405; after Note 9, add:

10. ***Traffic stops: effect of decriminalization.*** As pointed out in Jordan Woods, *Decriminalization, Police Authority, and Routine Traffic Stops*, 62 UCLA L.Rev. 672 (2015), "since 1970 twenty-two states have decriminalized minor traffic violations by removing criminal sanctions, reclassifying the violations as noncriminal offenses," though "[t]hese decriminalization reforms have centered on modifying sanctions and have rarely restricted police authority and discretion in routine traffic stop settings." The author proposes "statutory and doctrinal reforms" restricting "police authority and discretion to use specific investigative tactics at the inception, duration, and conclusion of noncriminal traffic stops," such as by restricting "police authority and discretion to use a decriminalized traffic violation as grounds to question drivers and passengers about nontraffic crime, to obtain a driver's consent to search a car, to request a comprehensive personal background check on drivers and passengers, to arrest drivers and passengers (and thus any searches of the person or vehicle incident to arrest), and to use drug-sniffing dogs to search the exterior of vehicles," citing "Rhode Island's Racial Profiling Prevention Act of 2004," id. at 754–55. Do you agree?

E. PROTECTIVE SEARCH

14th ed., p. 408; in lieu of third paragraph in Note 3, add:

What is the status of *Adams* now that the Supreme Court's Second Amendment precedents recognize "a right to carry a loaded gun outside the home," *Moore v. Madigan*, 702 F.3d 933 (7th Cir.2012)? Consider *United States v. Robinson*, 814 F.3d 201 (4th Cir.2016), where after a traffic stop of a vehicle the police frisked the passenger based upon information that a few minutes earlier he had been seen loading a gun and then placing it into his pocket. In overturning his conviction of being a felon in possession of a firearm, the court concluded "that in states like West Virginia, which broadly allow public possession of firearms, reasonable suspicion that a person is armed does not by itself give rise to reasonable suspicion that the person is dangerous for *Terry* purposes." But on rehearing en banc, 846 F.3d 694 (4th Cir.2017), 11 of the 16 judges concluded otherwise:

"Robinson's argument presumes that the legal possession of a firearm cannot pose a danger to police officers during a forced stop, and it collapses the requirements for making a stop with the requirements for conducting a frisk. It thus fails at several levels when considered under the Supreme Court's 'stop-and-frisk' jurisprudence. First, Robinson confuses the standard for making stops—which requires a reasonable suspicion that a crime or other infraction has been or is being committed—with the standard for conducting a frisk—which requires both a lawful investigatory stop and a reasonable suspicion that the person stopped is armed and dangerous. Second, he fails to recognize that traffic stops alone are inherently dangerous for police officers. Third, he also fails to recognize that traffic stops of persons who are armed, whether legally or illegally, pose yet a greater safety risk to police officers. And fourth, he argues illogically that when a person forcefully stopped may be legally permitted to possess a firearm, any risk of danger to police officers posed by the firearm is eliminated. * * *

"The Supreme Court applied *Terry* to circumstances analogous to those before us in *Mimms*, [14th ed., p. 331] where an officer, after making a routine traffic stop, 'noticed a large bulge' under the defendant's jacket and therefore conducted a frisk. Holding that the frisk was clearly justified, the *Mimms* Court explained that '[t]he bulge in the jacket permitted the officer to conclude that Mimms was armed and thus posed a serious and present danger to the safety of the officer,' adding that '[i]n these circumstances, any man of "reasonable caution" would likely have conducted the "pat down." ' The only evidence of Mimms' dangerousness was the bulge indicating that he was armed. It was thus Mimms' status of being armed during a forced police encounter (the traffic stop) that posed the danger justifying the frisk * * *.

"In short, established Supreme Court law imposes two requirements for conducting a frisk, but no more than two: first, that the officer have conducted a lawful stop, which includes both a traditional *Terry* stop as well as a traffic stop; and second, that during the valid but forced encounter, the officer reasonably suspect that the person is armed and therefore dangerous. In both *Terry* and *Mimms*, the Court deliberately linked 'armed' and 'dangerous,' recognizing that the frisks in those cases were lawful because the stops were valid and the officer reasonably believed that the person stopped 'was armed and thus' dangerous. The use of 'and thus' recognizes that the risk of danger is created simply because the person, who was forcibly stopped, is armed.

"In this case, both requirements—a lawful stop and a reasonable suspicion that Robinson was armed—were satisfied, thus justifying Captain Roberts' frisk under the Fourth Amendment as a matter of law.

"Robinson argues that *Mimms* is distinguishable because the frisk there took place in a jurisdiction that made it a crime to carry a concealed deadly weapon. West Virginia, on the other hand, generally permits its citizens to carry firearms. From this distinction, Robinson argues that when the person forcibly stopped may be legally permitted to possess a firearm, the risk of danger posed by the firearm is eliminated. This argument, however, fails under the Supreme Court's express recognition that the legality of the frisk does not depend on the illegality of the firearm's possession. Indeed, the Court has twice explained that '[t]he purpose of this limited search [i.e., the frisk] is not to discover evidence of crime, but to allow the officer to pursue his investigation without fear of violence, and thus the frisk for weapons might be equally necessary and reasonable, whether or not carrying a concealed weapon violated any applicable state law.' *Williams*, [14th ed., p. 408]; see also *Long*, [14th ed., p. 409] ('[W]e have expressly rejected the view that the validity of a *Terry* search [i.e., a frisk] depends on whether the weapon is possessed in accordance with state law'). Robinson's position directly conflicts with these observations."

A concurring judge objected to the unitary "armed and thus dangerous" approach because it would seemingly also apply in cases where the person was armed with a "weapon" of some other sort (e.g., "a knitting needle, a sharpened pencil"), and preferred retaining the separate "dangerous" element, deemed satisfied in the instant case because "individuals who carry firearms—lawfully or unlawfully—pose a risk of danger to themselves, law enforcement officers, and the public at large."

The remaining four judges, dissenting, objected: "Guns, of course, are in some sense intrinsically dangerous. But the question under *Terry* is whether a person carrying a gun is a danger to the police or others. And where the state legislature has decided that its citizens may be entrusted to safely carry firearms on public streets and during traffic stops, and law-abiding citizens have availed themselves of these rights, I do not see how we can presume that every one of those citizens necessarily poses a danger to the police. * * *

"But my biggest concern is that these 'special burdens'—most relevantly, the *Terry* frisks at issue here—will not be distributed evenly across the population. Allowing police officers making stops to frisk anyone thought to be armed, in a state where the carrying of guns is widely permitted, 'creates a serious and recurring threat to the privacy of countless individuals.' And, critically, it 'gives police officers unbridled discretion' to decide which of those legally armed citizens will be targeted for frisks, implicating concerns about the abuse of police discretion that are fundamental to the Fourth Amendment. * * *

"The government assures that we need not worry about these possible disproportionate effects because a *Terry* frisk may be conducted only after a stop on reasonable suspicion of 'criminal activity'—an 'objective standard' that 'prevents police stops on hunches alone.' But that simply is not so, and to understand why not, we need look no further than the facts of this very case. Robinson was not stopped for 'criminal activity,' at least as that term generally is understood. As a legal matter, he was stopped because Officer Hudson observed a seatbelt violation—the kind of minor and routine traffic infraction that does next to nothing to narrow the class of legally armed citizens who may be subjected to a frisk at police discretion. And in reality, as Officer Hudson candidly testified at the suppression hearing, Robinson was stopped so that the police could investigate the tip they had received about a black male carrying a concealed firearm. Though Robinson's gun possession was presumptively lawful in light of West Virginia's generous public-carry laws, Robinson was stopped precisely because the police had a hunch that his possession in fact might be unlawful.

"It is true, as the government argues, that under *Whren v. United States*, [14th ed., p. 323], the Fourth Amendment permits this kind of pretextual traffic stop, undertaken in order to explore some unsupported hunch. But that is exactly the problem: In light of *Whren*, the requirement that a valid stop precede a *Terry* frisk imposes no meaningful limit at all on police discretion. If the police in a public-carry jurisdiction want to target a particular armed citizen for an exploratory frisk, then they need do no more than wait and watch for a moving violation, as in this case—or a parking violation; or, for the pedestrians among us, a jaywalking infraction, as the government helpfully explained at oral argument—and then make a pretextual stop."

§ 9. ADMINISTRATIVE INSPECTIONS AND REGULATORY SEARCHES: MORE ON BALANCING THE NEED AGAINST THE INVASION OF PRIVACY

14th ed., p. 413; after Note 1, add:

1A. *Business inspections revisited.* Over a quarter of a century passed before the Court decided another business inspection case, *City of Los Angeles v. Patel*, 135 S.Ct. 1198 (2015). Motel operators brought a facial challenge[a] to § 41.49 of the L.A. Code requiring hotel operators to record and keep for 90 days information about their guests, detailed in nature,[b] and further asserting

---

[a]   In *Patel*, the majority held "that facial challenges under the Fourth Amendment are not categorically barred or especially disfavored," and emphasized that "when addressing a facial challenge to a statute authorizing warrantless searches, the proper focus of the constitutional inquiry is searches that the law actually authorizes, not those for which it is irrelevant. If exigency or a warrant justifies an officer's search, the subject of the search must permit it to proceed irrespective of whether it is authorized by statute. Statutes authorizing warrantless searches also do no work where the subject of a search has consented. Accordingly, the constitutional "applications" that petitioner claims prevent facial relief here are irrelevant to our analysis because they do not involve actual applications of the statute." Alito and Thomas, JJ., in a separate dissent, objected to the majority's conclusion that § 41.49 was facially unconstitutional, because "even if the Court were 100% correct" in its Fourth Amendment analysis, "many other applications of this law are constitutional," as, e.g., when police having probable cause get a search warrant for the records but the hotel operator then refuses to make the records available.

[b]   As the *Patel* majority noted, this information includes "the guest's name and address; the number of people in each guest's party; the make, model, and license plate number of any guest's vehicle parked on hotel property; the guest's date and time of arrival and scheduled departure date, the room number assigned to the guest, the rate charged and amount collected for the room; and the method of payment. Guests without reservations, those who pay for their rooms with cash, and any guests who rent a room for less than 12 hours must present photographic identification at the time of check-in, and hotel operators are required to record the number and expiration date of that document. For those guests who check in using an electronic kiosk, the hotel's records must also contain the guest's credit card information."

that such records "shall be made available to any officer of the Los Angeles Police Department for inspection * * * at a time and in a manner that minimizes any interference with the operation of the business"; failure to make those records available is a misdemeanor punishable by fine and imprisonment. The City relied upon *Burger* as justification for § 41.49, so the Court considered (A) whether hotels are "closely regulated" and (B) whether such warrantless inspections are sufficiently limited to constitute an "adequate substitute for a warrant," matters about which the 5-Justice majority, per Sotomayor, J., and a 3-Justice dissent, per Scalia, J., disagreed.

The majority treated issue (A) as having two aspects: (i) nature of the business; and (ii) nature of the regulation. Regarding (i), said the majority, unlike the "only four industries" the Court had previously placed in that category—liquor sales, firearms dealing, mining, and running an automobile junkyard—"nothing inherent in the operation of hotels poses a clear and significant risk to the public welfare." To this the dissent responded: "The reason closely regulated industries may be searched without a warrant has nothing to do with the risk of harm they pose; rather, it has to do with the expectations of those who enter such a line of work." In support, the dissent noted that "lower courts, which do not have the luxury of picking the cases they hear, have identified many more businesses as closely regulated," e.g., pharmacies, massage parlors, commercial-fishing operations, day-care facilities, nursing homes, jewelers, barbershops, and rabbit dealers. Regarding (ii), the majority in *Patel,* asserting this category is a "narrow exception," emphasized that *Burger* teaches the regulation must involve a "comprehensive" scheme putting hotel owners on notice that their "property will be subject to periodic inspections undertaken for specific purposes." It cannot be said, the majority concluded, "that regulations requiring hotels to, *inter alia,* maintain a license, collect taxes, conspicuously post their rates, and meet certain sanitary standards * * * establish a comprehensive scheme of regulation that distinguishes hotels from numerous other businesses." The dissenters, on the other hand, noting that in the past the Court has looked at such factors as "the duration of the regulatory tradition, the comprehensiveness of the regulatory regime, and the imposition of similar regulations by other jurisdictions," argued these factors exist as to hotels, for "[a]t the time of the founding, * * * warrantless searches of inns and similar places of public accommodation were commonplace," existing regulations "reach into the 'minutest detail[s]' of motel operations," and "more than 100 similar register-inspections laws [exist] across the country." Who has the best of these arguments?

Regarding issue (B), the *Patel* majority found § 41.49 "constitutionally deficient under the 'certainty and regularity' prong of the closely regulated industries test because it fails sufficiently to constrain police officers' discretion as to which hotels to search and under what circumstances.[c] While the Court has upheld inspection schemes of closely regulated industries that called for searches at least four times a year [as in *Donovan v. Dewey,* 452 U.S. 594 (1981)], or on a 'regular basis' [as in *Burger*], § 41.49 imposes no comparable standard." The dissent responded: "Without a trace of irony, the Court tries to distinguish Los Angeles's law from the laws upheld in *Dewey* and *Burger* by pointing out that the latter regimes required inspections at least four times a year and on a 'regular basis' respectively. But the warrantless police searches of a business '10 times a day, every day for three months' that the Court envisions under Los Angeles's regime are entirely consistent with the regimes in *Dewey* and *Burger*; 10 times a day, every day, is 'at least four times a year,' and on a (much too) 'regular basis.' " Query, does this call into question the *Patel* result, or the results in *Burger* and *Dewey*?

Noting that the Court had often taken the position "that absent consent, exigent circumstances, or the like, in order for an administrative search to be constitutional, the subject of the search must be afforded an opportunity to obtain precompliance review before a neutral

---

[c] As the majority observed at another point, the Code provision would not be violated "[e]ven if a hotel has been searched 10 times a day, every day, for three months, without any violation being found."

decisionmaker,"[d] the *Patel* majority found § 41.49 defective in this respect: "A hotel owner who refuses to give an officer access to his or her registry can be arrested on the spot. * * * Absent an opportunity for precompliance review, the ordinance creates an intolerable risk that searches authorized by it will exceed statutory limits, or be used as a pretext to harass hotel operators and their guests." The needed remedy, the Court added, was either an administrative subpoena system or some other process that likewise "alters the dynamic between the officer and the hotel to be searched, and reduces the risk that officers will use these administrative searches as a pretext to harass business owners." Under a subpoena system, for example, a hotel operator "could move to quash the subpoena before any search takes place," and a "neutral decisionmaker, including an administrative law judge, would then review the subpoenaed party's objections before deciding whether the subpoena is enforceable." The Court emphasized that it held "only that a hotel owner must be afforded an *opportunity* to have a neutral decisionmaker review an officer's demand to search the registry before he or she faces penalties for failing to comply. Actual review need only occur in those rare instances where a hotel operator objects to turning over the registry. Moreover, this opportunity can be provided without imposing onerous burdens on those charged with an administrative scheme's enforcement," as "the searches authorized * * * would be constitutional if they were performed pursuant to an administrative subpoena," which "can be issued by the individual seeking the record—here officers in the field—without probable cause that a regulation is being infringed."

As the *Patel* majority concluded, the system it envisioned would permit inspection of hotel registries accomplished in any one of four ways: (i) "a proper administrative warrant"; (ii) an "administrative subpoena"; (iii) via "consent"; or (iv) under "exigent circumstances." Query: As to (i), under the inspection scheme envisioned by § 41.49, what would constitute a "proper" warrant under the *Camara/Barlow's* standard? As to (ii), should it *always* be a permissible alternative re § 41.49 (held *not* to "fall within the administrative search exception to the warrant requirement"), and if so will the traditional view—that on a motion to quash the "burden of showing an abuse of the * * * process is on the" challenger,[e] and that the Fourth Amendment only "requires that the subpoena be sufficiently limited in scope, relevant in purpose, and specific in directive so that compliance will not be unreasonably burdensome"[f]—suffice, or should enforcement be ordered only "upon a sufficient showing [by the City] that inspection * * * is in accordance with reasonable legislative or administrative standards"[g]? As to (iii), is the general rule re consent that the consenting party need not first be advised of his rights, see 14th ed., p. 424, Note 7, applicable here, and does this mean an officer could simply appear at the hotel and display the language of § 41.49 sans the penalty provision and make no mention of the *Patel*-required "opportunity for precompliance review"? As for (iv), does this relate to some risk the hotel operator might destroy or alter the registry, or instead or in addition the kind of circumstances mentioned by Justice Scalia, i.e., when it is thought a hotel might be used as a "prison[ ] for migrants smuggled across the border and held for ransom"?

---

[d]   *Donovan v. Lone Steer, Inc.*, 464 U.S. 408 (1984) (noting administrative search via subpoena permissible where subpoenaed party sufficiently protected by opportunity to "question the reasonableness of the subpoena, before suffering any penalties for refusing to comply with it"); *See v. City of Seattle*, 387 U.S. 541 (1967) ("while the demand to inspect may be issued by the agency, in the form of an administrative subpoena, it may not be made and enforced by the inspector in the field, and the subpoenaed party may obtain judicial review of the reasonableness of the demand prior to suffering penalties for refusing to comply"); *Camara v. Municipal Court*, 387 U.S. 523 (1967) ("broad statutory safeguards are no substitute for individualized review, particularly when those safeguards may only be invoked at the risk of a criminal penalty").

[e]   *United States v. Powell*, 379 U.S. 48 (1964).

[f]   *See v. City of Seattle*, 387 U.S. 541 (1967).

[g]   Model Code of Pre-Arraignment Procedure § SS 250.3 (1975).

14th ed., p. 414; end of Note 2, add:

In *United States v. Kolsuz*, 890 F.3d 133 (4th Cir.2018), customs agents found firearms parts in defendant's luggage as he was about to board a flight to Turkey, and then "took possession of his smartphone and subjected it to a month-long, off-site forensic analysis, yielding a nearly 900-page report cataloguing the phone's data." After noting (1) that "the rationales underlying the border exception extend to exit as well as entry searches"; (2) that defendant did not "challenge the seizure of his phone," understandable because "he was in custody while the government undertook its month-long forensic analysis"; (3) that notwithstanding the fact that defendant "was arrested and his phone seized and transported miles from the airport," the search was properly characterized as a border search rather than a search incident to arrest; and (4) that defendant "does not challenge the manual search of his smartphone, undertaken on-site at the airport,"[h] the court agreed "with the district court that under *Riley*, the forensic examination of Kolsuz's phone must be considered a nonroutine border search, requiring some measure of individualized suspicion. What precisely that standard should be—whether reasonable suspicion is enough, as the district court concluded, or whether there must be a warrant based on probable cause, as Kolsuz suggests—is a question we need not resolve: Because the agents who conducted the search reasonably relied on precedent holding that no warrant was required, suppression of the report would be inappropriate even if we disagreed." A concurring judge, citing the analysis in Orin Kerr, *The Effect of Legislation on Fourth Amendment Protection,* 115 Mich.L.Rev. 1117 (2017), argued that "the legislative and executive branches * * * have a critical role to play in defining the standards for a border search, and they are much better equipped than we are to appreciate both the privacy interests at stake and the magnitude of the practical risks involved."

[h] Consider *United States v. Molina-Isidoro*, 884 F.3d 287 (5th Cir.2018), upholding a warrantless manual search on probable cause of a cell phone at the border by extending the *Davis* good faith principle, 14th ed., p. 224, to this post-*Riley* search to avoid "fix[ing] precedent in a rapidly changing area."

§ 10. CONSENT SEARCHES

A. THE NATURE OF "CONSENT"

14th ed., p. 426; replace Note 13:

13. *"Implied consent."* In BIRCHFIELD v. NORTH DAKOTA, 136 S.Ct. 2160 (2016), the Court, per Alito, J., concluded: "Drunk drivers take a grisly toll on the Nation's roads, claiming thousands of lives, injuring many more victims, and inflicting billions of dollars in property damage every year. To fight this problem, all States have laws that prohibit motorists from driving with a blood alcohol concentration (BAC) that exceeds a specified level. But determining whether a driver's BAC is over the legal limit requires a test, and many drivers stopped on suspicion of drunk driving would not submit to testing if given the option. So every State also has long had what are termed 'implied consent laws.' These laws impose penalties on motorists who refuse to undergo testing when there is sufficient reason to believe they are violating the State's drunk-driving laws.

"In the past, the typical penalty for noncompliance was suspension or revocation of the motorist's license. The cases now before us involve laws that go beyond that and make it a crime for a motorist to refuse to be tested after being lawfully arrested for driving while impaired. The question presented is whether such laws violate the Fourth Amendment's prohibition against unreasonable searches.

"[While each of the three cases collectively decided here involves a person arrested on drunk-driving charges and warned of the criminal penalties for refusal of a blood or breath test for blood alcohol concentration,] the cases differ in some respects. Petitioners Birchfield and Beylund were told that they were obligated to submit to a blood test, whereas petitioner Bernard was informed that a breath test was required. Birchfield and Bernard each refused to undergo a test and was convicted of a crime for his refusal. Beylund complied with the demand for a blood sample, and his license was then suspended in an administrative proceeding based on test results that revealed a very high blood alcohol level.

"Despite these differences, success for all three petitioners depends on the proposition that the criminal law ordinarily may not compel a motorist to submit to the taking of a blood sample or to a breath test unless a warrant authorizing such testing is issued by a magistrate. [The Court at this point, as discussed at Supp. p. 57, concluded that warrantless breath tests but not blood tests could be performed incident to arrest.]

"Having concluded that the search incident to arrest doctrine does not justify the warrantless taking of a blood sample, we must address respondents' alternative argument that such tests are justified based on the driver's legally implied consent to submit to them. It is well established that a search is reasonable when the subject consents, and that sometimes consent to a search need not be express but may be fairly inferred from context. Our prior opinions have referred approvingly to the general concept of implied-consent laws that impose civil penalties and evidentiary consequences on motorists who refuse to comply. Petitioners do not question the constitutionality of those laws, and nothing we say here should be read to cast doubt on them.

"It is another matter, however, for a State not only to insist upon an intrusive blood test, but also to impose criminal penalties on the refusal to submit to such a test. There must be a limit to the consequences to which motorists may be deemed to have consented by virtue of a decision to drive on public roads.

"Respondents and their amici all but concede this point. North Dakota emphasizes that its law makes refusal a misdemeanor and suggests that laws punishing refusal more severely would present a different issue. Borrowing from our Fifth Amendment jurisprudence, the United States suggests that motorists could be deemed to have consented to only those conditions that are "reasonable" in that they have a 'nexus' to the privilege of driving and entail penalties that are proportional to severity of the violation. But in the Fourth Amendment setting, this standard does not differ in substance from the one that we apply, since reasonableness is always the touchstone of Fourth Amendment analysis. And applying this standard, we conclude that motorists cannot be deemed to have consented to submit to a blood test on pain of committing a criminal offense.

"Our remaining task is to apply our legal conclusions to the three cases before us.

"Petitioner Birchfield was criminally prosecuted for refusing a warrantless blood draw, and therefore the search he refused cannot be justified as a search incident to his arrest or on the basis of implied consent. There is no indication in the record or briefing that a breath test would have failed to satisfy the State's interests in acquiring evidence to enforce its drunk-driving laws against Birchfield. And North Dakota has not presented any case-specific information to suggest that the exigent circumstances exception would have justified a warrantless search. Unable to see any other basis on which to justify a warrantless test of Birchfield's blood, we conclude that Birchfield was threatened with an unlawful search and that the judgment affirming his conviction must be reversed.

"Bernard, on the other hand, was criminally prosecuted for refusing a warrantless breath test. That test was a permissible search incident to Bernard's arrest for drunk driving, an arrest whose legality Bernard has not contested. Accordingly, the Fourth Amendment did not require officers to obtain a warrant prior to demanding the test, and Bernard had no right to refuse it.

"Unlike the other petitioners, Beylund was not prosecuted for refusing a test. He submitted to a blood test after police told him that the law required his submission, and his license was then suspended and he was fined in an administrative proceeding. The North Dakota Supreme Court held that Beylund's consent was voluntary on the erroneous assumption that the State could permissibly compel both blood and breath tests. Because voluntariness of consent to a search must be 'determined from the totality of all the circumstances,' we leave it to the state court on remand to reevaluate Beylund's consent given the partial inaccuracy of the officer's advisory."

In none of the three cases collectively decided in *Birchfield* does it appear there was ever an express claim that the implied-consent statute *itself* provides a basis for a warrantless search by, in effect, making the act of driving on the state's highways a sufficient manifestation of such consent. Thus there is post-*Birchfield* authority, regarding a statutory provision allowing, on an implied-consent theory, the warrantless taking and testing of blood from an unconscious person, that treating such a statute "as an irrevocable rule of implied consent does not comport with the consent exception of the warrant requirement because such treatment does not require an analysis of the voluntariness of consent." *State v. Romano*, 800 S.E.2d 644 (N.C.2017) (noting however that "*Birchfield* does not answer the specific question before us"). But the court in another state, *People v. Hyde,* 393 P.3d 962 (Colo.2017), likewise faced with a challenge to an implied-consent statute applicable to an unconscious person, concluded that in light of *Birchfield* such "statutory consent" was valid, given that the statute in question "imposes only civil, and not criminal penalties on drivers who refuse to submit to a blood test." Which court is correct?

B. THIRD PARTY CONSENT

14th ed., p. 433; end of Note 5, add:

In *State v. Vanhollenbeke*, 412 P.3d 1274 (Wash.2017), the court cautioned that a "general assertion that a driver of a vehicle owned by another person generally assumes the risk that the third-party owner will consent to a police search" of that vehicle is incorrect, as the "driver may be using the vehicle based on a lease, a rental, a sharing arrangement, or some other agreement" giving rise to "a property right [that] might also form the basis for an enforceable privacy right."

CHAPTER 8

NETWORK SURVEILLANCE

■ ■ ■

§ 1. THE FOURTH AMENDMENT

B. RIGHTS IN NON-CONTENT INFORMATION

14th ed., p. 481; replace Note 2 with the following and delete Note 7:

2. ***The Supreme Court modifies the third-party doctrine in Carpenter v. United States.*** In *Carpenter v. United States*, 138 S.Ct. 2206 (2018), the Supreme Court imposed important limits on the third-party doctrine. *Carpenter* involved government access to historical cell-site location information (CSLI). CSLI are records that cell phone providers automatically generate and store about which cell sites were used to route calls for a particular cellular phone number. Because providers know the location of each cell site, and phones typically use cell sites nearby, CSLI can be used to reconstruct the past location of a phone's user.

In *Carpenter*, investigators obtained orders requiring Carpenter's cell phone provider to disclose CSLI from his account to show Carpenter's involvement in a string of robberies. The records revealed that Carpenter's phone was in communication with cell towers near four robberies that occurred over a five-month window. In the decision below, the Sixth Circuit ruled that obtaining the CSLI was not a search that implicated Carpenter's rights because of the third-party doctrine. See *United States v. Carpenter*, 819 F.3d 880 (6th Cir. 2016). Before the Supreme Court, the government argued that cell phone users do not have Fourth Amendment rights in their CSLI because they voluntarily disclose their location to their cellular providers just like Smith revealed his numbers dialed to the phone company in *Smith v. Maryland* and *Miller* revealed his bank records to his bank in *United States v Miller*.

The Supreme Court disagreed. In an opinion authored by Chief Justice Roberts, joined by Justices Ginsburg, Breyer, Sotomayor, and Kagan, the Court held that the third-party doctrine does not apply in these circumstances:

"The Government's position fails to contend with the seismic shifts in digital technology that made possible the tracking of not only Carpenter's location but also everyone else's, not for a short period but for years and years. Sprint Corporation and its competitors are not your typical witnesses. Unlike the nosy neighbor who keeps an eye on comings and goings, they are ever alert, and their memory is nearly infallible. There is a world of difference between the limited types of personal information addressed in *Smith* and *Miller* and the exhaustive chronicle of location information casually collected by wireless carriers today. The Government thus is not asking for a straightforward application of the third-party doctrine, but instead a significant extension of it to a distinct category of information.

"The third-party doctrine partly stems from the notion that an individual has a reduced expectation of privacy in information knowingly shared with another. But the fact of diminished privacy interests does not mean that the Fourth Amendment falls out of the picture entirely. *Smith* and *Miller*, after all, did not rely solely on the act of sharing. Instead, they considered the nature of the particular documents sought to determine whether there is a legitimate 'expectation of privacy' concerning their contents. *Smith* pointed out the limited capabilities of a pen register;

as explained in *Riley*, telephone call logs reveal little in the way of "identifying information." *Miller* likewise noted that checks were "not confidential communications but negotiable instruments to be used in commercial transactions." In mechanically applying the third-party doctrine to this case, the Government fails to appreciate that there are no comparable limitations on the revealing nature of CSLI.

"The Court has in fact already shown special solicitude for location information in the third-party context. In *Knotts*, the Court relied on *Smith* to hold that an individual has no reasonable expectation of privacy in public movements that he "voluntarily conveyed to anyone who wanted to look." But when confronted with more pervasive tracking [in *Jones*], five Justices agreed that longer term GPS monitoring of even a vehicle traveling on public streets constitutes a search. Justice Gorsuch wonders [in dissent] why someone's location when using a phone is sensitive, and Justice Kennedy assumes that a person's discrete movements are not particularly private. Yet this case is not about "using a phone" or a person's movement at a particular time. It is about a detailed chronicle of a person's physical presence compiled every day, every moment, over several years. Such a chronicle implicates privacy concerns far beyond those considered in *Smith* and *Miller*.

"Neither does the second rationale underlying the third-party doctrine—voluntary exposure—hold up when it comes to CSLI. Cell phone location information is not truly "shared" as one normally understands the term. In the first place, cell phones and the services they provide are "such a pervasive and insistent part of daily life" that carrying one is indispensable to participation in modern society. *Riley*. Second, a cell phone logs a cell-site record by dint of its operation, without any affirmative act on the part of the user beyond powering up. Virtually any activity on the phone generates CSLI, including incoming calls, texts, or e-mails and countless other data connections that a phone automatically makes when checking for news, weather, or social media updates. Apart from disconnecting the phone from the network, there is no way to avoid leaving behind a trail of location data. As a result, in no meaningful sense does the user voluntarily assume the risk of turning over a comprehensive dossier of his physical movements.

"We therefore decline to extend *Smith* and *Miller* to the collection of CSLI. Given the unique nature of cell phone location information, the fact that the Government obtained the information from a third party does not overcome Carpenter's claim to Fourth Amendment protection. The Government's acquisition of the cell-site records was a search within the meaning of the Fourth Amendment."

The remaining Justices weighed in on the third-party doctrine in separate opinions. Although Justice Gorsuch dissented from the Court's ruling on other grounds, he suggested that the third-party doctrine should be rejected entirely as an unpersuasive application of *Katz*. "[T]he rationale of *Smith* and *Miller* is wrong," Justice Gorsuch concluded, and the Court was wrong "to keep *Smith* and *Miller* on life support and supplement them with a new and multilayered inquiry that seems to be only *Katz*-squared." Here is Justice Gorsuch's criticism of the third-party doctrine:

"Today the Court suggests that *Smith* and *Miller* distinguish between kinds of information disclosed to third parties and require courts to decide whether to "extend" those decisions to particular classes of information, depending on their sensitivity. But as the Sixth Circuit recognized and Justice Kennedy explains, no balancing test of this kind can be found in *Smith* and *Miller*. Those cases announced a categorical rule: Once you disclose information to third parties, you forfeit any reasonable expectation of privacy you might have had in it. And even if *Smith* and *Miller* did permit courts to conduct a balancing contest of the kind the Court now suggests, it's still hard to see how that would help the petitioner in this case. Why is someone's location when using a phone so much more sensitive than who he was talking to (*Smith*) or what financial transactions he engaged in (*Miller*)? I do not know and the Court does not say.

"The problem isn't with the Sixth Circuit's application of *Smith* and *Miller* but with the cases themselves. Can the government demand a copy of all your e-mails from Google or Microsoft without implicating your Fourth Amendment rights? Can it secure your DNA from 23andMe without a warrant or probable cause? *Smith* and *Miller* say yes it can—at least without running afoul of *Katz*. But that result strikes most lawyers and judges today—me included—as pretty unlikely. In the years since its adoption, countless scholars, too, have come to conclude that the "third-party doctrine is not only wrong, but horribly wrong." Kerr, The Case for the Third-Party Doctrine, 107 Mich. L. Rev. 561, 563, n. 5, 564 (2009) (collecting criticisms but defending the doctrine). The reasons are obvious. "As an empirical statement about subjective expectations of privacy," the doctrine is "quite dubious." Baude & Stern, The Positive Law Model of the Fourth Amendment, 129 Harv. L. Rev. 1821, 1872 (2016). People often do reasonably expect that information they entrust to third parties, especially information subject to confidentiality agreements, will be kept private. Meanwhile, if the third party doctrine is supposed to represent a normative assessment of when a person should expect privacy, the notion that the answer might be "never" seems a pretty unattractive societal prescription.

"What, then, is the explanation for our third party doctrine? The truth is, the Court has never offered a persuasive justification. The Court has said that by conveying information to a third party you " 'assume the risk' " it will be revealed to the police and therefore lack a reasonable expectation of privacy in it. But assumption of risk doctrine developed in tort law. It generally applies when "by contract or otherwise [one] expressly agrees to accept a risk of harm" or impliedly does so by "manifest[ing] his willingness to accept" that risk and thereby "take[s] his chances as to harm which may result from it." Restatement (Second) of Torts §§ 496B, 496C(1), and Comment b (1965). That rationale has little play in this context. Suppose I entrust a friend with a letter and he promises to keep it secret until he delivers it to an intended recipient. In what sense have I agreed to bear the risk that he will turn around, break his promise, and spill its contents to someone else? More confusing still, what have I done to "manifest my willingness to accept" the risk that the government will pry the document from my friend and read it without his consent?

"One possible answer concerns knowledge. I know that my friend might break his promise, or that the government might have some reason to search the papers in his possession. But knowing about a risk doesn't mean you assume responsibility for it. Whenever you walk down the sidewalk you know a car may negligently or recklessly veer off and hit you, but that hardly means you accept the consequences and absolve the driver of any damage he may do to you. Epstein, Privacy and the Third Hand: Lessons From the Common Law of Reasonable Expectations, 24 Berkeley Tech. L.J. 1199, 1204 (2009).

"Some have suggested the third party doctrine is better understood to rest on consent than assumption of risk. "So long as a person knows that they are disclosing information to a third party," the argument goes, "their choice to do so is voluntary and the consent valid." *Kerr*, supra, at 588. I confess I still don't see it. Consenting to give a third party access to private papers that remain my property is not the same thing as consenting to a search of those papers by the government. Perhaps there are exceptions, like when the third party is an undercover government agent. See Murphy, The Case Against the Case Against the Third-Party Doctrine: A Response to Epstein and Kerr, 24 Berkeley Tech. L.J. 1239, 1252 (2009); cf. Hoffa. But otherwise this conception of consent appears to be just assumption of risk relabeled—you've "consented" to whatever risks are foreseeable.

"Another justification sometimes offered for third party doctrine is clarity. You (and the police) know exactly how much protection you have in information confided to others: none. As rules go, "the king always wins" is admirably clear. But the opposite rule would be clear too: Third party disclosures never diminish Fourth Amendment protection (call it "the king always loses"). So clarity alone cannot justify the third party doctrine.

"In the end, what do *Smith* and *Miller* add up to? A doubtful application of *Katz* that lets the government search almost whatever it wants whenever it wants. The Sixth Circuit had to follow that rule and faithfully did just that, but it's not clear why we should."

Despite disagreeing with *Smith* and *Miller*, Justice Gorsuch nonetheless dissented in *Carpenter*. He reasoned that the Court should apply a "traditional approach" instead of the *Katz* test. The traditional approach should be rooted in some source of positive law sufficient to make "house, paper, or effect" sufficiently "yours" to invoke the Fourth Amendment. Exactly what that test should be must await a future case, Justice Gorsuch argued, because Carpenter had not sufficiently developed a theory on which a "legal interest is sufficient to make something yours" under the Fourth Amendment. According to Justice Gorsuch, "[m]uch work is needed to revitalize this area and answer these questions."

Justice Kennedy, joined by Justices Thomas and Alito, authored a dissent that defended the third-party doctrine of *Miller* and *Smith* and criticized the majority's refusal to apply it to the collection of CSLI:

"The principle established in *Miller* and *Smith* is correct for two reasons, the first relating to a defendant's attenuated interest in property owned by another, and the second relating to the safeguards inherent in the use of compulsory process.

"First, *Miller* and *Smith* placed necessary limits on the ability of individuals to assert Fourth Amendment interests in property to which they lack a requisite connection. Fourth Amendment rights, after all, are personal. The Amendment protects "[t]he right of the people to be secure in their . . . persons, houses, papers, and effects"—not the persons, houses, papers, and effects of others.

"The concept of reasonable expectations of privacy, first announced in *Katz*, sought to look beyond the arcane distinctions developed in property and tort law in evaluating whether a person has a sufficient connection to the thing or place searched to assert Fourth Amendment interests in it. Yet "property concepts" are, nonetheless, fundamental in determining the presence or absence of the privacy interests protected by that Amendment. This is so for at least two reasons. First, as a matter of settled expectations from the law of property, individuals often have greater expectations of privacy in things and places that belong to them, not to others. And second, the Fourth Amendment's protections must remain tethered to the text of that Amendment, which, again, protects only a person's own "persons, houses, papers, and effects."

"*Miller* and *Smith* set forth an important and necessary limitation on the *Katz* framework. They rest upon the commonsense principle that the absence of property law analogues can be dispositive of privacy expectations. The defendants in those cases could expect that the third-party businesses could use the records the companies collected, stored, and classified as their own for any number of business and commercial purposes. The businesses were not bailees or custodians of the records, with a duty to hold the records for the defendants' use. The defendants could make no argument that the records were their own papers or effects. The records were the business entities' records, plain and simple. The defendants had no reason to believe the records were owned or controlled by them and so could not assert a reasonable expectation of privacy in the records.

"The second principle supporting *Miller* and *Smith* is the longstanding rule that the Government may use compulsory process to compel persons to disclose documents and other evidence within their possession and control. A subpoena is different from a warrant in its force and intrusive power. While a warrant allows the Government to enter and seize and make the examination itself, a subpoena simply requires the person to whom it is directed to make the disclosure. A subpoena, moreover, provides the recipient the "opportunity to present objections" before complying, which further mitigates the intrusion. *Oklahoma Press Publishing Co. v. Walling*, 327 U.S. 186, 195 (1946).

"For those reasons this Court has held that a subpoena for records, although a "constructive" search subject to Fourth Amendment constraints, need not comply with the procedures applicable to warrants—even when challenged by the person to whom the records belong. Rather, a subpoena complies with the Fourth Amendment's reasonableness requirement so long as it is "sufficiently limited in scope, relevant in purpose, and specific in directive so that compliance will not be unreasonably burdensome." *Donovan v. Lone Steer, Inc.*, 464 U.S. 408, 415 (1984). Persons with no meaningful interests in the records sought by a subpoena, like the defendants in *Miller* and *Smith*, have no rights to object to the records' disclosure—much less to assert that the Government must obtain a warrant to compel disclosure of the records.

"Based on *Miller* and *Smith* and the principles underlying those cases, it is well established that subpoenas may be used to obtain a wide variety of records held by businesses, even when the records contain private information. Credit cards are a prime example. State and federal law enforcement, for instance, often subpoena credit card statements to develop probable cause to prosecute crimes ranging from drug trafficking and distribution to healthcare fraud to tax evasion. Subpoenas also may be used to obtain vehicle registration records, hotel records, employment records, and records of utility usage, to name just a few other examples.

"Carpenter does not question these traditional investigative practices. And he does not ask the Court to reconsider *Miller* and *Smith*. Carpenter argues only that, under *Miller* and *Smith*, the Government may not use compulsory process to acquire cell-site records from cell phone service providers.

"There is no merit in this argument. Cell-site records, like all the examples just discussed, are created, kept, classified, owned, and controlled by cell phone service providers, which aggregate and sell this information to third parties. As in *Miller*, Carpenter can "assert neither ownership nor possession" of the records and has no control over them.

"All this is not to say that *Miller* and *Smith* are without limits. *Miller* and *Smith* may not apply when the Government obtains the modern-day equivalents of an individual's own "papers" or "effects," even when those papers or effects are held by a third party. See *Ex parte Jackson*, 96 U.S. 727, 733 (1878) (letters held by mail carrier); *United States v. Warshak*, 631 F.3d 266, 283–288 (C.A.6 2010) (e-mails held by Internet service provider). As already discussed, however, this case does not involve property or a bailment of that sort. Here the Government's acquisition of cell-site records falls within the heartland of *Miller* and *Smith*.

"In fact, Carpenter's Fourth Amendment objection is even weaker than those of the defendants in *Miller* and *Smith*. Here the Government did not use a mere subpoena to obtain the cell-site records. It acquired the records only after it proved to a Magistrate Judge reasonable grounds to believe that the records were relevant and material to an ongoing criminal investigation. See 18 U.S.C. § 2703(d). So even if [a federal statute] gave Carpenter some attenuated interest in the records, the Government's conduct here would be reasonable under the standards governing subpoenas.

"Under *Miller* and *Smith*, then, a search of the sort that requires a warrant simply did not occur when the Government used court-approved compulsory process, based on a finding of reasonable necessity, to compel a cell phone service provider, as owner, to disclose cell-site records.

"The Court rejects a straightforward application of *Miller* and *Smith*. It concludes instead that applying those cases to cell-site records would work a "significant extension" of the principles underlying them, and holds that the acquisition of more than six days of cell-site records constitutes a search.

"In my respectful view the majority opinion misreads this Court's precedents, old and recent, and transforms *Miller* and *Smith* into an unprincipled and unworkable doctrine. The Court's newly conceived constitutional standard will cause confusion; will undermine traditional and important law enforcement practices; and will allow the cell phone to become a protected medium that dangerous persons will use to commit serious crimes."

Justice Kennedy was also unpersuaded that "cell-site records implicate greater privacy interests—and thus deserve greater Fourth Amendment protection—than financial records and telephone records." His dissent continues:

"Indeed, the opposite is true. A person's movements are not particularly private. As the Court recognized in *Knotts*, when the defendant there "traveled over the public streets he voluntarily conveyed to anyone who wanted to look the fact that he was traveling over particular roads in a particular direction, the fact of whatever stops he made, and the fact of his final destination." Today expectations of privacy in one's location are, if anything, even less reasonable than when the Court decided *Knotts* over 30 years ago. Millions of Americans choose to share their location on a daily basis, whether by using a variety of location-based services on their phones, or by sharing their location with friends and the public at large via social media.

"And cell-site records, as already discussed, disclose a person's location only in a general area. The records at issue here, for example, revealed Carpenter's location within an area covering between around a dozen and several hundred city blocks. Areas of this scale might encompass bridal stores and Bass Pro Shops, gay bars and straight ones, a Methodist church and the local mosque. These records could not reveal where Carpenter lives and works, much less his "familial, political, professional, religious, and sexual associations." *Jones* (Sotomayor, J., concurring).

"By contrast, financial records and telephone records do "reveal personal affairs, opinions, habits and associations." *Miller* (Brennan, J., dissenting); *Smith* (Marshall, J., dissenting). What persons purchase and to whom they talk might disclose how much money they make; the political and religious organizations to which they donate; whether they have visited a psychiatrist, plastic surgeon, abortion clinic, or AIDS treatment center; whether they go to gay bars or straight ones; and who are their closest friends and family members. The troves of intimate information the Government can and does obtain using financial records and telephone records dwarfs what can be gathered from cell-site records.

"Still, the Court maintains, cell-site records are "unique" because they are "comprehensive" in their reach; allow for retrospective collection; are "easy, cheap, and efficient compared to traditional investigative tools"; and are not exposed to cell phone service providers in a meaningfully voluntary manner. But many other kinds of business records can be so described. Financial records are of vast scope. Banks and credit card companies keep a comprehensive account of almost every transaction an individual makes on a daily basis. With just the click of a button, the Government can access each company's deep repository of historical financial information at practically no expense. And the decision whether to transact with banks and credit card companies is no more or less voluntary than the decision whether to use a cell phone. Today, just as when *Miller* was decided, "it is impossible to participate in the economic life of contemporary society without maintaining a bank account." *Miller* (Brennan, J., dissenting). But this Court, nevertheless, has held that individuals do not have a reasonable expectation of privacy in financial records."

After *Carpenter*, what kinds of third-party records collection should deserve Fourth Amendment protection? What test should courts use to determine whether a particular collection of records involves merely "limited" collection (to which the third-party doctrine applies) versus an "exhaustive" collection (to which it does not)? What is the standard for how limited is limited enough to eliminate Fourth Amendment rights? Should it depend on how much collection occurred in that case? Should it depend on how much collection occurs in a typical case using that technology? If it depends on the technology, how should courts define the category of relevant technology?

§ 2. STATUTORY PRIVACY LAWS

C. THE PEN REGISTER STATUTE

14th ed., p. 496; add the following new material at the end of Note 3:

Also see *Carpenter v. United States*, 138 S.Ct. 2206 (2018), which requires a search warrant under the Fourth Amendment for the government to acquire at least seven days' worth of historical cell-site records. See Supp. at 45–50.

D. THE STORED COMMUNICATIONS ACT

14th ed., p. 501; add the following new Notes 6 and 7:

6. ***Foreign government access to communications stored in the United States.*** It is common for individuals outside the United States to use U.S.-based social media sites like Facebook and Twitter as well as U.S.-based e-mail services like Gmail. As a result, criminal investigators for foreign governments conducting criminal investigations in their own countries often must seek records and contents of communications from providers in the United States. This raises an important question: Does United States law permit U.S.-based providers to disclose contents or records to foreign governments pursuant to foreign court orders?

The answer is simple with respect to non-content records. 18 U.S.C. § 2702(c)(6) permits providers to disclose non-content records to non-government entities. Because the statute defines government entities in a way that excludes foreign governments, see 18 U.S.C. § 2711(4), the disclosure of non-content records to foreign governments is permitted.

The answer is more complicated with respect to contents of communications. In March 2018, Congress created a new legal framework to resolve this issue by enacting the Clarifying Lawful Overseas Use of Data Act (CLOUD) Act. *See generally* Jennifer Daskal, *Microsoft Ireland, The Cloud Act, And International Lawmaking 2.0*, 71 Stan. L. Rev. Online 9 (2018). The CLOUD Act creates a new category, a "qualifying foreign government," that is pre-approved using a complex process within the executive branch with the possibility of congressional oversight. *See* 18 U.S.C. § 2523 (establishing the process).

A foreign government can be qualified if it is found that "the domestic law of the foreign government, including the implementation of that law, affords robust substantive and procedural protections for privacy and civil liberties in light of the data collection and activities of the foreign government that will be subject to the agreement." *Id.* at 2523(b)(1). U.S.-based providers are then permitted to disclose the contents of communications pursuant to the legal process of qualifying foreign governments. *See* 18 U.S.C. § 2702(b)(9). On the other hand, U.S.-based providers may not disclose the contents of communications pursuant to foreign legal process of governments that are not pre-approved. The basic idea is that U.S. providers can the disclose contents of communications to governments that have adequate privacy and civil liberties protections but not to governments that fail to have such protections.

7. ***Access to foreign-stored contents.*** An e-mail provider based in the United States might have servers around the world, and it might store files of its United States customers on servers outside the United States. In some cases, the very idea of e-mails being in a particular "place" is subject to question. When a user accesses her e-mail, the inbox that is assembled by the

provider might consist of files from servers all around the world. Some e-mails might come from servers in the United States; other e-mails might come from servers abroad; and some e-mails might come partly from servers in the United States and partly from servers abroad.

This practice raises an important question under the Stored Communications Act: When the government obtains legal process under 18 U.S.C. § 2703, can the provider refuse to comply, in whole or in part, on the ground that the relevant files are stored outside the United States?

The CLOUD Act described in Note 6 above created a new framework to answer this question. Under the statute, a U.S.-based provider ordinarily must comply with U.S.-based legal process even if information is stored outside the United States. *See* 18 U.S.C. § 2713 (requiring a provider to disclose contents or records "regardless of whether such communication, record, or other information is located within or outside the United States"). At the same time, providers can file a motion to modify or quash legal process if they have a reasonable belief that the customer is not a United States person and there is a material risk that the disclosure would violate the laws of a qualifying foreign government. *See* 18 U.S.C. § 2703(h)(2)(A). A court can modify or quash the legal process only if it finds, after hearing a response from the government, that the disclosure would violate the laws of the qualifying foreign government, the interests of justice dictate that the legal process should be modified or quashed, and the customer or subscriber is not a United States person and does not reside in the United States. *See id.* at § 2703(h)(2)(B).

CHAPTER 9

POLICE INTERROGATION AND CONFESSIONS

■ ■ ■

§ 2.   THE *MIRANDA* "REVOLUTION"

14th ed., p. 554; after Note (d), add:

(e)   *Timeless right to counsel warnings.* Is it sufficient if the police inform a suspect that she has "a right to an attorney" but the warnings never indicate that the suspect has the right to consult with that attorney or have the attorney present during questioning? *Compare Bridgers v. Dretke*, 431 F.3d 853 (5th Cir. 2005) ("[A] suspect must be explicitly warned that he has the right to counsel during interrogation.") *and People v. Mathews*, 2018 WL 2325206 (Mich. Ct. App. 2018) ("[W]e hold that a warning preceding a custodial interrogation is deficient when the warning contains only a broad reference to the 'right to an attorney' that does not, when the warning is read in its entirety, reasonably convey the suspect's right to consult with a lawyer and to have an attorney present during interrogation.") *with United States v. Warren*, 642 F.3d 182 (3d Cir. 2011) ("[I]t cannot be said that the *Miranda* court regarded an express reference to the temporal durability of [the right to an attorney] as elemental to a valid warning.") *and Carter v. People*, 398 P.3d 124 (Colo. 2017) ("[I]t would be highly counterintuitive for a reasonable suspect in a custodial setting, who has just been informed that the police cannot talk to him until after they advise him of his rights to remain silent and to have an attorney, to understand that an interrogation may then proceed without permitting him to exercise either of those rights.").

14th ed., p. 557; before Note 6, add:

5A.   *The growing need for* Miranda *warnings.* In *State v. Hubbard*, 118 A.3d 314 (N.J. 2015), the Court held that the defendant, charged with second-degree manslaughter of a three-month old child, and second-degree endangering the welfare of a child, should have been given the *Miranda* warnings, but never was. Therefore, the failure to administer the *Miranda* warnings required suppression of the recorded statement. One key factor in the custody determination was that a police officer had instructed the defendant to sit in a certain chair to permit the camera to obtain a full-face view of the defendant—without giving any *Miranda* warnings.

Justice Albin concurred in the result. He emphasized that "the law must adapt to technological advances. * * * Today, video cameras are mounted in many police vehicles recording motor vehicle stops and searches. Body cameras worn by police officers may soon be an integral part of an officer's uniform. In the near future, it may be that an officer's interaction with a suspect will be video-recorded from beginning to end, from a street arrest to an interrogation at police headquarters."

14th ed., p. 569; end of Note (b), add:

Innis says that courts should "focus primarily upon the perceptions of the suspect" when deciding whether police conduct amounts to the functional equivalent of express questioning. But, unlike the custody inquiry, the functional equivalent test is framed from the officers' perspective, asking what the police knew or should have known about the suspect. Lower courts differ with respect to whose perspective they emphasize. Consider *State v. Harris*, 892 N.W.2d 663 (Wis. 2017) ("positing a reasonable third-person observer and inquiring into how such a person would expect the suspect to react to the officer's words and actions"); *State v. Smith*, 995 A.2d 685 (Md. 2010) (holding that "there was no interrogation because an objective observer would not reasonably infer that [the officer's] statement or conduct was designed to elicit an incriminating response"). Welsh White, *Interrogation without Questions,* 78 Mich.L.Rev. 1209, 1231 (1980), argues that "the best reading of the *Innis* test is that it turns upon the *objective* purpose *manifested* by the police. Thus, an officer 'should know' that his speech or conduct will be 'reasonably likely to elicit an incriminating response' when he should realize that the speech or conduct will probably be viewed by the suspect as designed to achieve this purpose." *Id.* at 1232. Do you agree?

14th ed., p. 571; before Note 8, add:

7A. *Presenting a suspect with incriminating evidence.* Is presenting a suspect with incriminating evidence interrogation? *Compare United States v. Vallar*, 635 F.3d 271 (7th Cir. 2011) ("Merely apprising [the defendant] of the evidence against him by playing tapes implicating him in the conspiracy did not constitute interrogation."); *United States v. Genao,* 281 F.3d 305 (1st Cir. 2002) (holding that a detective's actions did not constitute interrogation where the detective showed the suspect contraband seized from his apartment and stated, "we've got a problem here"); *United States v. Payne,* 954 F.2d 199 (4th Cir. 1992) (holding that an officer's statement to the defendant that they found a gun in his house was not interrogation) *with Drury v. State*, 793 A.2d 567 (Md. 2002) (holding that there was interrogation when police arrested the defendant for burglary and theft of adult magazines, took him to the station, placed a tire iron and a trash bag with adult magazines on the table in front of him, and told him that they were going to send the evidence off for fingerprinting) *and Hill v. United States*, 858 A.2d 435 (D.C. 2004) (holding that a detective's statements that the defendant was going to be charged with second-degree murder and that his friend told the police what happened was interrogation).

7B. *Reading the suspect the charges.* Is it interrogation when police inform the defendant of the charges against him? *Compare United States v. Suggs,* 755 F.2d 1538 (11th Cir.1985) (no interrogation where defendant was shown a copy of his indictment and made a spontaneous exclamation concerning guilt) *with State v. Sawyer*, 156 S.W.3d 531 (Tenn. 2005) (holding that officer's action in reading the affidavit of complaint to the defendant was interrogation).

14th ed., p. 575; after Note 9, add:

9A. *The scope of the routine booking exception.* Lower courts are divided on the proper test to use to determine when the routine booking exception applies. *Compare United States v. Reyes*, 225 F.3d 71 (1st Cir. 2000) (using an objective test that permits officers to ask questions during booking unless the "officer should reasonably have expected the question to elicit an incriminating response") *with United States v. Virgen-Moreno*, 265 F.3d 276 (5th Cir. 2001) (focusing more on the officer's subjective intent and asking whether the "booking" question was designed to elicit incriminating statements) *and State v. Cruz*, 461 S.W.3d 531 (Tex. Crim. App. 2015) (adopting an objective standard that looks at "both the content of the question and the circumstances in which the question is asked" to determine if the question "reasonably relates to a legitimate administrative concern"). For an argument that the First and Fifth Circuit tests are misguided and the "legitimate administrative concern" standard is better, see George C. Thomas III, *Lost in the Fog of* Miranda, 64 Hastings L.J. 1501 (2013).

9B. *Questions about gang affiliation.* Can questions about gang affiliation be routine booking questions? *Compare United States v. Washington*, 462 F.3d 1124 (9th Cir. 2006) (yes; such questions are necessary "in order to ensure prisoner safety") *with People v. Elizalde*, 351 P.3d 1010 (Cal. 2015) (no; such questions are "reasonably likely to elicit an incriminating response"). Jurisdictions that permit such questions may prohibit them if the crime the suspect is accused of is gang-related. *See United States v. Williams*, 842 F.3d 1143 (9th Cir. 2016).

9C. *Questions about a suspect's drug and/or alcohol abuse.* Can the police ask routine booking questions about a suspect's drug or alcohol use without first giving *Miranda* warnings? *Compare State v. Chrisicos*, 813 A.2d 513 (N.H. 2002) (not in the context of a DWI offense) *with Colon v. State*, 568 S.E.2d 811 (Ga. App. 2002) (noting that "police officers have the responsibility to ask medical questions as part of routine booking in order to fulfill the government's obligation to provide medical treatment to one in custody" and holding that officer could ask DWI suspect what was wrong with him when he began vomiting).

14th ed., p. 579; replace Note (b) with the following:

(b)   *How speculative can the risk be?* How certain do the police need to be of the threat to public safety? Consider *United States v. Jones*, 154 F. Supp. 2d 617 (S.D.N.Y. 2001): "Nothing in the Supreme Court's opinion justifies a conclusion that officers are free to question the suspect about weapons before advising him of his rights whenever they arrest someone who has been implicated in possible firearms violations, or who has been seen at some prior time with a gun. Such a conclusion would blow a huge hole in *Miranda*'s protection against coercive interrogation, and would be completely inconsistent with the Court's statement that *Quarles* creates only a 'narrow exception' to *Miranda*. * * * In the context of searches for weapons, th[e public safety] doctrine requires, at a minimum, that the authorities have some real basis to believe that weapons are present, and some specific reason to believe that the weapon's undetected presence poses a danger to the police or to the public." *See also United States v. Brathwaite*, 458 F.3d 376 (5th Cir. 2006) (refusing to apply the exception when officers asked questions about guns in a private residence after police had swept the house and handcuffed the occupants). *But see United States v. Luker*, 395 F.3d 830 (8th Cir. 2005) (applying the exception to a question asking if there was "anything in [the defendant's] vehicle that shouldn't be there or that they should know about" based on the officer's knowledge that the defendant used drugs and concern about needles or substances associated with such use in his car); *United States v. Are*, 590 F.3d 499 (7th Cir. 2009) (applying the exception to questions posed to a handcuffed suspect even though "the officers had no specific reason to believe that [he] had a gun, only that he had prior weapons convictions and was involved in drug trafficking, which often involves weapons"); *United States v. Carillo*, 16 F.3d 1046 (9th Cir. 1994) (applying the exception to an officer's post-arrest question asking if the suspect (who had been arrested on drug charges) had any drugs or needles on his person and noting that the officer routinely asked this question to avoid contact with syringes (which had poked him in the past) and toxic substances (which had caused headaches and skin irritation in the past)).

14th ed., p. 580; replace Note (d) with the following:

(d)   *Rescue doctrine.* Somewhat similar to the "public safety" exception is the "rescue doctrine." Should statements obtained in violation of *Miranda* be admissible if police interrogation of a suspected kidnapper is motivated primarily by a desire to save the victim's life? Yes, answers *People v. Davis*, 208 P.3d 78 (Cal. 2009) ("[U]nder circumstances of extreme emergency where the possibility of saving the life of a missing victim exists, noncoercive questions may be asked of a material witness in custody even though answers to the questions may incriminate the witness."). *See also State v. Provost*, 490 N.W.2d 93 (Minn. 1992); *State v. Kunkel*, 404 N.W.2d 69 (Wis. 1987); William T. Pizzi, *The Privilege Against Self-Incrimination in a Rescue Situation,* 76 J.Crim.L. & C. 657 (1985). It is unsound, maintains Professor Pizzi, id. at 595–603, to approach the scope of the privilege against self-incrimination "solely from the defendant's point of view while totally ignoring the threat to the lives of others and the purpose and function of the police conduct"; the privilege and its attendant rules should not control "where the police are functioning in a situation which is primarily noninvestigative and where life is at stake."

Are there (should there be) any limits on what a police officer may do to a suspected kidnapper in order to get him to reveal the location of a kidnap victim? Consider Pizzi, supra, at 606: "[T]here are [due process] limits on the conduct of the police in their treatment of suspects even in an emergency situation where life is at stake," but "[i]n determining those limits [the] traditional scope of police conduct permitted in a purely investigative context is only a starting point."

14th ed., p. 595; after Note 23, add:

23A. *A Miranda app?* Andrew Guthrie Ferguson and Richard A. Leo, *The* Miranda *App: Metaphor and Machine*, 97 B.U. L. Rev. 935, 938 (2017), argue that police should replace the existing *Miranda* warnings and waiver regime with "a digital, scripted computer program of videos, text, and comprehension assessments [that is] accessible on a smartphone, computer tablet, iPad, or other system." They contend that a *Miranda* App has the following advantages: "First, by interposing a digital medium between the suspect and the Fifth Amendment, a *Miranda* App can reduce custodial pressure. The all too human pressure of a detective waiting for an answer dissipates when the detective is not in the room. Second, by signifying an independent source of legal rights, the *Miranda* App serves to rebalance constitutional power away from the police. Third, a *Miranda* App can ensure that a suspect 'understands' *Miranda* * * *. Fourth, building on the Supreme Court's recognition that *Miranda*'s 'core virtue' has been 'clarity and precision,' the App will establish a set procedure for police to follow, as well as clear instructions for suspects to follow. Finally, the *Miranda* App will be designed to collect helpful information for prosecutors, defense lawyers, and experts litigating the adequacy of warnings and waiver in individual cases, as well as to capture global data useful for academic researchers studying *Miranda* practice." *Id.* at 974.

14th ed., p. 597; before *Edwards v. Arizona*, add:

Mosley *in the lower courts.* After *Mosley*, it is clear that, once a suspect invokes her right to remain silent, the officers have to take a break and provide a fresh set of *Miranda* warnings before attempting to resume questioning. Just how long a break is required is unclear. *See, e.g., United States v. Oquendo-Rivas*, 750 F.3d 12, 17–18 (1st Cir. 2014) (finding a valid waiver of the right to remain silent when officers returned after twenty minutes, but noting that "[i]t would be both unwise and unworkable . . . to try and demarcate a one-time-fits-all limit for assessing reasonableness, which at its worst might only send interrogating officers running for their stopwatches"). And what about the other *Mosley* factors? Not all courts require that the resumed questioning be about a different offense. *See, e.g., Fleming v. Metrish*, 556 F.3d 520, 529 (6th Cir. 2009); *Flick v. Meko*, 2015 WL 13542567, at *3 (6th Cir. Oct. 20, 2015); *United States v. Morrison*, 2014 WL 3734253, at *6 (D. Minn. July 28, 2014); *United States v. Trapp*, 2014 WL 1117012, at *14 (D. Vt. Mar. 20, 2014). Nor do all courts require that the second interrogation take place in a different location, *see, e.g., United States v. Trapp*, 2014 WL 1117012, at *14 (D. Vt. Mar. 20, 2014), or with a different questioning officer, *see Fleming v. Metrish*, 556 F.3d 520, 529 (6th Cir. 2009). Which factors do you think should matter most and why?

14th ed., p. 605; after Note (ii), add:

(iii) *Re-initiation in the lower courts.* Court often reach different conclusions about whether similar words by a suspect evince "a willingness and a desire for a generalized discussion about the criminal investigation" under *Bradshaw. Compare U.S.A. v. Garcia*, 2014 WL 12626350, at *16 (C.D. Cal. July 8, 2014) (finding defendant's question "what are my alternatives" reopened dialogue) *and United States v. Bonilla*, 66 M.J. 654, 658 (C.G. Ct. Crim. App. 2008) (finding defendant's question "can you tell me what this is about" reopened dialogue) *with United States v. Daniels*, 225 F. Supp. 3d 1084, 1088 (N.D. Cal. 2016) (finding defendant's questions "what's going on" and "am I under arrest" did not reopen dialogue) *and People v. Flores*, 315 Ill. App. 3d 387, 393 (2000) (finding defendant's question "what was going on" did not reopen dialogue).

14th ed., p. 608; end of Note (a), add:

Courts regularly have trouble applying the *Davis* standard and often reach different conclusions about whether an invocation is ambiguous even when suspects use similar language. *Compare Wood v. Ercole*, 644 F.3d 83, 91 (2d Cir. 2011) ("I think I should get a lawyer" is an unambiguous invocation) *with United States v. Jenkins*, 2014 WL 12676281, at *4 (W.D. Mich. Nov. 6, 2014) ("I think I need a lawyer here before answering questions" is ambiguous); *United States v. Lee*, 413 F.3d 622, 625–27 (7th Cir. 2005) ("Can I have a lawyer?" is an unambiguous invocation) *with Sears v. Maryland*, 2017 WL 2778819, at *8–9 (D. Md. June 26, 2017) ("Is there a lawyer I can speak with?" is ambiguous); *and United States v. Seppala*, No. 16-CR-436 (KMW), 2017 WL 5633167, at *3 (S.D.N.Y. Nov. 22, 2017) ("Do I have an opportunity to call an attorney?" is an unambiguous invocation) *with State v. Demesme*, 228 So.3d 1206 (La. 2017) ("why don't you just give me a lawyer dog cause this is not what's up" is ambiguous). *See also* Levi James Grove, *Are You Sure You Need an Attorney: Invocation of the Fifth Amendment Right to Counsel by Suspects during Custodial Interrogations*, 64 Drake L. Rev. 919, 943 (2016) (concluding that "the *Davis* standard, as applied by the lower courts, has subjected similar statements to differing standards of clarity and thus yielded differing, inconsistent, and unpredictable results").

14th ed., p. 608; after Note (b), add:

(c) *More protective states.* Some states require police to seek clarification of ambiguous assertions of counsel as part of their state law. *See, e.g., State v. Hoey*, 881 P.2d 504 (Haw. 1994) (requiring clarification under the state constitution); *State v. Alston*, 10 A.3d 880 (N.J. 2011) (same); *State v. Risk*, 598 N.W.2d 642 (Minn. 1999) (same). As the *Hoey* court explained: "[T]wo precepts have commanded broad assent: that the *Miranda* safeguards exist to assure that the individual's right to choose between speech and silence remains unfettered throughout the interrogation process, and that the justification for *Miranda* rules, intended to operate in the real world, must be consistent with practical realities. A rule barring government agents from further interrogation until they determine whether a suspect's ambiguous statement was meant as a request for counsel fulfills both ambitions. It assures that a suspect's choice whether or not to deal with police through counsel will be scrupulously honored, and it faces both the real-world reasons why misunderstandings arise between suspect and interrogator and the real-world limitations on the capacity of police and trial courts to apply fine distinctions and intricate rules." The Supreme Court could have adopted a similar standard requiring clarification in *Davis* but chose not to. Why might it have made this decision?

14th ed., p. 622; after *Salinas v. Texas*, add:

For strong criticism of *Salinas v. Texas*, see Brandon L. Garrett, *Remaining Silent after Salinas*, 80 U. Chi. L. Rev. Dialogue 116 (2013); Yale Kamisar, *The* Miranda *Case Fifty Years Later*, 97 B.U.L. Rev. 1293 (2017); Tracey Maclin, *The Right to Silence v. the Fifth Amendment*, 2016 U. Chi. L. Forum 255 (2016).

30A. *Recent use of video recording devices.* Very recently, Professors Paul G. Cassell and Richard Fowles reported that "a growing number of police departments are requiring their officers to wear uniform-mounted body-cameras. Recent surveys suggest that about 25% of the nation's 17,000 police agencies are using video recording devices, with around 80% evaluating the technology. As of August 2016, of the 68 'major/city' police departments in the United States, about 43 have some type of body worn-camera programs in place." Paul G. Cassell & Richard Fowles,

Still Handcuffing the Cops? A Review of Fifty Years of Miranda's *Harmful Effects on Law Enforcement*, 97 B.U.L. Rev. 685, 839 (2017).

14th ed., p. 625; end of the Notes and Questions, before *McNeil v. Wisconsin*, add the following additional Notes and Questions:

2. ***Represented versus unrepresented suspects.*** *Montejo* suggests that *Miranda* warnings will adequately inform represented as well as unrepresented suspects of their Sixth Amendment rights. For an argument that "[t]his is contrary to a long line of precedent, stretching through the Warren, Burger, and Rehnquist Courts," see Craig Bradley, *What's Left of* Massiah?, 45 Tex. Tech. L. Rev. 237, 255 (2012). If the Sixth Amendment guarantees suspects the right to rely on counsel as a "medium" between them and the state, should the state have to go through counsel if it wants to obtain a waiver? Yes answers Eve Brensike Primus, *Disentangling* Miranda *and* Massiah: *How to Revive the Sixth Amendment Right to Counsel as a Tool for Regulating Confession Law*, 97 B.U.L. Rev. 1085, 1121 (2017). Do you agree?

3. ***What if a suspect clearly and unambiguously invokes her Sixth Amendment right to counsel?*** With the prophylactic protection of *Jackson* gone, what should police do if a noncustodial, post-indictment suspect asserts her Sixth Amendment right to counsel? Montejo did not actually invoke the right. Can the police ignore such an invocation? Must they leave? If so, can they come back and when? See Jonathan Witmer-Rich, *Interrogation and the Roberts Court*, 63 Fla. L. Rev. 1189, 1236–37 (2011) (arguing that an *Edwards*-like rule should apply to actual invocations of the Sixth Amendment right, but without the *Shatzer* 14-day rule).

4. ***More protective states.*** The *Montejo* Court emphasized states' abilities to provide additional protection to criminal defendants under state law, noting that "[i]f a State wishes to abstain from requesting interviews with represented defendants when counsel is not present, it obviously may continue to do so." Some states have done just that and rejected *Montejo* under their state law. *See, e.g., State v. Lawson*, 297 P.3d 1164, 1171–74 (Kan. 2013); *Keysor v. Kentucky*, 486 S.W.3d 273, 281–82 (Ky. 2016); *State v. Bevel*, 745 S.E.2d 237, 247 (W. Va. 2013).

14th ed., p. 649; after Note 7, add:

7A. ***Has Miranda harmed law enforcement?*** Paul G. Cassell & Richard Fowles, *Still Handcuffing the Cops? A Review of Fifty Years of Empirical Evidence of* Miranda's *Harmful Effects on Law Enforcement*, 97 B.U. L. Rev. 685 (2017), rely on decreases in FBI clearance rates to argue that "contrary to conventional academic opinion," *Miranda* has harmed law enforcement efforts to solve crime. *But see* Floyd Feeney, *Police Clearances: A Poor Way to Measure the Impact of* Miranda *on the Police*, 32 Rutgers L.J. 1, 4 (2000) (referring to an earlier iteration of the study as "fail[ing] to establish the conclusions that they reach"); John J. Donohue III, *Did* Miranda *Diminish Police Effectiveness?*, 50 Stan. L. Rev. 1147, 1156 (1998) (criticizing the reliance on clearance rates); Stephen J. Schulhofer, Miranda *and Clearance Rates*, 91 Nw. U. L. Rev. 278 (1996) (same).

§ 3. *MIRANDA*, THE PRIVILEGE AGAINST COMPELLED SELF-INCRIMINATION AND FOURTEENTH AMENDMENT DUE PROCESS: WHEN DOES A VIOLATION OF THESE SAFEGUARDS OCCUR?

14th ed., p. 657; after Note 3, add:

4. ***When does a criminal case begin?*** The Court in *Chavez v. Martinez* did not definitely answer this question and the lower courts disagree. The Third, Fourth, and Fifth Circuits have

stated that the Fifth Amendment is only a trial right whereas the Second, Seventh, Ninth, and Tenth Circuits have held that certain pretrial uses of compelled statements (at bail hearings, suppression hearings, arraignments, and probable cause hearings) can violate the Fifth Amendment. *See Vogt v. City of Hayes*, 844 F.3d 1235 (10th Cir. 2017) (summarizing the circuit split). If Martinez had been charged with a crime and the statements that he made to Chavez in the hospital had been offered against him at a pre-trial hearing, could he successfully argue that his Fifth Amendment rights were violated? For more discussion of *Vogt* and how the self-incrimination clause applies to compelled documents, *see infra* Chapter 15 of Supplement, pgs. 119–123.

§ 4.   THE *PATANE* AND *SEIBERT* CASES: IS PHYSICAL EVIDENCE OR A "SECOND CONFESSION" DERIVED FROM A FAILURE TO COMPLY WITH THE *MIRANDA* RULES ADMISSIBLE? THE COURT'S ANSWERS SHED LIGHT ON *DICKERSON*

14th ed., p. 663; after Note 4, add:

5.   **Patane *in the lower courts*.** Some states have rejected the rule in *Patane* and have chosen to exclude physical fruits of *Miranda* violations as a matter of state law. *See, e.g., State v. Peterson*, 923 A.2d 585 (Vt. 2007); *State v. Knapp*, 700 N.W.2d 899 (Wis. 2005); *Commonwealth v. Martin*, 827 N.E.2d 198 (Mass. 2005).

6.   ***Does* Patane *apply to a violation of* Edwards*?*** Lower courts are divided on whether *Patane* applies when the police ignore a suspect's invocation of his *Miranda* right to counsel. *Compare United States v. Gilkeson*, 431 F.Supp.2d 270, 292 (N.D.N.Y. 2006) (*Patane* does not apply to an *Edwards* violation) *with In re H.V.*, 252 S.W.3d 319, 328–29 (Tex. 2008) (*Patane* applies to an *Edwards* violation). In *Wisconsin v. Knapp*, 542 U.S. 952 (2004), the Supreme Court remanded a case involving an intentional *Edwards* violation for further consideration in light of *Patane*. Does that suggest that *Patane* permits the admission of physical fruits even if police ignore an invocation of rights? Consider the Court's response to deliberate police violations of *Miranda* rights in the case below (decided the same day as *Patane*):

14th ed., p. 668; insert the following as a new Note 1 and renumber the remaining Notes:

1.   ***What is the holding in* Seibert*?*** Under *Marks v. United States*, 430 U.S. 188, 193 (1977), when the Supreme Court issues a fractured decision, lower courts are instructed that the holding is the position "taken by those Members who concurred in judgments on the narrowest grounds." How would you apply the *Marks* formulation in *Seibert*? *Compare United States v. Capers*, 627 F.3d 470, 476 (2d. Cir. 2010) (explaining that most federal circuit courts agree that Justice Kennedy's test is the holding) *with United States v. Heron*, 564 F.3d 879, 884 (7th Cir. 2009) (declining to apply the *Marks* rule because Justice Kennedy's opinion failed to provide a "common denominator" for the judgment).

§ 6. THE "DUE PROCESS"—"VOLUNTARINESS" TEST REVISITED

A. *MILLER v. FENTON*: WHAT KINDS OF TRICKERY OR DECEPTION, IF ANY, MAY THE POLICE EMPLOY AFTER A SUSPECT HAS WAIVED HIS RIGHTS?

14th ed., p. 684; after Note 2, add:

2A. ***More on police deception in the lower courts.*** Courts typically do not find a confession involuntary merely because the police deceived the suspect. *See, e.g., United States v. Haak*, 884 F.3d 400, 409 (2d Cir. 2018) (noting that a "finding that police conduct is 'false, misleading, or intended to trick and cajole the defendant into confessing' does not necessarily render that confession involuntary"). However, some forms of police deception are so powerful that they "destroy the information required for a rational choice" and, in so doing, overcome the suspect's will and lead to an involuntary statement. *See, e.g., Aleman v. Village of Hanover Park*, 662 F.3d 897, 906 (7th Cir. 2011) (informing a father that three doctors concluded that his infant was injured as a result of being shaken rendered his resulting admission involuntary, because, "[n]ot being a medical expert, [the father] could not contradict what was represented to him as settled medical opinion . . . [He] had no rational basis, given his ignorance of medical science, to deny that he had been the cause"); *see also* Welsh White, *False Confessions and the Constitution: Safeguards Against Untrustworthy Confessions*, 32 Harv. C.R.-C.L. L. Rev. 105, 147 (1997) ("Deceiving the suspect into believing that forensic evidence establishes his guilt should be absolutely prohibited.").

B. *COLORADO v. CONNELLY*: DID THE COURT DECLINE TO EXPAND THE "VOLUNTARINESS" TEST OR DID IT REVISE THE TEST SIGNIFICANTLY?

14th ed., p. 692; replace Note 5 with the following:

5. ***Does the* Connelly *case mark the decline and fall of the "reliability" element?*** *Compare* George Dix, *Federal Constitutional Confession Law: The 1986 and 1987 Supreme Court Terms*, 67 Tex.L.Rev. 231, 272–76 (1988) (describing *Connelly* as "reject[ing] reliability as a relevant consideration in federal constitutional law") *with* Eve Brensike Primus, *The Future of Confession Law: Toward Rules for the Voluntariness Test*, 114 Mich. L. Rev. 1, 34 (2015) (arguing that *Connelly* is frequently misunderstood, that it does not reject reliability altogether as relevant, but simply notes that "[t]he question is not reliability simpliciter but rather whether the police have done something whose effect on the suspect reduces the reliability of the confession obtained").

Should the unreliability of a confession (or the absence of substantial indicia of reliability) render a confession inadmissible as a matter of federal constitutional law? Both Dix and Primus argue that reliability traditionally has played and should continue to play an important role in the constitutional analysis of a statement's voluntariness. But consider Albert Alschuler, *Constraint and Confession*, 74 Denv. U. L.Rev. 957, 959 (1997): "Just as the Constitution does not mandate the exclusion of unreliable eyewitness testimony, it does not mandate the exclusion of unreliable confessions. * * * The Constitution requires the exclusion of unreliable eyewitness testimony only when improper governmental conduct—for example, an impermissibly suggestive police line-up—has produced it. The rule should be no different for unreliable confessions. Unless improper governmental conduct has generated a confession, the Constitution should give the defendant only a right to present evidence of the confession's unreliability to the jury." Do you agree?

6.   *How could voluntariness develop going forward?* Consider Primus, *supra* note 5, at 55:

"As a matter of history and current practice, * * * there are two different strands within voluntariness doctrine—one deontological strand that focuses on the offensiveness of the police methods used and one consequentialist strand that is concerned with the problem of false confessions. Courts could profit from disentangling those strands and creating different tests for each. * * *

"Under the offensive-police methods variant, courts should identify those police tactics that offend our sense of justice and are inconsistent with fairness in an adversarial system. [For example, physical violence, threats of physical violence, and continuous interrogation beyond a specific time limit would qualify.] Courts should tell police outright that if they use those per se offensive tactics, the resulting confessions will be suppressed. When addressing claims that a combination of tactics is conscience shocking, the courts would continue to engage in a totality-of-the-circumstances analysis, but it would be more focused than it is at present: it would examine the police tactics at issue in light of what the police knew or reasonably should have known. It would not incorporate considerations going to aspects of the case not known to the police, such as the hidden characteristics of the suspects, nor would it consider the effect that the tactics actually had on the suspects.

"Under the effect-on-the-suspect variant, courts should identify those interrogation tactics that police know or should know are significantly likely to increase the chances of a false confession. If police use tactics that the social science has revealed significantly increase the likelihood of false confessions, the state should be required to produce clear and convincing evidence that the resulting confession is reliable. And if the police use tactics that they should know are significantly likely to increase the chance of a false confession given the particular circumstances of an individual case, that too should trigger reliability scrutiny."

Consider also Lawrence Rosenthal, *Compulsion*, 19 U. Pa. J. Const. L. 889, 889 & 960 (2017) (arguing that the due process voluntariness test should be replaced with a test that asks if a suspect was compelled, meaning that there was "an official undertaking to induce a witness to provide evidence by threat of punitive sanctions"); George C. Thomas & Richard A. Leo, *Confessions of Guilt: From Torture to* Miranda *and Beyond* 226 (2012) (positing a "moral choice theory" under which courts ask "whether [the alternative to talking that the suspect faced] is something that society believes police ought to be able to force on suspects"); Mark A. Godsey, *Rethinking the Involuntary Confession Rule: Toward a Workable Test for Identifying Compelled Self-Incrimination*, 93 Calif. L. Rev. 465, 515–39 (2005) (proposing an "objective penalty" approach under which the court begins with a baseline understanding of what a suspect should expect in an interrogation given reasonable practices and then asks whether the police moved the suspect below that baseline).

14th ed., p. 695–97; replace the final section of § 6 (starting with the Drizin & Leo excerpt on p. 695 and continuing until § 7) with the following:

NOTES AND QUESTIONS ON THE CENTRAL PARK JOGGER CASE

1.   *How prevalent are false confessions?* Steven A. Drizin & Richard A. Leo, *The Problem of False Confessions in the Post-DNA World*, 82 N.C.L.Rev. 891, 905 (2004), report that of 140 convicted prisoners released and exonerated as a result of DNA testing at the time they wrote their article, approximately 25% of these wrongful convictions were caused by false confessions. More recent studies suggest that false confessions are present in 15–20 percent of exonerations. *See, e.g.,* Richard A. Leo, *Interrogation and Confessions in* Academy for Justice, A Report on Scholarship and Criminal Justice Reform, Vol. 2, p. 234 (Erik Luna ed. 2017); Brandon L. Garrett, *Convicting the Innocent: Where Criminal Prosecutions Go Wrong* 18–19 (2011); Saul M. Kassin et al., *Police-Induced Confessions: Risk Factors and Recommendations*, 34 Law & Hum. Behav. 3, 3 (2010).

2. *How powerful are false confessions?* Professors Drizin and Leo reported and analyzed 125 proven false confessions, all of which occurred in the post-*Miranda* era (55% between 1993–2003) and were struck by the fact that "more than four-fifths (81%) of the innocent defendants who chose to take their case to trial were wrongfully convicted 'beyond a reasonable doubt' even though their confession was ultimately demonstrated to be false. [An] additional fourteen false confessions in this study * * * chose to accept a plea bargain rather than take their case to trial—despite their innocence—typically to avoid the death penalty. Remarkably, then, 86% (or almost nine of every ten) of the individuals in our sample whose false confessions were not discovered by police or dismissed by prosecutors before trial were eventually convicted. * * * This study adds to a growing body of research demonstrating the power of confession evidence to substantially prejudice a trier of fact's ability to even-handedly evaluate a criminal defendant's culpability." Drizin & Leo, supra, note 1 at 995–96.

3. *Homicide cases.* Professor Leo considers it highly significant that more than 80% of the 125 false confessions analyzed in the 2004 study he did with Professor Drizin occurred in homicide cases and that 80 percent of the false confessions studied by Professor Samuel Gross and his colleagues occurred in murder cases. See Richard A. Leo, *Police Interrogation and American Justice* 245 (2008). Professor Leo suggests why this is so: "Police are under greater institutional pressure to solve serious and high-profile cases and therefore put more time, effort and pressure into interrogating suspects—conducting longer and more intense interrogations—and trying to elicit confessions. Investigators are thus more likely to use psychologically coercive techniques or simply wear down a suspect. In homicides, the fact that the victim is dead and police frequently lack any eyewitnesses makes getting a confession even more important." *Id.* at 246.

CAUSES OF FALSE CONFESSIONS

"In the last twenty years, empiricists, criminologists, and psychologists have studied cases that we now know relied on false confessions to identify a number of interrogation techniques that are significantly correlated with false confessions. These tactics include lengthy interrogations, contamination of the resulting confession by feeding the suspect key details that only the perpetrator could have known, direct promises of lenient treatment if the suspect confesses, indirect promises of lenient treatment through minimization techniques, threats of harsh consequences if the suspect refuses to confess, false evidence ploys that make it appear that the police can already conclusively establish the suspect's guilt, and leading or suggestive questioning of vulnerable populations (juveniles, mentally disabled people, and the mentally ill)."

—Eve Brensike Primus, *The Future of Confession Law: Toward Rules for the Voluntariness Test*, 114 Mich. L. Rev. 1, 44 (2015).

1. *Length of interrogation.* Drizin and Leo deem it noteworthy that, of those cases in which the length of interrogation could be determined, most of the false confessors were subjected to questioning for an extraordinarily long time:

"More than 80% of the false confessors were interrogated for more than six hours, and 50% [were] interrogated for more than twelve hours. The average length of interrogation was 16.3 hours, and the median length of interrogation was twelve hours. These figures are especially striking when they are compared to studies of routine police interrogations in America, which suggest that more than 90% of normal interrogations last less than two hours. These figures support the observations of many researchers that interrogation-induced false observations tend to be correlated with lengthy interrogations in which the innocent suspect's resistance is worn down, coercive techniques are used, and the suspect is made to feel helpless, regardless of his innocence." Steven A. Drizin & Richard A. Leo, *The Problem of False Confessions in the Post-DNA World*, 82 N.C.L.Rev. 891, 948 (2004). According to Susan Saulny, *Why Confess to What You Didn't Do?*, N.Y.Times, Dec. 8, 2002, at 5, the five teenage suspects in the Central Park jogger case were questioned for fourteen to thirty hours.

2. *Police contamination of confessions.* Police can "contaminate" a confession by "leak[ing] and feed[ing] the innocent suspect unique and/or nonpublic details that the innocent suspect, once broken, then repeats back and incorporates into his (false) confession statement, which makes it appear true and persuasive." Richard A. Leo, *Interrogation and Confessions in* Academy for Justice, A Report on Scholarship and Criminal Justice Reform, Vol. 2, p. 250 (Erik Luna ed. 2017). But just how frequent is police contamination of confessions? Consider Brandon L. Garrett, *Convicting the Innocent: Where Criminal Prosecutions Go Wrong* 18–19 (2011):

"Forty of the first 250 DNA exoneration cases (16%) involved a false confession. I wondered what people who we now know are innocent reportedly said when they confessed. I used the trial transcripts to find out what was said during interrogations and how the confessions were described and litigated at trial. When I began this process, I expected to see confessions without much information. An innocent person might be able to say 'I did it,' but obviously could not say what exactly he did, since he was not there at the crime scene. I knew it was possible that a confession could be contaminated if police prompted the suspect on how the crime happened, and I thought that I might find a handful of cases where this had happened. * * *

"To my great surprise, when I analyzed these case materials I found that not just a few, but almost all, of these exonerees' confessions were contaminated. . . . All but two of the forty exonerees studied told police much more than just 'I did it.' Instead, police said that these innocent people gave rich, detailed, and accurate information about the crime, including what police described as 'inside information' that only the true culprit could have known."

3. *Promises of leniency and threats of punishment.* Professor Leo tells us that, "once interrogation commences, the primary cause of police-induced false confessions is psychologically coercive methods." Richard A. Leo, *Police Interrogation and American Justice* 230 (2008). Leo continues: "By psychological coercion, I mean either one of two things: police use of interrogation techniques that are regarded as inherently coercive in psychology and law; or police use of interrogation techniques that, cumulatively, cause a suspect to perceive that he has no choice but to comply with the interrogators' demands. Usually, these amount to the same thing."

More specifically, Professor Leo is quite troubled by police interrogators' promises of leniency and threats of punishment. Drawing upon an earlier study he did with Richard Ofshe, Leo maintains that "in the modern era" "promises of leniency and threats of punishment, whether implicit or explicit, are the primary cause of police-induced false confessions." *Id.* at 309.

4. *Indirect promises of leniency through minimization techniques.* Police are often trained to use minimization tactics during interrogation. "[M]inimization tactics are designed to provide the suspect with moral justification and face-saving excuses for having committed the crime in question. Using this approach, the interrogator offers sympathy and understanding; normalizes and minimizes the crime, often suggesting that he or she would have behaved similarly; and offers the suspect a choice of alternative explanations—for example, suggesting to the suspect that the murder was spontaneous, provoked, peer-pressured, or accidental rather than the work of a cold-blooded pre-meditated killer." Saul M. Kassin et al., *Police-Induced Confessions: Risk Factors and Recommendations*, 34 Law & Hum. Behav. 3, 12 (2010). According to researchers, "this tactic communicates by implication that leniency in punishment is forthcoming upon confession" and causes innocent people to confess. *Id.* at 12, 18–19.

5.   *False evidence ploys.* Police will sometimes try to overcome a suspect's denials of involvement in the crime by misrepresenting the evidence that they have to suggest the suspect's guilt. "Basic research shows that once people see an outcome as inevitable, cognitive and motivational forces conspire to promote their acceptance, compliance with, and even approval of that outcome." Kassin, *supra* note 4, at 17. In laboratory studies, false evidence ploys nearly doubled the incidence of false confessions. *Id.* at 16–18; *see also* Richard A. Leo, *Interrogation and Confessions in* Academy for Justice, A Report on Scholarship and Criminal Justice Reform, Vol. 2, p. 255 (Erik Luna ed. 2017) ("Experimental research indicates that false-evidence ploys are far more likely to elicit false confessions than true confessions, and archival/ documentary research indicates that false-evidence ploys are present in virtually all police interrogations leading to proven false confessions.").

6.   *Vulnerable populations.* "[O]f the first 200 DNA exonerations in the U.S., 35% of the false confessors were 18 years or younger and/or had a developmental disability." In their sample of wrongful convictions, Gross, Jacoby, Matheson, Montgomery, and Patel (2005) found that 44% of the exonerated juveniles and 69% of exonerated persons with mental disabilities were wrongly convicted because of false confessions." Kassin, *supra* note 4, at 19. Multiple studies conclude that juveniles and those with mental disabilities and/or mental illness are more likely to falsely confess. Professor Leo explains why:

"Juveniles are more likely to falsely confess because they tend to be developmentally immature, impulsive, naively trusting of authority, submissive, eager to please adult figures, and thus more easily pressured, manipulated, and persuaded to make or agree to false statements without fully understanding the nature or gravity of an interrogation or the long-term consequences of their responses to police accusations. Mentally handicapped individuals are more likely to confess falsely for a variety of reasons related to their low intelligence, short attention span, poor memory, and poor conceptual and communication skills, which cause them to become easily confused, highly suggestible and compliant, and easy to manipulate; in addition, people with intellectual disabilities have a tendency to mask or disguise their cognitive deficits and to look to others—particularly authority figures—for appropriate cues to behavior. People with mental illness possess any number of psychiatric symptoms that make them more likely to agree with, suggest, or confabulate false and misleading information to detectives during interrogation, including faulty reality monitoring, distorted perceptions and beliefs, an inability to distinguish fact from fantasy, proneness to feelings of guilt, heightened anxiety, mood disturbances, and a lack of self-control."

Richard A. Leo, *Interrogation and Confessions in* Academy for Justice, A Report on Scholarship and Criminal Justice Reform, Vol. 2, p. 248–49 (Erik Luna ed. 2017); *see also* Kassin, *supra* note 4, at 19–22.

7.   *The limits of false confession studies.* Consider Lawrence Rosenthal, *Against Orthodoxy:* Miranda *Is Not Prophylactic and the Constitution Is Not Perfect*, 10 Chapman L.Rev. 579, 616–17 (2007): "The problem with the empirical case for greater due process regulation [of confessions] is that we have no idea what rate of false confessions is produced by the [interrogation] tactics that the critics have targeted. * * * Maybe even more important, we do not even know if the tactics identified by the critics produce *disproportionate* numbers of false confessions. Perhaps they do not. * * * [It] would not surprise me if the vast majority of custodial interrogations involve the features condemned by critics. If so, the fact that a study of false confessions will frequently disclose the use of the interrogation tactics identified by [some professor] provides no basis to conclude that these features increase the likelihood that a confession is false."

PROPOSED REFORMS

1. *Recording requirements.* "The risk of harm caused by false confessions could be greatly reduced," maintain Professors Drizin and Leo, "if police were required to electronically record the entirety of all custodial interrogations of suspects." Steven A. Drizin & Richard A. Leo, *The Problem of False Confessions in the Post-DNA World*, 82 N.C.L.Rev. 891, 997 (2004). They give three reasons:

(1) taping "creates an objective comprehensive, and reviewable record of the interrogation";

(2) taping "leads to a higher level of scrutiny (by police officials as well as others) [that will] improve the quality of interrogation practices and thus increase the ability of police to separate the innocent from the guilty"; and

(3) a taping requirement "creates the opportunity for various criminal justice officials to more closely monitor both the quality of police interrogation and the reliability of confession statements" and to enable all the participants in the criminal justice system "to more easily detect false confessions and thus more easily prevent their admission into evidence."

Id.; *see also* Saul M. Kassin et al., *Police-Induced Confessions: Risk Factors and Recommendations*, 34 Law & Hum. Behav. 3, 26 (2010) (describing the "numerous advantages to a videotaping policy").

2. *Limits on the length of interrogations.* Many experts favor setting time limits for police interrogations. Consider Richard A. Leo, *Police Interrogation and American Justice* 311–12 (2008): "Lengthy incommunicado interrogation is not only inherently unfair, [but] far more common in false confession cases than other ones. * * * Specifying a time limit on interrogations of no more than four hours should diminish the risk of eliciting false confessions while maintaining the ability of police to elicit true confessions from the guilty. [For, as the authors of a widely-used police interrogation manual have] pointed out, 'rarely will a competent interrogator require more than approximately four hours to obtain a confession from an offender, even in cases of a very serious nature.'" *See also* Kassin, *supra* note 1, at 28 (arguing for time limits and noting that "[t]he vast majority of interrogations last from 30 minutes up to 2 hours").

3. *Prohibiting promises of leniency and threats.* Professor Leo argues that "[a]ppellate courts need to create an unambiguous, bright line rule prohibiting under all circumstances any implicit or explicit promise, offers, or suggestion of leniency in exchange for an admission. This would include any inducement that reasonably communicates a promise, suggestion, or offer of reduced charging, sentencing, or punishment; freedom; immunity; or police, prosecutorial, judicial, or juror leniency in exchange for an admission or confession. Appellate courts also need to create an unambiguous rule prohibiting, under all circumstances, any implicit or explicit threat or suggestion of harm in the absence of an admission. This would include any inducement that reasonably communicates higher charging, a longer prison sentence, or other harsher punishment in the absence of an admission or confession. * * * Appellate courts must exclude all promises of leniency (or their functional equivalents) because they create an unacceptable risk that police will elicit false, unreliable, or untrustworthy confessions." Leo, *supra* note 2, at 309–10; *see also* Welsh S. White, *What Is a Voluntary Confession Now?*, 50 Rutgers L. Rev. 2001, 2052–53 (1998).

After discussing *Leyra v. Denno* (1954) and *Lynumn v. Illinois* (1963), two pre-*Miranda* voluntariness cases "which suggest that interrogation tactics that threaten the suspect with harsh punishments if she does not confess or offer express or implied promises of significant sentencing advantages if she does may exert such unfair pressure on the suspect as to render the resulting confession involuntary," Professor White comments, "the Court could establish the rule that interrogation tactics that threaten harsh consequences if the suspect does not confess or suggest that she will receive significant leniency in terms of disposition [citing *Miller v. Fenton*] or sentence if she does will generally be sufficient to render a resulting confession involuntary." *Id.*

4. *Distinguishing among different kinds of trickery.* Professor White believes that the data "provide a clear basis for distinguishing among different kinds of trickery. Based on [the available data], a court applying the Due Process test could properly hold that certain types of misrepresentation should be strongly condemned and perhaps sufficient in themselves to render a resulting confession involuntary. Specifically, misrepresentations designed to convince the suspect that his guilt has been established by either forensic evidence or his failure to pass a lie detector test should be prohibited, or at least viewed as likely to render a resulting confession involuntary." White, *supra* note 3, at 2055; *see also* Kassin, *supra* note 1, at 28–29 (arguing that false evidence should not be used on vulnerable populations and should not be presented as incontrovertible and noting that analyses of false confession cases, one hundred years of basic psychology research, and numerous laboratory experiments provide "strong support for the proposition that outright lies can put innocents at risk to confess by leading them to feel trapped by the inevitability of the evidence against them").

5. *Protecting vulnerable populations.* Researchers have recommended special protections for members of vulnerable populations. *See, e.g.*, Kassin, *supra* note 1, at 30 (recommending that vulnerable population members be given attorneys before they are interrogated and/or that law enforcement personnel who are going to question them be given special training about their vulnerabilities and what tactics to avoid (like false evidence ploys)).

6. *Skepticism about constitutional reforms.* Lawrence Rosenthal, *Against Orthodoxy: Miranda is Not Prophylactic and the Constitution is Not Perfect*, 10 Chapman L.Rev. 579 (2007), has considerable difficulty understanding why the false confession studies should lead to greater due process regulation of confessions generally. He suggests that the police probably use the same interrogation techniques in the vast majority of custodial interrogations. Therefore the fact that these techniques appear in false confession cases "provides no basis to conclude that these [techniques] increase the likelihood that a confession is false." *Id.* at 617–18. Professor Rosenthal continues (at 618–20):

"At best, it is probably reasonable to presume that more aggressive interrogation techniques will produce a higher rate of confessions than more passive approaches, but it is entirely unclear that the rate of false confessions will also increase through more aggressive techniques.[167]

" * * * [Even] if courts could somehow divine error rates, how are they to decide what constitutes an unacceptable rate of error? Three percent? Ten percent? * * * And what about the large number of guilty offenders who will go unpunished if courts brand as impermissible investigative tactics that are far more likely to produce accurate than false convictions but that nevertheless produce error rates that are thought to be unacceptable?

" * * * The advocates of due process regulation of interrogation * * * seek additional protection, based on evidence that [certain interrogation] techniques produce some nontrivial (although as yet unascertained) error rate. As a doctrinal matter, the absence of any historical support for prophylactic due process regulation of interrogation techniques based on a presumed risk of error might itself doom the case for new regulation. Even putting that problem aside, however, no one could tenably read the Due Process Clause as a prohibition of error in the criminal justice system. Surely 'due process' accommodates that much reality."

7. *Nonconstitutional reforms.* Consider Eve Brensike Primus, *The Future of Confession Law: Toward Rules for the Voluntariness Test*, 114 Mich. L. Rev. 1, 54–55 (2015): "Scholars have

---

[167] To be sure, one can build an anecdotal case that investigators sometimes persuade a suspect that his position is so hopeless that he has no realistic chance but to confess, [citing several commentators], but this says nothing about the rate at which the same tactics induce a guilty suspect to provide an accurate confession.

rightly argued that the problem will need to be attacked from many different angles and have proposed other significant reforms including better police training, specialized procedures for interrogating vulnerable populations, protocols to ensure that interrogators do not know the facts of the crimes being investigated to prevent the possibility of contamination, pretrial reliability assessments under federal and state evidentiary rules or statutes, greater use of false-confession experts in criminal jury trials, and better jury instructions to educate jurors about reliability problems with confessions."

8. *Different police training.* Most American law enforcement personnel use the Reid method for interrogating suspects. Developed in 1947, "[t]he Reid method of interrogation consists of guilt-presumptive, accusatory, and confirmatory questioning that, relying on pressure and persuasion, seeks to move a suspect from denial to admission and then to elicit a full narrative confession of guilt." Leo, *supra* note 2, at 242. "First, investigators are advised to isolate the suspect in a small private room, which increases his or her anxiety and incentive to escape. A nine-step process then ensues in which an interrogator employs both negative and positive incentives. On one hand, the interrogator confronts the suspect with accusations of guilt, assertions that may be bolstered by evidence, real or manufactured, and refuses to accept alibis and denials. On the other hand, the interrogator offers sympathy and moral justification, introducing 'themes' that minimize the crime and lead suspects to see confession as an expedient means of escape." Kassin, *supra* note 1, at 7.

Some experts have argued that American police should move away from the Reid method to investigative interviewing approaches like those currently used in England and Canada. Consider Leo, *supra* note 2, at 256: "Investigative interviewing approaches emphasize truthful information-gathering as their goal rather than eliciting a confession of guilt; they emphasize establishing rapport and letting suspects first tell their story before being confronted with inconsistencies or truthful existing evidence rather than accusatory approaches based on psychological control and manipulation; investigative interviewing approaches do not permit false-evidence ploys and lies and do not rely on minimization techniques that implicitly communicate promises and threats; and investigative interviewing approaches rely on open-ended exploratory questioning rather than close-ended confirmatory questioning."

Do you agree that an investigative interviewing approach would be better? Consider Christopher Slobogin, *Manipulation of Suspects and Unrecorded Questioning: After Fifty Years of Miranda Jurisprudence, Still Two (or Maybe Three) Burning Issues*, 97 B.U. L. Rev. 1157, 1162–64 (2017):

"[T]he jury is still out as to how effective these [investigative interviewing] tactics are. It has been asserted that confession rates achieved using [England's investigative interviewing] technique are at least as high as those in the United States. But that claim can be disputed on a number of grounds. A stronger claim, based on research to date, is that [investigative interviewing] techniques produce a greater amount of information than more confrontational practices that might be met with denials and clam-ups. That is a decided advantage if * * * more information means a greater chance of exposing contradiction. A final claim that is likely true is that, given their relatively unaggressive posture, [investigative interviewing] techniques are less likely to cause false confessions.

"Nonetheless, yet to be proffered is solid evidence that, compared to [the Reid method], [investigative interviewing] techniques have superior 'diagnosticity'—that is, a similar or higher true confession rate combined with a lower false confession rate. [The Reid method] may be significantly better than [investigative interviewing] techniques at producing true confessions, and if any false confessions they generate can be exposed prior to use in adjudication * * *, their ultimate diagnosticity may be superior. If so, American police are justified in refusing to abandon [the Reid method] on effectiveness grounds."

9. *Should criminal suspects get the same statutory protections as police do when they are suspected of misconduct?* Yes, argues Professor Kate Levine, *Police Suspects*, 116 Colum. L. Rev. 1197 (2016). At least fourteen states have enacted statutes or have negotiated agreements providing affirmative protections for police suspects, known as Law Enforcement Officers' Bill of Rights (LEOBORs). The protections in LEOBORs often go far beyond constitutional requirements, providing that "police suspects may be questioned only during the day; that they may be questioned only by a limited number of interrogators; that they must be given time to attend to their personal needs; that they may not be threatened, subject to abusive language, or induced to confess through untrue promises of leniency; and that their choice to inculpate themselves must not be conditioned on losing their job or benefits." *Id.* at 1200. Professor Levine argues that extending the protections that police suspects receive to all criminal defendants "may increase the humanity with which suspects are treated and the accuracy of their confessions." *Id.* at 1258.

§ 7. *MASSIAH* REVISITED; *MASSIAH* AND *MIRANDA* COMPARED AND CONTRASTED

A. THE REVIVIFICATION OF *MASSIAH*

14th ed., p. 704; end of Note 2, add:

Some lower courts have suggested that the foci of the "interrogation" and "deliberate elicitation" inquiries are different. *See, e.g., United States v. Rommy*, 506 F.3d 108, 135 (2d Cir. 2007) (stating that the Fifth Amendment interrogation inquiry focuses on the suspect and the suspect's perception of the situation whereas the Sixth Amendment deliberate elicitation standard considers whether the government was intentionally seeking to obtain incriminating statements from the accused); *Hill v. United States*, 858 A.2d 435, 442 (D.C. 2004) ("For Sixth Amendment purposes, therefore, the focus is on the police officer's action and intent, not on an objective evaluation of the police actions' effect on the suspect that is relevant under the Fifth Amendment."). *But cf. Rhode Island v. Innis*, 446 U.S. 291, 301 n.7 (1980) (explaining that the intent of the police is not "irrelevant" to the interrogation inquiry).

14th ed., p. 706; after Note (b), add:

(c) *Was it wrong to import* Miranda *waiver doctrine into the Sixth Amendment context?* Eve Brensike Primus, *Disentangling* Miranda *and* Massiah*: How to Revive the Sixth Amendment Right to Counsel as a Tool for Regulating Confession Law*, 97 B.U.L. Rev. 1085, 1085, 1103–04 (2017), argues that the Supreme Court's importation of *Miranda* waiver doctrine into *Massiah* was misguided given the different purposes of the Fifth and Sixth Amendments:

"*Miranda* has always been focused on dispelling the inherent compulsion in the custodial interrogation environment in order to ensure that suspects are not being compelled to give testimony against themselves in violation of the Self-Incrimination Clause. In contrast, the Sixth Amendment pretrial right to counsel is grounded in concepts of fundamental fairness and equality and is designed to ensure that criminal defendants have attorneys to help them navigate the procedural and substantive complexities of the law and face the prosecutorial forces of organized society. * * *

"Advising a suspect of his rights, the consequences of speaking, and giving him the option to ask for help may be sufficient to dissipate the compulsion and prevent a Fifth Amendment violation, but * * * [s]aying that a confession will be used against him does not advise the suspect of how a lawyer could help him; it merely tells him what the state wants to do with his statement.

The suspect may not understand the nature of the charges, that complicity can be just as damning as actual perpetration of the offense, or that a lawyer could explain the legal elements to him. It is not always intuitive to a suspect that a lawyer might examine the indictment for legal sufficiency before permitting him to talk or that the lawyer might be better at negotiating a plea for him if he does not give an incriminating statement. In the world of sentencing guidelines with downward departures, an attorney might be able to negotiate a deal for a client who is inclined to cooperate with authorities. All of these are 'intricacies of [the] substantive and procedural criminal law' that an attorney could help the defendant understand and that a defendant might not understand are part of the attorney's job.

"The *Miranda* warnings also do nothing to inform the suspect of the equalizing role that attorneys are supposed to play in the adversarial system. The suspect might not understand what it means to be indicted * * * . He might think he can talk his way out of things * * *. An attorney could explain what an indictment is and what it means about the government's posture toward him * * *. By failing to consider the underlying rationales for the Sixth Amendment right to counsel, the *Patterson* Court imported a waiver regime that is ill suited to the purposes of that right."

(d)　*Adequacy of the warnings.* How much can the police modify the *Miranda* warnings and still adequately convey the Sixth Amendment right to counsel? Are there modifications that are permissible under the *Duckworth v. Eagan* line of cases for Fifth Amendment purposes that would be problematic under the Sixth Amendment? Consider Eda Katharine Tinto, *Wavering on Waiver: Montejo v. Louisiana and the Sixth Amendment Right to Counsel*, 48 Am. Crim. L. Rev. 1335, 1360–61 (2011) (arguing that the modification in *Duckworth* itself—involving language that the suspect had a right to a lawyer "if and when [he] went to court"—is misleading in the Sixth Amendment context, because it suggests no right to the presence of an attorney during post-indictment questioning in violation of *Massiah*).

(e)　*Implied waiver.* Can a Sixth Amendment waiver of the right to counsel be implied after *Miranda* warnings are read as long as the suspect understands the warnings and gives an uncoerced statement? *Cf. Berghuis v. Thompkins.* Lower courts are divided. *Compare United States v. Scarpa*, 897 F.2d 63, 68–69 (2d Cir. 1990) (yes) *with In re Darryl P.*, 63 A.3d 1142, 1191 (Md. Ct. Sp. App. 2013) (no).

(f)　*More protective states.* A number of states have rejected *Patterson* as a matter of state law. *See, e.g., People v. Grice*, 794 N.E.2d 9, 10 (N.Y. 2003) (holding that a criminal defendant who has been formally charged may not waive the right to counsel unless she does so in the presence of her attorney); *State v. Sanchez*, 609 A.2d 400, 408 (N.J. 1992) (requiring either the presence of an attorney to waive or a waiver following a judicial advisement of rights); *State v. Liulama*, 845 P.2d 1194, 1203 (Haw. Ct. App. 1993) (same). *See also* Michael C. Mims, *A Trap for the Unwary: The Sixth Amendment Right to Counsel after* Montejo v. Louisiana, 71 La. L. Rev. 345, 369–70 (2010) (arguing for more stringent waiver requirements that would parallel the waiver requirements for waiving the right to counsel at trial).

CHAPTER 10

LINEUPS, SHOWUPS AND OTHER PRE-TRIAL IDENTIFICATION PROCEDURES

■ ■ ■

§ 1. *WADE* AND *GILBERT*: CONSTITUTIONAL CONCERN ABOUT THE DANGERS INVOLVED IN EYEWITNESS IDENTIFICATIONS

14th ed., p. 724; replace Note 5 with the following:

5. *Excluding first-time in-court identifications.* Although courtroom identifications are highly suggestive (the defendant is sitting at counsel's table waiting to be identified), they are not highly regulated by the courts. Consider Garrett, supra note 4, at 461: "Courts generally reject arguments that in-court identifications are inherently suggestive.... Judges may view the courtroom identification as pure theater or a witness demonstration, but ... they also seem to think that the presence of counsel and the solemnity of testimony under oath in a courtroom makes the courtroom identification more, not less, reliable."

For a recent decision rejecting this view, see *State v. Dickson*, 141 A.3d 810 (Conn. 2016). After emphasizing that it was "hard-pressed to imagine how there could be a *more* suggestive identification procedure than placing a witness on the stand in open court, confronting the witness with the person who the state has accused of committing the crime, and then asking the witness if he can identify the person who committed the crime," the Connecticut Supreme Court held that "in cases in which identity is an issue, in-court identifications that are not preceded by a successful identification in a nonsuggestive identification procedure implicate due process principles and, therefore, must be prescreened by the trial court." The state must request permission before offering a first-time in-court identification, and the trial court may only grant permission if there is no factual dispute as to identity or the ability of the eyewitness to identify the defendant is not in dispute. If there is such a dispute, no first-time in-court identification will be admitted, and the state may instead request permission to conduct a nonsuggestive identification procedure (an out-of-court lineup or photographic array). The Connecticut Supreme Court recognized that its decision to exclude many first-time, in-court identifications conflicted with the approach of a number of other courts, *see id.* at 431 n.14.

§ 4. SOCIAL SCIENCE RESEARCH ON IDENTIFICATION PROCEDURES AND THE NEED FOR REFORM

14th ed., p. 744; replace the citation to 725 Ill. Comp. Stat. 5/107A–5 with the following citation:

725 Ill. Comp. Stat. 5/107A–2 (requiring blind identification procedures, fillers that match suspect description, pre-identification instructions to the witness, and recording or photographing of the identification procedure);

14th ed., p. 744; replace footnote d with the following:

d   As of 2013, approximately one-fifth of state and local law enforcement agencies reported using either audio or video recording to document photo arrays, and twenty-four percent reported using either audio or video recording to document live lineups. *See* Police Executive Research Foundation, *A National Survey of Eyewitness Identification Procedures in Law Enforcement Agencies* 88 (2013).

14th ed., p. 745; at the end of Note 3, add:

Failure to comply with statutory or policy requirements may also be admissible to support misidentification claims made to the jury, and some courts will instruct jurors that they may consider the failure to comply with established procedures when assessing the reliability of an identification. *See, e.g.*, N.C. Gen. Stat. § 15A–284.52(d).

States vary in their approaches to eyewitness identification reform with some states enacting top-down, command and control legislation that mandates a uniform statewide policy and other states enacting more flexible, bottom-up legislation that requires each agency to create its own policy on eyewitness identification in accordance with general scientific principles about ensuring accurate identifications. For a comprehensive description of these different approaches and a discussion of their effectiveness, see Keith A. Findley, *Implementing the Lessons from Wrongful Convictions: An Empirical Analysis of Eyewitness Identification Reform Strategies*, 81 Missouri L. Rev. 377 (2016).

In January of 2017, then-Deputy Attorney General Sally Yates issued a memorandum for all law enforcement and prosecutorial offices adopting the above-listed recommendations and directing law enforcement agencies to update their internal policies accordingly. A copy of the memorandum is available at https://www.justice.gov/file/923201/download.

3A. ***Should police need reasonable suspicion that someone committed an offense before they are permitted to put the suspect into a lineup?*** Yes, contends Gary L. Wells, Eyewitness Identification in Academy for Justice, A Report on Scholarship and Criminal Justice Reform, Vol. 2, p. 267–68 (Erik Luna ed. 2017): "[N]othing increases the chances of mistaken identification more than the mere absence of the culprit from the lineup. * * * [E]yewitnesses have a propensity to make affirmative identification decisions even when the culprit is not present in the lineup. This means that there is inherent risk to an innocent suspect from being placed in an eyewitness identification procedure. * * * Currently, there appear to be no jurisdictions in the U.S. for which there is a standard (e.g., reasonable suspicion) that should be met in order to put an individual's photo into a photo lineup to see if an eyewitness will identify that person. * * * [R]esearchers have shown that any jurisdiction that has a low base rate for the presence of the culprit in its lineups is risking a high rate of mistaken identifications. In the eyewitness-identification area, this is known as the base-rate problem. I have called for some kind of standard, such as reasonable suspicion, before placing a possible suspect into the jeopardy of an eyewitness-identification procedure."

14th ed., p. 745; in Note 6, before the citation to *State v. Ledbetter*, add the following:

Model Jury Instructions on Eyewitness Identification, Mass. Court System (Nov. 16, 2015), *available   at*   http://www.mass.gov/courts/docs/sjc/docs/model-jury-instructions-on-eyewitness-identification-november-2015.pdf (incorporating generally accepted scientific principles about eyewitness identification problems into jury instructions); *Commonwealth v. Bastaldo*, 32 N.E.3d 873 (Mass. 2015) (requiring an instruction on the difficulties of cross-racial identification when applicable);

14th ed., p. 745; at the end of Note 6, add:

See also Laurie N. Feldman, *The Unreliable Case Against the Reliability of Eyewitness Identifications: A Response to Judge Alex Kozinski*, 34 Quinnipiac L. Rev. 493, 505 (2016) (arguing that, "because eyewitness research is unsettled and nuanced, '[b]rief instructions may not . . . provide sufficient guidance to explain the relevant scientific evidence to the jury, but lengthy instructions may be cumbersome and complex,'" and noting that more focused instructions from New Jersey "have been found to cause jurors to *undervalue* strongly probative identification evidence, potentially letting guilty parties go free" (quoting the National Academy of Sciences Report, 14th ed. note 4 at p. 745)).

14th ed., p. 745; in Note 7, before the citation to *State v. Henderson*, add the following:

Young v. State, 374 P.3d 395 (Alaska 2016) (rejecting the *Brathwaite* framework as a matter of state constitutional law and requiring a pretrial reliability hearing whenever there is some evidence of suggestiveness that could lead to a mistaken identification);

14th ed., p. 746; after Note 8, add:

    9.   *Continued controversy about the social science.* There continues to be controversy over both the results of social science studies and the weight that should be given to them in the context of eyewitness identifications. Former Judge Alex Kozinski of the United States Court of Appeals for the Ninth Circuit relied on social science research to argue for the adoption of standardized and rigorous procedures for eyewitness identifications: "[The belief that eyewitnesses are highly reliable] is so much part of our culture that one often hears talk of a 'mere' circumstantial case as contrasted to a solid case based on eyewitness testimony. In fact, research shows that eyewitness identifications are highly unreliable, especially where the witness and the perpetrator are of different races. Eyewitness reliability is further compromised when the identification occurs under the stress of a violent crime, an accident or catastrophic event—which pretty much covers all situations where identity is in dispute at trial. In fact, mistaken eyewitness testimony was a factor in more than a third of wrongful conviction cases. Yet, courts have been slow in allowing defendants to present expert evidence on the fallibility of eyewitnesses; many courts still don't allow it. Few, if any, courts instruct juries on the pitfalls of eyewitness identification or caution them to be skeptical of eyewitness testimony." Hon. Alex Kozinski, *Criminal Law 2.0*, 44 Geo. L.J. Ann. Rev. Crim. Proc. iii–iv (2015).

    A prosecutor in Connecticut recently took issue with Kozinski's reliance on social science research noting that "findings [are] in flux" about the science, in part, because "researchers themselves admit that they cannot answer many questions about the reliability (or the statistical significance) of their laboratory studies as applied to real crimes, real eyewitnesses under oath, and real jurors." Laurie N. Feldman, *The Unreliable Case Against the Reliability of Eyewitness Identifications: A Response to Judge Alex Kozinski*, 34 Quinnipiac L. Rev. 493, 496–98 (2016). Moreover, Feldman argues that "the percentage of mistaken eyewitnesses in studies greatly exceeds the percentage of mistaken eyewitnesses who testify at trials," because "[p]olice and prosecutors do not proceed against wrongly identified 'fillers.'" *Id.* at 499.

Chapter 11

Grand Jury Investigations

■ ■ ■

§ 3. OTHER OBJECTIONS TO THE INVESTIGATION

14th ed., p. 770; at the end of Note 4, add:

Consider also the discussion in the majority opinion in *Carpenter v. United States*, Supp. p. 45, and Supp. p. 73 as to why the Fourth Amendment there demanded use of a search warrant rather than a court order compelling production. The government in *Carpenter* used a court order under § 2703(d) rather than a grand jury subpoena since the Stored Communication Act provisions authorizing use of grand jury subpoenas, § 2703(c) and § 2703(b), do not extend to the cell-site location information sought in *Carpenter*. Consider also the positions on the allowable use of "compulsory process," including grand jury subpoenas, advanced in the *Carpenter* dissents of Justice Kennedy and Justice Alito, and the majority's response to those positions.

§ 5. SELF-INCRIMINATION AND THE COMPELLED PRODUCTION OF DOCUMENTS

B. THE ACT-OF-PRODUCTION DOCTRINE

14th ed., p. 825; at the end of Note 5, add:

See also the discussion in Note 8 of Ch. 6, § 4, added at Supp., p. 55.

CHAPTER 12

THE SCOPE OF THE EXCLUSIONARY RULES

■ ■ ■

§ 1. "STANDING" TO OBJECT
TO THE ADMISSION OF EVIDENCE

A. THE FOURTH AMENDMENT

14th ed., p. 831; replace Note 1 with the following:

1. *Standing as a distinct inquiry.* Although Justice Rehnquist, writing in *Rakas*, believed that "standing" should not be distinct from the Fourth Amendment inquiry, the Supreme Court recently clarified in *Byrd v. United States*, 138 S. Ct. 1518, 1530 (2018), that "[t]he concept of standing in Fourth Amendment cases can be a useful shorthand for capturing the idea that a person must have a cognizable Fourth Amendment interest in the place searched before seeking relief for an unconstitutional search." Consider also SEARCHSZR, § 11.3 at 121: "[It] is important to keep in mind that the question traditionally labeled as standing (did the police intrude upon *this defendant's* justified expectation of privacy?) is not identical to, for example, the question of whether any Fourth Amendment search has occurred (did the police intrude upon *anyone's* justified expectation of privacy?), and that therefore the [issues traditionally called "standing" issues] are still rather discrete and deserving of separate attention, no matter what label is put on them."

14th ed., p. 835; replace Note 9 with the following:

9. *Can an unauthorized driver of a rental car have standing to object to a search of the car?* Yes, the Court answered in BYRD v. UNITED STATES, 138 S. Ct. 1518 (2018). After renting a car, Latasha Reed gave the keys to Terrence Byrd even though Byrd was not listed as an authorized driver on the rental agreement. When Byrd (who was driving the car alone) was later stopped by the police for a possible traffic infraction, officers searched the trunk and found body armor and heroin. Byrd moved to suppress the evidence, but the Government alleged that he did not have standing to object to the search of the vehicle, because he was not an authorized driver and therefore had no expectation of privacy. The Supreme Court unanimously disagreed. Justice Kennedy, writing for the Court, explained:

"Although the Court has not set forth a single metric or exhaustive list of considerations to resolve the circumstances in which a person can be said to have a reasonable expectation of privacy, it has explained that '[l]egitimation of expectations of privacy by law must have a source outside of the Fourth Amendment, either by reference to concepts of real or personal property law or to understandings that are recognized and permitted by society.' *Rakas.* The two concepts in cases like this one are often linked. 'One of the main rights attaching to property is the right to exclude others,' and, in the main, 'one who owns or lawfully possesses or controls property will in all likelihood have a legitimate expectation of privacy by virtue of the right to exclude.' *Ibid.* * * *

"This situation would be similar to the defendant in *Jones*, who * * * had a reasonable expectation of privacy in his friend's apartment because he 'had complete dominion and control over the apartment and could exclude other from it.' * * * The Court sees no reason why the expectation of privacy that comes from lawful possession and control and the attendant right to exclude would differ depending on whether the car in question is rented or privately owned by someone other than the person in current possession of it, much as it did not seem to matter whether the friend of the defendant in *Jones* owned or leased the apartment he permitted the defendant to use in his absence. Both would have the expectation of privacy that comes with the right to exclude. Indeed, the Government conceded at oral argument that an unauthorized driver in sole possession of a rental car would be permitted to exclude third parties from it, such as a carjacker."

Responding to the Government's argument that the violation of the rental agreement vitiated any expectation of privacy, the majority noted that "car-rental agreements are filled with long lists of restrictions. Examples include prohibitions on driving the car on unpaved roads or driving while using a handheld cellphone. Few would contend that violating provisions like these has anything to do with a driver's reasonable expectation of privacy in the rental car * * *."

The Court also used *Byrd* as an opportunity to correct the Government's overly-broad misreading of *Rakas*. The Government had argued that, because Byrd would not have had standing as a passenger under *Rakas* if the authorized driver was driving the car, he should not have standing now, having displaced the authorized driver. But, the Court responded, "[t]he Court in *Rakas* did not hold that passengers cannot have an expectation of privacy in automobiles. To the contrary, the Court disclaimed any intent to hold 'that a passenger lawfully in an automobile may not invoke the exclusionary rule and challenge a search of that vehicle unless he happens to own or have a possessory interest in it.'"

However, the Court would not go so far as to say that unauthorized drivers of rental cars *always* have standing to object to a search of the car. Citing footnote 12 in *Rakas*, the Court emphasized that "*Rakas* makes clear that 'wrongful' presence at the scene of a search would not enable a defendant to object to the legality of the search. * * * No matter the degree of possession and control, the car thief would not have a reasonable expectation of privacy in a stolen car." The Court then remanded for the lower court to address the Government's argument that Byrd was tantamount to a car thief, because (a) he intentionally used Reed to rent the car knowing that he would not have been able to do so based on his criminal record, and (b) he did so for the illegal purpose of transporting his heroin. The Court noted that "[i]t is unclear whether the Government's allegations, if true, would constitute a criminal offense in the acquisition of the rental car under applicable law. And it may be that there is no reason that the law should distinguish between one who obtains a vehicle through subterfuge of the type the Government alleges occurred here and one who steals the car outright. The Government did not raise this argument [below,] however. * * * And it is unclear from the record whether the Government's inferences paint an accurate picture of what occurred. [Thus, t]he proper course is to remand* * *."

The Court also indicated that the lower court could, on remand, choose to avoid the standing inquiry entirely if it believed that the police had probable cause that would have justified the vehicle search under the automobile exception: "Because Fourth Amendment standing is subsumed under substantive Fourth Amendment doctrine, it is not a jurisdictional question and hence need not be addressed before addressing other aspects of the merits * * *."

14th ed., p. 836; at the end of Note 10, add the following paragraph:

In *Byrd*, *supra* Note 9, the driver of the rental car raised an alternative argument that he had a common-law property interest in the rental car as a second bailee. The Supreme Court refused to address the issue, because Byrd had not raised it below. But Justice Thomas, joined by Justice Gorsuch, wrote a concurring opinion inviting that issue in a future case and noting that whether a rental car could be considered a person's "effect" under the Fourth Amendment "seems to turn on at least three threshold questions. First, what kind of property interest do individuals need before something can be considered 'their . . . effec[t]' under the original meaning of the

Fourth Amendment? Second, what body of law determines whether that property interest is present—modern state law, the common law of 1791, or something else? Third, is the unauthorized use of a rental car illegal or otherwise wrongful under the relevant law, and, if so, does that illegality or wrongfulness affect the Fourth Amendment analysis?" *Id.* at 1531.

14th ed., p. 841; after *Minnesota v. Carter*, add the following note:

14. ***Trespass doctrine applied to the home.*** How does the revival of the trespass doctrine in *Jones* and *Jardines* affect the standing inquiry with respect to searches of homes? Consider *United States v. Bain*, 874 F.3d 1 (1st Cir. 2017) (holding that an overnight guest had standing to object to the "trespass" by police of putting a key into the front door lock of his girlfriend's condo unit under common law property concepts as well as the reasonable expectation of privacy test). *But see State v. Talkington*, 345 P.3d 258 (Kan. 2015) (noting that the defendant, a social guest, did not have a property interest in the curtilage of the home, but holding that he could still assert a Fourth Amendment claim, because he did have a reasonable expectation of privacy under *Katz*).

§ 2. THE "FRUIT OF THE POISONOUS TREE"

A. FOURTH AMENDMENT VIOLATIONS

14th ed., p. 848; after Note 4, add:

4A. ***Does the discovery of an outstanding arrest warrant break the causal chain between an unconstitutional stop and the discovery of evidence found incident to an arrest based on the warrant?*** The Supreme Court answered this question in UTAH v. STRIEFF, 136 S.Ct. 2056 (2016). Utah police had received an anonymous tip reporting "narcotics activity" at a particular residence. Officer Fackrell saw Strieff leaving that home. Without any reasonable suspicion that Strieff had been engaged in criminal activity, Fackrell stopped him, asked him what he was doing at the house, requested his identification, and detained him while he relayed Strieff's information to a police dispatcher. Upon learning that Strieff had an outstanding arrest warrant for a traffic violation, Fackrell arrested him and found methamphetamine during a search incident to arrest. Justice Thomas, writing for a 5–3 majority, applied the factors from *Brown v. Illinois*, 422 U.S. 590 (1975), to find that the discovery of the arrest warrant was sufficiently attenuated from the illegal stop to permit admission of the methamphetamine evidence. All eight justices agreed that the *Brown v. Illinois* framework applied and that the first factor—temporal proximity between the initially unlawful stop and the search—favored suppression given that "Officer Fackrell discovered drug contraband on Strieff's person only minutes after the illegal stop." The primary disagreement between the majority and the dissents centered on the application of the other two *Brown* factors.

With respect to the second factor—the presence of intervening circumstances, Justice Thomas and the majority thought the outstanding arrest warrant was an intervening circumstance sufficient to dissipate the initial taint of the illegal stop. After clarifying that an intervening circumstance need not be an independent act by the defendant, the majority emphasized that "the warrant was valid, it predated Officer Fackrell's investigation, and it was entirely unconnected with the stop. . . . Officer Fackrell's arrest of Strieff thus was a ministerial act that was independently compelled by the pre-existing warrant."

The majority also felt that the third factor—the purpose and flagrancy of the official misconduct—strongly favored the State. Justice Thomas described Officer Fackrell's conduct as "at most negligent" and as involving "good-faith mistakes" or "errors in judgment [that] hardly rise to a purposeful or flagrant violation of Strieff's Fourth Amendment rights." According to the majority, "[f]or the violation to be flagrant, more severe police misconduct is required than the mere absence of proper cause for the seizure." The majority opinion also emphasized that "there is no indication that this unlawful stop was part of any systemic or recurrent police misconduct" and noted that, "were evidence of a dragnet search presented here, the application of the *Brown* factors could be different." Ultimately, the majority found that "[t]he discovery of the warrant broke the causal chain between the unconstitutional stop and the discovery of evidence." Because the evidence was sufficiently attenuated from the initial illegality, it was admissible.

Justices Ginsburg, Sotomayor, and Kagan dissented. Justice Kagan, writing for herself and Justice Ginsburg, explained that the exclusionary rule "serves a crucial function—to deter unconstitutional police conduct" and noted that the attenuation doctrine, as described through *Brown*'s factors, is "our effort to 'mark the point' at which the discovery of evidence 'become[s] so attenuated' from the police misconduct that the deterrent benefit of exclusion drops below its cost." Here, Justice Kagan felt, "[n]othing in Fackrell's discovery of an outstanding warrant so attenuated the connection between his wrongful behavior and his detection of drugs as to diminish the exclusionary rule's deterrent benefits."

Justice Kagan took issue with the majority's suggestion that the discovery of an outstanding warrant could be a sufficient intervening circumstance to break the causal chain: "The notion of such a disrupting event comes from the tort law doctrine of proximate causation. And as in the tort context, a circumstance counts as intervening only when it is unforeseeable—not when it can be seen coming from miles away. . . . Fackrell's discovery of an arrest warrant . . . was an eminently foreseeable consequence of stopping Strieff." It is "routine procedure" to check for warrants during a stop and there are a "staggering number of such warrants on the books"— particularly in those "cities, towns, and neighborhoods where stops are most likely to occur."

Justice Kagan also objected to the majority's conclusion that Fackrell's actions were not purposeful and flagrant, noting that the conduct in this case was much like that in the *Brown* case itself: "Fackrell's seizure of Strieff was a calculated decision, taken with so little justification that the State has never tried to defend its legality. At the suppression hearing, Fackrell acknowledged that the stop was designed for investigatory purposes [and he] frankly admitted that he had no basis for his action except that Strieff 'was coming out of the house.' "

Ultimately, Justice Kagan worried that "[t]he majority's misapplication of *Brown*'s three-part inquiry creates unfortunate incentives for the police—indeed, practically invites them to do what Fackrell did here. . . . Now the officer knows that [a stop unsupported by reasonable suspicion] may well yield admissible evidence: So long as the target is one of the many millions of people in this country with an outstanding arrest warrant, anything the officer finds in a search is fair game for use in a criminal prosecution. The officer's incentive to violate the Constitution thus increases: From here on, he sees potential advantage in stopping individuals without reasonable suspicion— exactly the temptation the exclusionary rule is supposed to remove."

Justice Sotomayor went even further in her separate dissent, noting that "this case tells everyone, white and black, guilty and innocent, that an officer can verify your legal status at any time. It says that your body is subject to invasion while courts excuse the violation of your rights. It implies that you are not a citizen of a democracy but the subject of a carceral state, just waiting to be cataloged." She noted that "[t]he States and Federal Government maintain databases with over 7.8 million outstanding warrants, the vast majority of which appear to be for minor offenses." While agreeing that "most officers act in 'good faith' and do not set out to break the law," she took issue with the majority's suggestion that these stops are "isolated instance[s] of negligence." Rather, she wrote, "[m]any are the product of institutionalized training procedures." As a result, "[w]e must not pretend that the countless people who are routinely targeted by police are 'isolated.' They are the canaries in the coal mine . . . who recognize that unlawful police stops corrode all our civil liberties and threaten all our lives. Until their voices matter too, our justice system will continue to be anything but." Justice Sotomayor's separate dissent is more fully excerpted *supra* Supp., p. 11.

D. SIXTH AMENDMENT VIOLATIONS

14th ed., p. 862; before § 3, add:

For an argument that the importation of the *Elstad-Patane-Seibert* line of cases into the Sixth Amendment context is "misguided" because it fails to consider the differences between the *Miranda* and *Massiah* doctrines, see Eve Brensike Primus, *Disentangling* Miranda *and* Massiah: *How to Revive the Sixth Amendment Right to Counsel as a Tool for Regulating Confession Law*, 97 B.U.L. Rev. 1085, 1109–1114 (2017).

PART 3

THE COMMENCEMENT OF FORMAL PROCEEDINGS

■ ■ ■

CHAPTER 13

PRETRIAL RELEASE

■ ■ ■

§ 1. THE RIGHT TO BAIL; PRETRIAL RELEASE PROCEDURES

14th ed., p. 882; before Note 8, add:

Sandra Thompson, *Do Prosecutors Matter? A Proposal to Ban One-Sided Bail Hearings*, 44 Hofstra L.Rev. 1161, 1164 (2016), noting that the ABA Standards for Criminal Justice, Prosecution Function § 3–5.1 (4th ed.2015), "take the position that defendants are better off if a prosecutor is present at the bail hearing, even if defense counsel is not," argues, id. at 1162, "that time has proven this approach to protecting the rights of defendants at bail hearings is unrealistic and that defendants are actually better off if prosecutors are ethically barred from participating unless defense counsel is present."

CHAPTER 14

THE DECISION WHETHER TO PROSECUTE

■ ■ ■

§ 2. SOME VIEWS ON DISCRETION IN THE CRIMINAL PROCESS AND THE PROSECUTOR'S DISCRETION IN PARTICULAR

14th ed., p. 910; replace A.B.A. Standards, 3d ed:

A.B.A. STANDARDS FOR CRIMINAL JUSTICE: PROSECUTION FUNCTION
(4th ed., 2017).

Standard 3–4.4   Discretion in Filing, Declining, Maintaining, and Dismissing Criminal Charges

(a) In order to fully implement the prosecutor's functions and duties, including the obligation to enforce the law while exercising sound discretion, the prosecutor is not obliged to file or maintain all criminal charges which the evidence might support. Among the factors which the prosecutor may properly consider in exercising discretion to initiate, decline, or dismiss a criminal charge, even though it meets the requirements of Standard 3–4.3, are:

(i)   the strength of the case;

(ii) the prosecutor's doubt that the accused is in fact guilty;

(iii) the extent or absence of harm caused by the offense;

(iv) the impact of prosecution or non-prosecution on the public welfare;

(v)   the background and characteristics of the offender, including any voluntary restitution or efforts at rehabilitation;

(vi) whether the authorized or likely punishment or collateral consequences are disproportionate in relation to the particular offense or the offender;

(vii) the views and motives of the victim or complainant;

(viii) any improper conduct by law enforcement;

(ix) unwarranted disparate treatment of similarly situated persons;

(x)   potential collateral impact on third parties, including witnesses or victims;

(xi) cooperation of the offender in the apprehension or conviction of others;

(xii) the possible influence of any cultural, ethnic, socioeconomic or other improper biases;

(xiii) changes in law or policy;

(xiv) the fair and efficient distribution of limited prosecutorial resources;

(xv) the likelihood of prosecution by another jurisdiction; and

(xvi) whether the public's interests in the matter might be appropriately vindicated by available civil, regulatory, administrative, or private remedies.

(b)   In exercising discretion to file and maintain charges, the prosecutor should not consider:

(i)   partisan or other improper political or personal considerations;

(ii)   hostility or personal animus towards a potential subject, or any other improper motive of the prosecutor; or

(iii)   the impermissible criteria described in Standard 1.6 above.

(c)   A prosecutor may file and maintain charges even if juries in the jurisdiction have tended to acquit persons accused of the particular kind of criminal act in question.

(d)   The prosecutor should not file or maintain charges greater in number or degree than can reasonably be supported with evidence at trial and are necessary to fairly reflect the gravity of the offense or deter similar conduct.

(e)   A prosecutor may condition a dismissal of charges, *nolle prosequi*, or similar action on the accused's relinquishment of a right to seek civil redress only if the accused has given informed consent, and such consent is disclosed to the court. A prosecutor should not use a civil waiver to avoid a bona fide claim of improper law enforcement actions, and a decision not to file criminal charges should be made on its merits and not for the purpose of obtaining a civil waiver.

(f)   The prosecutor should consider the possibility of a noncriminal disposition, formal or informal, or a deferred prosecution or other diversionary disposition, when deciding whether to initiate or prosecute criminal charges. The prosecutor should be familiar with the services and resources of other agencies, public or private, that might assist in the evaluation of cases for diversion or deferral from the criminal process.

§ 3.   CHALLENGING THE PROSECUTOR'S DISCRETION

B.   THE DECISION TO PROSECUTE

14th ed., p. 927; before Note 1, add:

0.1   *Discovery limitations.* As concluded in the en banc decision in UNITED STATES v. DAVIS, 793 F.3d 712 (7th Cir.2015), whether the *Armstrong* discovery limitations apply depends upon the locus of the suspected discrimination. The defendants in that case alleged that the prosecutor, the FBI, and the Bureau of Alcohol, Tobacco, Firearms and Explosives (ATF) had engaged in racial discrimination with respect to the investigation and prosecution of stash-house stings. To their request for discovery, the prosecutor responded that *Armstrong* "forbids discovery into prosecutorial selectivity unless the defense first shows that similarly situations persons have not been prosecuted," lacking here. The court of appeals concluded:

"To the extent that Davis and the other six defendants want information about how the United States Attorney has exercised prosecutorial discretion, *Armstrong* is an insuperable obstacle (at least on this record). But the defendants' principal targets are the ATF and the FBI. They maintain that these agencies offer lucrative-seeming opportunities to black and Hispanic suspects, yet not to those similarly situated in criminal background and interests but of other ethnicity. If the agencies do that, they have violated the Constitution—and the fact that the United States Attorney may have prosecuted every case the agencies presented, or chosen 25% of them in a race-blind lottery, would not matter, since the constitutional problem would have preceded the prosecutor's role and could not be eliminated by the fact that things didn't get worse at a later step. * * *

"Agents of the ATF and FBI are not protected by a powerful privilege or covered by a presumption of constitutional behavior. Unlike prosecutors, agents regularly testify in criminal cases, and their credibility may be relentlessly attacked by defense counsel. They also may have to testify in pretrial proceedings, such as hearings on motions to suppress evidence, and again their honesty is open to challenge. Statements that agents make in affidavits for search or arrest warrants may be contested, and the court may need their testimony to decide whether if shorn of untruthful statements the affidavits would have established probable cause. * * * Before holding hearings (or civil trials) district judges regularly, and properly, allow discovery into nonprivileged aspects of what agents have said or done. In sum, the sort of considerations that led to the outcome in *Armstrong* do not apply to a contention that agents of the FBI or ATF engaged in racial discrimination when selecting targets for sting operations, or when deciding which suspects to refer for prosecution."

C. THE DIVERSION DECISION

14th ed., p. 938; before Note 2, add:

1A. *Risks and remedies.* One of the dangers "attending the practice of pre-charge diversion * * * is the risk that individuals who would not otherwise be prosecuted or convicted will be persuaded to enter into deferred prosecution agreements, thus expanding the net of social control in the name of 'diversion.' The psychological pressure to resolve the matter as quickly as possible may also prevent accused individuals from invoking constitutional rights and other protections they would possess in a formal prosecution." Model Penal Code: Sentencing § 6.02A (Proposed Final Draft 2017). The Code's provision on deferred prosecution addresses those concerns in various ways, including by (1) limiting deferred prosecution to cases in which "a prosecutor has probable cause to believe that an individual has committed a crime and reasonably anticipates that sufficient admissible evidence can be developed to support conviction at trial"; (2) providing for right to counsel whenever a defendant is tendered a deferred prosecution agreement, even "before the initiation of formal charges"; and (3) providing that the existence of a deferred-prosecution agreement "does not relieve the prosecuting agency of any duty to disclose exculpatory evidence.".

CHAPTER 15

THE PRELIMINARY HEARING

■ ■ ■

§ 4. PRELIMINARY HEARING PROCEDURES

A. APPLICATION OF THE RULES OF EVIDENCE

14th ed., p. 967; after Note 3 add:

4. *Self-incrimination and compelled statements.* In CITY OF HAYS, KANSAS V. VOGT, ___ U.S. ___, 138 S.Ct. 55, 198 L.Ed.2d 781 (2017), the Supreme Court (with Gorsuch, J., not participating) granted the petition for writ of certiorari, which set forth the following "question presented":

> "Whether the Fifth Amendment is violated when allegedly compelled statements are used at a probable cause hearing but not a criminal trial."

Following oral argument, the Court dismissed the writ of certiorari as improvidently granted. This ruling left in place the Tenth Circuit ruling and opinion in *Vogt v. City of Hays, Kansas*, 844 F.3d 1235 (10th Cir. 2017). The Tenth Circuit had answered "yes" to the question presented, relying on a reading of the self-incrimination clause inconsistent with that adopted in several other circuits.

City of Hays presented a § 1983 action brought by Vogt, formerly a police officer in the Hays police department. Vogt's complaint, in numbered paragraphs 11–27, set for the following factual allegations:

> "[11] While still employed as a Hays police officer, Plaintiff [Vogt] sought employment with the Haysville, Kansas police department * * *; [12] During his Haysville hiring process, Plaintiff disclosed that he had kept a knife for his personal use after coming into possession of it while working as a Hays police officer; [13] [Haysville] extended Plaintiff a conditional offer of employment * * * which was conditioned upon Plaintiff reporting the above information, and tendering the knife, to the Hays police department; [14] Haysville warned Plaintiff that they would follow-up with Hays to ensure that Plaintiff had complied with this condition of employment; [15] * * * Plaintiff complied with the condition of employment imposed by the Haysville police department in order to obtain employment with Haysville; [16] Chief Scheibler [of the Hays department] immediately compelled Plaintiff to document the facts related to his possession of the knife as a condition of his employment with the Hays police department and opened an internal investigation seeking only administrative policy violations; [17] In compliance with Chief Scheibler's order, Plaintiff wrote a vague one-sentence report related to his possession of the knife; [18] Having satisfied Haysville's conditions, Plaintiff submitted two weeks' notice of his resignation to the Hays police department so that he could accept employment with the Haysville police department; [19] Lt. Wright, who is responsible for internal investigations conducted by the Hays police department, compelled Plaintiff to give a statement while he was still employed by Hays as a condition of employment, during which Lt. Wright assured Plaintiff that he was seeking only policy violations and was not conducting a criminal investigation; [20] During the internal statement, Lt. Wright elicited further information about Plaintiff's

possession of the knife, including the type of police call Plaintiff was handling when he came into possession of the knife; [21] Lt. Wright used the additional detail elicited in Plaintiff's compelled internal statement as an investigatory lead to locate * * * an audio recording which captured the circumstances of how Plaintiff came into possession of the knife; [22] Using Plaintiff's compelled statements and fruits thereof against him, Chief Scheibler requested the Kansas Bureau of Investigation to initiate a criminal investigation * * *; [23] Lt. Wright produced all evidence gathered in his internal investigation, including Plaintiff's compelled statements and fruits thereof, to the [Bureau's] criminal investigator for use in the criminal proceedings against Plaintiff; [24] Because of the criminal investigation, the Haysville police department withdrew its offer of employment to Plaintiff; [25] Using Plaintiff's compelled statements and fruits thereof against him, Plaintiff was charged in early 2014 with two felony counts related to his possession of the knife * * * in the Ellis County, Kansas district court; [26] At Plaintiff's probable cause hearing in late 2014, Plaintiff's compelled statements and fruits thereof were used against him in a criminal case; [27] In separate rulings, a state magistrate judge and a state district court judge both determined that probable cause did not exist to bind Plaintiff over for trial and Plaintiff was dismissed from the criminal charges in early 2015." 2015 WL13636538

Vogt argued that the above facts established the liability of the City of Hays for violating Vogt's privilege against self-incrimination. Initially, the Hays police department had compelled Vogt's statements under the concept of compulsion established in *Garrity v. New Jersey* (14th ed., fn. c, p. 679).[a] The State of Kansas (not a party to the action) had subsequently made Vogt "a witness against himself" in a "criminal case" when it used that statement and its fruits in a Kansas preliminary hearing (a hearing in which the magistrate is directed to determine whether there is "probable cause to believe a felony has been committed").[b] Since § 1983 applies to a state actor who "causes" the citizen "to be subjected * * * to the deprivation" of a constitutional right, Hays had § 1983 responsibility for this element of the constitutional violation (i.e., in submitting the file to the Bureau for criminal investigation, it could reasonable foresee a subsequent prosecution in which that statement and derivative evidence was introduce against Vogt).

Vogt's theory of the case was successfully challenged on a motion to dismiss in the district court. *Vogt v. City of Hays, Kansas*, 2015 WL5730331 (D.Kan. 2015). That ruling focused on whether Vogt's statements (assuming they were compelled) had been used in a "criminal case." The Supreme Court's ruling in *Chavez v. Martinez* [14th ed., p. 652] had held that compulsion alone did not violate the self-incrimination clause; the compelled statement must also be utilized in "a criminal case" to render the individual "a witness against himself." A Tenth Circuit opinion had noted that the *Chavez* plurality "explicitly declined to decide 'the precise movement when a criminal case commences' for the purposes of the Fifth Amendment." The *Chavez* plurality had noted that " 'criminal case' at the very least requires the initiation of legal proceedings," but that

---

[a] Vogt also claimed that the City of Haysville had violated his privilege against self-incrimination by conditioning its job offer on Vogt making an incriminating statement to the Hays police department. The 10th Circuit rejected that claim. It reasoned that *Garrity* compulsion only applied where the state actor threatened to deny "some benefit * * * or right" that the declarant "already enjoyed."

[b] Kansas is not a jurisdiction in which the rules of evidence flatly do not apply to the preliminary hearing. See 14th ed., ch. 14, § 4 at p. 966. The Kansas Supreme Court has held that the rules of evidence should be applied in the preliminary hearing except where relaxed by statute. State v. Cremer, 234 Kan. 594, 676 P.3d 59 (1984). While many of the states that apply the rules of evidence at preliminary hearings do not recognize exclusionary rule objections there, see 14th ed., Note 4, p. 967, Kansas allows a "motion to suppress [a] confession or admission" to be made "prior to the preliminary examination or trial." See Kan.Stat.Ann. § 22–2101; State v. Teeter, 249 Kan. 548, 819 P.2d 651 (1991) (reviewing successful motion to suppress made at a preliminary hearing). The Tenth Circuit did not address Vogt's opportunity to preclude admission of his statement (and its fruits) at the preliminary hearing. As discussed infra, that opportunity was discussed in oral argument before the Supreme Court, and may have played a role in the Court's decision to dismiss the writ as improvidently granted.

left open "whether use of the compelled statement at some point before trial but after the initiation of criminal proceedings was actionable." The district court took note of opinions from several circuits indicating that earlier proceedings were part of a criminal case. *Sornberger v. City of Knoxville*, Illinois, 434 F.3d 1006 (7th Cir. 2006), concluded that the self-incrimination clause was violated where compelled statements had been used in a variety of pretrial proceedings (a probable cause hearing, a bail hearing, and at an arraignment before the trial court). The Ninth and Second Circuits later agreed. See *Higazy v. Templeton*, 505 F.3d 161 (2d Cir. 2007) ("an initial appearance which included the determination of whether he would be detained or released was part of the criminal case against Higazy"); *Stoot v. City of Everett*, 582 F.3d 910 (9th Cir. 2009) (a coerced confession has been "used [in a criminal case] * * * when it has been relied on" to file formal charges against the declarant, to determine judicially that the prosecution may proceed, and to determine pretrial custody status). On the other hand, relying on Supreme Court references to the self-incrimination privilege as a "trial right," the Third, Fourth, and Fifth Circuits had held that the self-incrimination clause is not violated unless the compelled statements (or its fruits) is "introduced at trial." Looking to similar statements in Tenth Circuit opinions, the district court concluded that "Tenth Circuit precedent" similarly precluded finding a self-incrimination violation in the case before it.

The Tenth Circuit, on appeal, reversed the district court dismissal, holding that the Vogt "adequately pleaded" a Fifth Amendment violation. *Vogt v. City of Hays, Kansas*, 844 F.3d 1235 (10th Cir. 2017).[c] The court acknowledged that its "precedents provide conflicting signals on whether the term 'criminal case' includes pretrial proceedings as well as the trial." Although Vogt alleged use of his statements "(1) to start an [internal police] investigation * * *, (2) to initiate a criminal investigation, (3) to bring criminal charges, and (4) to support the prosecution during the probable cause hearing," it was only necessary to address "whether the term 'criminal case' covers at least one pretrial proceeding: a hearing to determine probable cause." Based on the "text of Fifth Amendment, * * * interpret[ed] in light of the common understanding of the phrase 'criminal case,' " and the "Framers' understanding of the right against self-incrimination," that right clearly is shown to be "more than a trial right." As *Counselman v. Hitchcock* (14th ed., Note 1, p. 788) had recognized, the term "criminal case" is broader than the Sixth Amendment's "criminal prosecution," and "appears to encompass all of the proceedings involved in a 'criminal prosecution.' " Relevant sources (founding-era dictionaries and caselaw) indicate that the terms "case" and "cause" were used synonymously. Also, "there was consensus that the right against self-incrimination was not limited to the suspect's trial," as the "right against self-accusation was understood to arise primarily in pretrial or pre-prosecution settings [e.g., the grand jury] rather than in the context of a person's own criminal trial, * * * [where] criminal defendants were then unable to testify." While it was true that "courts have held in other contexts that evidence may be used in pretrial proceedings [such as preliminary hearings] even if the evidence would be inadmissible at trial, * * * [t]he defendant's attempt to impart this practice into the Fifth Amendment context * * * avoids the question by assuming that use of compelled statements in pretrial proceedings is not rendered inadmissible by the Fifth Amendment."

---

[c]   A concurring opinion emphasized that the court had addressed "only issues raised by the parties," leaving unanswered four questions: (1) "Even though the Fifth Amendment privilege * * * can be violated by use of the defendant's statement at a probable cause hearing, can there be a violation when such use does not cause a criminal sanction to be imposed on the defendant (such as when, as here, the court does not find probable cause)"; (2) "When a person voluntarily disclosed information to a government agency, does he or she thereby waive any Fifth Amendment objection to disclosing that same information to another agency"; (3) "Under what circumstances can an employee who has given notice of resignation claim that a request for incriminatory information was coercive?" And "most significantly, (4) In light of post-*Garrity* developments in Fifth Amendment doctrine, if a public employee believes that he or she is being coerced * * *, must the employee invoke the privilege by refusing to provide information, or can the employee still, as in *Garrity*, provide the information and then demand immunity from use. See Peter Westen, *Answering Self-Incriminating Questions or be Fired*, 37 Am.J.Crim.L. 97 (2010).

After certiorari was granted, the Supreme Court granted the motion of the United States Solicitor General to participate in oral argument as amicus curiae (supporting petitioner City of Hays). In their briefs and oral arguments, neither Hays nor the Solicitor General challenged the conclusion that the probable cause hearing was part of the "criminal case." Rather, they argued, the critical issue was what use of the compelled statement required the declarant to be "a witness against himself." On that issue, they advanced the following position, as set forth in the Solicitor General's brief: "The text of the Self-Incrimination Clause, interpreted in light of its purpose, prohibits reliance on a criminal defendant's compelled statements to convict or punish him. Such use compel[s] the defendant to be a witness against himself in a criminal case. * * * But a defendant does not stand as 'a witness against himself' when his statements are used for other purposes in pretrial proceedings, such as to determine whether he is competent to stand trial or whether probable cause exists for the case to proceed. Those proceedings may remove procedural barriers to further prosecution, but they do not 'enlist the defendant as an instrument in his or her own condemnation' because they do not resolve the ultimate questions of guilt and punishment.[d] *Mitchell v. United States* [14th ed., Note 1(c)(iii), p. 1417]." 2017 WL 5592696.

The respondent Vogt's brief argued that looking to the "witness against" phrase did not undercut the Tenth Circuit's conclusion: "Petitioner does not dispute that 'criminal case' includes the probable cause hearing here, which was an adversarial proceeding before a judge that took place after Officer Vogt was criminally charged and was held for the purpose of assessing the evidence of his guilt. Petitioner now argues instead that the phrase 'witness against himself' limits the Clause's protection to criminal trials, but that phrase simply describes the type of evidence covered by the Clause—namely, evidence that is testimonial and incriminating in character. The phrase 'in a criminal case,' by contrast, describes the setting in which the proscription applies. A defendant is just as much a 'witness against himself' when his compelled, incriminating, and testimonial statement is admitted as evidence of his guilt at an in-court probable cause hearing as he would be if it were admitted at a subsequent trial. * * * The courtroom use of Officer Vogt's compelled testimony at the probable cause hearing to demonstrate his criminal guilt is directly contrary to the purpose of the Fifth Amendment, which is designed to prevent incriminating uses of statements throughout a criminal case, not just in the proceedings that ultimately determine guilt and punishment."[e]

In oral argument, apart from discussion of the appropriate interpretation of the Fifth Amendment, several Justices raised issues relating to the record. Justice Sotomayor initially asked what the record reflected as to "Respondent * * * [filing] a motion to suppress his statements or object at the probable cause hearing to their admission." She further noted, "If you don't object to the admission of a statement, you've waived that objection." Counsel for Hays noted that such a motion (which could be made in Kansas, see note b supra) was not reflected in the record and his "understanding" was that such a motion had not been filed. Justice Breyer noted that he could not find in the record before the Court any indication Vogt had objected at the preliminary hearing, and, indeed, "couldn't find any instance where any of the compelled statements were introduced into the preliminary hearing."[f] He further noted, with support from Chief Justice Roberts, that

[d]   The Solicitor General's brief noted that this focus on "exposure to criminal penalties, rather than procedural steps in a case" was not unique: "The [Supreme] Court's interpretation of the Confrontation Clause, which uses the same phrase 'witness against' to grant only a trial right, reinforces [the above interpretation]." As to the Confrontation Clause and the preliminary hearing, see 14th ed., Note 1, p. 667.

[e]   In the oral argument, several justices directed the attorneys to consider the scope of the pretrial proceedings that might be encompassed under this analysis—in particular, whether it would extend to the government's use of compelled statements in the grand jury proceeding (see Note 5, Supp., p. 127), the competency-to-stand-trial proceeding (and the bearing of *Estelle v. Smith*, 14th ed., Note 34, p. 633), and the *Gerstein* determination (14th ed., Note 8, p. 311).

[f]   The Tenth Circuit in footnote 7 of its opinion had rejected the "defendants argu[ment] that Mr. Vogt is not entitled to rely upon an inference that his alleged admissions were 'admitted into evidence through witness testimony' " in light of the magistrate's dismissal of the charges. The court responded that since Mr. Vogt's complaint

the matters not present in the record "in my mind raises the question as to whether this is, in fact, an appropriate case or controversy for the court to take." At another point, counsel for Vogt noted that a decision at this point might be premature, in light of the remaining questions (as noted in the concurring opinion, see fn. c supra) and "to 'DIG' the case as improvidently granted" might be appropriate. Of course, in later dismissing the case, the Court did not set forth its reasons for concluding that certiorari was improvidently granted.

stated that the "compelled statements and fruits thereof were used against him in a criminal case, we can reasonably infer that these statements were used to support probable cause."

CHAPTER 16

GRAND JURY REVIEW

■ ■ ■

§ 3. CHALLENGES TO THE EVIDENCE BEFORE THE GRAND JURY

14th ed., p. 991; after the first paragraph of Note 5, add:

The Supreme court opinions extending *Costello* to unconstitutionally obtained evidence included references to instances of grand jury consideration of statements produced through compulsion prohibited under the Fifth Amendment's self-incrimination clause. See CRIMPROC § 15.5(a). In the course of oral argument in *City of Hays v. Vogt*, Justice Breyer advanced a limited reading of the application of *Costello* to such evidence; while a challenge to the indictment is barred, presentation of a compelled statement before the grand jury still should constitute a self-incrimination violation, with other procedural avenues available to prevent or remedy that violation.

As discussed in Note 4 of Ch. 15, § 4(A), Supp., p. 119, certiorari was granted in *City of Hays* to review a § 1983 ruling in which the lower court concluded that prosecution use of an accused's compelled statement in a probable cause hearing violated the accused's privilege against self-incrimination. In the course of exploring whether the reasoning of that ruling would also apply to prosecution use in a grand jury proceeding, Justice Breyer initially noted: "[S]upreme Court cases refer to a grand jury proceeding as part of a criminal case, and you cannot introduce it in a criminal case. * * * [Y]ou can't attack a grand jury proceeding later, but that's different." Official Transcript, p. 8, 2018 WL136809. Subsequently, Justice Breyer added: "I don't know what the answer is in a grand jury proceeding. I do know that you can't attack that proceeding at trial, but I don't know whether, as in this case, somebody might, if they were used, bring a § 1983 claim * * *. And I don't know what would happen if, because of the circumstance, the defendant went before a judge [prior to the grand jury proceeding] and said: Judge, keep that piece of paper [i.e., the compelled statement] out of the grand jury proceedings." Official Transcript p. 15, 2018 WL1368609. Justice Alito subsequently asked petitioner's counsel whether he "was familiar with any cases * * * in federal law that allow a person who thinks that he or she may be under investigation by a grand jury to go to a federal judge and file a motion in limine regarding the evidence that may be presented to the grand jury?" Counsel replied, "I am not," and Justice Alito responded: "This would be revolutionary, wouldn't it?" Official Transcript, p. 21, 2018 WL136809.[2]

---

[2]   In an earlier dialogue with petitioner's counsel, Justice Breyer had noted: "Where are the cases that say that even though the person objected [in a preindictment proceeding], you can introduce it to the grand jury"; and counsel responded: "I agree that, I am not aware of any case where the defendant tries to stop the information from being presented to the grand jury." Official Transcript, p. 9, 2018 WL1368609. Neither the briefs nor the oral argument discussed the history in the federal courts of the action in equity to gain return of property obtained illegally by federal agents, sometimes to be accompanied by a court order prohibiting further use of the fruits of that illegal action.

Prior to the adoption of the Federal Rules of Criminal Procedures, the Supreme Court, in a series of rulings, recognized that an independent equity action could be brought preindictment to obtain the return of property that had been unconstitutionally seized by federal law enforcement officers. Moreover, the relief granted could include prohibiting those officers from making further use of that seizure, including related testimony before a grand jury. See CRIMPROC § 8.9(a). This position was later thought to be incorporated in Federal Rule 41(e), which provided for a "motion for return of property and to suppress evidence," available to "a person aggrieved by an unlawful search

---

and seizure." That motion did not specify the time for making the motion and was held to be available preindictment. As a result of amendments discussed infra, Rule 41 now separates the "motion to suppress," which is a pretrial motion, and the "motion to return property," which may be made preindictment and provides for both returning the property and "impos[ing] reasonable conditions to protect access to the property and its use in later proceedings." See Fed.R.Crim.P. 41(g) (motion to return), 41(h) motion to suppress.

In an action relying on the original version of Rule 41(e), a divided Second Circuit held that the district court had authority to entertain a preindictment petition for suppression of a confession allegedly obtained by police actions constituting coercion under the self-incrimination clause. *In re Fried*, 161 F.2d 453 (2d Cir. 1947), cert. granted, 331 U.S. 804, writ dismissed on motion of petitioner, 332 U.S. 807 (1947). The Second Circuit rejected the government's argument that the authority recognized in earlier Supreme Court cases and in Rule 41(e) did not apply because: "[It] rests on—is inseparably tied up with—the 'property' of the person from whom the article was taken, to have it returned to him, [while] a confession, even if written and signed, is an intangible which cannot be returned to the confessant [and] memory of its contents cannot be eradicated from members of the officials." That argument, the majority noted, failed to account for Rule 41(e)'s reference to a suppression remedy and failed to recognize that suppression following the issuance of an indictment is not a satisfactory remedy, as "a wrongful indictment" in itself causes great harm. This position was later supported by the Fourth Circuit, but questioned by the First Circuit. See CRIMPROC § 8.9(a).

Following the Supreme Court's ruling in *Calandra* and the references to *Costello* extending to unconstitutionally obtained evidence, Rule 41 was amended to separate the motion for return of property and the motion to suppress. The Advisory Committee noted: "Rule 41(e) is not intended to deny the United States the use of evidence permitted by the fourth amendment and federal statutes, even if the evidence might have been unlawfully seized. *United States v. Calandra*, 414 U.S. 338, 349 (1974) ('Rule 41(e) does not constitute a statutory expansion of the exclusionary rule')." The Committee also noted that, "if the United States has a need for the property in an investigation * * *, its retention of the property generally is reasonable." In light of this commentary, and a reading of *Calandra* as "clearly impl[ying] that the target of the government's investigation may not use * * * [the motion to return] to prevent the grand jury from having access to illegally obtained evidence," lower courts have shaped relief to preserve the government's continued use of the illegally seized property (e.g., providing copies to the owner in the case of documents or allowing the government to retain possession with the owner granted access). See CRIMPROC § 8.9(a).

CHAPTER 19

JOINDER AND SEVERANCE

∎ ∎ ∎

§ 2. FAILURE TO JOIN RELATED OFFENSES

14th ed., p. 1085; replacing Note 2, add:

2.   *Defendant-caused severance.* In CURRIER v. VIRGINIA, 138 S.Ct. 2144 (2018), Currier, charged with burglary, grand larceny and unlawful possession of a firearm by a convicted felon, sought a severance of the latter charge, concerned that certain evidence as to it, his prior burglary and larceny convictions, might prejudice the jury's consideration of the other charges. He and the government agreed to a severance and that the burglary and larceny charges should be tried first. Acquitted in the first trial, he then sought to stop the second trial, arguing that it would amount to double jeopardy, but the trial court disagreed, and Currier was then convicted on the felony-in-possession charge. Gorsuch, J., for five Justices, rejecting Currier's claim that the severance and conviction violated the Double Jeopardy Clause, concluded that *Jeffers v United States*, 14th ed., p. 1079, "points the other way":

"What was true in *Jeffers*, we hold, can be no less true here. If a defendant's consent to two trials can overcome concerns lying at the historic core of the Double Jeopardy Clause, so too we think it must overcome a double jeopardy complaint under *Ashe*. Nor does anything in *Jeffers* suggest that the outcome should be different if the first trial yielded an acquittal rather than a conviction when a defendant consents to severance. While we acknowledge that *Ashe*'s protections apply only to trials following acquittals, as a general rule, the Double Jeopardy Clause " 'protects against a second prosecution for the same offense after conviction' " as well as " 'against a second prosecution for the same offense after acquittal.' " Because the Clause applies equally in both situations, consent to a second trial should in general have equal effect in both situations. * * *

"Mr. Currier replies that he had no real choice but to seek two trials. Without a second trial, he says, evidence of his prior convictions would have tainted the jury's consideration of the burglary and larceny charges. And, he notes, Virginia law guarantees a severance in cases like his unless the defendant and prosecution agree to a single trial. But no one disputes that the Constitution permitted Virginia to try all three charges at once with appropriate cautionary instructions. So this simply isn't a case where the defendant had to give up one constitutional right to secure another. Instead, Mr. Currier faced a lawful choice between two courses of action that each bore potential costs and rationally attractive benefits. It might have been a hard choice. But litigants every day face difficult decisions."

Concluding that those points "suffice to resolve this case in a full and proper way," Justice Kennedy did not join the balance of the Gorsuch opinion, where four Justices went on to conclude that civil issue preclusion principles cannot be imported into the criminal law via the Double Jeopardy Clause to prevent parties from retrying any issue or retrying any evidence about a previously tried issue. Thus, even assuming Currier's consent to holding a second trial didn't more broadly imply consent to the manner in which it was conducted, his argument must be rejected.

A dissent by Justice Ginsburg, for four Justices, citing *Ashe* for the proposition that the Double Jeopardy Clause also shields "the issue-preclusion effect of an acquittal," and distinguishing *Jeffers* because it "presented a claim-preclusion question," rejected the notion "that

Currier surrendered his right to assert the issue-preclusive effect of his first-trial acquittals by consenting to two trials. * * *

"Currier took no action inconsistent with assertion of an issue-preclusion plea. To understand why, one must comprehend just what issue preclusion forecloses. Unlike the right against a second trial for the same offense (claim preclusion), issue preclusion prevents relitigation of a previously rejected theory of criminal liability without necessarily barring a successive trial. Take *Ashe*, for example. Issue preclusion prevented the prosecution from arguing, at a second trial, that Ashe was one of the robbers who held up the poker players at gunpoint. But if the prosecution sought to prove, instead, that Ashe waited outside during the robbery and then drove the getaway car, issue preclusion would not have barred that trial. Similarly here, the prosecution could not again attempt to prove that Currier participated in the break-in and theft of the safe at the Garrisons' residence. But a second trial could be mounted if the prosecution alleged, for instance, that Currier was present at the river's edge when others showed up to dump the safe in the river, and that Currier helped to empty out and replace the guns contained in the safe."

CHAPTER 20

SPEEDY TRIAL AND OTHER SPEEDY DISPOSITION

■ ■ ■

§ 2.   OTHER SPEEDY DISPOSITION

14th ed., p. 1120; end of Note 4, add:

Regarding the source and dimensions of any post-trial right to "speedy" disposition, consider BETTERMAN v. MONTANA, 136 S.Ct. 1609 (2016), holding that "the Sixth Amendment's speedy trial guarantee * * * does not apply once a defendant has been found guilty at trial or has pled guilty to criminal charges," for "[a]s a measure protecting the presumptively innocent, the speedy trial right—like other similarly aimed measures—loses force upon conviction." Such a reading of the Sixth Amendment, the Court emphasized, "comports with the historical understanding," as "[a]t the founding, 'accused' described a status preceding 'convicted,'" "[a]nd 'trial' meant a discrete episode after which judgment (i.e., sentencing) would follow."

"The sole remedy for a violation of the speedy trial right—dismissal of the charges—fits the preconviction focus of the Clause. It would be an unjustified windfall, in most cases, to remedy sentencing delay by vacating validly obtained convictions. Betterman concedes that a dismissal remedy ordinarily would not be in order once a defendant has been convicted. * * *

"As we have explained, at the third phase of the criminal-justice process, i.e., between conviction and sentencing, the Constitution's presumption-of-innocence-protective speedy trial right is not engaged. That does not mean, however, that defendants lack any protection against undue delay at this stage. The primary safeguard comes from statutes and rules. The federal rule on point directs the court to "impose sentence without unnecessary delay." Fed. Rule Crim. Proc. 32(b)(1). Many States have provisions to the same effect, and some States prescribe numerical time limits. Further, as at the prearrest stage, due process serves as a backstop against exorbitant delay. After conviction, a defendant's due process right to liberty, while diminished, is still present. He retains an interest in a sentencing proceeding that is fundamentally fair. But because Betterman advanced no due process claim here, we express no opinion on how he might fare under that more pliable standard."

PART 4

THE ADVERSARY SYSTEM AND THE DETERMINATION OF GUILT OR INNOCENCE

■ ■ ■

CHAPTER 22

GUILTY PLEAS

■ ■ ■

§ 1. SOME VIEWS OF NEGOTIATED PLEAS

C. ACCURATE AND FAIR RESULTS

14th ed., p. 1192; before Note 9, add:

Compare Albert Alschuler, *A Nearly Perfect System for Convicting the Innocent*, 79 Alb.L.Rev. 919, 919–21 (2016): "Convicting defendants who would be acquitted at trial is one of the principal goals of plea bargaining. 'Half a loaf is better than none,' prosecutors say. 'When we have a weak case for any reason, we'll reduce to almost anything rather than lose.' If the correlation between 'weak cases' and actual innocence is better than random, plea bargaining surely 'convict[s] defendants who are in fact innocent (and would be acquitted [at trial]).'

"Prosecutors engage in both 'odds bargaining' and 'costs bargaining.' That is, they bargain both to ensure conviction in doubtful cases and to save the costs of trial. Were a prosecutor to engage in odds bargaining alone, he might estimate a defendant's chance of conviction at trial at 50% and this defendant's probable sentence if convicted at trial at ten years. Splitting the difference, the prosecutor then might offer to recommend a sentence of five years in exchange for a plea of guilty. Five years is what economists would call the defendant's 'expected' sentence—his predicted post-trial sentence discounted by the possibility of acquittal.

"An offer of five years, however, would leave a risk-neutral defendant indifferent between pleading guilty and standing trial, and the prosecutor hopes to avoid a trial. He does not want the defendant to be indifferent. The prosecutor therefore engages in costs bargaining as well as odds bargaining. He tailors his final offer, not to balance, but to overbalance the defendant's chances of acquittal. This prosecutor may offer four years in exchange for a plea—or two or three. One can easily discover real-world cases in which prosecutors fearful of defeat at trial have struck bargains allowing defendants facing potential life sentences to plead guilty to misdemeanors.

"When a prosecutor has no chance of obtaining a conviction at trial, he may be unable to make an offer that will overbalance the defendant's chances of acquittal. In every other case, however, the prosecutor can reduce the offered punishment to the point that it will become advantageous for the defendant to plead guilty whether he is guilty or innocent."

§ 2. REJECTED, KEPT AND BROKEN BARGAINS; UNREALIZED EXPECTATIONS

14th ed., p. 1203; before Note 6, add:

5A. *FOIA Waivers.* In *Price v. U.S. Department of Justice Attorney Office*, 865 F.3d 676 (D.C.Cir.2017), the court (after quoting Justice O'Connor's concurrence in *Town of Newton v. Rummery*, 480 U.S. 386 (19876), stating that a "prosecutor is permitted to consider only legitimate criminal justice concerns in striking [a plea] bargain—concerns such as rehabilitation, allocation of criminal justice resources, the strength of the evidence against the defendant, and the extent of [a defendant's] cooperation with the authorities") declared that "[t]his set of legitimate interests places boundaries on the rights that can be bargained away in plea negotiations." Hence, the court deemed invalid a prosecutor's inclusion in a plea agreement of a requirement that the defendant waive his federal statutory right to seek records related to his case under the Freedom of Information Act, given the government's failure to assert "any legitimate criminal-justice interest served by allowing the FOIA waivers in plea agreements."

The court stated that "Price has shown, through real-world examples, that enforcing a FOIA waiver would make it harder for litigants in his position to discover potentially exculpatory information or material supporting an ineffective-assistance-of-counsel claim. This is especially true given that, 'with rare exceptions, only the waivor' in such cases 'has the requisite knowledge and interest to lodge a FOIA request in the first place.' On the other side of the scale, the government has offered us nothing more than the unsupported blanket assertion that FOIA waivers assist in effective and efficient prosecution, without any support or explanation how. Under these particular circumstances, and based on the briefing in this case, we have little trouble in concluding that the public interest in enforcing Price's waiver is outweighed by the harm to public policy that enforcement would cause.

The dissent asserted than "[w]hen overcharging defendants, withholding material information, and permitting defendants to misperceive the evidence against them are all acceptable means to achieve the 'legitimate criminal-justice' objectives of a knowing, voluntary, and intelligent guilty plea, it makes no sense to insist limited FOIA waivers require satisfying an additional 'legitimate criminal-justice' interest,' especially since as a general matter there are 'multiple 'legitimate criminal-justice' objectives served by FOIA waivers—including the safeguarding of both scarce investigative resources and information within FOIA material that an inmate could use to harm victims or third-parties."

14th ed., p. 1207; replace Note 4:

4.   *Varieties and benefits of judicial participation.* A 2016 study collected interviews of nearly one hundred judges, prosecutors, and defense attorneys from ten of the many states whose law does not prohibit judicial involvement before a plea is tendered, revealing a surprising variety of ways that judges participate in plea bargaining. Nancy J. King and Ronald F. Wright, *The Invisible Revolution in Plea Bargaining: Managerial Judging and Judicial Participation in Negotiations*, 95 Tex.L.Rev. 325 (2016).

Most commonly reported was a short meeting about sentencing early in the process, between the judge, prosecutor, and defense counsel. Usually the attorneys begin this conversation by summarizing key evidence, the defendant's criminal history, and scoring under sentencing guidelines, if applicable. If the parties have already reached a tentative sentence deal, the judge states whether that recommended or stipulated sentence would be acceptable. If the parties have not agreed on a recommended sentence, the judge responds with language along the lines of, "Based on the information I have now, this is what I would give him if he decides to plead guilty." The conference may be off the record in chambers, or on the record in open court or at the bench. A handful of interviewees reported that when these conversations take place in open court on the record, the defendant is sometimes present. In several states, judges hold group conferences with the attorneys for all of the cases on the day's docket present at once, allowing them to chime in on each other's cases. Case law, statutes, and court rules often control these conferences, regulating such features as whether or not the meeting may be initiated by the judge, what judges can and cannot say, provision of discovery to the defense, preparation of information for the judge, plea withdrawal if a judge who accepts a sentence at the conference later changes her mind at sentencing, and whether a different judge must preside should the defendant end up going to trial.

In many counties with multiple judges, the study revealed, these early conferences are part of a formal process called "differentiated case management," which tracks those cases that are more likely to settle to specialized dockets or to judges other than those who handle cases headed for trial. These settlement tracks have various names, including "home court," "early case resolution," "early disposition docket," and "administrative term." One jurisdiction reportedly has a settlement court set up at the jail. Maryland courts staff their "preliminary disposition dockets," or "resolution conferences" with retired judges. Cases that do not settle go to a different judge for trial.

In two of the states, Oregon and Kansas, interviewees reported full-fledged judicial mediation in felony cases. Led by a judge approved by both sides, these mediations may include detailed "Best Practice" guides for the judges, attorneys, and probation officers who participate; "shuttle diplomacy" where the judge meets with one side then the next; risk assessments for each defendant; and sometimes the participation of victims, defendants, or even the defendant's family. Another innovation is formal authorization for felony court judges to function as lower court judges so that they may talk to the parties about sentencing before the preliminary hearing.

Interviewees from jurisdictions that embraced judicial participation in the negotiation phase reported that by reducing uncertainty for both sides and prompting lawyers to evaluate their cases sooner, judicial involvement helps parties reach agreements earlier than they would without the judge's input. Earlier pleas help avoid the costs of eve-of-trial settlements that waste juror time, and unnecessary pretrial detention, for example. And when the parties seek an unusually low sentence, the opportunity to answer the judge's questions in advance helps prevent delays.

Judges reported that early involvement also allows them to suggest options for sentencing that the parties overlook, and to remedy attorney error. Prosecutors found the judge's input helped them manage relationships with police, victims, and the public. Interviewees were unconcerned that these conversations about sentence occurred without presentence reports, as the judge generally had access to information at the conference that was the same or better than information available at sentencing. Nor was there much concern that the judge's participation would force defendants to settle before they received the information they needed. Rather, most interviewees reported that the defense received discovery before the conference, and that the conference allowed the defense to hear the prosecutor answer questions from the judge, questions that the prosecutor might never address in negotiations with defense counsel alone. Judges, it was widely reported, sometimes indicated a preference for a sentence lower than the prosecutor's offer, or persuaded a prosecutor to accept more lenient sentence terms by pointing out evidentiary weaknesses, resisting draconian applications of rigid prosecutorial policy, or educating an inexperienced or overzealous assistant. Concluded the authors, "interviewees suggested that by increasing the information available to a defendant and creating a sentencing option that is often more moderate than the prosecutor's offer, judicial participation can make an already coercive situation a little less so."

But consider Darryl Brown, *The Judicial Role in Criminal Charging and Plea Bargaining*, 46 Hofstra L.Rev. 63, 81 (2017), taking note of the "general asymmetrical structure of judicial power over charges in this setting," as "judges have more discretion to reject charges in proposed plea bargains on public-interest grounds because they are too lenient than because they are too harsh. This is because prosecutors' initial charging decisions set an implicit baseline for judicial authority regarding guilty pleas (they set no such baseline for prosecutors themselves, who are generally free to file additional charges). Judges can and do reject plea bargains because the parties have proposed to dismiss too many charges (or the wrong charges) as part of a negotiated plea deal. That is, they can rule that the bargain is too lenient for the court to approve, judged against the initial charging document and the evidence in support of it. But judges are on much thinner ground if they want to reject bargains as against the public interest because a defendant has agreed to plead guilty to all filed charges, even if the judge views those as too severe in light of the defendant's conduct. To describe the law of judicial authority in this context differently, judges' power over plea bargains is generally structured more as a check against prosecutors departing from their initial charging decision in the direction of leniency than as a check against unduly severe charging and plea bargain decisions by prosecutors."

14th ed., p. 1208; before last paragraph in Note 5, add:

In those jurisdictions that permit a judge, either incident to or apart from plea bargaining, to provide what are variously characterized as nonbinding "indicated sentences" or "sentencing inclinations," it is generally agreed, as stated in *State v. Sanney,* 404 P.3d 280 (Haw.2017): "If a defendant pleads guilty or no contest in response to a court's sentencing inclination, but the court later decides not to follow the inclination, then the court must so advise the defendant and provide the defendant with the opportunity to affirm or withdraw the plea of guilty or no contest."

14th ed., p. 1211; before paragraph d, add:

cc. *Acquittal of related offender.* In *People v. Fisher*, 71 N.E.3d 932 (N.Y.2017), defendant, charged with hindering prosecution by hiding a gun used by Roche in a fatal shooting, pled guilty but thereafter sought to withdraw his plea after Roche was acquitted of murder, claiming that "his guilt is inextricably tied to Roche's criminal liability, rendering him innocent if Roche is acquitted." The court responded that "the elements of * * * hindering prosecution were established at defendant's plea allocution when he admitted rendering criminal assistance to Roche, who defendant further admitted had committed second-degree murder."

14th ed., p. 1215; paragraph b, after *Underwood*, add:

But consider *United States v. Doe*, 865 F.3d 1295 (10th Cir.2017) ("In order to trigger good-faith review of a prosecutor's discretionary refusal to file a substantial-assistance motion, a defendant must first allege that the government acted in bad faith. The government may then rebut that allegation by providing its reasons for refusing to file the motion. Assuming those reasons are at least facially plausible, we hold that a defendant is only entitled to good-faith review if he or she "produce[s] evidence giving reason to question the justification [the government] advanced."

14th ed., p. 1216; in lieu of *Freeman* case in paragraph d, add:

In HUGHES v. UNITED STATES, 138 S.Ct. 1765 (2018), Hughes, indicted on drug and gun charges, entered into a Type-C plea agreement, per Fed.R.Crim.P. 11 (c)(1)(C), which stipulated he would receive a sentence of 180 months but did not refer to a particular Sentencing Guidelines range. After his guilty plea, the district court accepted the agreement and sentenced him to 180 months, calculating his Guidelines range as 188–235 months and determining that the sentence was in accordance with the Guidelines and other factors the court was required to consider. Shortly thereafter, the Sentencing commission adopted, and made retroactive, an amendment reducing Hughes sentencing range to 151–188 months, but the lower courts denied his motion for a reduced sentence because his plea agreement did not expressly rely on a Guidelines range. Kennedy, J., for six Justices, concluded:

"A sentence imposed pursuant to a Type-C agreement is no exception to the general rule that a defendant's Guidelines range is both the starting point and a basis for his ultimate sentence. Although in a Type-C agreement the Government and the defendant may agree to a specific sentence, that bargain is contingent on the district court accepting the agreement and its stipulated sentence. The Sentencing Guidelines prohibit district courts from accepting Type-C agreements without first evaluating the recommended sentence in light of the defendant's Guidelines range. So in the usual case the court's acceptance of a Type-C agreement and the sentence to be imposed pursuant to that agreement are 'based on' the defendant's Guidelines range.

"To be sure, the Guidelines are advisory only, and so not every sentence will be consistent with the relevant Guidelines range. See *Koons v. United States*, [138 S.Ct. 1783 (2018)]. For example, in *Koons* the Court today holds that five defendants' sentences were not 'based on' subsequently lowered Guidelines ranges because in that case the Guidelines and the record make clear that the sentencing judge 'discarded' their sentencing ranges 'in favor of mandatory minimums and substantial-assistance factors.' * * *

"If the Guidelines range was not 'a relevant part of the analytic framework the judge used to determine the sentence or to approve the agreement,' then the defendant's sentence was not based on that sentencing range, and relief under § 3582(c)(2) is unavailable. * * * Still, cases like *Koons* are a narrow exception to the general rule that, in most cases, a defendant's sentence will be 'based on' his Guidelines range. In federal sentencing the Guidelines are a district court's starting point, so when the Commission lowers a defendant's Guidelines range the defendant will be eligible for relief under § 3582(c)(2) absent clear demonstration, based on the record as a whole, that the court would have imposed the same sentence regardless of the Guidelines.

"[T]he Government contends that allowing defendants who enter Type-C agreements to seek reduced sentences under § 3582(c)(2) would deprive the Government of one of the benefits of its bargain—namely, the defendant's agreement to a particular sentence. But that has nothing to do with whether a defendant's sentence was based on the Sentencing Guidelines under § 3582(c)(2). And in any event, '[w]hat is at stake in this case is a defendant's eligibility for relief, not the extent of that relief.' Even if a defendant is eligible for relief, before a district court grants a reduction it must consider "the factors set forth in section 3553(a) to the extent that they are applicable' and the Commission's 'applicable policy statements.' The district court can consider the benefits the defendant gained by entering a Type-C agreement when it decides whether a reduction is appropriate (or when it determines the extent of any reduction), 'for the statute permits but does not require the court to reduce a sentence.'"

Roberts, J., for the three dissenters, objected: "With a Type-C agreement, the sentence is set by the parties, not by a judge applying the Guidelines. Far from being 'artificial,' that distinction is central to what makes a Type-C plea a Type-C plea. * * *

"The Government may well be able to limit the frustrating effects of today's decision in the long run. Going forward, it presumably can add a provision to every Type-C agreement in which the defendant agrees to waive any right to seek a sentence reduction following future Guidelines amendments."

14th ed., p. 1217; before paragraph e, add:

As illustrated by *United States v. Ritchison*, 887 F.3d 365 (8th Cir.2018), the nature of the plea agreement may affect the extent to which a subsequent advantageous change in the law is deemed to require "adjustment" of the defendant's sentence. Ritchison was charged with one count of being a felon in possession of a firearm, and the indictment also alleged he had two prior felony convictions for burglary and one for robbery, but the parties entered into a Rule 11(c)(1)(C) plea agreement—that is, one in which the prosecutor "agree[s] that a specific sentence or sentencing range is the appropriate disposition of the case"—that if the Armed Career Criminal Act, 18 U.S.C.A. § 924(e)(1), applied he would receive a sentence of 15 years, but otherwise a sentence of 10 years. Because each of Ritchison's priors constituted a "violent felony" under the ACCA, his mandatory minimum sentence was 15 years and his Guidelines range was 180 to 210 months. But when, as a result of the Supreme Court's later decision in *Johnson v. United States*, 135 S.Ct. 2551 (2015), his two prior burglary convictions no longer qualified as ACCA predicate offenses, Ritchison moved to vacate his sentence pursuant to 28 U.S.C.A. § 2255. Upon being resentenced to 10 years, he objected, arguing that "the plea agreement was now null and void because it was based on a mutual mistake of the parties," and thus "requested a sentence within the revised

Guidelines range" of 63 to 78 months, to no avail. On appeal, the court noted Ritchison's argument "that in prior cases, we have held that revisiting the entire sentence was an acceptable option under § 2255," but responded that in those cases "the district court was faced with resentencing a defendant who had been sentenced based on multiple convictions that were interdependent," while in the instant case the parties "entered a binding plea agreement on one count of conviction." "Under these circumstances, an appropriate correction to the sentence was to enforce the parties binding agreement, which specifically contemplated the possibility that Ritchison's criminal history might not trigger the enhanced penalties of the ACCA." As for Ritchison's alternative argument that the plea agreement was voidable because "negotiated based on a mutual mistake regarding the validity of the ACCA's residual clause," the court responded: "One contract principle we have declined to extend to the plea agreement context is the doctrine of mutual mistake."

14th ed., p. 1218; add to fn. k:

Compare *People v. Shinaul*, 88 N.E.3d 760 (Ill.2017), where defendant pled guilty to aggravated use of a weapon in exchange for the state dropping all remaining charges, but four years later defendant was able to overturn his guilty plea on the ground that the applicable statute was facially unconstitutional. The state then attempted to reinstate some of the nol-prossed charges, but was unsuccessful because the statute of limitations had run. While the state objected such a result "could have a chilling effect on the plea bargaining process," the court was unsympathetic, noting "that prosecutors in other jurisdictions have contracted with defendants to avoid the statute of limitations defense."

§ 3. THE ROLE AND RESPONSIBILITY OF DEFENSE COUNSEL

14th ed., p. 1222; at end of fn. a, add:

Moody, deemed "binding precedent," was reluctantly followed in *Turner v. United States*, 848 F.3d 767 (6th Cir.2017), noting that at least nine other circuits follow either such a bright-line rule or a rebuttal presumption that the right to counsel attaches only after formal charges are filed. In *State v. Farfan-Galvan*, 161 Idaho 610, 389 P.3d 155 (2016), noting "the practice by certain prosecuting entities of initiating contact with defendants while they are in custody in advance of their initial appearance or arraignment in order to extend plea offers which, if not accepted, expire at the time of the initial appearance or arraignment," thus "dissuading indigent defendants from seeking the assistance of court-appointed counsel to evaluate the offer," the court concluded such conduct violated the state's Rules of Professional Conduct.

14th ed., p. 1229; before Note 3, add:

2A. *Negotiation.* "In the early phases of the negotiation, the defense attorney should begin with a competitive strategy, but in a cooperative style. Even though several practice manuals suggest that defense attorneys should be extremely cooperative and seek to achieve a guilty plea agreement early in plea bargaining, negotiation theory establishes at least four reasons that the defense attorney's early tactics should be competitive. First, the government's opening demand, usually characterized by overcharging and excessively long legislatively-determined prison sentences, is very competitive. [A] * * * negotiator who uses a cooperative strategy against a competitive negotiator is severely disadvantaged. Thus, a defense attorney risks exploitation if he begins negotiations with a cooperative strategy. Second, the defendant usually has low bargaining power; some social scientists recommend that the less powerful negotiator begin competitively and become more cooperative later in the negotiation. Third, it may be necessary to adopt a competitive strategy initially to communicate to the prosecutor that the attorney intends to zealously represent the client and that he will not 'cave in' because of his caseload or other personal or institutional pressures. Finally, early competitive moves often convince the client that his attorney intends to represent him vigorously; this improves client relations. * * * The defense attorney should attempt to obtain unilateral concessions from the prosecutor by asking the prosecutor about her sense of 'what the case is worth' and what charge reductions she can make, without indicating the defendant's willingness to plead to any charge at all." Donald Gifford, *A Content-Based Theory of Strategy Selection in Legal Negotiation*, 46 Ohio St.L.J. 41, 79–80 (1985).

"While the potential sentence at trial is obviously an important piece of information that defense counsel should gather before negotiating a plea bargain, it may not provide a strategic advantage if used in the negotiation as a criteria. Using the sentence at trial as criteria in the negotiation can be disadvantageous because a concrete sentence can anchor the negotiation at a point that is unfavorable for the defendant. An anchor is a number or outcome that focuses the other negotiator's attention and expectation. The power of anchors is substantial and affects even those with negotiation experience and expertise. Presuming that the plea negotiation is a discount from a the expected sentence at trial, starting from this point may anchor the negotiation at a high point and force the defense counsel to argue for downward leniency, rather than starting from a lower point and encouraging the prosecutor to bargain upwards." Wesley Oliver & Rishi Batra, *Standards of Legitimacy in Criminal Negotiations*, 20 Harv.Negotiations L.Rev. 61, 76–77 (2015).

14th ed., p. 1235; end of Note 10 in lieu of last two paragraphs, add:

The Court later addressed the second *Strickland* prong, prejudice, in this context in LEE v. UNITED STATES, 137 S.Ct. 1958 (2017). Lee, a noncitizen lawful permanent resident charged with possessing drugs with intent to distribute, opted to accept a plea offer carrying a lower sentence than he would have faced at trial after his counsel erroneously assured him he would not be deported. Lee later was not allowed to withdraw his guilty plea because of that ineffective assistance, on the ground he could not show prejudice. The Government asked the Supreme Court to "accept a *per se* rule that a defendant with no viable defense cannot show prejudice from the denial of his right to trial," a proposition the Court, per Roberts, C.J., deemed erroneous because (1) it utilizes a categorical rule when a "case-by-case examination" is called for; and (2) "more fundamentally, * * * the inquiry as presented in *Hill v. Lockhart* [see 11th ed., p. 1258, footnote b] "focuses on a defendant's decisionmaking, which may not turn solely on the likelihood of conviction after trial." But, the Court cautioned: "Courts should not upset a plea solely because of *post hoc* assertions from a defendant about how he would have pleaded but for his attorney's deficiencies. Judges should instead look to contemporaneous evidence to substantiate a defendant's expressed preferences."

Given the "unusual circumstances of this case," the Court held Lee had "adequately demonstrated a reasonable probability that he would have rejected the plea had he known that it would lead to mandatory deportation," considering that (a) Lee repeatedly asked his attorney about whether there was any risk of deportation; (b) both Lee and his counsel testified he would have gone to trial had he known the true deportation consequences; (c) Lee's responses at his plea colloquy indicated the importance he placed on deportation; (d) Lee had strong connections with the U.S., where he had lived nearly 30 years, most of his life, and had no ties to South Korea; and (e) it would not be irrational for someone in Lee's situation to risk an additional few years of prison time in exchange for even a rather remote chance of acquittal.

Noting that in *Padilla* the Supreme Court looked to "norms of practice as reflected in American Bar Association standards and the like," and taking account of "a proliferation of reference guides since the *Padilla* decision," the court in *Morales Diaz v. State*, 896 N.W.2d 723 (Iowa 2017), adopted the 2015 version of those standards, reading in part: "After determining the client's immigration status and potential adverse consequences from the criminal proceedings, including removal, exclusion, bars to relief from removal, immigration detention, denial of citizenship, and adverse consequences to the client's immediate family, counsel should advise the client of all such potential consequences and determine with the client the best course of action for the client's interests and how to pursue it."

§ 6. THE EFFECT OF A GUILTY PLEA

14th ed., p. 1258; replace all content in § 6:

CLASS V. UNITED STATES
583 U.S. ___, 138 S.Ct. 798, 200 L.Ed.2d 37 (2018).

JUSTICE BREYER delivered the opinion of the Court. * * *

[Rodney Class was indicted for violating federal law by possessing firearms in his vehicle while it was parked on the grounds of the U.S. Capitol. He unsuccessfully sought dismissal of the indictment, claiming (i) that the statute violated the Second Amendment and (ii) that in violation of due process he was denied fair notice weapons were banned in the parking lot. Class later pled guilty to the possession charge pursuant to a plea agreement listing five categories of rights he expressly agreed to waive and three categories he could raise on appeal, but which said nothing about the right to raise on direct appeal a claim that the statute of conviction was unconstitutional.]

The question is whether a guilty plea by itself bars a federal criminal defendant from challenging the constitutionality of the statute of conviction on direct appeal. We hold that it does not. Class did not relinquish his right to appeal the District Court's constitutional determinations simply by pleading guilty. As we shall explain, this holding flows directly from this Court's prior decisions.

Fifty years ago this Court directly addressed a similar claim (a claim that the statute of conviction was unconstitutional). And the Court stated that a defendant's "plea of guilty did not . . . waive his previous [constitutional] claim." *Haynes v. United States*, 390 U.S. 85 (1968). Though Justice Harlan's opinion for the Court in *Haynes* offered little explanation for this statement, subsequent decisions offered a rationale that applies here.

In *Blackledge v. Perry*, 417 U.S. 21 (1974), North Carolina indicted and convicted Jimmy Seth Perry on a misdemeanor assault charge. When Perry exercised his right under a North Carolina statute to a de novo trial in a higher court, the State reindicted him, but this time the State charged a felony, which carried a heavier penalty, for the same conduct. Perry pleaded guilty. He then sought habeas relief on the grounds that the reindictment amounted to an unconstitutional vindictive prosecution. The State argued that Perry's guilty plea barred him from raising his constitutional challenge. But this Court held that it did not.

The Court noted that a guilty plea bars appeal of many claims, including some " 'antecedent constitutional violations' " related to events (say, grand jury proceedings) that had " 'occurred prior to the entry of the guilty plea' "(quoting *Tollett v. Henderson*, 411 U.S. 258 (1973)). While *Tollett* claims were "of constitutional dimension," the Court explained that "the nature of the underlying constitutional infirmity is markedly different" from a claim of vindictive prosecution, which implicates "the very power of the State" to prosecute the defendant. Accordingly, the Court wrote that "the right" Perry "asserts and that we today accept is the right not to be haled into court at all upon the felony charge" since "[t]he very initiation of the proceedings" against Perry "operated to deprive him due process of law."

A year and a half later, in *Menna v. New York*, 423 U.S. 61 (1975), this Court repeated what it had said and held in *Blackledge*. After Menna served a 30-day jail term for refusing to testify before the grand jury on November 7, 1968, the State of New York charged him once again for (what Menna argued was) the same crime. Menna pleaded guilty, but subsequently appealed arguing that the new charge violated the Double Jeopardy Clause. U.S. Const., Amdt. 5. The lower courts held that Menna's constitutional claim had been "waived" by his guilty plea.

This Court reversed. Citing *Blackledge*, the Court held that "a plea of guilty to a charge does not waive a claim that—judged on its face—the charge is one which the State may not constitutionally prosecute." Menna's claim amounted to a claim that "the State may not convict" him "no matter how validly his factual guilt is established." Menna's "guilty plea, therefore, [did] not bar the claim." * * *

In more recent years, we have reaffirmed the *Menna-Blackledge* doctrine and refined its scope. In *United States v. Broce*, 488 U.S. 563 (1989), the defendants pleaded guilty to two separate indictments in a single proceeding which "on their face" described two separate bid-rigging conspiracies. They later sought to challenge their convictions on double jeopardy grounds, arguing that they had only admitted to one conspiracy. Citing *Blackledge* and *Menna*, this Court repeated that a guilty plea does not bar a claim on appeal "where on the face of the record the court had no power to enter the conviction or impose the sentence." However, because the defendants could not "prove their claim by relying on those indictments and the existing record" and "without contradicting those indictments," this Court held that their claims were "foreclosed by the admissions inherent in their guilty pleas."

Unlike the claims in *Broce*, Class' constitutional claims here, as we understand them, do not contradict the terms of the indictment or the written plea agreement. They are consistent with Class' knowing, voluntary, and intelligent admission that he did what the indictment alleged. Those claims can be "resolved without any need to venture beyond that record."

Nor do Class' claims focus upon case-related constitutional defects that " 'occurred prior to the entry of the guilty plea.' " *Blackledge*. They could not, for example, "have been 'cured' through a new indictment by a properly selected grand jury." Because the defendant has admitted the charges against him, a guilty plea makes the latter kind of constitutional claim "irrelevant to the constitutional validity of the conviction." *Haring v. Prosise*, 462 U.S. 306 (1983). But the cases to which we have referred make clear that a defendant's guilty plea does not make irrelevant the kind of constitutional claim Class seeks to make.

In sum, the claims at issue here do not fall within any of the categories of claims that Class' plea agreement forbids him to raise on direct appeal. They challenge the Government's power to criminalize Class' (admitted) conduct. They thereby call into question the Government's power to " 'constitutionally prosecute' " him. *Broce, supra* (quoting *Menna, supra*). A guilty plea does not bar a direct appeal in these circumstances. * * *

The Government and the dissent argue that [Fed.R.Crim.P.] 11(a)(2) means that "a defendant who pleads guilty cannot challenge his conviction on appeal on a forfeitable or waivable ground that he either failed to present to the district court or failed to reserve in writing."

The problem with this argument is that, by its own terms, the Rule itself does not say whether it sets forth the exclusive procedure for a defendant to preserve a constitutional claim following a guilty plea. At the same time, the drafters' notes acknowledge that the "Supreme Court has held that certain kinds of constitutional objections may be raised after a plea of guilty." The notes then specifically refer to the "*Menna-Blackledge* doctrine."

JUSTICE ALITO, with whom JUSTICE KENNEDY and JUSTICE THOMAS join, dissenting. * * *

I

There is no justification for the muddle left by today's decision. The question at issue is not conceptually complex. In determining whether a plea of guilty prevents a defendant in federal or state court from raising a particular issue on appeal, the first question is whether the Federal Constitution precludes waiver. If the Federal Constitution permits waiver, the next question is whether some other law nevertheless bars waiver. And if no law prevents waiver, the final question is whether the defendant knowingly and intelligently waived the right to raise the claim on appeal. * * *

Analyzing this case under the framework set out above, I think the Court of Appeals was clearly correct. First, the Federal Constitution does not prohibit the waiver of the rights Class asserts. We have held that most personal constitutional rights may be waived, and Class concedes that this is so with respect to the rights he is asserting.

Second, no federal statute or rule bars waiver. On the contrary, Rule 11 * * * makes it clear that, with one exception that I will discuss below, a defendant who enters an unconditional plea waives all nonjurisdictional claims. Although the Rule does not say this expressly, that is the unmistakable implication of subdivision (a)(2), which allows a defendant, "[w]ith the consent of the court and the government," to "enter a conditional plea of guilty or nolo contendere, reserving in writing the right to have an appellate court review an adverse determination of a specified pretrial motion." * * *

The Advisory Committee's Notes on Rule 11 make this clear, stating that an unconditional plea (with the previously mentioned exception) "constitutes a waiver of all nonjurisdictional defects." Advisory Committee's Notes on a federal rule of procedure "provide a reliable source of insight into the meaning of a rule, especially when, as here, the rule was enacted precisely as the Advisory Committee proposed." Subdivision (a)(2) was adopted against the backdrop of decisions of this Court holding that a guilty plea generally relinquishes all defenses to conviction, see, e.g., *Tollett v. Henderson*, 411 U.S. 258, 267,(1973), and Rule 11(a)(2) creates a limited exception to that general principle. Far from prohibiting the waiver of nonjurisdictional claims, Rule 11 actually bars the raising of such claims (once again, with the previously mentioned exception).

II

A

I now turn to the one exception mentioned in the Advisory Committee's Notes on Rule 11—what the Notes, rather grandly, term the "*Menna-Blackledge* doctrine." * * *

Because this doctrine is the only exception recognized in Rule 11 and because the doctrine figures prominently in the opinion of the Court, it is important to examine its foundation and meaning.

B

Blackledge and *Menna* represented marked departures from our prior decisions. Before they were handed down, our precedents were clear: When a defendant pleaded guilty to a crime, he relinquished his right to litigate all nonjurisdictional challenges to his conviction (except for the claim that his plea was not voluntary and intelligent), and the prosecution could assert this forfeiture to defeat a subsequent appeal. The theory was easy to understand. * * *

III

Blackledge and *Menna* diverged from these prior precedents, but neither case provided a clear or coherent explanation for the departure.

A

In *Blackledge*, the Court held that a defendant who pleaded guilty could nevertheless challenge his conviction on the ground that his right to due process was violated by a vindictive prosecution. The Court asserted that this right was "markedly different" from the equal protection and Fifth Amendment rights at stake in *Tollett* and the *Brady* trilogy because it "went to the very power of the State to bring the defendant into court to answer the charge brought against him." The meaning of this distinction, however, is hard to grasp.

The most natural way to understand *Blackledge*'s reference to "the very power of the State" would be to say that an argument survives a guilty plea if it attacks the court's jurisdiction. * * * But that cannot be what *Blackledge* meant.

First, the defendant in *Blackledge* had been tried in state court in North Carolina for a state-law offense, and the jurisdiction of state courts to entertain such prosecutions is purely a matter of state law * * *. Second, a rule that jurisdictional defects alone survive a guilty plea would not explain the result in *Blackledge* itself. Arguments attacking a court's subject-matter jurisdiction can neither be waived nor forfeited. But the due process right at issue in *Blackledge* was perfectly capable of being waived or forfeited—as is just about every other right that is personal to a criminal defendant.

So if the "very power to prosecute" theory does not refer to jurisdiction, what else might it mean? The only other possibility that comes to mind is that it might mean that a defendant can litigate a claim if it asserts a right not to be tried, as opposed to a right not to be convicted. But we have said that "virtually all rights of criminal defendants" are "merely . . . right[s] not to be convicted," as distinguished from "right[s] not to be tried." Even when a constitutional violation requires the dismissal of an indictment, that "does not mean that [the] defendant enjoy[ed] a 'right not to be tried' " on the charges.

The rule could hardly be otherwise. Most constitutional defenses (and plenty of statutory defenses), if successfully asserted in a pretrial motion, deprive the prosecution of the "power" to proceed to trial or secure a conviction. If that remedial consequence converted them all into rights not to be prosecuted, *Blackledge* would have no discernible limit. * * *

The upshot is that the supposed "right not to be prosecuted" has no intelligible meaning in this context. * * *

B

If the thinking behind *Blackledge* is hard to follow, *Menna* may be worse. In that case, the Court held that a defendant who pleaded guilty could challenge his conviction on double jeopardy grounds. The case was decided by a three-page per curiam opinion, its entire analysis confined to a single footnote[, where] the Court wrote:

"[A] counseled plea of guilty is an admission of factual guilt so reliable that, where voluntary and intelligent, it quite validly removes the issue of factual guilt from the case. In most cases, factual guilt is a sufficient basis for the State's imposition of punishment. A guilty plea, therefore, simply renders irrelevant those constitutional violations not logically inconsistent with the valid establishment of factual guilt."

The wording of the final sentence is not easy to parse, but I interpret the Court's reasoning as follows: A defendant who pleads guilty does no more than admit that he committed the essential conduct charged in the indictment; therefore a guilty plea allows the litigation on appeal of any claim that is not inconsistent with the facts that the defendant necessarily admitted. * * * A holding of that scope is not what one expects to see in a footnote in a per curiam opinion, but if the Court meant less, its meaning is unclear.

C

When the Court returned to *Blackledge* and *Menna* in *United States v. Broce*, 488 U.S. 563 (1989), the Court essentially repudiated the theories offered in those earlier cases. * * * Like *Menna*, *Broce* involved a defendant (actually two defendants) who pleaded guilty but then sought to attack their convictions on double jeopardy grounds. This time, however, the Court held that their guilty pleas prevented them from litigating their claims.

The Court began by specifically disavowing *Menna*'s suggestion that a guilty plea admits only " 'factual guilt,' " meaning "the acts described in the indictments." Instead, the Court explained, an unconditional guilty plea admits "all of the factual and legal elements necessary to sustain a binding, final judgment of guilt and a lawful sentence." "By entering a plea of guilty, the accused is not simply stating that he did the discrete acts described in the indictment; he is admitting guilt of a substantive crime." * * * Thus, the Court concluded, a defendant's decision to plead guilty necessarily extinguishes whatever "potential defense[s]" he might have asserted in an effort to show that it would be unlawful to hold him liable for his conduct. So much for *Menna*.

As for *Blackledge*, by holding that the defendants' double jeopardy rights were extinguished by their pleas, *Broce* necessarily rejected the idea that a right not to be tried survives an unconditional guilty plea.

While *Broce* thus rejected the reasoning in *Blackledge* and *Menna*, the Court was content to distinguish those cases on the ground that they involved defendants who could succeed on appeal without going beyond "the existing record," whereas the defendants in *Broce* would have to present new evidence.

IV

A

This is where the *Menna-Blackledge* doctrine stood when we heard this case. Now, instead of clarifying the law, the Court sows new confusion by reiterating with seeming approval a string of catchphrases. The Court repeats the line that an argument survives if it "implicates 'the very power of the State' to prosecute the defendant," but this shibboleth is no more intelligible now than it was when first incanted in *Blackledge*. The Court also parrots the rule set out in the *Menna* footnote—that the only arguments waived by a guilty plea are those that contradict the facts alleged in the charging document, even though that rule is inconsistent with *Tollett*, the *Brady* trilogy, and *Broce*—and even though this reading would permit a defendant who pleads guilty to raise an uncertain assortment of claims never before thought to survive a guilty plea.

For example, would this rule permit a defendant to argue that his prosecution is barred by a statute of limitations or by the Speedy Trial Act? Presumably the answer is yes. By admitting commission of the acts alleged in an indictment or complaint, a defendant would not concede that the charge was timely. What about the argument that a defendant's alleged conduct does not violate the statute of conviction? Here again, the rule barring only those claims inconsistent with the facts alleged in the indictment or complaint would appear to permit the issue to be raised on appeal, but the Court says that a defendant who pleads guilty "has admitted the charges against him." What does this mean, exactly? * * *

Approaching the question from the opposite direction, the Court says that a guilty plea precludes a defendant from litigating "the constitutionality of case-related government conduct that takes place before the plea is entered." This category is most mysterious. I thought Class was arguing that the Government violated the Constitution at the moment when it initiated his prosecution. That sounds like he is trying to attack "the constitutionality of case-related government conduct that [took] place before the plea [was] entered." Yet the Court holds that he may proceed. Why?

Finally, the majority instructs that "a valid guilty plea relinquishes any claim that would contradict the 'admissions necessarily made upon entry of a voluntary plea of guilty' "(quoting *Broce*). I agree with that statement of the rule, but what the Court fails to acknowledge is that the scope of this rule depends on the law of the particular jurisdiction in question. If a defendant in federal court is told that under Rule 11 an unconditional guilty plea waives all nonjurisdictional claims (or as *Broce* put it, admits "all of the factual and legal elements necessary to sustain a binding, final judgment of guilt and a lawful sentence"), then that is the scope of the admissions implicit in the plea. * * *

In sum, the governing law in the present case is Rule 11 * * *. Under that Rule, an unconditional guilty plea waives all nonjurisdictional claims with the possible exception of the "*Menna-Blackledge* doctrine" created years ago by this Court. That doctrine is vacuous, has no sound foundation, and produces nothing but confusion. At a minimum, I would limit the doctrine to the particular types of claims involved in those cases. I certainly would not expand its reach. * * *

NOTES AND QUESTIONS

1. **Freestanding claim of "actual innocence."** To what extent may/should states recognize a broader range of post-conviction challenges by guilty plea defendants than allowed under *Class*? In *Schmidt v. State*, 909 N.W.2d 778 (Iowa 2018), the court noted that "[a]t the state level, a number of jurisdictions acknowledge freestanding claims of actual innocence," that is, where such claims are unaccompanied by an assertion of any *legal* error in the process by which the defendant's conviction was obtained.[a] In these jurisdictions, the question has sometimes been raised as to whether such an "actual innocence" claim may be made by guilty plea defendants or only those defendants who asserted their innocence earlier by standing trial. The court in *Schmidt,* stating "we do not think *Class* * * * affects our decision today," rejected its earlier holding that "[n]otions of newly discovered evidence simply have no bearing on a knowing and voluntary admission of guilt." By "now examin[ing] the phenomenon of actually innocent people pleading guilty," as manifested by the fact that the "National Registry of Exonerations reported that seventy-four exonerations in 2016 arose from pleas," the court reached the conclusion "that actually innocent people plead guilty for many different reasons." The dissent in *Schmidt,* invoking *Class* in support, objected: "Reexamining a guilty plea years after the fact is far different from reviewing a trial. Unlike with a case that actually went to trial, no trial transcript can be relied on if the witnesses no longer are around, have forgotten the events, or no longer are motivated to remember them."

2. **Manner of proof.** In assessing the *Schmidt* position, should it make any difference in what manner the defendant's "actual innocence" is purportedly established? Acknowledging that the legislature had already provided a remedy for defendants who pled guilty where "DNA evidence exonerates them," the court responded: "We see no reason why we should treat people exonerated by DNA evidence differently from people exonerated by other reliable means. For example, when the court determines the police planted evidence, such as drugs, why should that defendant remain in prison simply because he or she pled guilty to a reduced charge in light of the overwhelming evidence of his or her guilt?" But that was not the instant case, where the defendant, who pled guilty to assault with intent to commit sexual abuse and incest, now relied upon "recantation by the victim." The dissent objected that courts would now see "applications by defendants who pled guilty to domestic assault and now bully the survivors into recanting."

3. **Alford *plea.*** Is *Schmidt* also applicable to an *Alford* plea, discussed at 14th ed., p. 1250, or is the dissent correct in asserting *Schmidt* does not reach such instances because "[s]uch a defendant always maintained he or she was innocent"?

4. **Guilty-plea defendants with different guilt or otherwise unconvictable.** In a state that agrees with *Schmidt* regarding a guilty-plea defendant's right to make (i) an "actual

---

[a] As noted in *Schmidt*, such a "freestanding claim" must be distinguished from a "gateway claim," by which a habeas petitioner may overcome a procedural bar to habeas review by bringing a gateway claim of actual innocence such that the petitioner may obtain review of the underlying constitutional merits of his or her procedurally defaulted claim." See 14th ed., p. 1468, Note 2.

innocence" claim, what then of such defendants more precisely characterized as having (ii) "different guilt" or being (iii) "otherwise unconvictable"? Consider: (i) *Ex parte Mable*, 443 S.W.3d 129 (Tex.Crim.App.2014) ("actual innocence" can be raised here, where after defendant's guilty plea to possession of controlled substance state lab tested the material and found it was not a controlled substance); (ii) *Ex parte Broussard*, 517 S.W.3d 814 (Tex.Crim.App.2017) (where defendant arrested for possession of less than a gram of an unidentified substance a field test determined was cocaine and thereafter defendant pled guilty to delivery of cocaine, but later a lab test of that substance revealed it was meth, in the same penalty group, defendant not entitled to plea withdrawal notwithstanding existing rule that "possession of *each* individual substance within the same penalty group [is] a separate and distinct offense," as "a guilty plea is not necessarily involuntary when a defendant misapprehends a known unknown"); (iii) *Ex parte Palmberg*, 491 S.W.3d 804 (Tex.Crim.App.2016) (a "guilty plea does not violate due process * * * even when the defendant enters it while operating under various misapprehensions about the nature or strength of the State's case," here unawareness that the arresting officer used up all of the substance found on defendant in preliminary testing, so that "there was no remaining unprocessed sample available for laboratory analysis," even though a test "performed by an officer in the field is inadmissible at trial."

CHAPTER 23

TRIAL BY JURY

■ ■ ■

§ 1. RIGHT TO JURY TRIAL

14th ed., p. 1271; Note 5, before last sentence, add:

Consider also the acquittals of six armed occupiers of a federal wildlife refuge, a standoff that "drew right-wing anti-government protesters from across the U.S. to protest the federal government's control of public land across the West." Reportedly, "During the trial, flag-waving supporters, some in boots and cowboy hats, marched around the courthouse, in part hoping jurors might see one of their signs stating 'Google: jury nullification'—effectively urging jurors to acquit the defendants out of a belief that the law under which they are charged is wrong." Pearce & Anderson, Leaders of Oregon National Wildlife Refuge are Acquitted of Federal Charges, Los Angeles Times, Oct 27, 2016, http://www.latimes.com/nation/nationnow/la-na-oregon-standoff-jury-acquits-20161027-story.html; https://www.nytimes.com/2016/10/28/us/bundy-brothers-acquitted-in-takeover-of-oregon-wildlife-refuge.html.

§ 2. JURY SELECTION

B. SELECTING THE JURY FROM THE VENIRE: VOIR DIRE

14th ed., p. 1282; Note 3, change heading to *"Limits on impeaching the verdict with juror testimony"* and replace last paragraph with:

The Court in PEÑA-RODRIGUEZ v. COLORADO, 137 S.Ct. 855 (2017), considered whether the Sixth Amendment required a state court to accept juror affidavits that reported another juror's anti-Mexican statements during deliberations. The affidavits, filed as support for a motion for new trial after a conviction for unlawful sexual contact, stated that the juror had said that "Mexican men are physically controlling of women because of their sense of entitlement," that the defendant was guilty because, in the juror's experience as an ex-law enforcement officer, "Mexican men had a bravado that caused them to believe they could do whatever they wanted with women" and "take whatever they want," and that "nine times out of ten Mexican men were guilty of being aggressive toward women and young girls." The Court's opinion, written by Justice Kennedy, held that "where a juror makes a clear statement that indicates he or she relied on racial stereotypes or animus to convict a criminal defendant, the Sixth Amendment requires that the no-impeachment rule give way in order to permit the trial court to consider the evidence of the juror's statement and any resulting denial of the jury trial guarantee."

"Racial bias of the kind alleged in this case differs in critical ways from * * * the drug and alcohol abuse in *Tanner*, or the pro-defendant bias in *Warger*," the Court reasoned. "The behavior in those cases is troubling and unacceptable, but each involved anomalous behavior from a single jury—or juror —gone off course. Jurors are presumed to follow their oath, and neither history nor common experience show that the jury system is rife with mischief of these or similar kinds. To attempt to rid the jury of every irregularity of this sort would be to expose it to unrelenting scrutiny. 'It is not at all clear . . . that the jury system could survive such efforts to perfect it.' *Tanner*. The same cannot be said about racial bias, a familiar and recurring evil that, if left unaddressed, would risk systemic injury to the administration of justice. This Court's decisions demonstrate that racial bias implicates unique historical, constitutional, and institutional concerns. An effort to address the most grave and serious statements of racial bias is not an effort to perfect the jury but to ensure that our legal system remains capable of coming ever closer to the promise of equal treatment under the law that is so central to a functioning democracy."

"Racial bias is distinct in a pragmatic sense as well. In past cases this Court has relied on other safeguards to protect the right to an impartial jury. Some of those safeguards, to be sure, can disclose racial bias. Voir dire at the outset of trial, observation of juror demeanor and conduct during trial, juror reports before the verdict, and nonjuror evidence after trial are important mechanisms for discovering bias. Yet their operation may be compromised, or they may prove insufficient. * * * Generic questions about juror impartiality may not expose specific attitudes or biases that can poison jury deliberations. Yet more pointed questions "could well exacerbate whatever prejudice might exist without substantially aiding in exposing it. * * * The stigma that attends racial bias may make it difficult for a juror to report inappropriate statements during the course of juror deliberations. It is one thing to accuse a fellow juror of having a personal experience that improperly influences her consideration of the case, as would have been required in *Warger*. It is quite another to call her a bigot."

The Court argued, "A constitutional rule that racial bias in the justice system must be addressed—including, in some instances, after the verdict has been entered—is necessary to prevent a systemic loss of confidence in jury verdicts, a confidence that is a central premise of the Sixth Amendment trial right." It explained, "Not every offhand comment indicating racial bias or hostility will justify setting aside the no-impeachment bar to allow further judicial inquiry. For the inquiry to proceed, there must be a showing that one or more jurors made statements exhibiting overt racial bias that cast serious doubt on the fairness and impartiality of the jury's deliberations and resulting verdict. To qualify, the statement must tend to show that racial animus was a significant motivating factor in the juror's vote to convict. Whether that threshold showing has been satisfied is a matter committed to the substantial discretion of the trial court in light of all the circumstances, including the content and timing of the alleged statements and the reliability of the proffered evidence."

Chief Justice Roberts and Justice Thomas joined Justice Alito in dissent, arguing that there are no principled grounds to prevent the expansion of the Court's holding and that that it will "tend to defeat full and vigorous discussion, expose jurors to harassment, and deprive verdicts of stability." "Nothing in the text or history of the [Sixth] Amendment or in the inherent nature of the jury trial right suggests that the extent of the protection provided by the Amendment depends on the nature of a jury's partiality or bias. * * * Recasting this as an equal protection case would not provide a ground for limiting the holding to cases involving racial bias. At a minimum, cases involving bias based on any suspect classification—such as national origin or religion—would merit equal treatment. So, I think, would bias based on sex, or the exercise of the First Amendment right to freedom of expression or association. Indeed, convicting a defendant on the basis of any irrational classification would violate the Equal Protection Clause." The dissent also noted the difficulty of identifying which statements are " 'clear[ly]' based on racial or ethnic bias." "Suppose that the allegedly biased juror in this case never made reference to Peña-Rodriguez's race or national origin but said that he had a lot of experience with 'this macho type' and knew that men of this kind felt that they could get their way with women. Suppose that other jurors testified that they were certain that 'this macho type' was meant to refer to Mexican or Hispanic men."

14th ed., p. 1293; Note 4(c), insert after subheading before *Miller-El*:

The Court has emphasized repeatedly that a " 'trial court is best situated to evaluate both the words and the demeanor of jurors who are peremptorily challenged, as well as the credibility of the prosecutor who exercised those strikes.' " *Davis v. Ayala*, 135 S.Ct. 2187 (2015). " '[T]hese determinations of credibility and demeanor lie peculiarly within a trial judge's province,' and 'in the absence of exceptional circumstances, we [will] defer to the trial court.' " *Id.* An example of one circumstance that will trigger greater appellate scrutiny is a prosecutor's reliance on a "race-neutral" reason for challenging a black juror that, if sincere, would have equally supported the challenge of seated white juror.

14th ed., p. 1294; end of Note 4(c), add:

The Court upended another capital judgment from Louisiana for similar reasons in *Foster v. Chatman*, 136 S.Ct. 1737 (2016), finding the state's strikes were "motivated in substantial part by discriminatory intent," when the neutral reasons provided by the prosecution had "no grounding in fact," were "difficult to credit in light of the State's acceptance" of similarly situated white jurors, and "shifted over time."

14th ed., p. 1296; replace first two paragraphs of Note 7 with:

A defendant has a due process right to an impartial judge. In *Williams v. Pennsylvania*, 136 S.Ct. 1899 (2016), Justice Kennedy explained for the Court that due process guarantees an absence of actual bias on the part of a judge, but this is determined using an objective standard that usually avoids having to determine whether actual bias is present. The Court asks "whether, as an objective matter, 'the average judge in his position is "likely" to be neutral, or whether there is an unconstitutional "potential for bias." ' " This standard requires recusal when the likelihood of bias on the part of the judge " 'is too high to be constitutionally tolerable.' "[3] In *Williams,* the majority struck down as violating due process a decision of the Pennsylvania Supreme Court rejecting relief for a death row prisoner who had filed a late state post-conviction petition raising several *Brady* claims. One of the justices on the State Supreme Court had nearly three decades earlier served as the District Attorney for Philadelphia, and had given his approval for his staff to seek the death penalty in Williams's case. When Williams moved for his recusal, he denied the motion, participated in the decision denying the stay of execution, and authored a concurring opinion denouncing the errors of the lower court and the anti-death penalty agenda of the defenders' office representing Williams.

The United States Supreme Court concluded that due process required the former prosecutor's recusal. It relied primarily on *In re Murchison*, 349 U.S. 133 (1955), where it had held that due process forbid a judge from first sitting as grand jury, accusing a witness of contempt, and then presiding as judge at trial on that charge. The *Williams* Court explained that when "a judge had a direct, personal role in the defendant's prosecution," there is "a risk that the judge 'would be so psychologically wedded' to his or her previous position as a prosecutor that the judge 'would consciously or unconsciously avoid the appearance of having erred or changed position,' " and that judge's "own personal knowledge and impression" of the case, acquired through his or her role in the prosecution, may carry far more weight with the judge than the parties' arguments to the court.' " "Even if decades intervene before the former prosecutor revisits the matter as a jurist, the case may implicate the effects and continuing force of his or her original decision." The Court reasoned that the state justice's "significant, personal involvement in a critical decision in Williams's case gave rise to an unacceptable risk of actual bias. This risk so endangered the appearance of neutrality that his participation in the case 'must be forbidden if the guarantee of due process is to be adequately implemented.' " The Court added that the "decision will not

---

[3]   The Court has emphasized that this due process standard may demand recusal even when a judge has no actual subjective bias, but, objectively speaking, considering all the circumstances alleged, the probability of actual bias is too high to be constitutionally tolerable. Rippo v. Baker, 137 S.Ct. 905 (2017).

occasion a significant change in recusal practice" because "many jurisdictions" have ethical rules that "already require disqualification under the circumstances of this case."

Three justices dissented. The Chief Justice and Justice Alito found the risk of bias constitutionally tolerable. The issue before the Pennsylvania justice was a procedural question about overcoming the state's procedural bar on filing an untimely habeas petition, they argued, and "neither the procedural question nor Williams's merits claim in any way concerns the pretrial decision to seek the death penalty." Also, unlike the judge in *Murchison,* the justice had not "made up his mind about the only issue in the case" before the proceeding had even begun, and there was no risk that he would call 'on his own personal knowledge and impression of what had occurred in the grand jury room,' rather than the evidence presented to him by the parties." Justice Thomas objected to the Court's test as well as its application. The Constitution, he maintained, does not require the recusal of a former prosecutor from a prisoner's post-conviction proceedings. Instead, due process historically requires only the recusal of a judge who had "a direct and substantial pecuniary interest" or had "served as counsel in the same case." Williams's state post-conviction proceeding, he argued, "is not part of the criminal proceeding" but is a separate case, "civil in nature," challenging a criminal judgment that is already final.

CHAPTER 25

THE CRIMINAL TRIAL

■ ■ ■

14th ed., p. 1335; in introductory paragraph, before last sentence, add:

The accused also has the right to a public trial.

§ 2. CONFRONTATION AND TESTIMONIAL HEARSAY

14th ed., p. 1342; after last sentence of Section 1, add:

Consider the competing views reflected in *United States v. Sanchez-Gomez*, 859 F.3d 649 (9th Cir.2017) (en banc). The majority held: "This right to be free from unwarranted shackles no matter the proceeding respects our foundational principle that defendants are innocent until proven guilty. The principle isn't limited to juries or trial proceedings. It includes the perception of any person who may walk into a public courtroom, as well as those of the jury, the judge and court personnel. A presumptively innocent defendant has the right to be treated with respect and dignity in a public courtroom, not like a bear on a chain. . . . The right also maintains courtroom decorum and dignity: The courtroom's formal dignity, which includes the respectful treatment of defendants, reflects the importance of the matter at issue, guilt or innocence, and the gravity with which Americans consider any deprivation of an individual's liberty through criminal punishment. And it reflects a seriousness of purpose that helps to explain the judicial system's power to inspire the confidence and to affect the behavior of a general public whose demands for justice our courts seek to serve. The most visible and public manifestation of our criminal justice system is the courtroom. Courtrooms are palaces of justice, imbued with a majesty that reflects the gravity of proceedings designed to deprive a person of liberty or even life. A member of the public who wanders into a criminal courtroom must immediately perceive that it is a place where justice is administered with due regard to individuals whom the law presumes to be innocent. That perception cannot prevail if defendants are marched in like convicts on a chain gang. Both the defendant and the public have the right to a dignified, inspiring and open court process. Thus, innocent defendants may not be shackled at any point in the courtroom unless there is an individualized showing of need."

The dissenting judges, siding with the Second and Eleventh Circuits, argued that the majority's rule unnecessarily put those in state and federal courtrooms at risk of violence. They argued that the Supreme Court limited *Deck* to jury proceedings, that "there is no rule regarding restraints on pretrial detainees in non-jury proceedings that has 'deep roots in the common law,'" and that "pretrial detainees enjoy no heightened interests when they appear in court outside of the presence of a jury." "[B]ecause there is no allegation that the restraint policy is intended as a punishment," the dissent stated, "the question is simply whether requiring detainees to wear restraints while attending their pretrial hearings 'is reasonably related to a legitimate governmental objective.'"

14th ed., p. 1355; substitute for Note 2:

2. *Statements by young children; statements to those who must report to law enforcement.* The Court applied its "primary purpose test" to statements made to "persons other than law enforcement officers" for the first time in *Ohio v. Clark,* 135 S.Ct. 2173 (2015). There it considered whether the Confrontation Clause barred introduction into evidence of a 3-year-old's statements about physical abuse to a preschool teacher, after the trial court determined the child was incompetent to testify at trial under state law. The Court reasoned:

" * * * Because at least some statements to individuals who are not law enforcement officers could conceivably raise confrontation concerns, we decline to adopt a categorical rule excluding them from the Sixth Amendment's reach. Nevertheless, such statements are much less likely to be testimonial than statements to law enforcement officers. And considering all the relevant circumstances here, L. P.'s statements clearly were not made with the primary purpose of creating evidence for Clark's prosecution. Thus, their introduction at trial did not violate the Confrontation Clause.

"L. P.'s statements occurred in the context of an ongoing emergency involving suspected child abuse. When L. P.'s teachers noticed his injuries, they rightly became worried that the 3-year-old was the victim of serious violence. Because the teachers needed to know whether it was safe to release L. P. to his guardian at the end of the day, they needed to determine who might be abusing the child. Thus, the immediate concern was to protect a vulnerable child who needed help. Our holding in *Bryant* is instructive. As in *Bryant*, the emergency in this case was ongoing, and the circumstances were not entirely clear. L. P.'s teachers were not sure who had abused him or how best to secure his safety. Nor were they sure whether any other children might be at risk. As a result, their questions and L. P.'s answers were primarily aimed at identifying and ending the threat. Though not as harried, the conversation here was also similar to the 911 call in *Davis*. The teachers' questions were meant to identify the abuser in order to protect the victim from future attacks. Whether the teachers thought that this would be done by apprehending the abuser or by some other means is irrelevant. And the circumstances in this case were unlike the interrogation in *Hammon*, where the police knew the identity of the assailant and questioned the victim after shielding her from potential harm.

"There is no indication that the primary purpose of the conversation was to gather evidence for Clark's prosecution. On the contrary, it is clear that the first objective was to protect L. P. At no point did the teachers inform L. P. that his answers would be used to arrest or punish his abuser. L. P. never hinted that he intended his statements to be used by the police or prosecutors. And the conversation between L. P. and his teachers was informal and spontaneous. The teachers asked L. P. about his injuries immediately upon discovering them, in the informal setting of a preschool lunchroom and classroom, and they did so precisely as any concerned citizen would talk to a child who might be the victim of abuse. This was nothing like the formalized station-house questioning in *Crawford* or the police interrogation and battery affidavit in *Hammon*.

"L. P.'s age fortifies our conclusion that the statements in question were not testimonial. Statements by very young children will rarely, if ever, implicate the Confrontation Clause. Few preschool students understand the details of our criminal justice system. Rather, '[r]esearch on children's understanding of the legal system finds that' young children 'have little understanding of prosecution.' * * * Thus, it is extremely unlikely that a 3-year-old child in L. P.'s position would intend his statements to be a substitute for trial testimony. On the contrary, a young child in these circumstances would simply want the abuse to end, would want to protect other victims, or would have no discernible purpose at all.

"As a historical matter, moreover, there is strong evidence that statements made in circumstances similar to those facing L. P. and his teachers were admissible at common law. * * *

And when 18th-century courts excluded statements of this sort, * * * they appeared to do so because the child should have been ruled competent to testify, not because the statements were otherwise inadmissible * * * It is thus highly doubtful that statements like L. P.'s ever would have been understood to raise Confrontation Clause concerns. Neither *Crawford* nor any of the cases that it has produced has mounted evidence that the adoption of the Confrontation Clause was understood to require the exclusion of evidence that was regularly admitted in criminal cases at the time of the founding. Certainly, the statements in this case are nothing like the notorious use of ex parte examination in Sir Walter Raleigh's trial for treason, which we have frequently identified as 'the principal evil at which the Confrontation Clause was directed.' *Crawford.*

"Finally, although we decline to adopt a rule that statements to individuals who are not law enforcement officers are categorically outside the Sixth Amendment, the fact that L. P. was speaking to his teachers remains highly relevant. Courts must evaluate challenged statements in context, and part of that context is the questioner's identity. Statements made to someone who is not principally charged with uncovering and prosecuting criminal behavior are significantly less likely to be testimonial than statements given to law enforcement officers. It is common sense that the relationship between a student and his teacher is very different from that between a citizen and the police. We do not ignore that reality. In light of these circumstances, the Sixth Amendment did not prohibit the State from introducing L.P.'s statements at trial.

"Clark's efforts to avoid this conclusion are all off-base. He emphasizes Ohio's mandatory reporting obligations, in an attempt to equate L. P.'s teachers with the police and their caring questions with official interrogations. But the comparison is inapt. The teachers' pressing concern was to protect L. P. and remove him from harm's way. Like all good teachers, they undoubtedly would have acted with the same purpose whether or not they had a state-law duty to report abuse. And mandatory reporting statutes alone cannot convert a conversation between a concerned teacher and her student into a law enforcement mission aimed primarily at gathering evidence for a prosecution. * * * Clark is also wrong to suggest that admitting L. P.'s statements would be fundamentally unfair given that Ohio law does not allow incompetent children to testify. In any Confrontation Clause case, the individual who provided the out-of-court statement is not available as an in-court witness, but the testimony is admissible under an exception to the hearsay rules and is probative of the defendant's guilt. The fact that the witness is unavailable because of a different rule of evidence does not change our analysis."

Justice Thomas concurred in the judgment, again rejecting the primary purpose test, and instead asking whether the statements "bear sufficient indicia of solemnity to qualify as testimonial." L.Ps statements "bear no resemblance to the historical practices that the that the Confrontation Clause aimed to eliminate," as they were not "contained in formalized testimonial materials, such as affidavits, depositions, prior testimony, or confessions", nor "obtained in 'a formalized dialogue'; after the issuance of the warnings required by *Miranda*; while in police custody; or in an attempt to evade confrontation."

§ 3.   RIGHTS TO REMAIN SILENT AND TO TESTIFY

14th ed., p. 1361; before Note 6, add:

5A. ***The impact of prior conviction impeachment on the right to testify.*** The accuracy of the inference that *Griffin* forbids—that a defendant who does not testify must be guilty—has been undermined by studies of convicted defendants later exonerated by DNA evidence. One study found 39% of those convicted but later exonerated did not testify at their trials. The primary reason these innocent defendants stayed off the stand, the author concluded, was "the fear of impeachment with their prior convictions. Virtually all the defendants who did not testify had a prior record that likely would have been disclosed to the jury had they taken the stand." John H.

Blume, The Dilemma of the Criminal Defendant with a Prior Record—Lessons from the Wrongfully Convicted, 5 J. Empirical Legal Stud. 477 (2008).

Almost all jurisdictions permit impeachment with prior convictions. In the federal courts and many states, in order to raise and preserve for review a claim of improper impeachment with a prior conviction, a defendant must testify. *Luce v. United States*, 469 U.S. 38 (1984). Jurors are instructed that they may consider a testifying defendant's prior conviction only when deciding whether to believe the defendant's testimony, not as evidence that the defendant must have committed the charged crime. But studies suggest that jurors continue to infer propensity from prior convictions anyway. For example, one study found that mock jurors convicted a burglary defendant 82% of the time when they learned that the defendant had a prior robbery conviction, 73% of the time when impeached with a fraud conviction, and only 62% of the time when no prior crimes were used for impeachment. Jeffrey Bellin, The Silence Penalty, 103 Iowa L. Rev. 395 (2018).

Defendants with prior convictions who go to trial must choose: stay off the stand knowing jurors may draw an improper adverse inference from silence; or testify knowing jurors may improperly infer criminal propensity from convictions introduced only for impeachment. The increased likelihood of conviction when jurors infer guilt from *silence* is about as strong as the increased likelihood of conviction when jurors infer guilt from *prior conviction*, concluded Professor Bellin. The choice also affects many more defendants today than it did back in the mid-20th Century, because of the enormous increase in the proportion of defendants, particularly African American defendants, with prior records. Writes Bellin, the "dilemma inevitably contributes to a steady increase in guilty pleas and a corresponding decrease in trials. . . . The cycle is self-perpetuating. Every new conviction leads to a decreased likelihood of success in a subsequent trial and a stronger incentive to plead guilty."

Do these studies or changed circumstances warrant modification of the rules concerning the right to testify, the right not to testify, or the use of convictions to impeach? Commentary and state law is collected in the sources cited above, as well as Anna Roberts, *Reclaiming the Importance of the Defendant's Testimony: Prior Conviction Impeachment and the Fight Against Implicit Stereotyping*, 83 U.Chi.L.Rev. 835 (2016), and Montré D. Carodine, 'The Mis-Characterization of the Negro': A Race Critique of the Prior Conviction Impeachment Rule (2009), 84 Indiana L.J. 521 (2009).

14th ed., p. 1361; Note 6, change heading to *"Other burdens on the right to testify."*

14th ed., p. 1368; at end of chapter, as new Section, add:

§ 5. THE RIGHT TO A PUBLIC TRIAL

PRESLEY V. GEORGIA
558 U.S. 209, 130 S.Ct. 721, 175 L.Ed.2d 675 (2010).

[Before selecting a jury in Presley's trial, the trial judge excluded the lone courtroom observer, Presley's uncle, over defense counsel's objection. The judge explained, stating " '[t]here just isn't space * * * . "Each of those rows will be occupied by jurors. And his uncle cannot sit and intermingle with members of the jury panel.' " After Presley was convicted, the trial judge denied his motion for a new trial based on the exclusion of the public from voir dire, and the ruling was affirmed by Georgia's appellate courts. On direct appeal, the Supreme Court reversed.]

PER CURIAM. * * *

This Court's rulings with respect to the public trial right rest upon two different provisions of the Bill of Rights, both applicable to the States via the Due Process Clause of the Fourteenth Amendment. * * * The Sixth Amendment directs, in relevant part, that "[i]n all criminal prosecutions, the accused shall enjoy the right to a speedy and public trial . . . ." * * * [T]he public trial right extends beyond the accused and can be invoked under the First Amendment. *Press-Enterprise I,* 464 U.S. 501 (1984) [14th ed., p. 1330]. [This case] is brought under the Sixth Amendment, for it is the accused who invoked his right to a public trial. An initial question is whether the right to a public trial in criminal cases extends to the jury selection phase of trial, and in particular the *voir dire* of prospective jurors. In the First Amendment context that question was answered in *Press-Enterprise I.* The Court there held that the *voir dire* of prospective jurors must be open to the public under the First Amendment. Later in the same Term as *Press-Enterprise I,* the Court considered a Sixth Amendment case concerning whether the public trial right extends to a pretrial hearing on a motion to suppress certain evidence. *Waller v. Georgia,* 467 U.S. 39 (1984) [14th ed., p. 1330]. The *Waller* Court relied heavily upon *Press-Enterprise I* in finding that the Sixth Amendment right to a public trial extends beyond the actual proof at trial. It ruled that the pretrial suppression hearing must be open to the public because "there can be little doubt that the explicit Sixth Amendment right of the accused is no less protective of a public trial than the implicit First Amendment right of the press and public."

* * * The extent to which the First and Sixth Amendment public trial rights are coextensive is an open question, and it is not necessary here to speculate whether or in what circumstances the reach or protections of one might be greater than the other. Still, there is no legitimate reason, at least in the context of juror selection proceedings, to give one who asserts a First Amendment privilege greater rights to insist on public proceedings than the accused has. "Our cases have uniformly recognized the public-trial guarantee as one created for the benefit of the defendant." There could be no explanation for barring the accused from raising a constitutional right that is unmistakably for his or her benefit. That rationale suffices to resolve the instant matter.

* * * While the accused does have a right to insist that the *voir dire* of the jurors be public, there are exceptions to this general rule. "[T]he right to an open trial may give way in certain cases to other rights or interests, such as the defendant's right to a fair trial or the government's interest in inhibiting disclosure of sensitive information." *Waller.* "Such circumstances will be rare, however, and the balance of interests must be struck with special care." *Waller* provided standards for courts to apply before excluding the public from any stage of a criminal trial: "[T]he party seeking to close the hearing must advance an overriding interest that is likely to be prejudiced, the closure must be no broader than necessary to protect that interest, the trial court must consider reasonable alternatives to closing the proceeding, and it must make findings adequate to support the closure."

In upholding exclusion of the public at juror *voir dire* in the instant case, the Supreme Court of Georgia concluded, despite our explicit statements to the contrary, that trial courts need not consider alternatives to closure absent an opposing party's proffer of some alternatives. * * * Trial courts are obligated to take every reasonable measure to accommodate public attendance at criminal trials. Nothing in the record shows that the trial court could not have accommodated the public at Presley's trial. Without knowing the precise circumstances, some possibilities include reserving one or more rows for the public; dividing the jury venire panel to reduce courtroom congestion; or instructing prospective jurors not to engage or interact with audience members.

Petitioner also argues that, apart from failing to consider alternatives to closure, the trial court erred because it did not even identify any overriding interest likely to be prejudiced absent the closure of *voir dire.* There is some merit to this complaint. The generic risk of jurors overhearing prejudicial remarks, unsubstantiated by any specific threat or incident, is inherent whenever members of the public are present during the selection of jurors. If broad concerns of this sort were sufficient to override a defendant's constitutional right to a public trial, a court could exclude the public from jury selection almost as a matter of course. As noted in the dissent below, "the majority's reasoning permits the closure of voir dire in *every criminal case* conducted in this courtroom whenever the trial judge decides, for whatever reason, that he or she would prefer to fill the courtroom with potential jurors rather than spectators."

There are no doubt circumstances where a judge could conclude that threats of improper communications with jurors or safety concerns are concrete enough to warrant closing *voir dire.* But in those cases, the particular interest, and threat to that interest, must "be articulated along with findings specific enough that a reviewing court can determine whether the closure order was properly entered." We need not rule on this second claim of error, because even assuming, *arguendo,* that the trial court had an overriding interest in closing *voir dire,* it was still incumbent upon it to consider all reasonable alternatives to closure. It did not, and that is all this Court needs to decide.[a]

NOTES AND QUESTIONS

1.   *The interests protected by the public trial right.* "The requirement of a public trial is for the benefit of the accused; that the public may see he is fairly dealt with and not unjustly condemned, and that the presence of interested spectators may keep his triers keenly alive to a sense of their responsibility and to the importance of their functions." *Waller* (quoting *In re Oliver*, 333 U.S. 257, 270, n. 25 (1948)). "In addition to ensuring that judge and prosecutor carry out their duties responsibly, a public trial encourages witnesses to come forward and discourages perjury."

In an earlier case applying the First Amendment public trial right, the Court explained, "Public scrutiny of a criminal trial enhances the quality and safeguards the integrity of the factfinding process, with benefits to both the defendant and to society as a whole. Moreover, public access to the criminal trial fosters an appearance of fairness, thereby heightening public respect for the judicial process. And in the broadest terms, public access to criminal trials permits the public to participate in and serve as a check upon the judicial process . . . ." *Globe Newspaper Co v. Superior Court*, 457 U.S. 596 (1982) [14th ed., p. 1329].

Also instructive is the discussion in *Weaver v. Massachusetts*, 137 S.Ct. 1899 [p. 25], this Supplement], where the Court considered potential harms from the closure of the courtroom during jury selection, resulting in the exclusion of the defendant's mother and her minister. The Court in *Weaver* confirmed that a public trial violation is a structural error that required relief on direct appeal without regard to harmlessness, but held that when a defendant fails to object to the violation at trial and raises that failure as the basis for a post-conviction claim of ineffective assistance of counsel, a showing of prejudice is required. After holding that Weaver did not show prejudice from the exclusion, the Court suggested various ways in which such a showing might have been made under different circumstances. "If, for instance, defense counsel errs in failing to object when the government's main witness testifies in secret, then the defendant might be able to show prejudice with little more detail. * * * [P]etitioner's trial was not conducted in secret or in a remote place. * * * [T]he courtroom remained open during the evidentiary phase of the trial; the closure decision apparently was made by court officers rather than the judge; there were many members of the venire who did not become jurors but who did observe the proceedings; and there was a record made of the proceedings that does not indicate any basis for concern, other than the closure itself. There has been no showing, furthermore, that the potential harms flowing from a courtroom closure came to pass in this case. For example, there is no suggestion that any juror lied during voir dire; no suggestion of misbehavior by the prosecutor, judge, or any other party;

---

[a]   Justice Thomas, joined by Justice Scalia, dissented.

and no suggestion that any of the participants failed to approach their duties with the neutrality and serious purpose that our system demands."

2.   *When closure is justified.* To avoid violating the defendant's Sixth Amendment right, explained the Court in *Waller*, "(1) the party seeking to close the hearing must advance an overriding interest that is likely to be prejudiced, (2) the closure must be no broader than necessary to protect that interest, (3) the trial court must consider reasonable alternatives to closing the proceeding, and (4) it must make findings adequate to support the closure." Lower courts have found that overriding interests supporting exclusion—if the other requirements of the *Waller* test are met—include protecting the welfare of a minor victim of crime, preventing harassment or physical harm to witnesses, protecting classified or confidential information, and preserving courtroom security.

3.   *A less demanding test for "trivial" closures?* Some lower courts have applied a less stringent test for "partial" or "trivial" closures, where (unlike in *Presley* and *Weaver)* not all members of the public are excluded, or the exclusion is quite brief. These courts require only a "substantial" or "important" rather than an "overriding" reason for restricting access in order to justify such a closure, and have reasoned that these limited exclusions do not implicate the same secrecy and fairness concerns that a total closure does. *E.g., United States v. Perry*, 479 F.3d 885 (D.C.Cir.2007) (no violation by exclusion of eight-year-old son of defendant on trial for unlawfully accessing a computer resulting in damage; closure was trivial when son was only person excluded, his presence would not have ensured fair proceedings, discouraged perjury, or encouraged witnesses to come forward). Other courts have rejected this watering down of the *Waller* standard. How should courts resolve this dispute over the meaning of the Sixth Amendment?

CHAPTER 26

REPROSECUTION AND DOUBLE JEOPARDY

■ ■ ■

§ 1. REPROSECUTION AFTER MISTRIAL

B. DEFENSE CONSENT TO MISTRIAL

14th ed., p. 1384; Note 1, substitute for *Batts*:

Thomas v. Eighth Judicial Dist. Court, 402 P.3d 619 (Nev. 2017) (barring retrial after mistrial declared for Brady violation, holding state constitution bars retrial after mistrial whenever a prosecutor intentionally proceeds in a course of egregious and improper conduct that causes prejudice to the defendant which cannot be cured by means short of a mistrial).

§ 4. REPROSECUTION BY A DIFFERENT SOVEREIGN

14th ed., p. 1400; substitute for *Heath*:

PUERTO RICO v. SANCHEZ VALLE ET AL.
__ U.S. __, 136 S.Ct. 1863, 195 L.Ed.2d 179 (2016).

[Luis Sánchez Valle and Jaime Gómez Vázquez (on separate occasions) each sold a gun to an undercover police officer. Commonwealth prosecutors indicted them for, among other things, selling a firearm without a permit in violation of the Puerto Rico Arms Act of 2000. While those charges were pending, federal grand juries indicted Sánchez Valle and Gómez Vázquez, based on the same transactions, for violations of analogous U.S. gun trafficking statutes. Both defendants pleaded guilty to those federal charges. The Court granted certiorari to determine whether the Double Jeopardy Clause bars the Federal Government and Puerto Rico from successively prosecuting a defendant on like charges for the same conduct.]

JUSTICE KAGAN delivered the opinion of the Court.[a]

The Double Jeopardy Clause of the Fifth Amendment prohibits more than one prosecution for the "same offence." But under what is known as the dual-sovereignty doctrine, a single act gives rise to distinct offenses—and thus may subject a person to successive prosecutions—if it violates the laws of separate sovereigns. To determine whether two prosecuting authorities are different sovereigns for double jeopardy purposes, this Court asks a narrow, historically focused question. The inquiry does not turn, as the term "sovereignty" sometimes suggests, on the degree to which the second entity is autonomous from the first or sets its own political course. Rather, the issue is only whether the prosecutorial powers of the two jurisdictions have independent origins—or, said conversely, whether those powers derive from the same "ultimate source." *United States v. Wheeler*, 435 U.S. 313, 320 (1978). In this case, we must decide if, under that test, Puerto Rico and the United States may successively prosecute a single defendant for the same criminal

---

[a]   The dissenting opinion of Justice Breyer, joined by Justice Sotomayor, is omitted, as well as the separate concurring opinion by Justice Thomas.

conduct. We hold they may not, because the oldest roots of Puerto Rico's power to prosecute lie in federal soil.

I A

Puerto Rico became a territory of the United States in 1898, as a result of the Spanish-American War. The treaty concluding that conflict ceded the island, then a Spanish colony, to the United States, and tasked Congress with determining "[t]he civil rights and political status" of its inhabitants. * * * Acting pursuant to the U.S. Constitution's Territory Clause, Congress initially established a "civil government" for Puerto Rico possessing significant authority over internal affairs. The U.S. President, with the advice and consent of the Senate, appointed the governor, supreme court, and upper house of the legislature; the Puerto Rican people elected the lower house themselves. Federal statutes generally applied (as they still do) in Puerto Rico, but the newly constituted legislature could enact local laws in much the same way as the then-45 States. Over time, Congress granted Puerto Rico additional autonomy. * * * Public Law 600, "recognizing the principle of government by consent," authorized the island's people to "organize a government pursuant to a constitution of their own adoption." * * * The Puerto Rico Constitution created a new political entity, the Commonwealth of Puerto Rico—or, in Spanish, Estado Libre Asociado de Puerto Rico. * * *

II A

* * * The ordinary rule under that Clause is that a person cannot be prosecuted twice for the same offense.[1] But two prosecutions, this Court has long held, are not for the same offense if brought by different sovereigns—even when those actions target the identical criminal conduct through equivalent criminal laws As we have put the point: "[W]hen the same act transgresses the laws of two sovereigns, it cannot be truly averred that the offender has been twice punished for the same offence; but only that by one act he has committed two offences." *Heath v. Alabama*, 474 U.S. 82, 88 (1985). The Double Jeopardy Clause thus drops out of the picture when the "entities that seek successively to prosecute a defendant for the same course of conduct [are] separate sovereigns."

Truth be told, however, "sovereignty" in this context does not bear its ordinary meaning. For whatever reason, the test we have devised to decide whether two governments are distinct for double jeopardy purposes overtly disregards common indicia of sovereignty. * * * [T]he inquiry (despite its label) does not probe whether a government possesses the usual attributes, or acts in the common manner, of a sovereign entity. Rather, * * * our test hinges on a single criterion: the "ultimate source" of the power undergirding the respective prosecutions. Whether two prosecuting entities are dual sovereigns in the double jeopardy context, we have stated, depends on "whether [they] draw their authority to punish the offender from distinct sources of power." *Heath*. The inquiry is thus historical, not functional—looking at the deepest wellsprings, not the current exercise, of prosecutorial authority. If two entities derive their power to punish from wholly independent sources (imagine here a pair of parallel lines), then they may bring successive prosecutions. Conversely, if those entities draw their power from the same ultimate source (imagine now two lines emerging from a common point, even if later diverging), then they may not.[3]

---

[1]   Because the parties in this case agree that the Double Jeopardy Clause applies to Puerto Rico, we have no occasion to consider that question here.

[3]   The Court has never explained its reasons for adopting this historical approach to the dual-sovereignty doctrine. It may appear counter-intuitive, even legalistic, as compared to an inquiry focused on a governmental entity's functional autonomy. But that alternative would raise serious problems of application. It would require deciding exactly how much autonomy is sufficient for separate sovereignty and whether a given entity's exercise of self-rule exceeds that level. The results, we suspect, would often be uncertain, introducing error and inconsistency into our double jeopardy law. By contrast, as we go on to show, the Court has easily applied

Under that approach, the States are separate sovereigns from the Federal Government (and from one another). See *Abbate v. United States*, 359 U.S. 187, 195 (1959); *Bartkus v. Illinois*, 359 U.S. 121, 132–137 (1959). The States' "powers to undertake criminal prosecutions," we have explained, do not "derive[ ] . . . from the Federal Government." Instead, the States rely on "authority originally belonging to them before admission to the Union and preserved to them by the Tenth Amendment." Said otherwise: Prior to forming the Union, the States possessed "separate and independent sources of power and authority," which they continue to draw upon in enacting and enforcing criminal laws. *Heath.* State prosecutions therefore have their most ancient roots in an "inherent sovereignty" unconnected to, and indeed pre-existing, the U.S. Congress.[4]

For similar reasons, Indian tribes also count as separate sovereigns under the Double Jeopardy Clause. Originally, this Court has noted, "the tribes were self-governing sovereign political communities," possessing (among other capacities) the "inherent power to prescribe laws for their members and to punish infractions of those laws." *Wheeler*, 435 U.S., at 322–323. After the formation of the United States, the tribes became "domestic dependent nations," subject to plenary control by Congress—so hardly "sovereign" in one common sense. But unless and until Congress withdraws a tribal power—including the power to prosecute—the Indian community retains that authority in its earliest form. The "ultimate source" of a tribe's "power to punish tribal offenders" thus lies in its "primeval" or, at any rate, "pre-existing" sovereignty: A tribal prosecution, like a State's, is "attributable in no way to any delegation . . . of federal authority." * * *

Conversely, this Court has held that a municipality cannot qualify as a sovereign distinct from a State—no matter how much autonomy over criminal punishment the city maintains. See *Waller* [*v. Florida*], 397 U.S. 387, 395 (1970). Florida law, we recognized in our pivotal case on the subject, treated a municipality as a "separate sovereign entit[y]" for all relevant real-world purposes: The city possessed broad home-rule authority, including the power to enact criminal ordinances and prosecute offenses. But that functional control was not enough to escape the double jeopardy bar; indeed, it was wholly beside the point. * * * Because the municipality, in the first instance, had received its power from the State, those two entities could not bring successive prosecutions for a like offense.

And most pertinent here, this Court concluded in the early decades of the last century that U.S. territories—including an earlier incarnation of Puerto Rico itself—are not sovereigns distinct from the United States. * * *

B

* * * [I]f we go back as far as our doctrine demands—to the "ultimate source" of Puerto Rico's prosecutorial power,—we once again discover the U.S. Congress. * * * [I]f our double jeopardy decisions hinged on measuring an entity's self-governance, the emergence of the Commonwealth would have resulted as well in the capacity to bring the kind of successive prosecutions attempted

---

the "ultimate source" test to classify broad classes of governments as either sovereign or not for purposes of barring retrials.

[4]   Literalists might object that only the original 13 States can claim such an independent source of authority; for the other 37, Congress played some role in establishing them as territories, authorizing or approving their constitutions, or (at the least) admitting them to the Union. And indeed, that is the tack the dissent takes. But this Court long ago made clear that a new State, upon entry, necessarily becomes vested with all the legal characteristics and capabilities of the first 13. That principle of "equal footing," we have held, is essential to ensure that the nation remains "a union of States [alike] in power, dignity and authority, each competent to exert that residuum of sovereignty not delegated to the United States." Thus, each later-admitted State exercises its authority to enact and enforce criminal laws by virtue not of congressional grace, but of the independent powers that its earliest counter- parts both brought to the Union and chose to maintain. The dissent's contrary view—that, say, Texas's or California's powers (including the power to make and enforce criminal law) derive from the Federal Government—contradicts the most fundamental conceptual premises of our constitutional order, indeed the very bedrock of our Union

here. But as already explained, the dual-sovereignty test we have adopted focuses on a different question: not on the fact of self-rule, but on where it came from. We do not care, for example, that the States presently exercise autonomous control over criminal law and other local affairs; instead, we treat them as separate sovereigns because they possessed such control as an original matter, rather than deriving it from the Federal Government. * * *

* * * [N]o one argues that when the United States gained possession of Puerto Rico, its people possessed independent prosecutorial power, in the way that the States or tribes did upon becoming part of this country. Puerto Rico was until then a colony "under Spanish sovereignty." And local prosecutors in the ensuing decades, as petitioner itself acknowledges, exercised only such power as was "delegated by Congress" through federal statutes. Their authority derived from, rather than pre-existed association with, the Federal Government.

And contrary to petitioner's claim, Puerto Rico's transformative constitutional moment does not lead to a different conclusion. * * * Back of the Puerto Rican people and their Constitution, the "ultimate" source of prosecutorial power remains the U.S. Congress, just as back of a city's charter lies a state government. * * * Put simply, Congress conferred the authority to create the Puerto Rico Constitution, which in turn confers the authority to bring criminal charges. That makes Congress the original source of power for Puerto Rico's prosecutors—as it is for the Federal Government's. The island's Constitution, significant though it is, does not break the chain.

* * * So the Double Jeopardy Clause bars both Puerto Rico and the United States from prosecuting a single person for the same conduct under equivalent criminal laws.

JUSTICE GINSBURG, with whom JUSTICE THOMAS joins, concurring.

I join in full the Court's opinion, which cogently applies long prevailing doctrine. I write only to flag a larger question that bears fresh examination in an appropriate case. The double jeopardy proscription is intended to shield individuals from the harassment of multiple prosecutions for the same misconduct. Current "separate sovereigns" doctrine hardly serves that objective. States and Nation are "kindred systems," yet "parts of ONE WHOLE." The Federalist No. 82, p. 245 (J. Hopkins ed., 2d ed. 1802) (reprint 2008). Within that whole is it not "an affront to human dignity," "inconsistent with the spirit of [our] Bill of Rights," to try or punish a person twice for the same offense? Several jurists and commentators have suggested that the question should be answered with a resounding yes: Ordinarily, a final judgment in a criminal case, just as a final judgment in a civil case, should preclude renewal of the fray anyplace in the Nation. The matter warrants attention in a future case in which a defendant faces successive prosecutions by parts of the whole USA.

CHAPTER 27

SENTENCING

■ ■ ■

§ 1. INTRODUCTION TO SENTENCING

A. PURPOSES OF PUNISHMENT

14th ed., p. 1405; at end of Note 1, add:

In 2017, after fifteen years of research, drafting, and debate, the American Law Institute approved the final draft of Model Penal Code: Sentencing, a comprehensive work providing guidance to states for sentencing and sentencing procedure. The Comments and Reporters' Notes provide a rich compendium of research on sentencing law, policy, and practice across the nation. Section 1.02(2)(a) defines four purposes for sentencing decisions:

(i) to render sentences in all cases within a range of severity proportionate to the gravity of offenses, the harms done to crime victims, and the blameworthiness of offenders;

(ii) when reasonably feasible, to achieve offender rehabilitation, general deterrence, incapacitation of dangerous offenders, restitution to crime victims, preservation of families, and reintegration of offenders into the law-abiding community, provided these goals are pursued within the boundaries of proportionality in subsection (a)(i);

(iii) to render sentences no more severe than necessary to achieve the applicable purposes in subsections (a)(i) and (a)(ii); and

(iv) to avoid the use of sanctions that increase the likelihood offenders will engage in future criminal conduct.

The Comment to this section explains: "Under the new Code's scheme, no crime reductive or other utilitarian purpose of sentencing may justify a punishment outside the 'range of severity' proportionate to the gravity of the offense, the harm to the crime victim, and the blameworthiness of the offender. . . . [It is] intended to encourage rather than stamp out the pursuit of utilitarian ends, in an expanding universe of cases, and with ever-greater attention to proper implementation and evaluation . . . ."

B. TYPES OF SENTENCES

14th ed., p. 1406; Note 2, between "parole authorities." and "A *determinate*", add:

Most states have retained a parole board or other entity to exercise release discretion. Of the half million prisoners paroled in 2012, about 40% were released through discretionary decision-making. Paroling authorities deciding whether to grant release typically use parole release guidelines or other scoring instruments, and a growing number include "risk and needs" assessment tools to estimate a prisoner's statistical likelihood of recidivism based upon the recidivism history of prisoners with similar risk-factor profiles. See resources collected at http://nationalparoleresourcecenter.org.

14th ed., p. 1407; Note 5, before last sentence, add:

In misdemeanor and traffic offenses, fees often dwarf the fine authorized as punishment for the offense. For example, an Illinois report noted a defendant in McLean County convicted of Driving Under the Influence and fined $150, would in addition to the fine, be assessed a $75 "base fee," a $20 Court Automation fee, a $15 Court Document Storage Fund fee, $30 Circuit Court Fund fee, $25 Court Security fee, $5 E-Citation fee, $2 State's Attorney Records fee, $10 State's Attorney fee, and 15 state and local add-on fees totaling $1,560 (including fees for Children's Advocacy Centers, County Jail Medical Costs, Drug Court, Traffic School, Drivers' Education, Fire Prevention, Spinal Cord Injury, and Roadside Memorial Funds). The total $1,742 was more than ten times the $150 fine. In addition, a DUI defendant may also have to pay court ordered treatment and/or probation costs, which can cost several thousand dollars. Illinois Statutory Court Task Force, Findings and Recommendations for Addressing Barriers to Access to Justice and Additional Issues Associated with Fees and Other Court Costs in Civil, Criminal, and Traffic Proceedings 27–29 (2016).

"The vast majority of states impose 'user fees' for services commonly understood to be part of criminal justice expenditures, such as for use of a public defender, for 'room and board' for jail and prison, and for the arrested individual's probation and parole supervision. Criminal courts seek revenue from arrested individuals through booking fees at the time of arrest, bail administrative fees, dismissal fees, public defender application fees, court fees, disability and translation fees, jail and administrative fees, and postconviction fees. . . . Two-thirds of states . . . permit judges to charge defendants for at least a portion of the cost of their own public defender. . . .The fees create incentives for localities to run the criminal justice system like a business, one that creates value through imposing costs, tracking payments, and imposing additional sanctions for failure to pay. The risk is that arrest decisions are based on the institution's own organizational interest in generating revenue, rather than public considerations about safety." Elsa Jain, *Capitalizing on Criminal Justice*, 67 Duke L. J. 1381 (2018). Professor Beth Colgan summarized the findings of recent research: "Separate and distinct from the potential that inadequately designed systems for fines, fees, and forfeitures will distort criminal justice incentives, such systems can also undermine other governmental aims due to their inherently regressive nature. By entrenching or exacerbating the financial vulnerability of people and their families, fines, fees, and forfeitures can create long-term instability and familial disruption, increase criminal justice involvement, aggravate jail overcrowding, and—perhaps ironically—decrease net revenue." Colgan, "Fine, Fees and Forfeitures," in Academy for Justice (2017) (collecting research), http://academyforjustice.org.

Litigation is beginning to expose and challenge these practices. The Department of Justice report on the municipal courts in Ferguson, Missouri is the most well-known example. Another example is Cain v. City of New Orleans, 281 F. Supp. 3d 624 (E.D. La. 2017), granting summary judgment to civil rights plaintiffs for their claims that 1) assessments of fees by the judges of the Orleans Parish Criminal District Court violated due process when "governing law . . . force[d] the Judges to generate revenue from the criminal defendants they sentence, creating a substantial conflict of interest, and 2) judges routinely imprisoned indigent defendants for the failure to pay court debts without any ability-to-pay inquiry, violating their due process rights.

The ALI's MPC Sentencing recommends: "No economic sanction may be imposed unless the offender would retain sufficient means for reasonable living expenses and family obligations after compliance with the sanction," and "agencies or entities charged with collection of economic sanctions may not be the recipients of monies collected and may not impose fees on offenders for delinquent payments or services rendered." MPC Sentencing § 6.04 (ALI, Final Draft 2017).

14th ed., p. 1407; at end of Note 5, add:

For an example of one decision taking collateral consequences into account when setting a sentence, see *United States v. Nesbeth*, 188 F.Supp.3d 179 (E.D.N.Y. 2016) (noting collateral consequences following a federal conviction "can be particularly disruptive to an ex-convict's efforts at rehabilitation and reintegration into society," and describing legal prohibitions on certain employment, the "reluctance of private employers to hire ex-convicts," as well as ineligibility for educational, tax, housing, Social Security, and nutritional benefits).

C. WHO SETS THE SENTENCE?

14th ed., p. 1408; at end of last paragraph in Section 1, add:

Consider the ALI's position: "Long experience has shown that the use of jurors as sentencers is antithetical to policies of rationality, proportionality, and restraint in the imposition of criminal sanctions, and is fundamentally inconsistent with the Code's philosophy that the public policies of sentencing should be applied consistently and even-handedly in all cases." MPC Sentencing § 6.02, Comment (ALI, Final Draft 2017).

§ 2. ALLOCATING AND CONTROLLING SENTENCING DISCRETION

A. MANDATORY MINIMUM SENTENCES

14th ed., p. 1409; Note 3, after first paragraph, add:

The Comment to MPC Sentencing § 6.06 (ALI, Final Draft 2017) summarized the research: "Empirical research and policy analyses have shown time and again that mandatory minimum penalties fail to promote uniformity in punishment and instead exacerbate sentencing disparities, lead to disproportionate and even bizarre sanctions in individual cases, are ineffective measures for advancing deterrent and incapacitative objectives, distort the plea-bargaining process, shift sentencing authority from courts to prosecutors, result in pronounced geographic disparities due to uneven enforcement patterns in different prosecutors' offices, coerce some innocent defendants to plead guilty to lesser charges to avoid the threat of a mandatory term, undermine the rational ordering of graduated sentencing guidelines, penalize low-level and unsophisticated offenders more so than those in leadership roles, provoke nullification of the law by lawyers, judges, and jurors, and engender public perceptions in some communities that the criminal law lacks moral legitimacy."

B. SENTENCING GUIDELINES

14th ed., p. 1411; Note 2, before Section C, replace citation to "tentative draft" with:

MPC Sentencing § 6A.01–6B.11 (ALI, Final Draft, 2017).

§ 3. CONSTITUTIONAL LIMITS ON SENTENCING PROCEDURE

A. INFORMATION CONSIDERED IN SETTING THE SENTENCE

14th ed., p. 1415; Note 1.b., at end of first paragraph, add:

See also *Buck v. Davis,* 137 S.Ct. 759 (2017), finding ineffective assistance by defense counsel at the defendant's capital sentencing hearing. There, the jury had to determine whether the defendant was likely to be a future danger, and counsel allowed an expert to testify that the defendant's race increased the probability of future violence. The Court stated "when a jury hears expert testimony that expressly makes a defendant's race directly pertinent on the question of life or death, the impact of that evidence cannot be measured simply by how much air time it received at trial or how many pages it occupies in the record. Some toxins can be deadly in small doses."

D. JURY TRIAL AND BURDEN OF PROOF

14th ed., p. 1426; at end of Note 1, add:

The jury itself must find each fact necessary to impose a death sentence. The Sixth Amendment does not allow a sentencing scheme that requires a judge to determine those facts, even if the jury makes an advisory recommendation. *Hurst v. Florida,* 136 S.Ct. 616 (2016).

14th ed., p. 1433; at end of Note 5, add:

The Supreme Court of Hawaii has rejected the exception for prior convictions, interpreting the state's constitution to require that the government allege in the charging instrument any prior conviction triggering a mandatory minimum sentence, and that the jury find that conviction beyond a reasonable doubt. *State v. Auld,* 136 Hawai'i 244, 361 P.3d 471 (2015).

14th ed., p. 1435; at the end of Note 9, add:

The Commentary to MPC Sentencing provision on appellate review warns: "So long as the sentence review process has a gestalt character that does not turn on hard decision rules, and so long as the legal adequacy of the factual record is weighed against the judgment of appellate courts rather than the criteria of some other decisionmaking body, the practice of substantive sentence review has so far been allowed to coexist with the *Blakely* immunity granted to advisory sentencing systems. Beyond what has been specifically allowed by the Supreme Court, it is unclear how far the practice of appellate sentence review may be taken in an advisory-guidelines system without running afoul of *Blakely*." MPC: Sentencing § 7.09, Comment (ALI, Final Draft 2017).

PART 5

APPEALS, POST-CONVICTION REVIEW

■ ■ ■

CHAPTER 28

APPEALS

■ ■ ■

§ 1. THE DEFENDANT'S RIGHT TO APPEAL

14th ed., p. 1437; Note 1, substitute for last sentence:

Using data from a nationwide study of state criminal appeals (see Nicole A. Waters, *et al.*, Bureau of Justice Statistics Bulletin: Criminal Appeals in State Courts (Sept. 2015)), one study found that on average, defendants received a favorable outcome in 14.9% of appeals of-right by defendants, but less than 3% of appeals to courts of last resort that exercised discretion whether to review the case. Michael Heise, Nancy J. King & Nicole A. Heise, *State Criminal Appeals Revealed*, 70 Vand. L. Rev. 1939 (2017). Just over half of the appeals of right produced a reasoned judicial opinion; the remainder received a summary or memorandum decision. Less than 20% received oral argument. Sentencing challenges and insufficient evidence claims were most frequently raised (nearly 30% of first appeals of-right).

14th ed., p. 1438; after Note 3 add new Note 3A:

3a. *Inherent waiver by guilty plea.* A guilty plea "inherently waives" many potential appellate claims of error, as the Court explained in *Class v. United States,* 583 U.S. ___, 138 S.Ct. 798, 200 L.Ed.2d 37 (2018), p. 140 this Supplement. Claims inherently waived by a guilty plea include claims involving the "right to fair trial" and "accompanying constitutional guarantees," claims of "case related government conduct that takes place before plea," and claims "that would contradict the 'admissions necessarily made upon entry of a voluntary plea of guilty.' "

§ 4. REVIEW FOR CLAIMS NOT RAISED ON TIME

14th ed., p. 1448; at end of page, after "proceeding," add:

For a sentencing error, the defendant must "show a reasonable probability that the district court would have imposed a different sentence" had the error not occurred. *Molina-Martinez v. United States*, 136 S.Ct. 1338 (2016).

14th ed., 1449; Note 3.c., at end, add:

The Court in *Weaver v. Massachusetts,* 137 S.Ct. 1899 (2017), p. 25 this Supplement, addressed a somewhat related question, and its decision suggested that the Court is unlikely to find that every unraised "structural" error will necessarily satisfy the "prejudice" requirement of the plain error analysis. In *Weaver*, the Court held that a defendant raising a claim of ineffective assistance based on counsel's failure to raise a public trial violation must demonstrate "prejudice" under *Strickland,* even though a violation of the right to a public trial is considered a "structural error" on direct review. The Court emphasized that its decision was restricted to the context of an ineffective assistance claim alleging counsel's failure to object to closure of jury selection. The court's rationale, however, suggests that an unpreserved public trial right claim raised on direct appeal would also require a defendant to demonstrate "prejudice" for plain error relief, and that possibly other structural errors would require a showing of prejudice if not timely raised as well.

First, the Court rejected the dissenting justices' view that attempting to show prejudice from a violation of this structural error would be an impossible task. The Court assumed that in some cases a defendant would be able to make such a showing, stating that "not every public-trial violation will in fact lead to a fundamentally unfair trial" or deprive "the defendant of a reasonable probability of a different outcome." Weaver failed to demonstrate prejudice, it concluded, noting as support that the proceedings were not conducted in secret or in a remote place; that the remainder of the trial after jury selection was open; that the decision to close voir dire and exclude defendant's mother and her minister to make room for veniremembers was made by court officers, not the judge; that during closure, the proceedings were on the record and observed by many veniremembers who were not chosen; and that nothing in the record raised any suggestion that any juror, prosecutor, judge, or any other party misbehaved or that any of "the potential harms flowing from a courtroom closure came to pass." This part of the Court's rationale for demanding a showing of prejudice when the underlying error is structural will vary with the right at issue. Ruling out a reasonable probability of prejudice from other types of structural error, such as a biased judge, may not be so easy.

In addition to concluding that it was not impossible for reviewing courts to gauge the likelihood of prejudice from this particular structural error, the Court argued that the ineffective assistance context in which the claim was raised supported a requirement that the defendant demonstrate prejudice. Not raising the error until after trial deprives trial courts of the chance to cure such violations either by opening the courtroom or by explaining the reasons for closure, the Court said. Preserving the claim and raising it on direct review, the Court added, would have allowed reviewing courts to "give instruction to the trial courts in a familiar context that allows for elaboration of the relevant principles based on review of an adequate record." Both of these rationales are important for the plain error context, because quite often when a structural error is not raised in the trial court, the trial judge loses the opportunity to cure that error, and the reviewing court loses its fully developed record.[a]

[a]   The Court also mentioned that when a claim is raised in postconviction review, the costs and uncertainties of a new trial are greater than they are when a claim is raised on direct review. On direct review, "there may be a reasonable chance that not too much time will have elapsed for witness memories still to be accurate and physical evidence not to be lost." This argument would support requiring prejudice for at least some structural errors under the "cause and prejudice" test for avoiding procedural default in federal habeas review, another context where the application of a "prejudice" requirement to structural errors has divided courts. See Ch. 29, Section 4, and Note 2, p. 1478.

14th ed., p. 1450; at the end of Note 3.d. add:

Applying this standard (and rejecting a more stringent "shock-the-conscience" standard), the Court in *Rosales-Mireles v. United States*, 138 S.Ct. 1897 (2018), concluded that a miscalculation of the US Sentencing Guidelines range will ordinarily require a court of appeals to exercise its discretion to vacate the defendant's sentence. Noting that a defendant bears the burden of persuading the reviewing court that the error seriously affected the fairness, integrity or public reputation of judicial proceedings, Justice Sotomayor explained for the Court that an "error resulting in a higher range than the Guidelines provide usually establishes a reasonable probability that a defendant will serve a prison sentence that is more than 'necessary' to fulfill the purposes of incarceration." In asserting that any amount of actual jail time is significant to both the defendant and society, the Court relied upon social science studies of perceptions of fairness of the justice system. The Court also reasoned that the error in miscalculating the Guidelines range was a mistake by the judiciary (through its Probation Office), not a strategic error of counsel, and quoted an earlier opinion by then court of appeals Judge Gorsuch: "[W]hat reasonable citizen wouldn't bear a rightly diminished view of the judicial process and its integrity if courts refused to correct obvious errors of their own devise that threaten to require individuals to linger longer in federal prison than the law demands?" Finally, it noted that " 'remand for resentencing, while not costless, does not invoke the same difficulties as a remand for retrial does.' "

Responding to Justice Thomas's argument in dissent that the majority's decision invited sandbagging by defendants, the Court stated, "It is hard to imagine that defense counsel would 'deliberately forgo objection now' to a plain Guidelines error that would subject her client to a higher Guidelines range, 'because [counsel] perceives some slightly expanded chance to argue for "plain error" later.' " (quoting Henderson [p. 1448, Note 3b.]). "Even setting aside the conflict such a strategy would create with defense counsel's ethical obligations to represent her client vigorously and her duty of candor toward the court," the Court wrote, "any benefit from such a strategy is highly speculative. There is no guarantee that a court of appeals would agree to a remand, and no basis to believe that a district court would impose a lower sentence upon resentencing than the court would have imposed at the original sentencing proceedings had it been aware of the plain Guidelines error."

§ 5.   THE HARMLESS ERROR RULE

B.   CONSTITUTIONAL ERROR

14th ed., p. 1454; Note 2, before last sentence, add, as new paragraph:

The current Court's understanding of what makes an error "structural" appears in Part II of the Court's opinion in *Weaver v. Massachusetts*, 137 S.Ct. 1899 (2017), p. 25, this Supplement.

14th ed., p. 1460; at end of Note 2, add:

The appearance of fair adjudication also featured prominently in the Court's explanation of why an unconstitutional failure to recuse constitutes structural error even if the judge in question did not cast a deciding vote. In *Williams v. Pennsylvania,* 136 S.Ct. 1899 (2016), the Court held this was "a defect 'not amenable' to harmless-error review, regardless of whether the judge's vote was dispositive." Justice Kennedy, writing for the Court reasoned: "The deliberations of an appellate panel, as a general rule, are confidential. As a result, it is neither possible nor productive to inquire whether the jurist in question might have influenced the views of his or her colleagues during the decisionmaking process. Indeed, one purpose of judicial confidentiality is to assure jurists that they can reexamine old ideas and suggest new ones, while both seeking to persuade and being open to persuasion by their colleagues. As Justice Brennan wrote in his *Lavoie* concurrence,

> "The description of an opinion as being 'for the court' connotes more than merely that the opinion has been joined by a majority of the participating judges. It reflects the fact that these judges have exchanged ideas and arguments in deciding the case. It reflects the collective process of deliberation which shapes the court's perceptions of which issues must be addressed and, more importantly, how they must be addressed. And, while the influence of any single participant in this process can never be measured with precision, experience teaches us that each member's involvement plays a part in shaping the court's ultimate disposition." 475 U.S., at 831.

These considerations illustrate, moreover, that it does not matter whether the disqualified judge's vote was necessary to the disposition of the case. The fact that the interested judge's vote was not dispositive may mean only that the judge was successful in persuading most members of the court to accept his or her position. That outcome does not lessen the unfairness to the affected party.

A multimember court must not have its guarantee of neutrality undermined, for the appearance of bias demeans the reputation and integrity not just of one jurist, but of the larger institution of which he or she is a part. An insistence on the appearance of neutrality is not some artificial attempt to mask imperfection in the judicial process, but rather an essential means of ensuring the reality of a fair adjudication. Both the appearance and reality of impartial justice are necessary to the public legitimacy of judicial pronouncements and thus to the rule of law itself. When the objective risk of actual bias on the part of a judge rises to an unconstitutional level, the failure to recuse cannot be deemed harmless. * * * Williams must be granted an opportunity to present his claims to a court unburdened by any "possible temptation . . . not to hold the balance nice, clear and true between the State and the accused." *Tumey.* * * *

CHAPTER 29

POST-CONVICTION REVIEW: FEDERAL HABEAS CORPUS

■ ■ ■

§ 2. ISSUES COGNIZABLE

14th ed., p. 1469; Note 2, at end, add:

For a different and promising approach for investigating cases of actual innocence, see Robert P. Mosteller, *N.C. Innocence Inquiry Commission's First Decade: Impressive Successes and Lessons Learned*, 94 N.C.L.Rev. 1725 (2016). On whether a plea of guilty inherently waives such a claim in state post-conviction, see Note 1, p. 145 this Supplement.

§ 4. CLAIMS FORECLOSED BY PROCEDURAL DEFAULT

14th ed., p. 1477; Note 1.d., second paragraph, between "*trial* counsel," and "and also," insert new footnote a:

[a] The Court later declined "to extend *Martinez* to allow a federal court to hear a substantial, but procedurally defaulted, claim of ineffective assistance of appellate counsel when a prisoner's state postconviction counsel provides ineffective assistance by failing to raise that claim." Davila v. Davis, 137 S.Ct. 2058 (2017). It reasoned that such an extension is "not required to ensure that meritorious claims of trial error receive review by at least one state or federal court—the chief concern identified by this Court in *Martinez*" and "could ultimately knock down the procedural barriers to federal habeas review of nearly any defaulted claim of trial error," likely generating "high systemic costs and low systemic benefits."

14th ed., p. 1480; Note 4, end of first paragraph after "under § 2255," insert new footnote a:

[a] The Court's earlier ruling interpreting the scope of the federal statute applied retroactively to Bousley's conviction because that ruling "affected the reach of the underlying statute rather than the judicial procedures by which the statute is applied." See Note 1.c., p. 1489.

§ 5. RETROACTIVITY—WHICH LAW APPLIES?

14th ed., p. 1489; Note 1.c., replace third sentence (between "narrow." and "As for") with the following text and paragraph break:

One *Teague* exception requires retroactive application of "substantive" rulings. Substantive rulings "affect the reach of the underlying statute rather than the judicial procedures by which the statute is applied." They include decisions that "decriminalize a class of conduct" or narrow the scope of a criminal statute, see *Bousley v. United States*, p. 1480; *Welch v. United States,* 136 S.Ct. 1257 (2016) (applying retroactively earlier ruling that held a federal sentencing provision was void for vagueness), as well as decisions that prohibit "a certain category of punishment for a class of defendants because of their status or offense," such as the Court's rulings invalidating the mandatory application of life-without-parole sentences to juveniles. *Montgomery v. Louisiana,* 136 S.Ct. 718 (2016). Indeed, *Montgomery* held, "the Constitution requires state collateral review courts to give retroactive effect" to such rules.

§ 6. STANDARDS FOR REVIEWING STATE COURT INTERPRETATIONS AND APPLICATIONS OF FEDERAL LAW

A. CONTRARY DECISIONS AND UNREASONABLE APPLICATIONS

14th ed., p. 1499; after Note 8, add:

    9.   *Unreasonable determinations of fact.* In *Brumfield v. Cain,* 135 S.Ct. 2269 (2015), the Court applied § 2254(d)(2), limiting habeas relief based on faulty state court fact finding. A state post-conviction court had concluded that "Brumfield's IQ score was inconsistent with a diagnosis of intellectual disability" and that he had presented "no evidence of adaptive impairment." Based on its findings, the state court had denied Brumfield an evidentiary hearing and rejected his claim under *Atkins v. Virginia,* 536 U.S. 304 (2002), in which he Supreme Court held that the execution of the intellectually disabled contravenes the Eighth Amendment's prohibition on cruel and unusual punishment.

    Writing for the Court in *Brumfield*, Justice Sotomayor explained that a federal court reviewing a state court's factual findings in habeas may not characterize state-court factual determinations as unreasonable "merely because [it] would have reached a different conclusion in the first instance." Relief is not allowed just because " '[r]easonable minds reviewing the record might disagree' about the finding." The state court record in this case, however, "contained sufficient evidence to raise a question as to whether Brumfield met [the] criteria" for intellectual disability, including placement in special education classes, low reading level, low birth weight, and commitment to mental health facilities at a young age where he received antipsychotic and sedative drugs. "To conclude, as the state trial court did, that Brumfield's reported IQ score of 75 somehow demonstrated that he could not possess subaverage intelligence * * * reflected an unreasonable determination of the facts."

    Dissenting, four justices argued that it was inappropriate to evaluate this issue as a determination of fact under § 2254(d)(2). Instead, "the question whether Brumfield has met the legal standard for relief on, or at least an evidentiary hearing with regard to, his *Atkins* claim requires the application of law to those facts." Under 2254(d)(1), the dissenting justices argued, the state court's decision was not "contrary to" *Atkins,* where "this Court did not so much as mention an evidentiary hearing, let alone hold that prisoners raising *Atkins* claims are entitled to one." Moreover, the dissenters argued, the state court reasonably applied the general rule announced in *Atkins* when it found "that Brumfield had not come forward with evidence that he fell within the category of mentally retarded offenders about whom a national consensus against execution had developed." "Even if one were to mischaracterize *Atkins* as clearly establishing a right to an evidentiary hearing upon a substantial threshold showing of mental retardation, the state court did not unreasonably apply that rule. *Atkins* did not define the showing necessary, and the state court reasonably concluded that, on this record, Brumfield had not met it".

APPENDIX A

SELECTED PROVISIONS OF THE UNITED STATES CONSTITUTION

■ ■ ■

Section 9. * * *

[2] The privilege of the Writ of Habeas Corpus shall not be suspended, unless when in Cases of Rebellion or Invasion the public Safety may require it.

[3] No Bill of Attainder or ex post facto Law shall be passed.

ARTICLE III

Section 1. The judicial Power of the United States, shall be vested in one supreme Court, and in such inferior Courts as the Congress may from time to time ordain and establish. The Judges, both of the supreme and inferior Courts, shall hold their Offices during good Behaviour, and shall, at stated Times, receive for their Services a Compensation, which shall not be diminished during their Continuance in Office.

Section 2. [1] The judicial Power shall extend to all Cases, in Law and Equity, arising under this Constitution, the Laws of the United States, and Treaties made, or which shall be made, under their Authority;—to all Cases affecting Ambassadors, other public Ministers and Consuls;—to all Cases of admiralty and maritime Jurisdiction;—to Controversies to which the United States shall be a Party;—to Controversies between two or more States;—between a State and Citizens of another State;—between Citizens of different States;—between Citizens of the same State claiming Lands under the Grants of different States, and between a State, or the Citizens thereof, and foreign States, Citizens or Subjects.

[3] The trial of all Crimes, except in Cases of Impeachment, shall be by Jury; and such Trial shall be held in the State where the said Crimes shall have been committed; but when not committed within any State, the Trial shall be at such Place or Places as the Congress may by Law have directed.

Section 3.[1] Treason against the United States, shall consist only in levying War against them, or, in adhering to their Enemies, giving them Aid and Comfort. No Person shall be convicted of Treason unless on the Testimony of two Witnesses to the same overt Act, or on Confession in open Court.

[2] The Congress shall have Power to declare the Punishment of Treason, but no Attainder of Treason shall work Corruption of Blood, or Forfeiture except during the Life of the Person attainted.

ARTICLE IV

Section 2. [1] The Citizens of each State shall be entitled to all Privileges and Immunities of Citizens in the several States.

[2] A Person charged in any State with Treason, Felony, or other Crime, who shall flee from Justice, and be found in another State, shall on demand of the executive Authority of the State from which he fled, be delivered up, to be removed to the State having Jurisdiction of the Crime.

ARTICLE VI

[2] This Constitution, and the Laws of the United States which shall be made in Pursuance thereof; and all Treaties made, or which shall be made, under the Authority of the United States, shall be the supreme Law.

AMENDMENT I [1791]

Congress shall make no law respecting an establishment of religion, or prohibiting the free exercise thereof; or abridging the freedom of speech, or of the press; or the right of the people peaceably to assemble, and to petition the Government for a redress of grievances.

AMENDMENT II [1791]

A well regulated Militia, being necessary to the security of a free State, the right of the people to keep and bear Arms, shall not be infringed.

AMENDMENT III [1791]

No Soldier shall, in time of peace be quartered in any house, without the consent of the Owner, nor in time of war, but in a manner to be prescribed by law.

AMENDMENT IV [1791]

The right of the people to be secure in their persons, houses, papers, and effects, against unreasonable searches and seizures, shall not be violated, and no Warrants shall issue, but upon probable cause, supported by Oath or affirmation, and particularly describing the place to be searched, and the persons or things to be seized.

AMENDMENT V [1791]

No person shall be held to answer for a capital, or otherwise infamous crime, unless on a presentment or indictment of a Grand Jury, except in cases arising in the land or naval forces, or in the Militia, when in actual service in time of War or public danger; nor shall any person be subject for the same offence to be twice put in jeopardy of life or limb; nor shall be compelled in any criminal case to be a witness against himself, nor be deprived of life, liberty, or property, without due process of law; nor shall private property be taken for public use, without just compensation.

AMENDMENT VI [1791]

In all criminal prosecutions, the accused shall enjoy the right to a speedy and public trial, by an impartial jury of the State and district wherein the crime shall have been committed, which district shall have been previously ascertained by law, and to be informed of the nature and cause of the accusation; to be confronted with the witnesses against him; to have compulsory process for obtaining witnesses in his favor, and to have the Assistance of Counsel for his defence.

AMENDMENT VII [1791]

In Suits at common law, where the value in controversy shall exceed twenty dollars, the right of trial by jury shall be preserved, and no fact tried by jury, shall be otherwise re-examined in any Court of the United States, than according to the rules of the common law.

AMENDMENT VIII [1791]

Excessive bail shall not be required, nor excessive fines imposed, nor cruel and unusual punishments inflicted.

AMENDMENT IX [1791]

The enumeration in the Constitution, of certain rights, shall not be construed to deny or disparage others retained by the people.

AMENDMENT X [1791]

The powers not delegated to the United States by the Constitution, nor prohibited by it to the States, are reserved to the States respectively, or to the people.

AMENDMENT XIII [1865]

Section 1.   Neither slavery nor involuntary servitude, except as a punishment for crime whereof the party shall have been duly convicted, shall exist within the United States, or any place subject to their jurisdiction.

Section 2.   Congress shall have power to enforce this article by appropriate legislation.

AMENDMENT XIV [1868]

Section 1.   All persons born or naturalized in the United States, and subject to the jurisdiction thereof, are citizens of the United States and of the State wherein they reside. No State shall make or enforce any law which shall abridge the privileges or immunities of citizens of the United States; nor shall any State deprive any person of life, liberty, or property, without due process of law; nor deny to any person within its jurisdiction the equal protection of the laws.

Section 5.   The Congress shall have power to enforce, by appropriate legislation, the provisions of the article.

AMENDMENT XV [1870]

Section 1.   The right of citizens of the United States to vote shall not be denied or abridged by the United States or by any State on account of race, color, or previous condition of servitude.

Section 2.   The Congress shall have power to enforce this article by appropriate legislation.

APPENDIX B

SELECTED FEDERAL STATUTORY PROVISIONS

■ ■ ■

Analysis

Statute	Page
Wire and Electronic Communications Interception and Interception of Oral Communications (18 U.S.C. §§ 2510–2511, 2515–2518, 2520–2521)	179
Stored Wire and Electronic Communications and Transactional Records Access (18 U.S.C. §§ 2702, 2703, 2707, 2708, 2713)	197
Searches and Seizures (18 U.S.C. §§ 3103a, 3105, 3109)	204
Bail Reform Act of 1984 (18 U.S.C. §§ 3141–3150)	205
Speedy Trial Act of 1974 (As Amended) (18 U.S.C. §§ 3161–3162, 3164)	215
Jencks Act (18 U.S.C. § 3500)	220
Litigation Concerning Sources of Evidence (18 U.S.C. § 3504)	221
Criminal Appeals Act of 1970 (As Amended) (18 U.S.C. § 3731)	222
Crime Victims' Rights (18 U.S.C. § 3771)	222
Jury Selection and Service Act of 1968 (As Amended) (28 U.S.C. §§ 1861–1863, 1865–1867)	225
Habeas Corpus (28 U.S.C. §§ 2241–2244, 2253–2255, 2261–2266)	230
Privacy Protection Act of 1980 (42 U.S.C. §§ 2000aa–2000aa–12)	241
Guidelines (28 C.F.R. § 59.4)	245
Foreign Intelligence Surveillance Act (50 U.S.C. § 1861)	247

WIRE AND ELECTRONIC COMMUNICATIONS INTERCEPTION AND INTERCEPTION OF ORAL COMMUNICATIONS

(18 U.S.C. §§ 2510–2511, 2515–2518, 2520–2521).

§ 2510. Definitions

As used in this chapter

(1) "wire communication means any aural transfer made in whole or in part through the use of facilities for the transmission of communications by the aid of wire, cable, or other like connection between the point of origin and the point of reception (including the use of

179

such connection in a switching station) furnished or operated by any person engaged in providing or operating such facilities for the transmission of interstate or foreign communications or communications affecting interstate or foreign commerce;

(2) "oral communication" means any oral communication uttered by a person exhibiting an expectation that such communication is not subject to interception under circumstances justifying such expectation, but such term does not include any electronic communication;

(3) "State" means any State of the United States, the District of Columbia, the Commonwealth of Puerto Rico, and any territory or possession of the United States;

(4) "intercept" means the aural or other acquisition of the contents of any wire, electronic, or oral communication through the use of any electronic, mechanical, or other device.

(5) "electronic, mechanical, or other device" means any device or apparatus which can be used to intercept a wire, oral, or electronic communication other than—

(a) any telephone or telegraph instrument, equipment or facility, or any component thereof, (i) furnished to the subscriber or user by a provider of wire or electronic communication service in the ordinary course of its business and being used by the subscriber or user in the ordinary course of its business or furnished by such subscriber or user for connection to the facilities of such service and used in the ordinary course of its business; or (ii) being used by a provider of wire or electronic communication service in the ordinary course of its business, or by an investigative or law enforcement officer in the ordinary course of his duties;

(b) a hearing aid or similar device being used to correct subnormal hearing to not better than normal;

(6) "person" means any employee, or agent of the United States or any State or political subdivision thereof, and any individual, partnership, association, joint stock company, trust, or corporation;

(7) "Investigative or law enforcement officer" means any officer of the United States or of a State or political subdivision thereof, who is empowered by law to conduct investigations of or to make arrests for offenses enumerated in this chapter, and any attorney authorized by law to prosecute or participate in the prosecution of such offenses;

(8) "contents", when used with respect to any wire, oral, or electronic communication, includes any information concerning the substance, purport, or meaning of that communication;

(9) "Judge of competent jurisdiction" means—

(a) a judge of a United States district court or a United States court of appeals; and

(b) a judge of any court of general criminal jurisdiction of a State who is authorized by a statute of that State to enter orders authorizing interceptions of wire, oral, or electronic communications;

(10) "communication common carrier" has the meaning given that term in section 3 of the Communications Act of 1934;

(11) "aggrieved person" means a person who was a party to any intercepted wire, oral, or electronic communication or a person against whom the interception was directed;

(12) "electronic communication" means any transfer of signs, signals, writing, images, sounds, data, or intelligence of any nature transmitted in whole or in part by a wire, radio, electromagnetic, photoelectronic or photooptical system that affects interstate or foreign commerce, but does not include—

(A) any wire or oral communication;

(B) any communication made through a tone-only paging device;

(C) any communication from a tracking device (as defined in section 3117 of this title); or

(D) electronic funds transfer information stored by a financial institution in a communications system used for the electronic storage and transfer of funds;

(13) "user" means any person or entity who—

(A) uses an electronic communication service; and

(B) is duly authorized by the provider of such service to engage in such use;

(14) "electronic communications system" means any wire, radio, electromagnetic, photooptical or photoelectronic facilities for the transmission of wire or electronic communications, and any computer facilities or related electronic equipment for the electronic storage of such communications;

(15) "electronic communication service" means any service which provides to users thereof the ability to send or receive wire or electronic communications;

(16) "readily accessible to the general public" means, with respect to a radio communication, that such communication is not—

(A) scrambled or encrypted;

(B) transmitted using modulation techniques whose essential parameters have been withheld from the public with the intention of preserving the privacy of such communication;

(C) carried on a subcarrier or other signal subsidiary to a radio transmission;

(D) transmitted over a communication system provided by a common carrier, unless the communication is a tone only paging system communication; or

(E) transmitted on frequencies allocated under part 25, subpart D, E, or F of part 74, or part 94 of the Rules of the Federal Communications Commission, unless, in the case of a communication transmitted on a frequency allocated under part 74 that is not exclusively allocated to broadcast auxiliary services, the communication is a two-way voice communication by radio;

(17) "electronic storage" means—

(A) any temporary, intermediate storage of a wire or electronic communication incidental to the electronic transmission thereof; and

(B) any storage of such communication by an electronic communication service for purposes of backup protection of such communication;

(18) "aural transfer" means a transfer containing the human voice at any point between and including the point of origin and the point of reception;

(19) "foreign intelligence information", for purposes of section 2517(6) of this title, means—

(A)   information, whether or not concerning a United States person, that relates to the ability of the United States to protect against—

(i)   actual or potential attack or other grave hostile acts of a foreign power or an agent of a foreign power;

(ii)   sabotage or international terrorism by a foreign power or an agent of a foreign power; or

(iii)   clandestine intelligence activities by an intelligence service or network of a foreign power or by an agent of a foreign power; or

(B)   information, whether or not concerning a United States person, with respect to a foreign power or foreign territory that relates to—

(i)   the national defense or the security of the United States; or

(ii)   the conduct of the foreign affairs of the United States;

(20)   "protected computer" has the meaning set forth in section 1030; and

(21)   "computer trespasser"—

(A)   means a person who accesses a protected computer without authorization and thus has no reasonable expectation of privacy in any communication transmitted to, through, or from the protected computer; and

(B)   does not include a person known by the owner or operator of the protected computer to have an existing contractual relationship with the owner or operator of the protected computer for access to all or part of the protected computer.

§ 2511. Interception and disclosure of wire, oral, or electronic communications prohibited

(1)   Except as otherwise specifically provided in this chapter any person who—

(a)   intentionally intercepts, endeavors to intercept, or procures any other person to intercept or endeavor to intercept, any wire, oral, or electronic communication;

(b)   intentionally uses, endeavors to use, or procures any other person to use or endeavor to use any electronic, mechanical, or other device to intercept any oral communication when—

(i)   such device is affixed to, or otherwise transmits a signal through, a wire, cable, or other like connection used in wire communication; or

(ii)   such device transmits communications by radio, or interferes with the transmission of such communication; or

(iii)   such person knows, or has reason to know, that such device or any component thereof has been sent through the mail or transported in interstate or foreign commerce; or

(iv)   such use or endeavor to use (A) takes place on the premises of any business or other commercial establishment the operations of which affect interstate or foreign commerce; or (B) obtains or is for the purpose of obtaining information relating to the operations of any business or other commercial establishment the operations of which affect interstate or foreign commerce; or

(v)   such person acts in the District of Columbia, the Commonwealth of Puerto Rico, or any territory or possession of the United States;

(c)   intentionally discloses, or endeavors to disclose, to any other person the contents of any wire, oral, or electronic communication, knowing or having reason to know that the information was obtained through the interception of a wire, oral, or electronic communication in violation of this subsection;

(d)   intentionally uses, or endeavors to use, the contents of any wire, oral, or electronic communication, knowing or having reason to know that the information was obtained through the interception of a wire, oral, or electronic communication in violation of this subsection; or

(e)(i) intentionally discloses, or endeavors to disclose, to any other person the contents of any wire, oral, or electronic communication, intercepted by means authorized by sections 2511(2)(a)(ii), 2511(2)(b)–(c), 2511(2)(e), 2516, and 2518 of this chapter, (ii) knowing or having reason to know that the information was obtained through the interception of such a communication in connection with a criminal investigation, (iii) having obtained or received the information in connection with a criminal investigation, and (iv) with intent to improperly obstruct, impede, or interfere with a duly authorized criminal investigation,

shall be punished as provided in subsection (4) or shall be subject to suit as provided in subsection (5).

(2)(a)(i)   It shall not be unlawful under this chapter for an operator of a switchboard, or an officer, employee, or agent of a provider of wire or electronic communication service, whose facilities are used in the transmission of a wire or electronic communication, to intercept, disclose, or use that communication in the normal course of his employment while engaged in any activity which is a necessary incident to the rendition of his service or to the protection of the rights or property of the provider of that service, except that a provider of wire communication service to the public shall not utilize service observing or random monitoring except for mechanical or service quality control checks.

(ii)   Notwithstanding any other law, providers of wire or electronic communication service, their officers, employees, and agents, landlords, custodians, or other persons, are authorized to provide information, facilities, or technical assistance to persons authorized by law to intercept wire, oral, or electronic communications or to conduct electronic surveillance, as defined in section 101 of the Foreign Intelligence Surveillance Act of 1978, if such provider, its officers, employees, or agents, landlord, custodian, or other specified person, has been provided with—

(A)   a court order directing such assistance or a court order pursuant to section 704 of the Foreign Intelligence Surveillance Act of 1978 signed by the authorizing judge, or

(B)   a certification in writing by a person specified in section 2518(7) of this title or the Attorney General of the United States that no warrant or court order is required by law, that all statutory requirements have been met, and that the specified assistance is required,

setting forth the period of time during which the provision of the information, facilities, or technical assistance is authorized and specifying the information, facilities, or technical assistance required. No provider of wire or electronic communication service, officer, employee, or agent thereof, or landlord, custodian, or other specified person shall disclose the existence of any interception or surveillance or the device used to accomplish the interception or surveillance with respect to which the person has been furnished a court order or certification under this chapter, except as may otherwise be required by legal process and then only after prior notification to the Attorney General or to the principal prosecuting attorney of a State or any political subdivision of a State, as may be appropriate. Any such disclosure, shall render such person liable for the civil damages provided for in section 2520. No cause of action shall lie in any court against any provider of wire or electronic communication service, its officers, employees, or agents, landlord, custodian, or other specified person for providing information, facilities, or assistance in accordance with the terms of a court order, statutory authorization, or certification under this chapter.

(iii) If a certification under subparagraph (ii)(B) for assistance to obtain foreign intelligence information is based on statutory authority, the certification shall identify the specific statutory provision and shall certify that the statutory requirements have been met.

(b) It shall not be unlawful under this chapter for an officer, employee, or agent of the Federal Communications Commission, in the normal course of his employment and in discharge of the monitoring responsibilities exercised by the Commission in the enforcement of chapter 5 of title 47 of the United States Code, to intercept a wire or electronic communication, or oral communication transmitted by radio, or to disclose or use the information thereby obtained.

(c) It shall not be unlawful under this chapter for a person acting under color of law to intercept a wire, oral, or electronic communication, where such person is a party to the communication or one of the parties to the communication has given prior consent to such interception.

(d) It shall not be unlawful under this chapter for a person not acting under color of law to intercept a wire, oral, or electronic communication where such person is a party to the communication or where one of the parties to the communication has given prior consent to such interception unless such communication is intercepted for the purpose of committing any criminal or tortious act in violation of the Constitution or laws of the United States or of any State.

(e) Notwithstanding any other provision of this title or section 705 or 706 of the Communications Act of 1934, it shall not be unlawful for an officer, employee, or agent of the United States in the normal course of his official duty to conduct electronic surveillance, as defined in section 101 of the Foreign Intelligence Surveillance Act of 1978, as authorized by that Act.

(f) Nothing contained in this chapter or chapter 121 or 206 of this title, or section 705 of the Communications Act of 1934, shall be deemed to affect the acquisition by the United States Government of foreign intelligence information from international or foreign communications, or foreign intelligence activities conducted in accordance with otherwise applicable Federal law involving a foreign electronic communications system, utilizing a means other than electronic surveillance as defined in section 101 of the Foreign Intelligence Surveillance Act of 1978, and procedures in this chapter or chapter 121 and the Foreign Intelligence Surveillance Act of 1978 shall be the exclusive means by which electronic surveillance, as defined in section 101 of such Act, and the interception of domestic wire, oral, and electronic communications may be conducted.

(g) It shall not be unlawful under this chapter or chapter 121 of this title for any person—

(i) to intercept or access an electronic communication made through an electronic communication system that is configured so that such electronic communication is readily accessible to the general public;

(ii) to intercept any radio communication which is transmitted—

(I) by any station for the use of the general public, or that relates to ships, aircraft, vehicles, or persons in distress;

(II) by any governmental, law enforcement, civil defense, private land mobile, or public safety communications system, including police and fire, readily accessible to the general public;

(III) by a station operating on an authorized frequency within the bands allocated to the amateur, citizens band, or general mobile radio services; or

(IV) by any marine or aeronautical communications system;

(iii) to engage in any conduct which—

(I)   is prohibited by section 633 of the Communications Act of 1934; or

(II)   is excepted from the application of section 705(a) of the Communications Act of 1934 by section 705(b) of that Act;

(iv) to intercept any wire or electronic communication the transmission of which is causing harmful interference to any lawfully operating station or consumer electronic equipment, to the extent necessary to identify the source of such interference; or

(v)   for other users of the same frequency to intercept any radio communication made through a system that utilizes frequencies monitored by individuals engaged in the provision or the use of such system, if such communication is not scrambled or encrypted.

(h)   It shall not be unlawful under this chapter—

(i)   to use a pen register or a trap and trace device (as those terms are defined for the purposes of chapter 206 (relating to pen registers and trap and trace devices) of this title); or

(ii)   for a provider of electronic communication service to record the fact that a wire or electronic communication was initiated or completed in order to protect such provider, another provider furnishing service toward the completion of the wire or electronic communication, or a user of that service, from fraudulent, unlawful or abusive use of such service.

(i)   It shall not be unlawful under this chapter for a person acting under color of law to intercept the wire or electronic communications of a computer trespasser transmitted to, through, or from the protected computer, if—

(I)   the owner or operator of the protected computer authorizes the interception of the computer trespasser's communications on the protected computer;

(II)   the person acting under color of law is lawfully engaged in an investigation;

(III) the person acting under color of law has reasonable grounds to believe that the contents of the computer trespasser's communications will be relevant to the investigation; and

(IV) such interception does not acquire communications other than those transmitted to or from the computer trespasser.

(j)   It shall not be unlawful under this chapter for a provider of electronic communication service to the public or remote computing service to intercept or disclose the contents of a wire or electronic communication in response to an order from a foreign government that is subject to an executive agreement that the Attorney General has determined and certified to Congress satisfies section 2523.

(3)(a)   Except as provided in paragraph (b) of this subsection, a person or entity providing an electronic communication service to the public shall not intentionally divulge the contents of any communication (other than one to such person or entity, or an agent thereof) while in transmission on that service to any person or entity other than an addressee or intended recipient of such communication or an agent of such addressee or intended recipient.

(b)   A person or entity providing electronic communication service to the public may divulge the contents of any such communication—

(i)   as otherwise authorized in section 2511(2)(a) or 2517 of this title;

(ii)   with the lawful consent of the originator or any addressee or intended recipient of such communication;

(iii)   to a person employed or authorized, or whose facilities are used, to forward such communication to its destination; or

(iv)   which were inadvertently obtained by the service provider and which appear to pertain to the commission of a crime, if such divulgence is made to a law enforcement agency.

(4)(a)   Except as provided in paragraph (b) of this subsection or in subsection (5), whoever violates subsection (1) of this section shall be fined under this title or imprisoned not more than five years, or both.

(b)   Conduct otherwise an offense under this subsection that consists of or relates to the interception of a satellite transmission that is not encrypted or scrambled and that is transmitted—

(i)   to a broadcasting station for purposes of retransmission to the general public; or

(ii)   as an audio subcarrier intended for redistribution to facilities open to the public, but not including data transmissions or telephone calls,

is not an offense under this subsection unless the conduct is for the purposes of direct or indirect commercial advantage or private financial gain.

[(c)   Redesignated (b)]

(5)(a)(i)   If the communication is—

(A)   a private satellite video communication that is not scrambled or encrypted and the conduct in violation of this chapter is the private viewing of that communication and is not for a tortious or illegal purpose or for purposes of direct or indirect commercial advantage or private commercial gain; or

(B)   a radio communication that is transmitted on frequencies allocated under subpart D of part 74 of the rules of the Federal Communications Commission that is not scrambled or encrypted and the conduct in violation of this chapter is not for a tortious or illegal purpose or for purposes of direct or indirect commercial advantage or private commercial gain,

then the person who engages in such conduct shall be subject to suit by the Federal Government in a court of competent jurisdiction.

(ii)   In an action under this subsection—

(A)   if the violation of this chapter is a first offense for the person under paragraph (a) of subsection (4) and such person has not been found liable in a civil action under section 2520 of this title, the Federal Government shall be entitled to appropriate injunctive relief; and

(B)   if the violation of this chapter is a second or subsequent offense under paragraph (a) of subsection (4) or such person has been found liable in any prior civil action under section 2520, the person shall be subject to a mandatory $500 civil fine.

(b) The court may use any means within its authority to enforce an injunction issued under paragraph (ii)(A), and shall impose a civil fine of not less than $500 for each violation of such an injunction.

§ 2515.   Prohibition of use as evidence of intercepted wire or oral communications

Whenever any wire or oral communication has been intercepted, no part of the contents of such communication and no evidence derived therefrom may be received in evidence in any trial, hearing, or other proceeding in or before any court, grand jury, department, officer, agency, regulatory body, legislative committee, or other authority of the United States, a State, or a political subdivision thereof if the disclosure of that information would be in violation of this chapter.

§ 2516. Authorization for interception of wire, oral, or electronic communications

(1) The Attorney General, Deputy Attorney General, Associate Attorney General, or any Assistant Attorney General, any acting Assistant Attorney General, or any Deputy Assistant Attorney General or acting Deputy Assistant Attorney General in the Criminal Division or National Security Division specially designated by the Attorney General, may authorize an application to a Federal judge of competent jurisdiction for, and such judge may grant in conformity with section 2518 of this chapter an order authorizing or approving the interception of wire or oral communications by the Federal Bureau of Investigation, or a Federal agency having responsibility for the investigation of the offense as to which the application is made, when such interception may provide or has provided evidence of—

(a) any offense punishable by death or by imprisonment for more than one year under sections 2122 and 2274 through 2277 of title 42 of the United States Code (relating to the enforcement of the Atomic Energy Act of 1954), section 2284 of title 42 of the United States Code (relating to sabotage of nuclear facilities or fuel), or under the following chapters of this title: chapter 10 (relating to biological weapons), chapter 37 (relating to espionage), chapter 55 (relating to kidnapping), chapter 90 (relating to protection of trade secrets), chapter 105 (relating to sabotage), chapter 115 (relating to treason), chapter 102 (relating to riots), chapter 65 (relating to malicious mischief), chapter 111 (relating to destruction of vessels), or chapter 81 (relating to piracy);

(b) a violation of section 186 or section 501(c) of title 29, United States Code (dealing with restrictions on payments and loans to labor organizations), or any offense which involves murder, kidnapping, robbery, or extortion, and which is punishable under this title;

(c) any offense which is punishable under the following sections of this title: section 37 (relating to violence at international airports), section 43 (relating to animal enterprise terrorism), section 81 (arson within special maritime and territorial jurisdiction), section 201 (bribery of public officials and witnesses), section 215 (relating to bribery of bank officials), section 224 (bribery in sporting contests), subsection (d), (e), (f), (g), (h), or (i) of section 844 (unlawful use of explosives), section 1032 (relating to concealment of assets), section 1084 (transmission of wagering information), section 751 (relating to escape), section 832 (relating to nuclear and weapons of mass destruction threats), section 842 (relating to explosive materials), section 930 (relating to possession of weapons in Federal facilities), section 1014 (relating to loans and credit applications generally; renewals and discounts), section 1114 (relating to officers and employees of the United States), section 1116 (relating to protection of foreign officials), sections 1503, 1512, and 1513 (influencing or injuring an officer, juror, or witness generally), section 1510 (obstruction of criminal investigations), section 1511 (obstruction of State or local law enforcement), section 1581 (peonage), section 1584 (involuntary servitude), section 1589 (forced labor), section 1590 (trafficking with respect to peonage, slavery, involuntary servitude, or forced labor), section 1591 (sex trafficking of children by force, fraud, or coercion), section 1592 (unlawful conduct with respect to documents in furtherance of trafficking, peonage, slavery, involuntary servitude, or forced labor), section 1751 (Presidential and Presidential staff assassination, kidnapping, and assault), section 1951 (interference with commerce by threats or violence), section 1952 (interstate and foreign travel or transportation in aid of racketeering enterprises), section 1958 (relating to use of interstate commerce facilities in the commission of murder for hire), section 1959 (relating to violent crimes in aid of racketeering activity), section 1954 (offer, acceptance, or solicitation to influence operations of employee benefit plan), section 1955 (prohibition of business enterprises of gambling), section 1956 (laundering of monetary instruments), section 1957 (relating to engaging in monetary transactions in property derived from specified unlawful activity), section 659 (theft from interstate shipment), section 664 (embezzlement from pension and welfare funds), section 1343 (fraud by wire, radio, or television), section 1344 (relating to bank fraud), section 1992 (relating to terrorist attacks against mass transportation), sections 2251 and 2252 (sexual exploitation of children), section 2251A (selling or buying of children), section 2252A (relating to material constituting or containing child pornography), section 1466A (relating to child obscenity), section 2260 (production of sexually explicit depictions of a minor for importation into the United States), sections 2421, 2422, 2423, and 2425 (relating to transportation for illegal sexual activity and related crimes), sections 2312, 2313, 2314, and 2315 (interstate transportation of stolen property), section 2321 (relating to trafficking in certain motor vehicles or motor vehicle parts), section 2340A (relating to torture), section 1203 (relating to hostage taking), section 1029 (relating to fraud and related activity in connection with access devices), section 3146 (relating to penalty for failure to appear), section 3521(b)(3) (relating to witness relocation and assistance), section 32 (relating to destruction of aircraft or aircraft facilities), section 38 (relating to aircraft parts fraud), section 1963 (violations with respect to racketeer influenced and corrupt organizations), section 115 (relating to threatening or retaliating against a Federal official), section 1341 (relating to mail fraud), a felony violation of section 1030 (relating to computer fraud and abuse), section 351 (violations with respect to congressional, Cabinet, or Supreme Court assassinations, kidnapping, and assault), section 831 (relating to prohibited transactions involving nuclear materials), section 33 (relating to destruction of motor vehicles or motor vehicle facilities), section 175 (relating to biological weapons), section 175c (relating to variola virus), section 956 (conspiracy to harm persons or property overseas), a felony violation of section 1028 (relating to production of false identification documentation), section 1425 (relating to the procurement of citizenship or nationalization unlawfully), section 1426 (relating to the reproduction of naturalization or citizenship papers), section 1427 (relating to the sale of naturalization or citizenship papers), section 1541 (relating to passport issuance without authority), section 1542 (relating to false statements in passport applications), section 1543 (relating to forgery or false use of passports), section 1544 (relating to misuse of passports), section 1546 (relating to fraud and misuse of visas, permits, and other documents), or section 555 (relating to construction or use of international border tunnels);

(d)   any offense involving counterfeiting punishable under section 471, 472, or 473 of this title;

(e)   any offense involving fraud connected with a case under title 11 or the manufacture, importation, receiving, concealment, buying, selling, or otherwise dealing in narcotic drugs, marihuana, or other dangerous drugs, punishable under any law of the United States;

(f)   any offense including extortionate credit transactions under sections 892, 893, or 894 of this title;

(g)   a violation of section 5322 of title 31, United States Code (dealing with the reporting of currency transactions), or section 5324 of title 31, United States Code (relating to structuring transactions to evade reporting requirement prohibited);

(h)   any felony violation of sections 2511 and 2512 (relating to interception and disclosure of certain communications and to certain intercepting devices) of this title;

(i)   any felony violation of chapter 71 (relating to obscenity) of this title;

(j)   any violation of section 60123(b) (relating to destruction of a natural gas pipeline), section 46502 (relating to aircraft piracy), the second sentence of section 46504 (relating to assault on a flight crew with dangerous weapon), or section 46505(b)(3) or (c) (relating to explosive or incendiary devices, or endangerment of human life, by means of weapons on aircraft) of title 49;

(k)   any criminal violation of section 2778 of title 22 (relating to the Arms Export Control Act);

(*l*)   the location of any fugitive from justice from an offense described in this section;

(m)   a violation of section 274, 277, or 278 of the Immigration and Nationality Act (8 U.S.C. 1324, 1327, or 1328) (relating to the smuggling of aliens);

(n)   any felony violation of sections 922 and 924 of title 18, United States Code (relating to firearms);

(o)   any violation of section 5861 of the Internal Revenue Code of 1986 (relating to firearms);

(p)   a felony violation of section 1028 (relating to production of false identification documents), section 1542 (relating to false statements in passport applications), section 1546 (relating to fraud and misuse of visas, permits, and other documents), section 1028A (relating to aggravated identity theft) of this title or a violation of section 274, 277, or 278 of the Immigration and Nationality Act (relating to the smuggling of aliens);

(q)   any criminal violation of section 229 (relating to chemical weapons) or section 2332, 2332a, 2332b, 2332d, 2332f, 2332g, 2332h, 2339, 2339A, 2339B, 2339C, or 2339D of this title (related to terrorism);

(r)   any criminal violation of section 1 (relating to illegal restraints of trade or commerce), 2 (relating to illegal monopolizing of trade or commerce), or 3 (relating to illegal restraints of trade or commerce in territories or the District of Columbia) of the Sherman Act (15 U.S.C. 1, 2, 3);

(s)   any violation of section 670 (relating to theft of medical products); or

(t)   any conspiracy to commit any offense described in any subparagraph of this paragraph.

(2)   The principal prosecuting attorney of any State, or the principal prosecuting attorney of any political subdivision thereof, if such attorney is authorized by a statute of that State to make application to a State court judge of competent jurisdiction for an order authorizing or approving the interception of wire, oral, or electronic communications, may apply to such judge for, and such judge may grant in conformity with section 2518 of this chapter and with the applicable State statute an order authorizing, or approving the interception of wire, oral, or electronic communications by investigative or law enforcement officers having responsibility for the investigation of the offense as to which the application is made, when such interception may provide or has provided evidence of the commission of the offense of murder, kidnapping, human trafficking, child sexual exploitation, child pornography production, gambling, robbery, bribery, extortion, or dealing in narcotic drugs, marihuana or other dangerous drugs, or other crime dangerous to life, limb, or property, and punishable by imprisonment for more than one year, designated in any applicable State statute authorizing such interception, or any conspiracy to commit any of the foregoing offenses.

(3)   Any attorney for the Government (as such term is defined for the purposes of the Federal Rules of Criminal Procedure) may authorize an application to a Federal judge of competent jurisdiction for, and such judge may grant, in conformity with section 2518 of this title, an order authorizing or approving the interception of electronic communications by an investigative or law enforcement officer having responsibility for the investigation of the offense as to which the

application is made, when such interception may provide or has provided evidence of any Federal felony.

§ 2517. Authorization for disclosure and use of intercepted wire, oral, or electronic communications

(1) Any investigative or law enforcement officer who, by any means authorized by this chapter, has obtained knowledge of the contents of any wire, oral, or electronic communication, or evidence derived therefrom, may disclose such contents to another investigative or law enforcement officer to the extent that such disclosure is appropriate to the proper performance of the official duties of the officer making or receiving the disclosure.

(2) Any investigative or law enforcement officer who, by any means authorized by this chapter, has obtained knowledge of the contents of any wire, oral, or electronic communication or evidence derived therefrom may use such contents to the extent such use is appropriate to the proper performance of his official duties.

(3) Any person who has received, by any means authorized by this chapter, any information concerning a wire, oral, or electronic communication, or evidence derived therefrom intercepted in accordance with the provisions of this chapter may disclose the contents of that communication or such derivative evidence while giving testimony under oath or affirmation in any proceeding held under the authority of the United States or of any State or political subdivision thereof.

(4) No otherwise privileged wire, oral, or electronic communication intercepted in accordance with, or in violation of, the provisions of this chapter shall lose its privileged character.

(5) When an investigative or law enforcement officer, while engaged in intercepting wire, oral, or electronic communications in the manner authorized herein, intercepts wire, oral, or electronic communications relating to offenses other than those specified in the order of authorization or approval, the contents thereof, and evidence derived therefrom, may be disclosed or used as provided in subsections (1) and (2) of this section. Such contents and any evidence derived therefrom may be used under subsection (3) of this section when authorized or approved by a judge of competent jurisdiction where such judge finds on subsequent application that the contents were otherwise intercepted in accordance with the provisions of this chapter. Such application shall be made as soon as practicable.

(6) Any investigative or law enforcement officer, or attorney for the Government, who by any means authorized by this chapter, has obtained knowledge of the contents of any wire, oral, or electronic communication, or evidence derived therefrom, may disclose such contents to any other Federal law enforcement, intelligence, protective, immigration, national defense, or national security official to the extent that such contents include foreign intelligence or counterintelligence (as defined in section 3 of the National Security Act of 1947 (50 U.S.C. 401a)), or foreign intelligence information (as defined in subsection (19) of section 2510 of this title), to assist the official who is to receive that information in the performance of his official duties. Any Federal official who receives information pursuant to this provision may use that information only as necessary in the conduct of that person's official duties subject to any limitations on the unauthorized disclosure of such information.

(7) Any investigative or law enforcement officer, or other Federal official in carrying out official duties as such Federal official, who by any means authorized by this chapter, has obtained knowledge of the contents of any wire, oral, or electronic communication, or evidence derived therefrom, may disclose such contents or derivative evidence to a foreign investigative or law enforcement officer to the extent that such disclosure is appropriate to the proper performance of the official duties of the officer making or receiving the disclosure, and foreign investigative or law enforcement officers may use or disclose such contents or derivative evidence to the extent such use or disclosure is appropriate to the proper performance of their official duties.

(8)   Any investigative or law enforcement officer, or other Federal official in carrying out official duties as such Federal official, who by any means authorized by this chapter, has obtained knowledge of the contents of any wire, oral, or electronic communication, or evidence derived therefrom, may disclose such contents or derivative evidence to any appropriate Federal, State, local, or foreign government official to the extent that such contents or derivative evidence reveals a threat of actual or potential attack or other grave hostile acts of a foreign power or an agent of a foreign power, domestic or international sabotage, domestic or international terrorism, or clandestine intelligence gathering activities by an intelligence service or network of a foreign power or by an agent of a foreign power, within the United States or elsewhere, for the purpose of preventing or responding to such a threat. Any official who receives information pursuant to this provision may use that information only as necessary in the conduct of that person's official duties subject to any limitations on the unauthorized disclosure of such information, and any State, local, or foreign official who receives information pursuant to this provision may use that information only consistent with such guidelines as the Attorney General and Director of Central Intelligence shall jointly issue.

§ 2518.   Procedure for interception of wire, oral, or electronic communications

(1)   Each application for an order authorizing or approving the interception of a wire, oral, or electronic communication under this chapter shall be made in writing upon oath or affirmation to a judge of competent jurisdiction and shall state the applicant's authority to make such application. Each application shall include the following information:

(a)   the identity of the investigative or law enforcement officer making the application, and the officer authorizing the application;

(b)   a full and complete statement of the facts and circumstances relied upon by the applicant, to justify his belief that an order should be issued, including (i) details as to the particular offense that has been, is being, or is about to be committed, (ii) except as provided in subsection (11), a particular description of the nature and location of the facilities from which or the place where the communication is to be intercepted, (iii) a particular description of the type of communications sought to be intercepted, (iv) the identity of the person, if known, committing the offense and whose communications are to be intercepted;

(c)   a full and complete statement as to whether or not other investigative procedures have been tried and failed or why they reasonably appear to be unlikely to succeed if tried or to be too dangerous;

(d)   a statement of the period of time for which the interception is required to be maintained. If the nature of the investigation is such that the authorization for interception should not automatically terminate when the described type of communication has been first obtained, a particular description of facts establishing probable cause to believe that additional communications of the same type will occur thereafter;

(e)   a full and complete statement of the facts concerning all previous applications known to the individual authorizing and making the application, made to any judge for authorization to intercept, or for approval of interceptions of, wire, oral, or electronic communications involving any of the same persons, facilities or places specified in the application, and the action taken by the judge on each such application; and

(f)   where the application is for the extension of an order, a statement setting forth the results thus far obtained from the interception, or a reasonable explanation of the failure to obtain such results.

(2)   The judge may require the applicant to furnish additional testimony or documentary evidence in support of the application.

(3)   Upon such application the judge may enter an ex parte order, as requested or as modified, authorizing or approving interception of wire, oral, or electronic communications within the territorial jurisdiction of the court in which the judge is sitting (and outside that jurisdiction but within the United States in the case of a mobile interception device authorized by a Federal court within such jurisdiction), if the judge determines on the basis of the facts submitted by the applicant that—

(a)   there is probable cause for belief that an individual is committing, has committed, or is about to commit a particular offense enumerated in section 2516 of this chapter;

(b)   there is probable cause for belief that particular communications concerning that offense will be obtained through such interception;

(c)   normal investigative procedures have been tried and have failed or reasonably appear to be unlikely to succeed if tried or to be too dangerous;

(d)   except as provided in subsection (11), there is probable cause for belief that the facilities from which, or the place where, the wire, oral, or electronic communications are to be intercepted are being used, or are about to be used, in connection with the commission of such offense, or are leased to, listed in the name of, or commonly used by such person.

(4)   Each order authorizing or approving the interception of any wire, oral, or electronic communication under this chapter shall specify—

(a)   the identity of the person, if known, whose communications are to be intercepted;

(b)   the nature and location of the communications facilities as to which, or the place where, authority to intercept is granted;

(c)   a particular description of the type of communication sought to be intercepted, and a statement of the particular offense to which it relates;

(d)   the identity of the agency authorized to intercept the communications, and of the person authorizing the application; and

(e)   the period of time during which such interception is authorized, including a statement as to whether or not the interception shall automatically terminate when the described communication has been first obtained.

An order authorizing the interception of a wire, oral, or electronic communication under this chapter shall, upon request of the applicant, direct that a provider of wire or electronic communication service, landlord, custodian or other person shall furnish the applicant forthwith all information, facilities, and technical assistance necessary to accomplish the interception unobtrusively and with a minimum of interference with the services that such service provider, landlord, custodian, or person is according the person whose communications are to be intercepted. Any provider of wire or electronic communication service, landlord, custodian or other person furnishing such facilities or technical assistance shall be compensated therefor by the applicant for reasonable expenses incurred in providing such facilities or assistance. Pursuant to section 2522 of this chapter, an order may also be issued to enforce the assistance capability and capacity requirements under the Communications Assistance for Law Enforcement Act.

(5)   No order entered under this section may authorize or approve the interception of any wire, oral, or electronic communication for any period longer than is necessary to achieve the objective of the authorization, nor in any event longer than thirty days. Such thirty-day period begins on the earlier of the day on which the investigative or law enforcement officer first begins to conduct an interception under the order or ten days after the order is entered. Extensions of an order may be granted, but only upon application for an extension made in accordance with subsection (1) of this section and the court making the findings required by subsection (3) of this

section. The period of extension shall be no longer than the authorizing judge deems necessary to achieve the purposes for which it was granted and in no event for longer than thirty days. Every order and extension thereof shall contain a provision that the authorization to intercept shall be executed as soon as practicable, shall be conducted in such a way as to minimize the interception of communications not otherwise subject to interception under this chapter, and must terminate upon attainment of the authorized objective, or in any event in thirty days. In the event the intercepted communication is in a code or foreign language, and an expert in that foreign language or code is not reasonably available during the interception period, minimization may be accomplished as soon as practicable after such interception. An interception under this chapter may be conducted in whole or in part by Government personnel, or by an individual operating under a contract with the Government, acting under the supervision of an investigative or law enforcement officer authorized to conduct the interception.

(6)   Whenever an order authorizing interception is entered pursuant to this chapter, the order may require reports to be made to the judge who issued the order showing what progress has been made toward achievement of the authorized objective and the need for continued interception. Such reports shall be made at such intervals as the judge may require.

(7)   Notwithstanding any other provision of this chapter, any investigative or law enforcement officer, specially designated by the Attorney General, the Deputy Attorney General, the Associate Attorney General, or by the principal prosecuting attorney of any State or subdivision thereof acting pursuant to a statute of that State, who reasonably determines that—

(a)   an emergency situation exists that involves—

(i)   immediate danger of death or serious physical injury to any person,

(ii)   conspiratorial activities threatening the national security interest, or

(iii)   conspiratorial activities characteristic of organized crime,

that requires a wire, oral, or electronic communication to be intercepted before an order authorizing such interception can, with due diligence, be obtained, and

(b)   there are grounds upon which an order could be entered under this chapter to authorize such interception,

may intercept such wire, oral, or electronic communication if an application for an order approving the interception is made in accordance with this section within forty-eight hours after the interception has occurred, or begins to occur. In the absence of an order, such interception shall immediately terminate when the communication sought is obtained or when the application for the order is denied, whichever is earlier. In the event such application for approval is denied, or in any other case where the interception is terminated without an order having been issued, the contents of any wire, oral, or electronic communication intercepted shall be treated as having been obtained in violation of this chapter, and an inventory shall be served as provided for in subsection (d) of this section on the person named in the application.

(8)(a)   The contents of any wire, oral, or electronic communication intercepted by any means authorized by this chapter shall, if possible, be recorded on tape or wire or other comparable device. The recording of the contents of any wire, oral, or electronic communication under this subsection shall be done in such a way as will protect the recording from editing or other alterations. Immediately upon the expiration of the period of the order, or extensions thereof, such recordings shall be made available to the judge issuing such order and sealed under his directions. Custody of the recordings shall be wherever the judge orders. They shall not be destroyed except upon an order of the issuing or denying judge and in any event shall be kept for ten years. Duplicate recordings may be made for use or disclosure pursuant to the provisions of subsections (1) and (2) of section 2517 of this chapter for investigations. The presence of the seal provided for by this subsection, or a satisfactory explanation for the absence thereof, shall be a prerequisite for the use or disclosure of the contents of any wire, oral, or electronic communication or evidence derived therefrom under subsection (3) of section 2517.

(b)   Applications made and orders granted under this chapter shall be sealed by the judge. Custody of the applications and orders shall be wherever the judge directs. Such applications and orders shall be disclosed only upon a showing of good cause before a judge of competent jurisdiction and shall not be destroyed except on order of the issuing or denying judge, and in any event shall be kept for ten years.

(c)   Any violation of the provisions of this subsection may be punished as contempt of the issuing or denying judge.

(d)   Within a reasonable time but not later than ninety days after the filing of an application for an order of approval under section 2518(7)(b) which is denied or the termination of the period of an order or extensions thereof, the issuing or denying judge shall cause to be served, on the persons named in the order or the application, and such other parties to intercepted communications as the judge may determine in his discretion that is in the interest of justice, an inventory which shall include notice of—

(1)   the fact of the entry of the order or the application;

(2)   the date of the entry and the period of authorized, approved or disapproved interception, or the denial of the application; and

(3)   the fact that during the period wire, oral, or electronic communications were or were not intercepted.

The judge, upon the filing of a motion, may in his discretion make available to such person or his counsel for inspection such portions of the intercepted communications, applications and orders as the judge determines to be in the interest of justice. On an ex parte showing of good cause to a judge of competent jurisdiction the serving of the inventory required by this subsection may be postponed.

(9)   The contents of any wire, oral, or electronic communication intercepted pursuant to this chapter or evidence derived therefrom shall not be received in evidence or otherwise disclosed in any trial, hearing, or other proceeding in a Federal or State court unless each party, not less than ten days before the trial, hearing, or proceeding, has been furnished with a copy of the court order, and accompanying application, under which the interception was authorized or approved. This ten-day period may be waived by the judge if he finds that it was not possible to furnish the party with the above information ten days before the trial, hearing, or proceeding and that the party will not be prejudiced by the delay in receiving such information.

(10)(a)   Any aggrieved person in any trial, hearing, or proceeding in or before any court, department, officer, agency, regulatory body, or other authority of the United States, a State, or a political subdivision thereof, may move to suppress the contents of any wire or oral communication intercepted pursuant to this chapter, or evidence derived therefrom, on the grounds that—

(i)   the communication was unlawfully intercepted;

(ii)   the order of authorization or approval under which it was intercepted is insufficient on its face; or

(iii)   the interception was not made in conformity with the order of authorization or approval.

Such motion shall be made before the trial, hearing, or proceeding unless there was no opportunity to make such motion or the person was not aware of the grounds of the motion. If the motion is granted, the contents of the intercepted wire or oral communication, or evidence derived therefrom, shall be treated as having been obtained in violation of this chapter. The judge, upon the filing of such motion by the aggrieved person, may in his discretion make available to the aggrieved person or his counsel for inspection such portions of the intercepted communication or evidence derived therefrom as the judge determines to be in the interests of justice.

(b)   In addition to any other right to appeal, the United States shall have the right to appeal from an order granting a motion to suppress made under paragraph (a) of this subsection, or the denial of an application for an order of approval, if the United States attorney shall certify to the judge or other official granting such motion or denying such application that the appeal is not taken for purposes of delay. Such appeal shall be taken within thirty days after the date the order was entered and shall be diligently prosecuted.

(c)   The remedies and sanctions described in this chapter with respect to the interception of electronic communications are the only judicial remedies and sanctions for nonconstitutional violations of this chapter involving such communications.

(11) The requirements of subsections (1)(b)(ii) and (3)(d) of this section relating to the specification of the facilities from which, or the place where, the communication is to be intercepted do not apply if—

(a)   in the case of an application with respect to the interception of an oral communication—

(i)   the application is by a Federal investigative or law enforcement officer and is approved by the Attorney General, the Deputy Attorney General, the Associate Attorney General, an Assistant Attorney General, or an acting Assistant Attorney General;

(ii)   the application contains a full and complete statement as to why such specification is not practical and identifies the person committing the offense and whose communications are to be intercepted; and

(iii)   the judge finds that such specification is not practical; and

(b)   in the case of an application with respect to a wire or electronic communication—

(i)   the application is by a Federal investigative or law enforcement officer and is approved by the Attorney General, the Deputy Attorney General, the Associate Attorney General, an Assistant Attorney General, or an acting Assistant Attorney General;

(ii)   the application identifies the person believed to be committing the offense and whose communications are to be intercepted and the applicant makes a showing that there is probable cause to believe that the person's actions could have the effect of thwarting interception from a specified facility;

(iii)   the judge finds that such showing has been adequately made; and

(iv)   the order authorizing or approving the interception is limited to interception only for such time as it is reasonable to presume that the person identified in the application is or was reasonably proximate to the instrument through which such communication will be or was transmitted.

(12) An interception of a communication under an order with respect to which the requirements of subsections (1)(b)(ii) and (3)(d) of this section do not apply by reason of subsection (11)(a) shall not begin until the place where the communication is to be intercepted is ascertained by the person implementing the interception order. A provider of wire or electronic communications service that has received an order as provided for in subsection (11)(b) may move the court to modify or quash the order on the ground that its assistance with respect to the

interception cannot be performed in a timely or reasonable fashion. The court, upon notice to the government, shall decide such a motion expeditiously.

§ 2520. Recovery of civil damages authorized

(a) In general.—Except as provided in section 2511(2)(a)(ii), any person whose wire, oral, or electronic communication is intercepted, disclosed, or intentionally used in violation of this chapter may in a civil action recover from the person or entity, other than the United States, which engaged in that violation such relief as may be appropriate.

(b) Relief.—In an action under this section, appropriate relief includes—

(1) such preliminary and other equitable or declaratory relief as may be appropriate;

(2) damages under subsection (c) and punitive damages in appropriate cases; and

(3) a reasonable attorney's fee and other litigation costs reasonably incurred.

(c) Computation of damages.—(1) In an action under this section, if the conduct in violation of this chapter is the private viewing of a private satellite video communication that is not scrambled or encrypted or if the communication is a radio communication that is transmitted on frequencies allocated under subpart D of part 74 of the rules of the Federal Communications Commission that is not scrambled or encrypted and the conduct is not for a tortious or illegal purpose or for purposes of direct or indirect commercial advantage or private commercial gain, then the court shall assess damages as follows:

(A) If the person who engaged in that conduct has not previously been enjoined under section 2511(5) and has not been found liable in a prior civil action under this section, the court shall assess the greater of the sum of actual damages suffered by the plaintiff, or statutory damages of not less than $50 and not more than $500.

(B) If, on one prior occasion, the person who engaged in that conduct has been enjoined under section 2511(5) or has been found liable in a civil action under this section, the court shall assess the greater of the sum of actual damages suffered by the plaintiff, or statutory damages of not less than $100 and not more than $1000.

(2) In any other action under this section, the court may assess as damages whichever is the greater of—

(A) the sum of the actual damages suffered by the plaintiff and any profits made by the violator as a result of the violation; or

(B) statutory damages of whichever is the greater of $100 a day for each day of violation or $10,000.

(d) Defense.—A good faith reliance on—

(1) a court warrant or order, a grand jury subpoena, a legislative authorization, or a statutory authorization;

(2) a request of an investigative or law enforcement officer under section 2518(7) of this title; or

(3) a good faith determination that section 2511(3) 2511(2)(i), or 2511(2)(j) of this title permitted the conduct complained of;

is a complete defense against any civil or criminal action brought under this chapter or any other law.

(e)　Limitation.—A civil action under this section may not be commenced later than two years after the date upon which the claimant first has a reasonable opportunity to discover the violation.

(f)　Administrative discipline.—If a court or appropriate department or agency determines that the United States or any of its departments or agencies has violated any provision of this chapter, and the court or appropriate department or agency finds that the circumstances surrounding the violation raise serious questions about whether or not an officer or employee of the United States acted willfully or intentionally with respect to the violation, the department or agency shall, upon receipt of a true and correct copy of the decision and findings of the court or appropriate department or agency promptly initiate a proceeding to determine whether disciplinary action against the officer or employee is warranted. If the head of the department or agency involved determines that disciplinary action is not warranted, he or she shall notify the Inspector General with jurisdiction over the department or agency concerned and shall provide the Inspector General with the reasons for such determination.

(g)　Improper disclosure is violation.—Any willful disclosure or use by an investigative or law enforcement officer or governmental entity of information beyond the extent permitted by section 2517 is a violation of this chapter for purposes of section 2520(a).

§ 2521.　Injunction against illegal interception

Whenever it shall appear that any person is engaged or is about to engage in any act which constitutes or will constitute a felony violation of this chapter, the Attorney General may initiate a civil action in a district court of the United States to enjoin such violation. The court shall proceed as soon as practicable to the hearing and determination of such an action, and may, at any time before final determination, enter such a restraining order or prohibition, or take such other action, as is warranted to prevent a continuing and substantial injury to the United States or to any person or class of persons for whose protection the action is brought. A proceeding under this section is governed by the Federal Rules of Civil Procedure, except that, if an indictment has been returned against the respondent, discovery is governed by the Federal Rules of Criminal Procedure.

STORED WIRE AND ELECTRONIC COMMUNICATIONS AND TRANSACTIONAL RECORDS ACCESS

§ 2702.　Voluntary disclosure of customer communications or records

(a)　Prohibitions.—Except as provided in subsection (b) or (c)—

(1)　a person or entity providing an electronic communication service to the public shall not knowingly divulge to any person or entity the contents of a communication while in electronic storage by that service; and

(2)　a person or entity providing remote computing service to the public shall not knowingly divulge to any person or entity the contents of any communication which is carried or maintained on that service—

(A)　on behalf of, and received by means of electronic transmission from (or created by means of computer processing of communications received by means of electronic transmission from), a subscriber or customer of such service;

(B)　solely for the purpose of providing storage or computer processing services to such subscriber or customer, if the provider is not authorized to access the contents of any such communications for purposes of providing any services other than storage or computer processing; and

(3)   a provider of remote computing service or electronic communication service to the public shall not knowingly divulge a record or other information pertaining to a subscriber to or customer of such service (not including the contents of communications covered by paragraph (1) or (2)) to any governmental entity.

(b)   Exceptions for disclosure of communications.—A provider described in subsection (a) may divulge the contents of a communication—

(1)   to an addressee or intended recipient of such communication or an agent of such addressee or intended recipient;

(2)   as otherwise authorized in section 2517, 2511(2)(a), or 2703 of this title;

(3)   with the lawful consent of the originator or an addressee or intended recipient of such communication, or the subscriber in the case of remote computing service;

(4)   to a person employed or authorized or whose facilities are used to forward such communication to its destination;

(5)   as may be necessarily incident to the rendition of the service or to the protection of the rights or property of the provider of that service;

(6)   to the National Center for Missing and Exploited Children, in connection with a report submitted thereto under section 2258A;

(7)   to a law enforcement agency—

(A)   if the contents—

(i)   were inadvertently obtained by the service provider; and

(ii)   appear to pertain to the commission of a crime; or

[(B)   Repealed. Pub.L. 108–21, Title V, § 508(b)(1)(A), Apr. 30, 2003, 117 Stat. 684]

[(C)   Repealed. Pub.L. 107–296, Title II, § 225(d)(1)(C), Nov. 25, 2002, 116 Stat. 2157]

(8)   to a governmental entity, if the provider, in good faith, believes that an emergency involving danger of death or serious physical injury to any person requires disclosure without delay of communications relating to the emergency;

(9)   to a foreign government pursuant to an order from a foreign government that is subject to an executive agreement that the Attorney General has determined and certified to Congress satisfies section 2523.

(c)   Exceptions for disclosure of customer records.—A provider described in subsection (a) may divulge a record or other information pertaining to a subscriber to or customer of such service (not including the contents of communications covered by subsection (a)(1) or (a)(2))—

(1)   as otherwise authorized in section 2703;

(2)   with the lawful consent of the customer or subscriber;

(3)   as may be necessarily incident to the rendition of the service or to the protection of the rights or property of the provider of that service;

(4)   to a governmental entity, if the provider, in good faith, believes that an emergency involving danger of death or serious physical injury to any person requires disclosure without delay of information relating to the emergency;

(5)   to the National Center for Missing and Exploited Children, in connection with a report submitted thereto under section 2258A;

(6)   to any person other than a governmental entity; or

(7)   to a foreign government pursuant to an order from a foreign government that is subject to an executive agreement that the Attorney General has determined and certified to Congress satisfies section 2523.

(d)   Reporting of emergency disclosures.—On an annual basis, the Attorney General shall submit to the Committee on the Judiciary of the House of Representatives and the Committee on the Judiciary of the Senate a report containing—

(1)   the number of accounts from which the Department of Justice has received voluntary disclosures under subsection (b)(8); and

(2)   a summary of the basis for disclosure in those instances where—

(A)   voluntary disclosures under subsection (b)(8) were made to the Department of Justice; and

(B)   the investigation pertaining to those disclosures was closed without the filing of criminal charges.

§ 2703.   Required disclosure of customer communications or records

(a)   Contents of wire or electronic communications in electronic storage.—A governmental entity may require the disclosure by a provider of electronic communication service of the contents of a wire or electronic communication, that is in electronic storage in an electronic communications system for one hundred and eighty days or less, only pursuant to a warrant issued using the procedures described in the Federal Rules of Criminal Procedure (or, in the case of a State court, issued using State warrant procedures) by a court of competent jurisdiction. A governmental entity may require the disclosure by a provider of electronic communications services of the contents of a wire or electronic communication that has been in electronic storage in an electronic communications system for more than one hundred and eighty days by the means available under subsection (b) of this section.

(b)   Contents of wire or electronic communications in a remote computing service.—

(1)   A governmental entity may require a provider of remote computing service to disclose the contents of any wire or electronic communication to which this paragraph is made applicable by paragraph (2) of this subsection—

(A)   without required notice to the subscriber or customer, if the governmental entity obtains a warrant issued using the procedures described in the Federal Rules of Criminal Procedure (or, in the case of a State court, issued using State warrant procedures) by a court of competent jurisdiction; or

(B)   with prior notice from the governmental entity to the subscriber or customer if the governmental entity—

(i)   uses an administrative subpoena authorized by a Federal or State statute or a Federal or State grand jury or trial subpoena; or

(ii)   obtains a court order for such disclosure under subsection (d) of this section; except that delayed notice may be given pursuant to section 2705 of this title.

(2)   Paragraph (1) is applicable with respect to any wire or electronic communication that is held or maintained on that service—

(A)   on behalf of, and received by means of electronic transmission from (or created by means of computer processing of communications received by means of electronic transmission from), a subscriber or customer of such remote computing service; and

(B)   solely for the purpose of providing storage or computer processing services to such subscriber or customer, if the provider is not authorized to access the contents of any such communications for purposes of providing any services other than storage or computer processing.

(c)   Records concerning electronic communication service or remote computing service.—

(1)   A governmental entity may require a provider of electronic communication service or remote computing service to disclose a record or other information pertaining to a subscriber to or customer of such service (not including the contents of communications) only when the governmental entity—

(A)   obtains a warrant issued using the procedures described in the Federal Rules of Criminal Procedure (or, in the case of a State court, issued using State warrant procedures) by a court of competent jurisdiction;

(B)   obtains a court order for such disclosure under subsection (d) of this section;

(C)   has the consent of the subscriber or customer to such disclosure;

(D)   submits a formal written request relevant to a law enforcement investigation concerning telemarketing fraud for the name, address, and place of business of a subscriber or customer of such provider, which subscriber or customer is engaged in telemarketing (as such term is defined in section 2325 of this title); or

(E)   seeks information under paragraph (2).

(2)   A provider of electronic communication service or remote computing service shall disclose to a governmental entity the—

(A)   name;

(B)   address;

(C)   local and long distance telephone connection records, or records of session times and durations;

(D)   length of service (including start date) and types of service utilized;

(E)   telephone or instrument number or other subscriber number or identity, including any temporarily assigned network address; and

(F)   means and source of payment for such service (including any credit card or bank account number),

of a subscriber to or customer of such service when the governmental entity uses an administrative subpoena authorized by a Federal or State statute or a Federal or State grand jury or trial subpoena or any means available under paragraph (1).

(3)   A governmental entity receiving records or information under this subsection is not required to provide notice to a subscriber or customer.

(d)   Requirements for court order.—A court order for disclosure under subsection (b) or (c) may be issued by any court that is a court of competent jurisdiction and shall issue only if the governmental entity offers specific and articulable facts showing that there are reasonable grounds to believe that the contents of a wire or electronic communication, or the records or other information sought, are relevant and material to an ongoing criminal investigation. In the case of a State governmental authority, such a court order shall not issue if prohibited by the law of such State. A court issuing an order pursuant to this section, on a motion made promptly by the service provider, may quash or modify such order, if the information or records requested are unusually voluminous in nature or compliance with such order otherwise would cause an undue burden on such provider.

(e)   No cause of action against a provider disclosing information under this chapter.—No cause of action shall lie in any court against any provider of wire or electronic communication service, its officers, employees, agents, or other specified persons for providing information, facilities, or assistance in accordance with the terms of a court order, warrant, subpoena, statutory authorization, or certification under this chapter.

(f)   Requirement to preserve evidence.—

(1)   In general.—A provider of wire or electronic communication services or a remote computing service, upon the request of a governmental entity, shall take all necessary steps to preserve records and other evidence in its possession pending the issuance of a court order or other process.

(2)   Period of retention.—Records referred to in paragraph (1) shall be retained for a period of 90 days, which shall be extended for an additional 90-day period upon a renewed request by the governmental entity.

(g)   Presence of officer not required.—Notwithstanding section 3105 of this title, the presence of an officer shall not be required for service or execution of a search warrant issued in accordance with this chapter requiring disclosure by a provider of electronic communications service or remote computing service of the contents of communications or records or other information pertaining to a subscriber to or customer of such service.

(h)   Comity analysis and disclosure of information regarding legal process seeking contents of fire or electronic communication.

(1)   Definitions. In this subsection

(A)   the term 'qualifying foreign government' means a foreign government

(i)   with which the United States has an executive agreement that has entered into force under section2523; and

(ii)   the laws of which provide to electronic communication service providers and remote computing service providers substantive and procedural opportunities similar to those provided under paragraphs (2) and (5); and

(B)   the term 'United States person' has the meaning given the term in section 2523.

(2)   Motions to quash or modify.

(A) A provider of electronic communication service to the public or remote computing service, including a foreign electronic communication service or remote computing service, that is being required to disclose pursuant to legal process issued under this section the contents of a wire or electronic communication of a subscriber or customer, may file a motion to modify or quash the legal process where the provider reasonably believes

(i)   that the customer or subscriber is not a United States person and does not reside in the United States; and

(ii)   that the required disclosure would create a material risk that the provider would violate the laws of a qualifying foreign government.

Such a motion shall be filed not later than 14 days after the date on which the provider was served with the legal process, absent agreement with the government or permission from the court to extend the deadline based on an application made within the 14 days. The right to move to quash is without prejudice to any other grounds to move to quash or defenses thereto, but it shall be the sole basis for moving to quash on the grounds of a conflict of law related to a qualifying foreign government.

(B)   Upon receipt of a motion filed pursuant to subparagraph (A), the court shall afford the governmental entity that applied for or issued the legal process under this section the opportunity to respond. The court may modify or quash the legal process, as appropriate, only if the court finds that—

(i)   the required disclosure would cause the provider to violate the laws of a qualifying foreign government;

(ii)   based on the totality of the circumstances, the interests of justice dictate that the legal process should be modified or quashed; and

(iii)   the customer or subscriber is not a United States person and does not reside in the United States.

(3)   Comity Analysis. For purposes of making a determination under paragraph (2)(B)(ii), the court shall take into account, as appropriate

(A)   the interests of the United States, including the investigative interests of the governmental entity seeking to require the disclosure;

(B)   the interests of the qualifying foreign government in preventing any prohibited disclosure;

(C)   the likelihood, extent, and nature of penalties to the provider or any employees of the provider as a result of inconsistent legal requirements imposed on the provider;

(D)   the location and nationality of the subscriber or customer whose communications are being sought, if known, and the nature and extent of the subscriber or customer's connection to the United States, or if the legal process has been sought on behalf of a foreign authority pursuant to section 3512, the nature and extent of the subscriber or customer's connection to the foreign authority's country;

(E)   the nature and extent of the provider's ties to and presence in the United States;

(F)   the importance to the investigation of the information required to be disclosed;

(G)   the likelihood of timely and effective access to the information required to disclosed through means that would cause less serious negative consequences; and

(H)   if the legal process has been sought on behalf of a foreign authority pursuant to section 3512, the investigative interests of the foreign authority making the request for assistance.

(4)   Disclosure obligations during pendency of challenge. A service provider shall preserve, but not be obligated to produce, information sought during the pendency of a motion brought under this subsection, unless the court finds that immediate production is necessary to prevent an adverse result identified in section 705(a)(2).

(5)   Disclosure to qualifying foreign government.

(A)   It shall not constitute a violation of a protective order issued under section 2705 for a provider of electronic communication service to the public or remote computing service to disclose to the entity within a qualifying foreign government, designated in an executive agreement under section 2523, the fact of the existence of legal process issued under this section seeking the contents of a wire or electronic communication of a customer or subscriber who is a national or resident of the qualifying foreign government.

(B)   Nothing in this paragraph shall be construed to modify or otherwise affect any other authority to make a motion to modify or quash a protective order issued under section 2705.

§ 2707.   Civil action

(a)   Cause of action.—Except as provided in section 2703(e), any provider of electronic communication service, subscriber, or other person aggrieved by any violation of this chapter in which the conduct constituting the violation is engaged in with a knowing or intentional state of mind may, in a civil action, recover from the person or entity, other than the United States, which engaged in that violation such relief as may be appropriate.

(b)   Relief.—In a civil action under this section, appropriate relief includes—

(1)   such preliminary and other equitable or declaratory relief as may be appropriate;

(2)   damages under subsection (c); and

(3)   a reasonable attorney's fee and other litigation costs reasonably incurred.

(c)   Damages.—The court may assess as damages in a civil action under this section the sum of the actual damages suffered by the plaintiff and any profits made by the violator as a result of the violation, but in no case shall a person entitled to recover receive less than the sum of $1,000. If the violation is willful or intentional, the court may assess punitive damages. In the case of a successful action to enforce liability under this section, the court may assess the costs of the action, together with reasonable attorney fees determined by the court.

(d)   Administrative discipline.—If a court or appropriate department or agency determines that the United States or any of its departments or agencies has violated any provision of this chapter, and the court or appropriate department or agency finds that the circumstances surrounding the violation raise serious questions about whether or not an officer or employee of the United States acted willfully or intentionally with respect to the violation, the department or agency shall, upon receipt of a true and correct copy of the decision and findings of the court or appropriate department or agency promptly initiate a proceeding to determine whether disciplinary action against the officer or employee is warranted. If the head of the department or agency involved determines that disciplinary action is not warranted, he or she shall notify the Inspector General with jurisdiction over the department or agency concerned and shall provide the Inspector General with the reasons for such determination.

(e)   Defense.—A good faith reliance on—

(1)   a court warrant or order, a grand jury subpoena, a legislative authorization, or a statutory authorization (including a request of a governmental entity under section 2703(f) of this title);

(2)   a request of an investigative or law enforcement officer under section 2518(7) of this title; or

(3)   a good faith determination that section 2511(3), section 2702(b)(9), or section 2702(c)(7) of this title permitted the conduct complained of.

(f)   Limitation.—A civil action under this section may not be commenced later than two years after the date upon which the claimant first discovered or had a reasonable opportunity to discover the violation.

(g)   Improper disclosure.—Any willful disclosure of a "record", as that term is defined in section 552a(a) of title 5, United States Code, obtained by an investigative or law enforcement officer, or a governmental entity, pursuant to section 2703 of this title, or from a device installed pursuant to section 3123 or 3125 of this title, that is not a disclosure made in the proper performance of the official functions of the officer or governmental entity making the disclosure, is a violation of this chapter. This provision shall not apply to information previously lawfully disclosed (prior to the commencement of any civil or administrative proceeding under this chapter) to the public by a Federal, State, or local governmental entity or by the plaintiff in a civil action under this chapter.

§ 2708.   Exclusivity of remedies

The remedies and sanctions described in this chapter are the only judicial remedies and sanctions for nonconstitutional violations of this chapter.

§ 2713.   Required preservation and disclosure of communications and records

A provider of electronic communication service or remote computing service shall comply with the obligations of this chapter to preserve, backup, or disclose the contents of a wire or electronic communication and any record or other information pertaining to a customer or subscriber within such provider's possession, custody, or control, regardless of whether such communication, record, or other information is located within or outside of the United States.

SEARCHES AND SEIZURES

(18 U.S.C. §§ 3103a, 3105, 3109).

§ 3103a.   Additional grounds for issuing warrant

(a)   In general.—In addition to the grounds for issuing a warrant in section 3103 of this title, a warrant may be issued to search for and seize any property that constitutes evidence of a criminal offense in violation of the laws of the United States.

(b)   Delay.—With respect to the issuance of any warrant or court order under this section, or any other rule of law, to search for and seize any property or material that constitutes evidence of a criminal offense in violation of the laws of the United States, any notice required, or that may be required, to be given may be delayed if—

     (1)   the court finds reasonable cause to believe that providing immediate notification of the execution of the warrant may have an adverse result (as defined in section 2705, except if the adverse results consist only of unduly delaying a trial);

     (2)   the warrant prohibits the seizure of any tangible property, any wire or electronic communication (as defined in section 2510), or, except as expressly provided in chapter 121, any stored wire or electronic information, except where the court finds reasonable necessity for the seizure; and

     (3)   the warrant provides for the giving of such notice within a reasonable period not to exceed 30 days after the date of its execution, or on a later date certain if the facts of the case justify a longer period of delay.

(c)   Extensions of delay.—Any period of delay authorized by this section may be extended by the court for good cause shown, subject to the condition that extensions should only be granted upon an updated showing of the need for further delay and that each additional delay should be limited to periods of 90 days or less, unless the facts of the case justify a longer period of delay.

(d) Reports.—

(1) Report by judge.—Not later than 30 days after the expiration of a warrant authorizing delayed notice (including any extension thereof) entered under this section, or the denial of such warrant (or request for extension), the issuing or denying judge shall report to the Administrative Office of the United States Courts—

(A) the fact that a warrant was applied for;

(B) the fact that the warrant or any extension thereof was granted as applied for, was modified, or was denied;

(C) the period of delay in the giving of notice authorized by the warrant, and the number and duration of any extensions; and

(D) the offense specified in the warrant or application.

(2) Report by administrative office of the United States courts.—Beginning with the fiscal year ending September 30, 2007, the Director of the Administrative Office of the United States Courts shall transmit to Congress annually a full and complete report summarizing the data required to be filed with the Administrative Office by paragraph (1), including the number of applications for warrants and extensions of warrants authorizing delayed notice, and the number of such warrants and extensions granted or denied during the preceding fiscal year.

(3) Regulations.—The Director of the Administrative Office of the United States Courts, in consultation with the Attorney General, is authorized to issue binding regulations dealing with the content and form of the reports required to be filed under paragraph (1).

§ 3105. Persons authorized to serve search warrant

A search warrant may in all cases be served by any of the officers mentioned in its direction or by an officer authorized by law to serve such warrant, but by no other person, except in aid of the officer on his requiring it, he being present and acting in its execution.

§ 3109. Breaking doors or windows for entry or exit

The officer may break open any outer or inner door or window of a house, or any part of a house, or anything therein, to execute a search warrant, if, after notice of his authority and purpose, he is refused admittance or when necessary to liberate himself or a person aiding him in the execution of the warrant.

BAIL REFORM ACT OF 1984

(18 U.S.C. §§ 3141–3150).

§ 3141. Release and detention authority generally

(a) Pending trial.—A judicial officer authorized to order the arrest of a person under section 3041 of this title before whom an arrested person is brought shall order that such person be released or detained, pending judicial proceedings, under this chapter.

(b) Pending sentence or appeal.—A judicial officer of a court of original jurisdiction over an offense, or a judicial officer of a Federal appellate court, shall order that, pending imposition or execution of sentence, or pending appeal of conviction or sentence, a person be released or detained under this chapter.

§ 3142. Release or detention of a defendant pending trial

(a) In general.—Upon the appearance before a judicial officer of a person charged with an offense, the judicial officer shall issue an order that, pending trial, the person be—

(1) released on personal recognizance or upon execution of an unsecured appearance bond, under subsection (b) of this section;

(2) released on a condition or combination of conditions under subsection (c) of this section;

(3) temporarily detained to permit revocation of conditional release, deportation, or exclusion under subsection (d) of this section; or

(4) detained under subsection (e) of this section.

(b) Release on personal recognizance or unsecured appearance bond.—The judicial officer shall order the pretrial release of the person on personal recognizance, or upon execution of an unsecured appearance bond in an amount specified by the court, subject to the condition that the person not commit a Federal, State, or local crime during the period of release and subject to the condition that the person cooperate in the collection of a DNA sample from the person if the collection of such a sample is authorized pursuant to section 3 of the DNA Analysis Backlog Elimination Act of 2000 (42 U.S.C. 14135a), unless the judicial officer determines that such release will not reasonably assure the appearance of the person as required or will endanger the safety of any other person or the community.

(c) Release on conditions.—

(1) If the judicial officer determines that the release described in subsection (b) of this section will not reasonably assure the appearance of the person as required or will endanger the safety of any other person or the community, such judicial officer shall order the pretrial release of the person—

(A) subject to the condition that the person not commit a Federal, State, or local crime during the period of release and subject to the condition that the person cooperate in the collection of a DNA sample from the person if the collection of such a sample is authorized pursuant to section 3 of the DNA Analysis Backlog Elimination Act of 2000 (42 U.S.C. 14135a); and

(B) subject to the least restrictive further condition, or combination of conditions, that such judicial officer determines will reasonably assure the appearance of the person as required and the safety of any other person and the community, which may include the condition that the person—

(i) remain in the custody of a designated person, who agrees to assume supervision and to report any violation of a release condition to the court, if the designated person is able reasonably to assure the judicial officer that the person will appear as required and will not pose a danger to the safety of any other person or the community;

(ii) maintain employment, or, if unemployed, actively seek employment;

(iii) maintain or commence an educational program;

(iv) abide by specified restrictions on personal associations, place of abode, or travel;

(v) avoid all contact with an alleged victim of the crime and with a potential witness who may testify concerning the offense;

(vi) report on a regular basis to a designated law enforcement agency, pretrial services agency, or other agency;

(vii) comply with a specified curfew;

(viii)refrain from possessing a firearm, destructive device, or other dangerous weapon;

(ix) refrain from excessive use of alcohol, or any use of a narcotic drug or other controlled substance, as defined in section 102 of the Controlled Substances Act (21 U.S.C. 802), without a prescription by a licensed medical practitioner;

(x) undergo available medical, psychological, or psychiatric treatment, including treatment for drug or alcohol dependency, and remain in a specified institution if required for that purpose;

(xi) execute an agreement to forfeit upon failing to appear as required, property of a sufficient unencumbered value, including money, as is reasonably necessary to assure the appearance of the person as required, and shall provide the court with proof of ownership and the value of the property along with information regarding existing encumbrances as the judicial office may require;

(xii) execute a bail bond with solvent sureties; who will execute an agreement to forfeit in such amount as is reasonably necessary to assure appearance of the person as required and shall provide the court with information regarding the value of the assets and liabilities of the surety if other than an approved surety and the nature and extent of encumbrances against the surety's property; such surety shall have a net worth which shall have sufficient unencumbered value to pay the amount of the bail bond;

(xiii)return to custody for specified hours following release for employment, schooling, or other limited purposes; and

(xiv) satisfy any other condition that is reasonably necessary to assure the appearance of the person as required and to assure the safety of any other person and the community.

In any case that involves a minor victim under section 1201, 1591, 2241, 2242, 2244(a)(1), 2245, 2251, 2251A, 2252(a)(1), 2252(a)(2), 2252(a)(3), 2252A(a)(1), 2252A(a)(2), 2252A(a)(3), 2252A(a)(4), 2260, 2421, 2422, 2423, or 2425 of this title, or a failure to register offense under section 2250 of this title, any release order shall contain, at a minimum, a condition of electronic monitoring and each of the conditions specified at subparagraphs (iv), (v), (vi), (vii), and (viii).

(2) The judicial officer may not impose a financial condition that results in the pretrial detention of the person.

(3) The judicial officer may at any time amend the order to impose additional or different conditions of release.

(d) Temporary detention to permit revocation of conditional release, deportation, or exclusion.—If the judicial officer determines that—

(1) such person—

(A) is, and was at the time the offense was committed, on—

(i) release pending trial for a felony under Federal, State, or local law;

(ii) release pending imposition or execution of sentence, appeal of sentence or conviction, or completion of sentence, for any offense under Federal, State, or local law; or

(iii) probation or parole for any offense under Federal, State, or local law; or

(B) is not a citizen of the United States or lawfully admitted for permanent residence, as defined in section 101(a)(20) of the Immigration and Nationality Act (8 U.S.C. 1101(a)(20)); and

(2) such person may flee or pose a danger to any other person or the community;

such judicial officer shall order the detention of such person, for a period of not more than ten days, excluding Saturdays, Sundays, and holidays, and direct the attorney for the Government to notify the appropriate court, probation or parole official, or State or local law enforcement official, or the appropriate official of the Immigration and Naturalization Service. If the official fails or declines to take such person into custody during that period, such person shall be treated in accordance with the other provisions of this section, notwithstanding the applicability of other provisions of law governing release pending trial or deportation or exclusion proceedings. If temporary detention is sought under paragraph (1)(B) of this subsection, such person has the burden of proving to the court such person's United States citizenship or lawful admission for permanent residence.

(e) Detention.—

(1) If, after a hearing pursuant to the provisions of subsection (f) of this section, the judicial officer finds that no condition or combination of conditions will reasonably assure the appearance of the person as required and the safety of any other person and the community, such judicial officer shall order the detention of the person before trial.

(2) In a case described in subsection (f)(1) of this section, a rebuttable presumption arises that no condition or combination of conditions will reasonably assure the safety of any other person and the community if such judicial officer finds that—

(A) the person has been convicted of a Federal offense that is described in subsection (f)(1) of this section, or of a State or local offense that would have been an offense described in subsection (f)(1) of this section if a circumstance giving rise to Federal jurisdiction had existed;

(B) the offense described in subparagraph (A) of this subsection was committed while the person was on release pending trial for a Federal, State, or local offense; and

(C) a period of not more than five years has elapsed since the date of conviction, or the release of the person from imprisonment, for the offense described in subparagraph (A) of this subsection, whichever is later.

(3) Subject to rebuttal by the person, it shall be presumed that no condition or combination of conditions will reasonably assure the appearance of the person as required and the safety of the community if the judicial officer finds that there is probable cause to believe that the person committed—

(A) an offense for which a maximum term of imprisonment of ten years or more is prescribed in the Controlled Substances Act (21 U.S.C. 801 et seq.), the Controlled Substances Import and Export Act (21 U.S.C. 951 et seq.), or chapter 705 of title 46;

(B) an offense under section 924(c), 956(a), or 2332b of this title;

(C) an offense listed in section 2332b(g)(5)(B) of title 18, United States Code, for which a maximum term of imprisonment of 10 years or more is prescribed;

(D)   an offense under chapter 77 of this title for which a maximum term of imprisonment of 20 years or more is prescribed; or

(E)   an offense involving a minor victim under section 1201, 1591, 2241, 2242, 2244(a)(1), 2245, 2251, 2251A, 2252(a)(1), 2252(a)(2), 2252(a)(3), 2252A(a)(1), 2252A(a)(2), 2252A(a)(3), 2252A(a)(4), 2260, 2421, 2422, 2423, or 2425 of this title.

(f)   Detention hearing.—The judicial officer shall hold a hearing to determine whether any condition or combination of conditions set forth in subsection (c) of this section will reasonably assure the appearance of such person as required and the safety of any other person and the community—

(1)   upon motion of the attorney for the Government, in a case that involves—

(A)   a crime of violence*, a violation of section 1591, or an offense listed in section 2332b(g)(5)(B) for which a maximum term of imprisonment of 10 years or more is prescribed;

(B)   an offense for which the maximum sentence is life imprisonment or death;

(C)   an offense for which a maximum term of imprisonment of ten years or more is prescribed in the Controlled Substances Act (21 U.S.C. 801 et seq.), the Controlled Substances Import and Export Act (21 U.S.C. 951 et seq.), or chapter 705 of title 46

(D)   any felony if such person has been convicted of two or more offenses described in subparagraphs (A) through (C) of this paragraph, or two or more State or local offenses that would have been offenses described in subparagraphs (A) through (C) of this paragraph if a circumstance giving rise to Federal jurisdiction had existed, or a combination of such offenses; or

(E)   any felony that is not otherwise a crime of violence that involves a minor victim or that involves the possession or use of a firearm or destructive device (as those terms are defined in section 921), or any other dangerous weapon, or involves a failure to register under section 2250 of title 18, United States Code; or

(2)   Upon motion of the attorney for the Government or upon the judicial officer's own motion, in a case that involves—

(A)   a serious risk that such person will flee; or

(B)   a serious risk that such person will obstruct or attempt to obstruct justice, or threaten, injure, or intimidate, or attempt to threaten, injure, or intimidate, a prospective witness or juror.

The hearing shall be held immediately upon the person's first appearance before the judicial officer unless that person, or the attorney for the Government, seeks a continuance. Except for good cause, a continuance on motion of such person may not exceed five days (not including any intermediate Saturday, Sunday, or legal holiday), and a continuance on motion of the attorney for the Government may not exceed three days (not including any intermediate Saturday, Sunday, or legal holiday). During a continuance, such person shall be detained, and the judicial officer, on motion of the attorney for the Government or sua sponte, may order that, while in custody, a person who appears to be a narcotics addict receive a medical examination to determine whether such person is an addict. At the hearing, such person has the right to be represented by counsel, and, if financially unable to obtain adequate representation, to have counsel appointed. The person

---

*   The phrase "crime of violence" is defined in 18 U.S.C. § 3156(a)(4) as meaning: "(A) an offense that has an element of the offense the use, attempted use, or threatened use of physical force against the person or property of another, or (B) any other offense that is a felony and that, by its nature, involves a substantial risk that physical force against the person or property of another may be used in the course of committing the offense."

shall be afforded an opportunity to testify, to present witnesses, to cross-examine witnesses who appear at the hearing, and to present information by proffer or otherwise. The rules concerning admissibility of evidence in criminal trials do not apply to the presentation and consideration of information at the hearing. The facts the judicial officer uses to support a finding pursuant to subsection (e) that no condition or combination of conditions will reasonably assure the safety of any other person and the community shall be supported by clear and convincing evidence. The person may be detained pending completion of the hearing. The hearing may be reopened, before or after a determination by the judicial officer, at any time before trial if the judicial officer finds that information exists that was not known to the movant at the time of the hearing and that has a material bearing on the issue whether there are conditions of release that will reasonably assure the appearance of such person as required and the safety of any other person and the community.

(g)   Factors to be considered.—The judicial officer shall, in determining whether there are conditions of release that will reasonably assure the appearance of the person as required and the safety of any other person and the community, take into account the available information concerning—

(1)   the nature and circumstances of the offense charged, including whether the offense is a crime of violence, a violation of section 1591, a Federal crime of terrorism, or involves a minor victim or a controlled substance, firearm, explosive, or destructive device;

(2)   the weight of the evidence against the person;

(3)   the history and characteristics of the person, including—

(A)   the person's character, physical and mental condition, family ties, employment, financial resources, length of residence in the community, community ties, past conduct, history relating to drug or alcohol abuse, criminal history, and record concerning appearance at court proceedings; and

(B)   whether, at the time of the current offense or arrest, the person was on probation, on parole, or on other release pending trial, sentencing, appeal, or completion of sentence for an offense under Federal, State, or local law; and

(4)   the nature and seriousness of the danger to any person or the community that would be posed by the person's release. In considering the conditions of release described in subsection (c)(1)(B)(xi) or (c)(1)(B)(xii) of this section, the judicial officer may upon his own motion, or shall upon the motion of the Government, conduct an inquiry into the source of the property to be designated for potential forfeiture or offered as collateral to secure a bond, and shall decline to accept the designation, or the use as collateral, of property that, because of its source, will not reasonably assure the appearance of the person as required.

(h)   Contents of release order.—In a release order issued under subsection (b) or (c) of this section, the judicial officer shall—

(1)   include a written statement that sets forth all the conditions to which the release is subject, in a manner sufficiently clear and specific to serve as a guide for the person's conduct; and

(2)   advise the person of—

(A)   the penalties for violating a condition of release, including the penalties for committing an offense while on pretrial release;

(B)   the consequences of violating a condition of release, including the immediate issuance of a warrant for the person's arrest; and

(C) sections 1503 of this title (relating to intimidation of witnesses, jurors, and officers of the court), 1510 (relating to obstruction of criminal investigations), 1512 (tampering with a witness, victim, or an informant), and 1513 (retaliating against a witness, victim, or an informant).

(i) Contents of detention order.—In a detention order issued under subsection (e) of this section, the judicial officer shall—

(1) include written findings of fact and a written statement of the reasons for the detention;

(2) direct that the person be committed to the custody of the Attorney General for confinement in a corrections facility separate, to the extent practicable, from persons awaiting or serving sentences or being held in custody pending appeal;

(3) direct that the person be afforded reasonable opportunity for private consultation with counsel; and

(4) direct that, on order of a court of the United States or on request of an attorney for the Government, the person in charge of the corrections facility in which the person is confined deliver the person to a United States marshal for the purpose of an appearance in connection with a court proceeding.

The judicial officer may, by subsequent order, permit the temporary release of the person, in the custody of a United States marshal or another appropriate person, to the extent that the judicial officer determines such release to be necessary for preparation of the person's defense or for another compelling reason.

(j) Presumption of innocence.—Nothing in this section shall be construed as modifying or limiting the presumption of innocence.

§ 3143. Release or detention of a defendant pending sentence or appeal

(a) Release or detention pending sentence.—

(1) Except as provided in paragraph (2), the judicial officer shall order that a person who has been found guilty of an offense and who is awaiting imposition or execution of sentence, other than a person for whom the applicable guideline promulgated pursuant to 28 U.S.C. 994 does not recommend a term of imprisonment, be detained, unless the judicial officer finds by clear and convincing evidence that the person is not likely to flee or pose a danger to the safety of any other person or the community if released under section 3142(b) or (c). If the judicial officer makes such a finding, such judicial officer shall order the release of the person in accordance with section 3142(b) or (c).

(2) The judicial officer shall order that a person who has been found guilty of an offense in a case described in subparagraph (A), (B), or (C) of subsection (f)(1) of section 3142 and is awaiting imposition or execution of sentence be detained unless—

(A)(i) the judicial officer finds there is a substantial likelihood that a motion for acquittal or new trial will be granted; or

(ii) an attorney for the Government has recommended that no sentence of imprisonment be imposed on the person; and

(B) the judicial officer finds by clear and convincing evidence that the person is not likely to flee or pose a danger to any other person or the community.

(b) Release or detention pending appeal by the defendant.—(1) Except as provided in paragraph (2), the judicial officer shall order that a person who has been found guilty of an offense and sentenced to a term of imprisonment, and who has filed an appeal or a petition for a writ of certiorari, be detained, unless the judicial officer finds—

    (A) by clear and convincing evidence that the person is not likely to flee or pose a danger to the safety of any other person or the community if released under section 3142(b) or (c) of this title; and

    (B) that the appeal is not for the purpose of delay and raises a substantial question of law or fact likely to result in—

        (i)   reversal,

        (ii) an order for a new trial,

        (iii) a sentence that does not include a term of imprisonment, or

        (iv) a reduced sentence to a term of imprisonment less than the total of the time already served plus the expected duration of the appeal process.

If the judicial officer makes such findings, such judicial officer shall order the release of the person in accordance with section 3142(b) or (c) of this title, except that in the circumstance described in subparagraph (B)(iv) of this paragraph, the judicial officer shall order the detention terminated at the expiration of the likely reduced sentence.

    (2)   The judicial officer shall order that a person who has been found guilty of an offense in a case described in subparagraph (A), (B), or (C) of subsection (f)(1) of section 3142 and sentenced to a term of imprisonment, and who has filed an appeal or a petition for a writ of certiorari, be detained.

    (c)   Release or detention pending appeal by the government.—The judicial officer shall treat a defendant in a case in which an appeal has been taken by the United States under section 3731 of this title, in accordance with section 3142 of this title, unless the defendant is otherwise subject to a release or detention order.

Except as provided in subsection (b) of this section, the judicial officer, in a case in which an appeal has been taken by the United States under section 3742, shall—

    (1) if the person has been sentenced to a term of imprisonment, order that person detained; and

    (2) in any other circumstance, release or detain the person under section 3142.

§ 3144.   Release or detention of a material witness

If it appears from an affidavit filed by a party that the testimony of a person is material in a criminal proceeding, and if it is shown that it may become impracticable to secure the presence of the person by subpoena, a judicial officer may order the arrest of the person and treat the person in accordance with the provisions of section 3142 of this title. No material witness may be detained because of inability to comply with any condition of release if the testimony of such witness can adequately be secured by deposition, and if further detention is not necessary to prevent a failure of justice. Release of a material witness may be delayed for a reasonable period of time until the deposition of the witness can be taken pursuant to the Federal Rules of Criminal Procedure.

§ 3145.   Review and appeal of a release or detention order

    (a)   Review of a release order.—If a person is ordered released by a magistrate judge, or by a person other than a judge of a court having original jurisdiction over the offense and other than a Federal appellate court—

(1) the attorney for the Government may file, with the court having original jurisdiction over the offense, a motion for revocation of the order or amendment of the conditions of release; and

(2) the person may file, with the court having original jurisdiction over the offense, a motion for amendment of the conditions of release.

The motion shall be determined promptly.

(b) Review of a detention order.—If a person is ordered detained by a magistrate judge, or by a person other than a judge of a court having original jurisdiction over the offense and other than a Federal appellate court, the person may file, with the court having original jurisdiction over the offense, a motion for revocation or amendment of the order. The motion shall be determined promptly.

(c) Appeal from a release or detention order.—An appeal from a release or detention order, or from a decision denying revocation or amendment of such an order, is governed by the provisions of section 1291 of title 28 and section 3731 of this title. The appeal shall be determined promptly. A person subject to detention pursuant to section 3143(a)(2) or (b)(2), and who meets the conditions of release set forth in section 3143(a)(1) or (b)(1), may be ordered released, under appropriate conditions, by the judicial officer, if it is clearly shown that there are exceptional reasons why such person's detention would not be appropriate.

§ 3146.   Penalty for failure to appear

(a) Offense.—Whoever, having been released under this chapter knowingly—

(1) fails to appear before a court as required by the conditions of release; or

(2) fails to surrender for service of sentence pursuant to a court order;

shall be punished as provided in subsection (b) of this section.

(b) Punishment.—(1) The punishment for an offense under this section is—

(A) if the person was released in connection with a charge of, or while awaiting sentence, surrender for service of sentence, or appeal or certiorari after conviction for—

(i) an offense punishable by death, life imprisonment, or imprisonment for a term of 15 years or more, a fine under this title or imprisonment for not more than ten years, or both;

(ii) an offense punishable by imprisonment for a term of five years or more, a fine under this title or imprisonment for not more than five years, or both;

(iii) any other felony, a fine under this title or imprisonment for not more than two years, or both; or

(iv) a misdemeanor, a fine under this title or imprisonment for not more than one year, or both; and

(B) if the person was released for appearance as a material witness, a fine under this chapter or imprisonment for not more than one year, or both.

(2) A term of imprisonment imposed under this section shall be consecutive to the sentence of imprisonment for any other offense.

(c) Affirmative defense.—It is an affirmative defense to a prosecution under this section that uncontrollable circumstances prevented the person from appearing or surrendering, and that the person did not contribute to the creation of such circumstances in reckless disregard of the requirement to appear or surrender, and that the person appeared or surrendered as soon as such circumstances ceased to exist.

(d)   Declaration of forfeiture.—If a person fails to appear before a court as required, and the person executed an appearance bond pursuant to section 3142(b) of this title or is subject to the release condition set forth in clause (xi) or (xii) of section 3142(c)(1)(B) of this title, the judicial officer may, regardless of whether the person has been charged with an offense under this section, declare any property designated pursuant to that section to be forfeited to the United States.

§ 3147.   Penalty for an offense committed while on release

A person convicted of an offense committed while released under this chapter shall be sentenced, in addition to the sentence prescribed for the offense to—

(1)   a term of imprisonment of not more than ten years if the offense is a felony; or

(2)   a term of imprisonment of not more than one year if the offense is a misdemeanor.

A term of imprisonment imposed under this section shall be consecutive to any other sentence of imprisonment.

§ 3148.   Sanctions for violation of a release condition

(a)   Available sanctions.—A person who has been released under section 3142 of this title, and who has violated a condition of his release, is subject to a revocation of release, an order of detention, and a prosecution for contempt of court.

(b)   Revocation of release.—The attorney for the Government may initiate a proceeding for revocation of an order of release by filing a motion with the district court. A judicial officer may issue a warrant for the arrest of a person charged with violating a condition of release, and the person shall be brought before a judicial officer in the district in which such person's arrest was ordered for a proceeding in accordance with this section. To the extent practicable, a person charged with violating the condition of release that such person not commit a Federal, State, or local crime during the period of release, shall be brought before the judicial officer who ordered the release and whose order is alleged to have been violated. The judicial officer shall enter an order of revocation and detention if, after a hearing, the judicial officer—

(1)   finds that there is—

(A)   probable cause to believe that the person has committed a Federal, State, or local crime while on release; or

(B)   clear and convincing evidence that the person has violated any other condition of release; and

(2)   finds that—

(A)   based on the factors set forth in section 3142(g) of this title, there is no condition or combination of conditions of release that will assure that the person will not flee or pose a danger to the safety of any other person or the community; or

(B)   the person is unlikely to abide by any condition or combination of conditions of release.

If there is probable cause to believe that, while on release, the person committed a Federal, State, or local felony, a rebuttable presumption arises that no condition or combination of conditions will assure that the person will not pose a danger to the safety of any other person or the community. If the judicial officer finds that there are conditions of release that will assure that the person will not flee or pose a danger to the safety of any other person or the community, and that the person will abide by such conditions, the judicial officer shall treat the person in accordance with the provisions of section 3142 of this title and may amend the conditions of release accordingly.

(c)   Prosecution for contempt.—The judicial officer may commence a prosecution for contempt, under section 401 of this title, if the person has violated a condition of release.

§ 3149.   Surrender of an offender by a surety

A person charged with an offense, who is released upon the execution of an appearance bond with a surety, may be arrested by the surety, and if so arrested, shall be delivered promptly to a United States marshal and brought before a judicial officer. The judicial officer shall determine in accordance with the provisions of section 3148(b) whether to revoke the release of the person, and may absolve the surety of responsibility to pay all or part of the bond in accordance with the provisions of Rule 46 of the Federal Rules of Criminal Procedure. The person so committed shall be held in official detention until released pursuant to this chapter or another provision of law.

§ 3150.   Applicability to a case removed from a State court

The provisions of this chapter apply to a criminal case removed to a Federal court from a State court.

SPEEDY TRIAL ACT OF 1974 (AS AMENDED)

(18 U.S.C. §§ 3161–3162, 3164).

§ 3161.   Time limits and exclusions

(a)   In any case involving a defendant charged with an offense, the appropriate judicial officer, at the earliest practicable time, shall, after consultation with the counsel for the defendant and the attorney for the Government, set the case for trial on a day certain, or list it for trial on a weekly or other short-term trial calendar at a place within the judicial district, so as to assure a speedy trial.

(b)   Any information or indictment charging an individual with the commission of an offense shall be filed within thirty days from the date on which such individual was arrested or served with a summons in connection with such charges. If an individual has been charged with a felony in a district in which no grand jury has been in session during such thirty-day period, the period of time for filing of the indictment shall be extended an additional thirty days.

(c)(1)   In any case in which a plea of not guilty is entered, the trial of a defendant charged in an information or indictment with the commission of an offense shall commence within seventy days from the filing date (and making public) of the information or indictment, or from the date the defendant has appeared before a judicial officer of the court in which such charge is pending, whichever date last occurs. If a defendant consents in writing to be tried before a magistrate judge on a complaint, the trial shall commence within seventy days from the date of such consent.

(2)   Unless the defendant consents in writing to the contrary, the trial shall not commence less than thirty days from the date on which the defendant first appears through counsel or expressly waives counsel and elects to proceed pro se.

(d)(1)   If any indictment or information is dismissed upon motion of the defendant, or any charge contained in a complaint filed against an individual is dismissed or otherwise dropped, and thereafter a complaint is filed against such defendant or individual charging him with the same offense or an offense based on the same conduct or arising from the same criminal episode, or an information or indictment is filed charging such defendant with the same offense or an offense based on the same conduct or arising from the same criminal episode, the provisions of subsections

(b) and (c) of this section shall be applicable with respect to such subsequent complaint, indictment, or information, as the case may be.

(2)   If the defendant is to be tried upon an indictment or information dismissed by a trial court and reinstated following an appeal, the trial shall commence within seventy days from the date the action occasioning the trial becomes final, except that the court retrying the case may extend the period for trial not to exceed one hundred and eighty days from the date the action occasioning the trial becomes final if the unavailability of witnesses or other factors resulting from the passage of time shall make trial within seventy days impractical. The periods of delay enumerated in section 3161(h) are excluded in computing the time limitations specified in this section. The sanctions of section 3162 apply to this subsection.

(e)   If the defendant is to be tried again following a declaration by the trial judge of a mistrial or following an order of such judge for a new trial, the trial shall commence within seventy days from the date the action occasioning the retrial becomes final. If the defendant is to be tried again following an appeal or a collateral attack, the trial shall commence within seventy days from the date the action occasioning the retrial becomes final, except that the court retrying the case may extend the period for retrial not to exceed one hundred and eighty days from the date the action occasioning the retrial becomes final if unavailability of witnesses or other factors resulting from passage of time shall make trial within seventy days impractical. The periods of delay enumerated in section 3161(h) are excluded in computing the time limitations specified in this section. The sanctions of section 3162 apply to this subsection.

(f)   Notwithstanding the provisions of subsection (b) of this section, for the first twelve-calendar-month period following the effective date of this section as set forth in section 3163(a) of this chapter the time limit imposed with respect to the period between arrest and indictment by subsection (b) of this section shall be sixty days, for the second such twelve-month period such time limit shall be forty-five days and for the third such period such time limit shall be thirty-five days.

(g)   Notwithstanding the provisions of subsection (c) of this section, for the first twelve-calendar-month period following the effective date of this section as set forth in section 3163(b) of this chapter, the time limit with respect to the period between arraignment and trial imposed by subsection (c) of this section shall be one hundred and eighty days, for the second such twelve-month period such time limit shall be one hundred and twenty days, and for the third such period such time limit with respect to the period between arraignment and trial shall be eighty days.

(h)   The following periods of delay shall be excluded in computing the time within which an information or an indictment must be filed, or in computing the time within which the trial of any such offense must commence:

(1)   Any period of delay resulting from other proceedings concerning the defendant, including but not limited to—

(A)   delay resulting from any proceeding, including any examinations, to determine the mental competency or physical capacity of the defendant;

(B)   delay resulting from trial with respect to other charges against the defendant;

(C)   delay resulting from any interlocutory appeal;

(D)   delay resulting from any pretrial motion, from the filing of the motion through the conclusion of the hearing on, or other prompt disposition of, such motion;

(E)   delay resulting from any proceeding relating to the transfer of a case or the removal of any defendant from another district under the Federal Rules of Criminal Procedure;

(F)   delay resulting from transportation of any defendant from another district, or to and from places of examination or hospitalization, except that any time consumed in excess of ten days from the date an order of removal or an order directing such transportation, and the defendant's arrival at the destination shall be presumed to be unreasonable;

(G)   delay resulting from consideration by the court of a proposed plea agreement to be entered into by the defendant and the attorney for the Government; and

(H)   delay reasonably attributable to any period, not to exceed thirty days, during which any proceeding concerning the defendant is actually under advisement by the court.

(2)   Any period of delay during which prosecution is deferred by the attorney for the Government pursuant to written agreement with the defendant, with the approval of the court, for the purpose of allowing the defendant to demonstrate his good conduct.

(3)(A)   Any period of delay resulting from the absence or unavailability of the defendant or an essential witness.

(B)   For purposes of subparagraph (A) of this paragraph, a defendant or an essential witness shall be considered absent when his whereabouts are unknown and, in addition, he is attempting to avoid apprehension or prosecution or his whereabouts cannot be determined by due diligence. For purposes of such subparagraph, a defendant or an essential witness shall be considered unavailable whenever his whereabouts are known but his presence for trial cannot be obtained by due diligence or he resists appearing at or being returned for trial.

(4)   Any period of delay resulting from the fact that the defendant is mentally incompetent or physically unable to stand trial.

(5)   If the information or indictment is dismissed upon motion of the attorney for the Government and thereafter a charge is filed against the defendant for the same offense, or any offense required to be joined with that offense, any period of delay from the date the charge was dismissed to the date the time limitation would commence to run as to the subsequent charge had there been no previous charge.

(6)   A reasonable period of delay when the defendant is joined for trial with a codefendant as to whom the time for trial has not run and no motion for severance has been granted.

(7)(A)   Any period of delay resulting from a continuance granted by any judge on his own motion or at the request of the defendant or his counsel or at the request of the attorney for the Government, if the judge granted such continuance on the basis of his findings that the ends of justice served by taking such action outweigh the best interest of the public and the defendant in a speedy trial. No such period of delay resulting from a continuance granted by the court in accordance with this paragraph shall be excludable under this subsection unless the court sets forth, in the record of the case, either orally or in writing, its reasons for finding that the ends of justice served by the granting of such continuance outweigh the best interests of the public and the defendant in a speedy trial.

(B)   The factors, among others, which a judge shall consider in determining whether to grant a continuance under subparagraph (A) of this paragraph in any case are as follows:

(i)   Whether the failure to grant such a continuance in the proceeding would be likely to make a continuation of such proceeding impossible, or result in a miscarriage of justice.

(ii)   Whether the case is so unusual or so complex, due to the number of defendants, the nature of the prosecution, or the existence of novel questions of fact or law, that it is unreasonable to expect adequate preparation for pretrial proceedings or for the trial itself within the time limits established by this section.

(iii)   Whether, in a case in which arrest precedes indictment, delay in the filing of the indictment is caused because the arrest occurs at a time such that it is unreasonable to expect return and filing of the indictment within the period specified in section 3161(b), or because the facts upon which the grand jury must base its determination are unusual or complex.

(iv)   Whether the failure to grant such a continuance in a case which, taken as a whole, is not so unusual or so complex as to fall within clause (ii), would deny the defendant reasonable time to obtain counsel, would unreasonably deny the defendant or the Government continuity of counsel, or would deny counsel for the defendant or the attorney for the Government the reasonable time necessary for effective preparation, taking into account the exercise of due diligence.

(C)   No continuance under subparagraph (A) of this paragraph shall be granted because of general congestion of the court's calendar, or lack of diligent preparation or failure to obtain available witnesses on the part of the attorney for the Government.

(8)   Any period of delay, not to exceed one year, ordered by a district court upon an application of a party and a finding by a preponderance of the evidence that an official request, as defined in section 3292 of this title, has been made for evidence of any such offense and that it reasonably appears, or reasonably appeared at the time the request was made, that such evidence is, or was, in such foreign country.

(i)   If trial did not commence within the time limitation specified in section 3161 because the defendant had entered a plea of guilty or nolo contendere subsequently withdrawn to any or all charges in an indictment or information, the defendant shall be deemed indicted with respect to all charges therein contained within the meaning of section 3161, on the day the order permitting withdrawal of the plea becomes final.

(j)(1)   If the attorney for the Government knows that a person charged with an offense is serving a term of imprisonment in any penal institution, he shall promptly—

(A)   undertake to obtain the presence of the prisoner for trial; or

(B)   cause a detainer to be filed with the person having custody of the prisoner and request him to so advise the prisoner and to advise the prisoner of his right to demand trial.

(2)   If the person having custody of such prisoner receives a detainer, he shall promptly advise the prisoner of the charge and of the prisoner's right to demand trial. If at any time thereafter the prisoner informs the person having custody that he does demand trial, such person shall cause notice to that effect to be sent promptly to the attorney for the Government who caused the detainer to be filed.

(3)   Upon receipt of such notice, the attorney for the Government shall promptly seek to obtain the presence of the prisoner for trial.

(4)   When the person having custody of the prisoner receives from the attorney for the Government a properly supported request for temporary custody of such prisoner for trial, the prisoner shall be made available to that attorney for the Government (subject, in cases of interjurisdictional transfer, to any right of the prisoner to contest the legality of his delivery).

(k)(1)   If the defendant is absent (as defined by subsection (h)(3)) on the day set for trial, and the defendant's subsequent appearance before the court on a bench warrant or other process or surrender to the court occurs more than 21 days after the day set for trial, the defendant shall be deemed to have first appeared before a judicial officer of the court in which the information or indictment is pending within the meaning of subsection (c) on the date of the defendant's subsequent appearance before the court.

(2) If the defendant is absent (as defined by subsection (h)(3)) on the day set for trial, and the defendant's subsequent appearance before the court on a bench warrant or other process or surrender to the court occurs not more than 21 days after the day set for trial, the time limit required by subsection (c), as extended by subsection (h), shall be further extended by 21 days.

§ 3162. Sanctions

(a)(1) If, in the case of any individual against whom a complaint is filed charging such individual with an offense, no indictment or information is filed within the time limit required by section 3161(b) as extended by section 3161(h) of this chapter, such charge against that individual contained in such complaint shall be dismissed or otherwise dropped. In determining whether to dismiss the case with or without prejudice, the court shall consider, among others, each of the following factors: the seriousness of the offense; the facts and circumstances of the case which led to the dismissal; and the impact of a reprosecution on the administration of this chapter and on the administration of justice.

(2) If a defendant is not brought to trial within the time limit required by section 3161(c) as extended by section 3161(h), the information or indictment shall be dismissed on motion of the defendant. The defendant shall have the burden of proof of supporting such motion but the Government shall have the burden of going forward with the evidence in connection with any exclusion of time under subparagraph 3161(h) (3). In determining whether to dismiss the case with or without prejudice, the court shall consider, among others, each of the following factors: the seriousness of the offense; the facts and circumstances of the case which led to the dismissal; and the impact of a reprosecution on the administration of this chapter and on the administration of justice. Failure of the defendant to move for dismissal prior to trial or entry of a plea of guilty or nolo contendere shall constitute a waiver of the right to dismissal under this section.

(b) In any case in which counsel for the defendant or the attorney for the Government (1) knowingly allows the case to be set for trial without disclosing the fact that a necessary witness would be unavailable for trial; (2) files a motion solely for the purpose of delay which he knows is totally frivolous and without merit; (3) makes a statement for the purpose of obtaining a continuance which he knows to be false and which is material to the granting of a continuance; or (4) otherwise willfully fails to proceed to trial without justification consistent with section 3161 of this chapter, the court may punish any such counsel or attorney, as follows:

(A) in the case of an appointed defense counsel, by reducing the amount of compensation that otherwise would have been paid to such counsel pursuant to section 3006A of this title in an amount not to exceed 25 per centum thereof;

(B) in the case of a counsel retained in connection with the defense of a defendant, by imposing on such counsel a fine of not to exceed 25 per centum of the compensation to which he is entitled in connection with his defense of such defendant;

(C) by imposing on any attorney for the Government a fine of not to exceed $250;

(D) by denying any such counsel or attorney for the Government the right to practice before the court considering such case for a period of not to exceed ninety days; or

(E) by filing a report with an appropriate disciplinary committee.

The authority to punish provided for by this subsection shall be in addition to any other authority or power available to such court.

(c)   The court shall follow procedures established in the Federal Rules of Criminal Procedure in punishing any counsel or attorney for the Government pursuant to this section.

§ 3164.   Persons detained or designated as being of high risk

(a)   The trial or other disposition of cases involving—

(1)   a detained person who is being held in detention solely because he is awaiting trial, and

(2)   a released person who is awaiting trial and has been designated by the attorney for the Government as being of high risk,

shall be accorded priority.

(b)   The trial of any person described in subsection (a) (1) or (a) (2) of this section shall commence not later than ninety days following the beginning of such continuous detention or designation of high risk by the attorney for the Government. The periods of delay enumerated in section 3161(h) are excluded in computing the time limitation specified in this section.

(c)   Failure to commence trial of a detainee as specified in subsection (b), through no fault of the accused or his counsel, or failure to commence trial of a designated releasee as specified in subsection (b), through no fault of the attorney for the Government, shall result in the automatic review by the court of the conditions of release. No detainee, as defined in subsection (a), shall be held in custody pending trial after the expiration of such ninety-day period required for the commencement of his trial. A designated releasee, as defined in subsection (a), who is found by the court to have intentionally delayed the trial of his case shall be subject to an order of the court modifying his nonfinancial conditions of release under this title to insure that he shall appear at trial as required.

JENCKS ACT

(18 U.S.C. § 3500).

§ 3500.   Demands for production of statements and reports of witnesses

(a)   In any criminal prosecution brought by the United States, no statement or report in the possession of the United States which was made by a Government witness or prospective Government witness (other than the defendant) shall be the subject of subpena, discovery, or inspection until said witness has testified on direct examination in the trial of the case.

(b)   After a witness called by the United States has testified on direct examination, the court shall, on motion of the defendant, order the United States to produce any statement (as hereinafter defined) of the witness in the possession of the United States which relates to the subject matter as to which the witness has testified. If the entire contents of any such statement relate to the subject matter of the testimony of the witness, the court shall order it to be delivered directly to the defendant for his examination and use.

(c)   If the United States claims that any statement ordered to be produced under this section contains matter which does not relate to the subject matter of the testimony of the witness, the court shall order the United States to deliver such statement for the inspection of the court in camera. Upon such delivery the court shall excise the portions of such statement which do not relate to the subject matter of the testimony of the witness. With such material excised, the court shall then direct delivery of such statement to the defendant for his use. If, pursuant to such procedure, any portion of such statement is withheld from the defendant and the defendant objects to such withholding, and the trial is continued to an adjudication of the guilt of the defendant, the entire text of such statement shall be preserved by the United States and, in the event the defendant appeals, shall be made available to the appellate court for the purpose of determining the correctness of the ruling of the trial judge. Whenever any statement is delivered to a defendant pursuant to this section, the court in its discretion, upon application of said defendant, may recess proceedings in the trial for such time as it may determine to be reasonably required for the examination of such statement by said defendant and his preparation for its use in the trial.

(d) If the United States elects not to comply with an order of the court under subsection (b) or (c) hereof to deliver to the defendant any such statement, or such portion thereof as the court may direct, the court shall strike from the record the testimony of the witness, and the trial shall proceed unless the court in its discretion shall determine that the interests of justice require that a mistrial be declared.

(e) The term "statement", as used in subsections (b), (c), and (d) of this section in relation to any witness called by the United States, means—

(1) a written statement made by said witness and signed or otherwise adopted or approved by him;

(2) a stenographic, mechanical, electrical, or other recording, or a transcription thereof, which is a substantially verbatim recital of an oral statement made by said witness and recorded contemporaneously with the making of such oral statement; or

(3) a statement, however taken or recorded, or a transcription thereof, if any, made by said witness to a grand jury.

LITIGATION CONCERNING SOURCES OF EVIDENCE

(18 U.S.C. § 3504).

§ 3504. Litigation concerning sources of evidence

(a) In any trial, hearing, or other proceeding in or before any court, grand jury, department, officer, agency, regulatory body, or other authority of the United States—

(1) upon a claim by a party aggrieved that evidence is inadmissible because it is the primary product of an unlawful act or because it was obtained by the exploitation of an unlawful act, the opponent of the claim shall affirm or deny the occurrence of the alleged unlawful act;

(2) disclosure of information for a determination if evidence is inadmissible because it is the primary product of an unlawful act occurring prior to June 19, 1968, or because it was obtained by the exploitation of an unlawful act occurring prior to June 19, 1968, shall not be required unless such information may be relevant to a pending claim of such inadmissibility; and

(3) no claim shall be considered that evidence of an event is inadmissible on the ground that such evidence was obtained by the exploitation of an unlawful act occurring prior to June 19, 1968, if such event occurred more than five years after such allegedly unlawful act.

(b) As used in this section "unlawful act" means any act the use of any electronic, mechanical, or other device (as defined in section 2510(5) of this title) in violation of the Constitution or laws of the United States or any regulation or standard promulgated pursuant thereto.

CRIMINAL APPEALS ACT OF 1970
(AS AMENDED)
(18 U.S.C. § 3731).

§ 3731. Appeal by United States

In a criminal case an appeal by the United States shall lie to a court of appeals from a decision, judgment, or order of a district court dismissing an indictment or information or granting a new trial after verdict or judgment, as to any one or more counts, or any part thereof, except that no appeal shall lie where the double jeopardy clause of the United States Constitution prohibits further prosecution.

An appeal by the United States shall lie to a court of appeals from a decision or order of a district court suppressing or excluding evidence or requiring the return of seized property in a criminal proceeding, not made after the defendant has been put in jeopardy and before the verdict or finding on an indictment or information, if the United States attorney certifies to the district court that the appeal is not taken for purpose of delay and that the evidence is a substantial proof of a fact material in the proceeding.

An appeal by the United States shall lie to a court of appeals from a decision or order, entered by a district court of the United States, granting the release of a person charged with or convicted of an offense, or denying a motion for revocation of, or modification of the conditions of, a decision or order granting release.

The appeal in all such cases shall be taken within thirty days after the decision, judgment or order has been rendered and shall be diligently prosecuted.

The provisions of this section shall be liberally construed to effectuate its purposes.

CRIME VICTIMS' RIGHTS
(18 U.S.C. § 3771).

§ 3771. Crime victims' rights

(a) Rights of crime victims.—A crime victim has the following rights:

(1) The right to be reasonably protected from the accused.

(2) The right to reasonable, accurate, and timely notice of any public court proceeding, or any parole proceeding, involving the crime or of any release or escape of the accused.

(3) The right not to be excluded from any such public court proceeding, unless the court, after receiving clear and convincing evidence, determines that testimony by the victim would be materially altered if the victim heard other testimony at that proceeding.

(4) The right to be reasonably heard at any public proceeding in the district court involving release, plea, sentencing, or any parole proceeding.

(5) The reasonable right to confer with the attorney for the Government in the case.

(6) The right to full and timely restitution as provided in law.

(7) The right to proceedings free from unreasonable delay.

(8) The right to be treated with fairness and with respect for the victim's dignity and privacy.

(b)   Rights afforded.—

(1)   In general.—

In any court proceeding involving an offense against a crime victim, the court shall ensure that the crime victim is afforded the rights described in subsection (a). Before making a determination described in subsection (a)(3), the court shall make every effort to permit the fullest attendance possible by the victim and shall consider reasonable alternatives to the exclusion of the victim from the criminal proceeding. The reasons for any decision denying relief under this chapter shall be clearly stated on the record.

(2)   Habeas corpus proceedings.—

(A)   In general.—In a Federal habeas corpus proceeding arising out of a State conviction, the court shall ensure that a crime victim is afforded the rights described in paragraphs (3), (4), (7), and (8) of subsection (a).

(B)   Enforcement.—

(i)   In general.—These rights may be enforced by the crime victim or the crime victim's lawful representative in the manner described in paragraphs (1) and (3) of subsection (d).

(ii)   Multiple victims.—In a case involving multiple victims, subsection (d)(2) shall also apply.

(C)   Limitation.—This paragraph relates to the duties of a court in relation to the rights of a crime victim in Federal habeas corpus proceedings arising out of a State conviction, and does not give rise to any obligation or requirement applicable to personnel of any agency of the Executive Branch of the Federal Government.

(D)   Definition.—For purposes of this paragraph, the term "crime victim" means the person against whom the State offense is committed or, if that person is killed or incapacitated, that person's family member or other lawful representative.

(c)   Best efforts to accord rights.—

(1)   Government.—Officers and employees of the Department of Justice and other departments and agencies of the United States engaged in the detection, investigation, or prosecution of crime shall make their best efforts to see that crime victims are notified of, and accorded, the rights described in subsection (a).

(2)   Advice of attorney.—The prosecutor shall advise the crime victim that the crime victim can seek the advice of an attorney with respect to the rights described in subsection (a).

(3)   Notice.—Notice of release otherwise required pursuant to this chapter shall not be given if such notice may endanger the safety of any person.

(d)   Enforcement and limitations.—

(1)   Rights.—The crime victim or the crime victim's lawful representative, and the attorney for the Government may assert the rights described in subsection (a). A person accused of the crime may not obtain any form of relief under this chapter.

(2)   Multiple crime victims.—In a case where the court finds that the number of crime victims makes it impracticable to accord all of the crime victims the rights described in subsection (a), the court shall fashion a reasonable procedure to give effect to this chapter that does not unduly complicate or prolong the proceedings.

(3) Motion for relief and writ of mandamus.—The rights described in subsection (a) shall be asserted in the district court in which a defendant is being prosecuted for the crime or, if no prosecution is underway, in the district court in the district in which the crime occurred. The district court shall take up and decide any motion asserting a victim's right forthwith. If the district court denies the relief sought, the movant may petition the court of appeals for a writ of mandamus. The court of appeals may issue the writ on the order of a single judge pursuant to circuit rule or the Federal Rules of Appellate Procedure. The court of appeals shall take up and decide such application forthwith within 72 hours after the petition has been filed. In no event shall proceedings be stayed or subject to a continuance of more than five days for purposes of enforcing this chapter. If the court of appeals denies the relief sought, the reasons for the denial shall be clearly stated on the record in a written opinion.

(4) Error.—In any appeal in a criminal case, the Government may assert as error the district court's denial of any crime victim's right in the proceeding to which the appeal relates.

(5) Limitation on relief.—In no case shall a failure to afford a right under this chapter provide grounds for a new trial. A victim may make a motion to re-open a plea or sentence only if—

(A) the victim has asserted the right to be heard before or during the proceeding at issue and such right was denied;

(B) the victim petitions the court of appeals for a writ of mandamus within 14 days; and

(C) in the case of a plea, the accused has not pled to the highest offense charged.

This paragraph does not affect the victim's right to restitution as provided in title 18, United States Code.

(6) No cause of action.—Nothing in this chapter shall be construed to authorize a cause of action for damages or to create, to enlarge, or to imply any duty or obligation to any victim or other person for the breach of which the United States or any of its officers or employees could be held liable in damages. Nothing in this chapter shall be construed to impair the prosecutorial discretion of the Attorney General or any officer under his direction.

(e) Definitions.—For the purposes of this chapter, the term "crime victim" means a person directly and proximately harmed as a result of the commission of a Federal offense or an offense in the District of Columbia. In the case of a crime victim who is under 18 years of age, incompetent, incapacitated, or deceased, the legal guardians of the crime victim or the representatives of the crime victim's estate, family members, or any other persons appointed as suitable by the court, may assume the crime victim's rights under this chapter, but in no event shall the defendant be named as such guardian or representative.

(f) Procedures to promote compliance.—

(1) Regulations.—Not later than 1 year after the date of enactment of this chapter, the Attorney General of the United States shall promulgate regulations to enforce the rights of crime victims and to ensure compliance by responsible officials with the obligations described in law respecting crime victims.

(2) Contents.—The regulations promulgated under paragraph (1) shall—

(A) designate an administrative authority within the Department of Justice to receive and investigate complaints relating to the provision or violation of the rights of a crime victim;

(B) require a course of training for employees and offices of the Department of Justice that fail to comply with provisions of Federal law pertaining to the treatment of crime victims, and otherwise assist such employees and offices in responding more effectively to the needs of crime victims;

(C) contain disciplinary sanctions, including suspension or termination from employment, for employees of the Department of Justice who willfully or wantonly fail to comply with provisions of Federal law pertaining to the treatment of crime victims; and

(D) provide that the Attorney General, or the designee of the Attorney General, shall be the final arbiter of the complaint, and that there shall be no judicial review of the final decision of the Attorney General by a complainant.

JURY SELECTION AND SERVICE ACT OF 1968 (AS AMENDED)

(28 U.S.C. §§ 1861–1863, 1865–1867).

§ 1861. Declaration of policy

It is the policy of the United States that all litigants in Federal courts entitled to trial by jury shall have the right to grand and petit juries selected at random from a fair cross section of the community in the district or division wherein the court convenes. It is further the policy of the United States that all citizens shall have the opportunity to be considered for service on grand and petit juries in the district courts of the United States, and shall have an obligation to serve as jurors when summoned for that purpose.

§ 1862. Discrimination prohibited

No citizen shall be excluded from service as a grand or petit juror in the district courts of the United States or in the Court of International Trade on account of race, color, religion, sex, national origin, or economic status.

§ 1863. Plan for random jury selection

(a) Each United States district court shall devise and place into operation a written plan for random selection of grand and petit jurors that shall be designed to achieve the objectives of sections 1861 and 1862 of this title, and that shall otherwise comply with the provisions of this title. The plan shall be placed into operation after approval by a reviewing panel consisting of the members of the judicial council of the circuit and either the chief judge of the district whose plan is being reviewed or such other active district judge of that district as the chief judge of the district may designate. The panel shall examine the plan to ascertain that it complies with the provisions of this title. If the reviewing panel finds that the plan does not comply, the panel shall state the particulars in which the plan fails to comply and direct the district court to present within a reasonable time an alternative plan remedying the defect or defects. Separate plans may be adopted for each division or combination of divisions within a judicial district. The district court may modify a plan at any time and it shall modify the plan when so directed by the reviewing panel. The district court shall promptly notify the panel, the Administrative Office of the United States Courts, and the Attorney General of the United States, of the initial adoption and future modifications of the plan by filing copies therewith. Modifications of the plan made at the instance of the district court shall become effective after approval by the panel. Each district court shall submit a report on the jury selection process within its jurisdiction to the Administrative Office of the United States Courts in such form and at such times as the Judicial Conference of the United States may specify. The Judicial Conference of the United States may, from time to time, adopt rules and regulations governing the provisions and the operation of the plans formulated under this title.

(b) Among other things, such plan shall—

(1) either establish a jury commission, or authorize the clerk of the court, to manage the jury selection process. If the plan establishes a jury commission, the district court shall appoint one citizen to serve with the clerk of the court as the jury commission: *Provided, however,* That the plan for the District of Columbia may establish a jury commission consisting of three citizens. The citizen jury commissioner shall not belong to the same political party as the clerk serving with him. The clerk or the jury commission, as the case may be, shall act under the supervision and control of the chief judge of the district court or such other judge of the district court as the plan may provide. Each jury commissioner shall, during his tenure in office, reside in the judicial district or division for which he is appointed. Each citizen jury commissioner shall receive compensation to be fixed by the district court plan at a rate not to exceed $50 per day for each day necessarily employed in the performance of his duties, plus reimbursement for travel, subsistence, and other necessary expenses incurred by him in the performance of such duties. The Judicial Conference of the United States may establish standards for allowance of travel, subsistence, and other necessary expenses incurred by jury commissioners.

(2) specify whether the names of prospective jurors shall be selected from the voter registration lists or the lists of actual voters of the political subdivisions within the district or division. The plan shall prescribe some other source or sources of names in addition to voter lists where necessary to foster the policy and protect the rights secured by sections 1861 and 1862 of this title. The plan for the District of Columbia may require the names of prospective jurors to be selected from the city directory rather than from voter lists. The plans for the districts of Puerto Rico and the Canal Zone may prescribe some other source or sources of names of prospective jurors in lieu of voter lists, the use of which shall be consistent with the policies declared and rights secured by sections 1861 and 1862 of this title. The plan for the district of Massachusetts may require the names of prospective jurors to be selected from the resident list provided for in chapter 234A, Massachusetts General Laws, or comparable authority, rather than from voter lists.

(3) specify detailed procedures to be followed by the jury commission or clerk in selecting names from the sources specified in paragraph (2) of this subsection. These procedures shall be designed to ensure the random selection of a fair cross section of the persons residing in the community in the district or division wherein the court convenes. They shall ensure that names of persons residing in each of the counties, parishes, or similar political subdivisions within the judicial district or division are placed in a master jury wheel; and shall ensure that each county, parish, or similar political subdivision within the district or division is substantially proportionally represented in the master jury wheel for that judicial district, division, or combination of divisions. For the purposes of determining proportional representation in the master jury wheel, either the number of actual voters at the last general election in each county, parish, or similar political subdivision, or the number of registered voters if registration of voters is uniformly required throughout the district or division, may be used.

(4) provide for a master jury wheel (or a device similar in purpose and function) into which the names of those randomly selected shall be placed. The plan shall fix a minimum number of names to be placed initially in the master jury wheel, which shall be at least one-half of 1 per centum of the total number of persons on the lists used as a source of names for the district or division; but if this number of names is believed to be cumbersome and unnecessary, the plan may fix a smaller number of names to be placed in the master wheel,

but in no event less than one thousand. The chief judge of the district court, or such other district court judge as the plan may provide, may order additional names to be placed in the master jury wheel from time to time as necessary. The plan shall provide for periodic emptying and refilling of the master jury wheel at specified times, the interval for which shall not exceed four years.

(5)(A) except as provided in subparagraph (B), specify those groups of persons or occupational classes whose members shall, on individual request therefor, be excused from jury service. Such groups or classes shall be excused only if the district court finds, and the plan states, that jury service by such class or group would entail undue hardship or extreme inconvenience to the members thereof, and excuse of members thereof would not be inconsistent with sections 1861 and 1862 of this title.

(B) specify that volunteer safety personnel, upon individual request, shall be excused from jury service. For purposes of this subparagraph, the term "volunteer safety personnel" means individuals serving a public agency (as defined in section 1203(6) of title I of the Omnibus Crime Control and Safe Streets Act of 1968) in an official capacity, without compensation, as firefighters or members of a rescue squad or ambulance crew.

(6) specify that the following persons are barred from jury service on the ground that they are exempt: (A) members in active service in the Armed Forces of the United States; (B) members of the fire or police departments of any State, the District of Columbia, any territory or possession of the United States, or any subdivision of a State, the District of Columbia, or such territory or possession; (C) public officers in the executive, legislative, or judicial branches of the Government of the United States, or of any State, the District of Columbia, any territory or possession of the United States, or any subdivision of a State, the District of Columbia, or such territory or possession, who are actively engaged in the performance of official duties

(7) fix the time when the names drawn from the qualified jury wheel shall be disclosed to parties and to the public. If the plan permits these names to be made public, it may nevertheless permit the chief judge of the district court, or such other district court judge as the plan may provide, to keep these names confidential in any case where the interests of justice so require.

(8) specify the procedures to be followed by the clerk or jury commission in assigning persons whose names have been drawn from the qualified jury wheel to grand and petit jury panels.

(c) The initial plan shall be devised by each district court and transmitted to the reviewing panel specified in subsection (a) of this section within one hundred and twenty days of the date of enactment of the Jury Selection and Service Act of 1968. The panel shall approve or direct the modification of each plan so submitted within sixty days thereafter. Each plan or modification made at the direction of the panel shall become effective after approval at such time thereafter as the panel directs, in no event to exceed ninety days from the date of approval. Modifications made at the instance of the district court under subsection (a) of this section shall be effective at such time thereafter as the panel directs, in no event to exceed ninety days from the date of modification.

(d) State, local, and Federal officials having custody, possession, or control of voter registration lists, lists of actual voters, or other appropriate records shall make such lists and records available to the jury commission or clerks for inspection, reproduction, and copying at all reasonable times as the commission or clerk may deem necessary and proper for the performance of duties under this title. The district courts shall have jurisdiction upon application by the

Attorney General of the United States to compel compliance with this subsection by appropriate process.

§ 1865.   Qualifications for jury service

(a)   The chief judge of the district court, or such other district court judge as the plan may provide, on his initiative or upon recommendation of the clerk or jury commission, or the clerk under supervision of the court if the court's jury selection plan so authorizes, shall determine solely on the basis of information provided on the juror qualification form and other competent evidence whether a person is unqualified for, or exempt, or to be excused from jury service. The clerk shall enter such determination in the space provided on the juror qualification form and in any alphabetical list of names drawn from the master jury wheel. If a person did not appear in response to a summons, such fact shall be noted on said list.

(b)   In making such determination the chief judge of the district court, or such other district court judge as the plan may provide, or the clerk if the court's jury selection plan so provides, shall deem any person qualified to serve on grand and petit juries in the district court unless he—

(1)   is not a citizen of the United States eighteen years old who has resided for a period of one year within the judicial district;

(2)   is unable to read, write, and understand the English language with a degree of proficiency sufficient to fill out satisfactorily the juror qualification form;

(3)   is unable to speak the English language;

(4)   is incapable, by reason of mental or physical infirmity, to render satisfactory jury service; or

(5)   has a charge pending against him for the commission of, or has been convicted in a State or Federal court of record of, a crime punishable by imprisonment for more than one year and his civil rights have not been restored.

§ 1866.   Selection and summoning of jury panels

(a)   The jury commission, or in the absence thereof the clerk, shall maintain a qualified jury wheel and shall place in such wheel names of all persons drawn from the master jury wheel who are determined to be qualified as jurors and not exempt or excused pursuant to the district court plan. From time to time, the jury commission or the clerk shall draw at random from the qualified jury wheel such number of names of persons as may be required for assignment to grand and petit jury panels. The clerk or jury commission shall post a general notice for public review in the clerk's office and on the court's website explaining the process by which names are periodically and randomly drawn. The jury commission or the clerk shall prepare a separate list of names of persons assigned to each grand and petit jury panel.

(b)   When the court orders a grand or petit jury to be drawn, the clerk or jury commission or their duly designated deputies shall issue summonses for the required number of jurors.

Each person drawn for jury service may be served personally, or by registered, certified, or first-class mail addressed to such person at his usual residence or business address.

If such service is made personally, the summons shall be delivered by the clerk or the jury commission or their duly designated deputies to the marshal who shall make such service.

If such service is made by mail, the summons may be served by the marshal or by the clerk, the jury commission or their duly designated deputies, who shall make affidavit of service and shall attach thereto any receipt from the addressee for a registered or certified summons.

(c)   Except as provided in section 1865 of this title or in any jury selection plan provision adopted pursuant to paragraph (5) or (6) of section 1863(b) of this title, no person or class of persons shall be disqualified, excluded, excused, or exempt from service as jurors: *Provided*, That any person summoned for jury service may be (1) excused by the court, or by the clerk under supervision of the court if the court's jury selection plan so authorizes, upon a showing of undue hardship or extreme inconvenience, for such period as the court deems necessary, at the conclusion of which such person either shall be summoned again for jury service under subsections (b) and (c) of this section or, if the court's jury selection plan so provides, the name of such person shall be reinserted into the qualified jury wheel for selection pursuant to subsection (a) of this section, or (2) excluded by the court on the ground that such person may be unable to render impartial jury service or that his service as a juror would be likely to disrupt the proceedings, or (3) excluded upon peremptory challenge as provided by law, or (4) excluded pursuant to the procedure specified by law upon a challenge by any party for good cause shown, or (5) excluded upon determination by the court that his service as a juror would be likely to threaten the secrecy of the proceedings, or otherwise adversely affect the integrity of jury deliberations. No person shall be excluded under clause (5) of this subsection unless the judge, in open court, determines that such is warranted and that exclusion of the person will not be inconsistent with sections 1861 and 1862 of this title. The number of persons excluded under clause (5) of this subsection shall not exceed one per centum of the number of persons who return executed jury qualification forms during the period, specified in the plan, between two consecutive fillings of the master jury wheel. The names of persons excluded under clause (5) of this subsection, together with detailed explanations for the exclusions, shall be forwarded immediately to the judicial council of the circuit, which shall have the power to make any appropriate order, prospective or retroactive, to redress any misapplication of clause (5) of this subsection, but otherwise exclusions effectuated under such clause shall not be subject to challenge under the provisions of this title. Any person excluded from a particular jury under clause (2), (3), or (4) of this subsection shall be eligible to sit on another jury if the basis for his initial exclusion would not be relevant to his ability to serve on such other jury.

(d)   Whenever a person is disqualified, excused, exempt, or excluded from jury service, the jury commission or clerk shall note in the space provided on his juror qualification form or on the juror's card drawn from the qualified jury wheel the specific reason therefor.

(e)   In any two-year period, no person shall be required to (1) serve or attend court for prospective service as a petit juror for a total of more than thirty days, except when necessary to complete service in a particular case, or (2) serve on more than one grand jury, or (3) serve as both a grand and petit juror.

(f)   When there is an unanticipated shortage of available petit jurors drawn from the qualified jury wheel, the court may require the marshal to summon a sufficient number of petit jurors selected at random from the voter registration lists, lists of actual voters, or other lists specified in the plan, in a manner ordered by the court consistent with sections 1861 and 1862 of this title.

(g)   Any person summoned for jury service who fails to appear as directed may be ordered by the district court to appear forthwith and show cause for failure to comply with the summons. Any person who fails to show good cause for noncompliance with a summons may be fined not more than $1,000, imprisoned not more than three days, ordered to perform community service, or any combination thereof.

§ 1867.   Challenging compliance with selection procedures

(a)   In criminal cases, before the voir dire examination begins, or within seven days after the defendant discovered or could have discovered, by the exercise of diligence, the grounds therefor, whichever is earlier, the defendant may move to dismiss the indictment or stay the proceedings against him on the ground of substantial failure to comply with the provisions of this title in selecting the grand or petit jury.

(b)   In criminal cases, before the voir dire examination begins, or within seven days after the Attorney General of the United States discovered or could have discovered, by the exercise of diligence, the grounds therefor, whichever is earlier, the Attorney General may move to dismiss the indictment or stay the proceedings on the ground of substantial failure to comply with the provisions of this title in selecting the grand or petit jury.

(c)   In civil cases, before the voir dire examination begins, or within seven days after the party discovered or could have discovered, by the exercise of diligence, the grounds therefor, whichever is earlier, any party may move to stay the proceedings on the ground of substantial failure to comply with the provisions of this title in selecting the petit jury.

(d)   Upon motion filed under subsection (a), (b), or (c) of this section, containing a sworn statement of facts which, if true, would constitute a substantial failure to comply with the provisions of this title, the moving party shall be entitled to present in support of such motion the testimony of the jury commission or clerk, if available, any relevant records and papers not public or otherwise available used by the jury commissioner or clerk, and any other relevant evidence. If the court determines that there has been a substantial failure to comply with the provisions of this title in selecting the grand jury, the court shall stay the proceedings pending the selection of a grand jury in conformity with this title or dismiss the indictment, whichever is appropriate. If the court determines that there has been a substantial failure to comply with the provisions of this title in selecting the petit jury, the court shall stay the proceedings pending the selection of a petit jury in conformity with this title.

(e)   The procedures prescribed by this section shall be the exclusive means by which a person accused of a Federal crime, the Attorney General of the United States or a party in a civil case may challenge any jury on the ground that such jury was not selected in conformity with the provisions of this title. Nothing in this section shall preclude any person or the United States from pursuing any other remedy, civil or criminal, which may be available for the vindication or enforcement of any law prohibiting discrimination on account of race, color, religion, sex, national origin or economic status in the selection of persons for service on grand or petit juries.

(f)   The contents of records or papers used by the jury commission or clerk in connection with the jury selection process shall not be disclosed, except pursuant to the district court plan or as may be necessary in the preparation or presentation of a motion under subsection (a), (b), or (c) of this section, until after the master jury wheel has been emptied and refilled pursuant to section 1863(b)(4) of this title and all persons selected to serve as jurors before the master wheel was emptied have completed such service. The parties in a case shall be allowed to inspect, reproduce, and copy such records or papers at all reasonable times during the preparation and pendency of such a motion. Any person who discloses the contents of any record or paper in violation of this subsection may be fined not more than $1,000 or imprisoned not more than one year, or both.

HABEAS CORPUS

(28 U.S.C. §§ 2241–2244, 2253–2255, 2261–2266).

§ 2241.   Power to grant writ

(a)   Writs of habeas corpus may be granted by the Supreme Court, any justice thereof, the district courts and any circuit judge within their respective jurisdictions. The order of a circuit judge shall be entered in the records of the district court of the district wherein the restraint complained of is had.

(b)   The Supreme Court, any justice thereof, and any circuit judge may decline to entertain an application for a writ of habeas corpus and may transfer the application for hearing and determination to the district court having jurisdiction to entertain it.

(c) The writ of habeas corpus shall not extend to a prisoner unless—

(1) He is in custody under or by color of the authority of the United States or is committed for trial before some court thereof; or

(2) He is in custody for an act done or omitted in pursuance of an Act of Congress, or an order, process, judgment or decree of a court or judge of the United States; or

(3) He is in custody in violation of the Constitution or laws or treaties of the United States; or

(4) He, being a citizen of a foreign state and domiciled therein is in custody for an act done or omitted under any alleged right, title, authority, privilege, protection, or exemption claimed under the commission, order or sanction of any foreign state, or under color thereof, the validity and effect of which depend upon the law of nations; or

(5) It is necessary to bring him into court to testify or for trial.

(d) Where an application for a writ of habeas corpus is made by a person in custody under the judgment and sentence of a State court of a State which contains two or more Federal judicial districts, the application may be filed in the district court for the district wherein such person is in custody or in the district court for the district within which the State court was held which convicted and sentenced him and each of such district courts shall have concurrent jurisdiction to entertain the application. The district court for the district wherein such an application is filed in the exercise of its discretion and in furtherance of justice may transfer the application to the other district court for hearing and determination.

(e)(1) No court, justice, or judge shall have jurisdiction to hear or consider an application for a writ of habeas corpus filed by or on behalf of an alien detained by the United States who has been determined by the United States to have been properly detained as an enemy combatant or is awaiting such determination.

(2) Except as provided in paragraphs (2) and (3) of section 1005(e) of the Detainee Treatment Act of 2005 (10 U.S.C. 801 note), no court, justice, or judge shall have jurisdiction to hear or consider any other action against the United States or its agents relating to any aspect of the detention, transfer, treatment, trial, or conditions of confinement of an alien who is or was detained by the United States and has been determined by the United States to have been properly detained as an enemy combatant or is awaiting such determination.

§ 2242.   Application

Application for a writ of habeas corpus shall be in writing signed and verified by the person for whose relief it is intended or by someone acting in his behalf.

It shall allege the facts concerning the applicant's commitment or detention, the name of the person who has custody over him and by virtue of what claim or authority, if known.

It may be amended or supplemented as provided in the rules of procedure applicable to civil actions.

If addressed to the Supreme Court, a justice thereof or a circuit judge it shall state the reasons for not making application to the district court of the district in which the applicant is held.

§ 2243.   Issuance of writ; return; hearing; decision

A court, justice or judge entertaining an application for a writ of habeas corpus shall forthwith award the writ or issue an order directing the respondent to show cause why the writ should not be granted, unless it appears from the application that the applicant or person detained is not entitled thereto.

The writ, or order to show cause shall be directed to the person having custody of the person detained. It shall be returned within three days unless for good cause additional time, not exceeding twenty days, is allowed.

The person to whom the writ or order is directed shall make a return certifying the true cause of the detention.

When the writ or order is returned a day shall be set for hearing, not more than five days after the return unless for good cause additional time is allowed.

Unless the application for the writ and the return present only issues of law the person to whom the writ is directed shall be required to produce at the hearing the body of the person detained.

The applicant or the person detained may, under oath, deny any of the facts set forth in the return or allege any other material facts.

The return and all suggestions made against it may be amended, by leave of court, before or after being filed.

The court shall summarily hear and determine the facts, and dispose of the matter as law and justice require.

§ 2244. Finality of determination

(a)   No circuit or district judge shall be required to entertain an application for a writ of habeas corpus to inquire into the detention of a person pursuant to a judgment of a court of the United States if it appears that the legality of such detention has been determined by a judge or court of the United States on a prior application for a writ of habeas corpus, except as provided in section 2255.

(b)(1)   A claim presented in a second or successive habeas corpus application under section 2254 that was presented in a prior application shall be dismissed.

(2)   A claim presented in a second or successive habeas corpus application under section 2254 that was not presented in a prior application shall be dismissed unless—

(A)   the applicant shows that the claim relies on a new rule of constitutional law, made retroactive to cases on collateral review by the Supreme Court, that was previously unavailable; or

(B)(i) the factual predicate for the claim could not have been discovered previously through the exercise of due diligence; and

(ii)   the facts underlying the claim, if proven and viewed in light of the evidence as a whole, would be sufficient to establish by clear and convincing evidence that, but for constitutional error, no reasonable factfinder would have found the applicant guilty of the underlying offense.

(3)(A) Before a second or successive application permitted by this section is filed in the district court, the applicant shall move in the appropriate court of appeals for an order authorizing the district court to consider the application.

(B)   A motion in the court of appeals for an order authorizing the district court to consider a second or successive application shall be determined by a three-judge panel of the court of appeals.

(C)   The court of appeals may authorize the filing of a second or successive application only if it determines that the application makes a prima facie showing that the application satisfies the requirements of this subsection.

(D)   The court of appeals shall grant or deny the authorization to file a second or successive application not later than 30 days after the filing of the motion.

(E)   The grant or denial of an authorization by a court of appeals to file a second or successive application shall not be appealable and shall not be the subject of a petition for rehearing or for a writ of certiorari.

(4)   A district court shall dismiss any claim presented in a second or successive application that the court of appeals has authorized to be filed unless the applicant shows that the claim satisfies the requirements of this section.

(c)   In a habeas corpus proceeding brought in behalf of a person in custody pursuant to the judgment of a State court, a prior judgment of the Supreme Court of the United States on an appeal or review by a writ of certiorari at the instance of the prisoner of the decision of such State court, shall be conclusive as to all issues of fact or law with respect to an asserted denial of a Federal right which constitutes ground for discharge in a habeas corpus proceeding, actually adjudicated by the Supreme Court therein, unless the applicant for the writ of habeas corpus shall plead and the court shall find the existence of a material and controlling fact which did not appear in the record of the proceeding in the Supreme Court and the court shall further find that the applicant for the writ of habeas corpus could not have caused such fact to appear in such record by the exercise of reasonable diligence.

(d)(1)   A 1-year period of limitation shall apply to an application for a writ of habeas corpus by a person in custody pursuant to the judgment of a State court. The limitation period shall run from the latest of—

(A)   the date on which the judgment became final by the conclusion of direct review or the expiration of the time for seeking such review;

(B)   the date on which the impediment to filing an application created by State action in violation of the Constitution or laws of the United States is removed, if the applicant was prevented from filing by such State action;

(C)   the date on which the constitutional right asserted was initially recognized by the Supreme Court, if the right has been newly recognized by the Supreme Court and made retroactively applicable to cases on collateral review; or

(D)   the date on which the factual predicate of the claim or claims presented could have been discovered through the exercise of due diligence.

(2)   The time during which a properly filed application for State post-conviction or other collateral review with respect to the pertinent judgment or claim is pending shall not be counted toward any period of limitation under this subsection.

§ 2253.   Appeal

(a)   In a habeas corpus proceeding or a proceeding under section 2255 before a district judge, the final order shall be subject to review, on appeal, by the court of appeals for the circuit in which the proceeding is held.

(b)   There shall be no right of appeal from a final order in a proceeding to test the validity of a warrant to remove to another district or place for commitment or trial a person charged with a criminal offense against the United States, or to test the validity of such person's detention pending removal proceedings.

(c)(1)   Unless a circuit justice or judge issues a certificate of appealability, an appeal may not be taken to the court of appeals from—

(A)   the final order in a habeas corpus proceeding in which the detention complained of arises out of process issued by a State court; or

(B)   the final order in a proceeding under section 2255.

(2)   A certificate of appealability may issue under paragraph (1) only if the applicant has made a substantial showing of the denial of a constitutional right.

(3)   The certificate of appealability under paragraph (1) shall indicate which specific issue or issues satisfy the showing required by paragraph (2).

§ 2254.   State custody; remedies in Federal courts

(a)   The Supreme Court, a Justice thereof, a circuit judge, or a district court shall entertain an application for a writ of habeas corpus in behalf of a person in custody pursuant to the judgment of a State court only on the ground that he is in custody in violation of the Constitution or laws or treaties of the United States.

(b)(1)   An application for a writ of habeas corpus on behalf of a person in custody pursuant to the judgment of a State court shall not be granted unless it appears that—

(A)   the applicant has exhausted the remedies available in the courts of the State; or

(B)(i)   there is an absence of available State corrective process; or

(ii)   circumstances exist that render such process ineffective to protect the rights of the applicant.

(2)   An application for a writ of habeas corpus may be denied on the merits, notwithstanding the failure of the applicant to exhaust the remedies available in the courts of the State.

(3)   A State shall not be deemed to have waived the exhaustion requirement or be estopped from reliance upon the requirement unless the State, through counsel, expressly waives the requirement.

(c)   An applicant shall not be deemed to have exhausted the remedies available in the courts of the State, within the meaning of this section, if he has the right under the law of the State to raise, by any available procedure, the question presented.

(d)   An application for a writ of habeas corpus on behalf of a person in custody pursuant to the judgment of a State court shall not be granted with respect to any claim that was adjudicated on the merits in State court proceedings unless the adjudication of the claim—

(1)   resulted in a decision that was contrary to, or involved an unreasonable application of, clearly established Federal law, as determined by the Supreme Court of the United States; or

(2)   resulted in a decision that was based on an unreasonable determination of the facts in light of the evidence presented in the State court proceeding.

(e)(1)   In a proceeding instituted by an application for a writ of habeas corpus by a person in custody pursuant to the judgment of a State court, a determination of a factual issue made by a State court shall be presumed to be correct. The applicant shall have the burden of rebutting the presumption of correctness by clear and convincing evidence.

(2)   If the applicant has failed to develop the factual basis of a claim in State court proceedings, the court shall not hold an evidentiary hearing on the claim unless the applicant shows that—

(A)   the claim relies on—

(i)   a new rule of constitutional law, made retroactive to cases on collateral review by the Supreme Court, that was previously unavailable; or

(ii)   a factual predicate that could not have been previously discovered through the exercise of due diligence; and

(B)   the facts underlying the claim would be sufficient to establish by clear and convincing evidence that but for constitutional error, no reasonable factfinder would have found the applicant guilty of the underlying offense.

(f)   If the applicant challenges the sufficiency of the evidence adduced in such State court proceeding to support the State court's determination of a factual issue made therein, the applicant, if able, shall produce that part of the record pertinent to a determination of the sufficiency of the evidence to support such determination. If the applicant, because of indigency or other reason is unable to produce such part of the record, then the State shall produce such part of the record and the Federal court shall direct the State to do so by order directed to an appropriate State official. If the State cannot provide such pertinent part of the record, then the court shall determine under the existing facts and circumstances what weight shall be given to the State court's factual determination.

(g)   A copy of the official records of the State court, duly certified by the clerk of such court to be a true and correct copy of a finding, judicial opinion, or other reliable written indicia showing such a factual determination by the State court shall be admissible in the Federal court proceeding.

(h)   Except as provided in section 408 of the Controlled Substances Act, in all proceedings brought under this section, and any subsequent proceedings on review, the court may appoint counsel for an applicant who is or becomes financially unable to afford counsel, except as provided by a rule promulgated by the Supreme Court pursuant to statutory authority. Appointment of counsel under this section shall be governed by section 3006A of title 18.

(i)   The ineffectiveness or incompetence of counsel during Federal or State collateral post-conviction proceedings shall not be a ground for relief in a proceeding arising under section 2254.

§ 2255.   Federal custody; remedies on motion attacking sentence

(a)   A prisoner in custody under sentence of a court established by Act of Congress claiming the right to be released upon the ground that the sentence was imposed in violation of the Constitution or laws of the United States, or that the court was without jurisdiction to impose such sentence, or that the sentence was in excess of the maximum authorized by law, or is otherwise subject to collateral attack, may move the court which imposed the sentence to vacate, set aside or correct the sentence.

(b)   Unless the motion and the files and records of the case conclusively show that the prisoner is entitled to no relief, the court shall cause notice thereof to be served upon the United States attorney, grant a prompt hearing thereon, determine the issues and make findings of fact and conclusions of law with respect thereto. If the court finds that the judgment was rendered without jurisdiction, or that the sentence imposed was not authorized by law or otherwise open to collateral attack, or that there has been such a denial or infringement of the constitutional rights of the prisoner as to render the judgment vulnerable to collateral attack, the court shall vacate and set the judgment aside and shall discharge the prisoner or resentence him or grant a new trial or correct the sentence as may appear appropriate.

(c)   A court may entertain and determine such motion without requiring the production of the prisoner at the hearing.

(d)   An appeal may be taken to the court of appeals from the order entered on the motion as from a final judgment on application for a writ of habeas corpus.

(e)   An application for a writ of habeas corpus in behalf of a prisoner who is authorized to apply for relief by motion pursuant to this section, shall not be entertained if it appears that the applicant has failed to apply for relief, by motion, to the court which sentenced him, or that such court has denied him relief, unless it also appears that the remedy by motion is inadequate or ineffective to test the legality of his detention.

(f)   A 1-year period of limitation shall apply to a motion under this section. The limitation period shall run from the latest of—

(1)   the date on which the judgment of conviction becomes final;

(2)   the date on which the impediment to making a motion created by governmental action in violation of the Constitution or laws of the United States is removed, if the movant was prevented from making a motion by such governmental action;

(3)   the date on which the right asserted was initially recognized by the Supreme Court, if that right has been newly recognized by the Supreme Court and made retroactively applicable to cases on collateral review; or

(4)   the date on which the facts supporting the claim or claims presented could have been discovered through the exercise of due diligence.

(g)   Except as provided in section 408 of the Controlled Substances Act, in all proceedings brought under this section, and any subsequent proceedings on review, the court may appoint counsel, except as provided by a rule promulgated by the Supreme Court pursuant to statutory authority. Appointment of counsel under this section shall be governed by section 3006A of title 18.

(h)   A second or successive motion must be certified as provided in section 2244 by a panel of the appropriate court of appeals to contain—

(1)   newly discovered evidence that, if proven and viewed in light of the evidence as a whole, would be sufficient to establish by clear and convincing evidence that no reasonable factfinder would have found the movant guilty of the offense; or

(2)   a new rule of constitutional law, made retroactive to cases on collateral review by the Supreme Court, that was previously unavailable.

§ 2261.   Prisoners in State custody subject to capital sentence; appointment of counsel; requirement of rule of court or statute; procedures for appointment

(a)   This chapter shall apply to cases arising under section 2254 brought by prisoners in State custody who are subject to a capital sentence. It shall apply only if the provisions of subsections (b) and (c) are satisfied.

(b)   Counsel.—This chapter is applicable if—

(1)   the Attorney General of the United States certifies that a State has established a mechanism for providing counsel in postconviction proceedings as provided in section 2265; and

(2)   counsel was appointed pursuant to that mechanism, petitioner validly waived counsel, petitioner retained counsel, or petitioner was found not to be indigent.

(c)   Any mechanism for the appointment, compensation, and reimbursement of counsel as provided in subsection (b) must offer counsel to all State prisoners under capital sentence and must provide for the entry of an order by a court of record—

(1)   appointing one or more counsels to represent the prisoner upon a finding that the prisoner is indigent and accepted the offer or is unable competently to decide whether to accept or reject the offer;

(2)   finding, after a hearing if necessary, that the prisoner rejected the offer of counsel and made the decision with an understanding of its legal consequences; or

(3)   denying the appointment of counsel upon a finding that the prisoner is not indigent.

(d)   No counsel appointed pursuant to subsections (b) and (c) to represent a State prisoner under capital sentence shall have previously represented the prisoner at trial in the case for which the appointment is made unless the prisoner and counsel expressly request continued representation.

(e)   The ineffectiveness or incompetence of counsel during State or Federal post-conviction proceedings in a capital case shall not be a ground for relief in a proceeding arising under section 2254. This limitation shall not preclude the appointment of different counsel, on the court's own motion or at the request of the prisoner, at any phase of State or Federal post-conviction proceedings on the basis of the ineffectiveness or incompetence of counsel in such proceedings.

§ 2262.   Mandatory stay of execution; duration; limits on stays of execution; successive petitions

(a)   Upon the entry in the appropriate State court of record of an order under section 2261(c), a warrant or order setting an execution date for a State prisoner shall be stayed upon application to any court that would have jurisdiction over any proceedings filed under section 2254. The application shall recite that the State has invoked the post-conviction review procedures of this chapter and that the scheduled execution is subject to stay.

(b)   A stay of execution granted pursuant to subsection (a) shall expire if—

(1)   a State prisoner fails to file a habeas corpus application under section 2254 within the time required in section 2263;

(2)   before a court of competent jurisdiction, in the presence of counsel, unless the prisoner has competently and knowingly waived such counsel, and after having been advised of the consequences, a State prisoner under capital sentence waives the right to pursue habeas corpus review under section 2254; or

(3)   a State prisoner files a habeas corpus petition under section 2254 within the time required by section 2263 and fails to make a substantial showing of the denial of a Federal right or is denied relief in the district court or at any subsequent stage of review.

(c)   If one of the conditions in subsection (b) has occurred, no Federal court thereafter shall have the authority to enter a stay of execution in the case, unless the court of appeals approves the filing of a second or successive application under section 2244(b).

§ 2263.   Filing of habeas corpus application; time requirements; tolling rules

(a)   Any application under this chapter for habeas corpus relief under section 2254 must be filed in the appropriate district court not later than 180 days after final State court affirmance of the conviction and sentence on direct review or the expiration of the time for seeking such review.

(b)   The time requirements established by subsection (a) shall be tolled—

(1)   from the date that a petition for certiorari is filed in the Supreme Court until the date of final disposition of the petition if a State prisoner files the petition to secure review by the Supreme Court of the affirmance of a capital sentence on direct review by the court of last resort of the State or other final State court decision on direct review;

(2) from the date on which the first petition for post conviction review or other collateral relief is filed until the final State court disposition of such petition; and

(3) during an additional period not to exceed 30 days, if—

(A) a motion for an extension of time is filed in the Federal district court that would have jurisdiction over the case upon the filing of a habeas corpus application under section 2254; and

(B) a showing of good cause is made for the failure to file the habeas corpus application within the time period established by this section.

§ 2264. Scope of Federal review; district court adjudications

(a) Whenever a State prisoner under capital sentence files a petition for habeas corpus relief to which this chapter applies, the district court shall only consider a claim or claims that have been raised and decided on the merits in the State courts, unless the failure to raise the claim properly is—

(1) the result of State action in violation of the Constitution or laws of the United States;

(2) the result of the Supreme Court's recognition of a new Federal right that is made retroactively applicable; or

(3) based on a factual predicate that could not have been discovered through the exercise of due diligence in time to present the claim for State or Federal post-conviction review.

(b) Following review subject to subsections (a), (d), and (e) of section 2254, the court shall rule on the claims properly before it.

§ 2265. Certification and judicial review

(a) Certification.—

(1) In general.—If requested by an appropriate State official, the Attorney General of the United States shall determine—

(A) whether the State has established a mechanism for the appointment, compensation, and payment of reasonable litigation expenses of competent counsel in State postconviction proceedings brought by indigent prisoners who have been sentenced to death;

(B) the date on which the mechanism described in subparagraph (A) was established; and

(C) whether the State provides standards of competency for the appointment of counsel in proceedings described in subparagraph (A).

(2) Effective date.—The date the mechanism described in paragraph (1)(A) was established shall be the effective date of the certification under this subsection.

(3) Only express requirements.—There are no requirements for certification or for application of this chapter other than those expressly stated in this chapter.

(b) Regulations.—The Attorney General shall promulgate regulations to implement the certification procedure under subsection (a).

(c) Review of certification.—

(1)   In general.—The determination by the Attorney General regarding whether to certify a State under this section is subject to review exclusively as provided under chapter 158 of this title.

(2)   Venue.—The Court of Appeals for the District of Columbia Circuit shall have exclusive jurisdiction over matters under paragraph (1), subject to review by the Supreme Court under section 2350 of this title.

(3)   Standard of review.—The determination by the Attorney General regarding whether to certify a State under this section shall be subject to de novo review.

§ 2266.   Limitation periods for determining applications and motions

(a)   The adjudication of any application under section 2254 that is subject to this chapter, and the adjudication of any motion under section 2255 by a person under sentence of death, shall be given priority by the district court and by the court of appeals over all noncapital matters.

(b)(1)(A) A district court shall render a final determination and enter a final judgment on any application for a writ of habeas corpus brought under this chapter in a capital case not later than 450 days after the date on which the application is filed, or 60 days after the date on which the case is submitted for decision, whichever is earlier.

(B)   A district court shall afford the parties at least 120 days in which to complete all actions, including the preparation of all pleadings and briefs, and if necessary, a hearing, prior to the submission of the case for decision.

(C)(i)   A district court may delay for not more than one additional 30-day period beyond the period specified in subparagraph (A), the rendering of a determination of an application for a writ of habeas corpus if the court issues a written order making a finding, and stating the reasons for the finding, that the ends of justice that would be served by allowing the delay outweigh the best interests of the public and the applicant in a speedy disposition of the application.

(ii)   The factors, among others, that a court shall consider in determining whether a delay in the disposition of an application is warranted are as follows:

(I)   Whether the failure to allow the delay would be likely to result in a miscarriage of justice.

(II)   Whether the case is so unusual or so complex, due to the number of defendants, the nature of the prosecution, or the existence of novel questions of fact or law, that it is unreasonable to expect adequate briefing within the time limitations established by subparagraph (A).

(III) Whether the failure to allow a delay in a case that, taken as a whole, is not so unusual or so complex as described in subclause (II), but would otherwise deny the applicant reasonable time to obtain counsel, would unreasonably deny the applicant or the government continuity of counsel, or would deny counsel for the applicant or the government the reasonable time necessary for effective preparation, taking into account the exercise of due diligence.

(iii) No delay in disposition shall be permissible because of general congestion of the court's calendar.

(iv) The court shall transmit a copy of any order issued under clause (i) to the Director of the Administrative Office of the United States Courts for inclusion in the report under paragraph (5).

(2)   The time limitations under paragraph (1) shall apply to—

(A)   an initial application for a writ of habeas corpus;

(B)   any second or successive application for a writ of habeas corpus; and

(C)   any redetermination of an application for a writ of habeas corpus following a remand by the court of appeals or the Supreme Court for further proceedings, in which case the limitation period shall run from the date the remand is ordered.

(3)(A)   The time limitations under this section shall not be construed to entitle an applicant to a stay of execution, to which the applicant would otherwise not be entitled, for the purpose of litigating any application or appeal.

(B)   No amendment to an application for a writ of habeas corpus under this chapter shall be permitted after the filing of the answer to the application, except on the grounds specified in section 2244(b).

(4)(A)   The failure of a court to meet or comply with a time limitation under this section shall not be a ground for granting relief from a judgment of conviction or sentence.

(B)   The State may enforce a time limitation under this section by petitioning for a writ of mandamus to the court of appeals. The court of appeals shall act on the petition for a writ of mandamus not later than 30 days after the filing of the petition.

(5)(A)   The Administrative Office of the United States Courts shall submit to Congress an annual report on the compliance by the district courts with the time limitations under this section.[*]

(B)   The report described in subparagraph (A) shall include copies of the orders submitted by the district courts under paragraph (1)(B)(iv).

(c)(1)(A) A court of appeals shall hear and render a final determination of any appeal of an order granting or denying, in whole or in part, an application brought under this chapter in a capital case not later than 120 days after the date on which the reply brief is filed, or if no reply brief is filed, not later than 120 days after the date on which the answering brief is filed.

(B)(i)   A court of appeals shall decide whether to grant a petition for rehearing or other request for rehearing en banc not later than 30 days after the date on which the petition for rehearing is filed unless a responsive pleading is required, in which case the court shall decide whether to grant the petition not later than 30 days after the date on which the responsive pleading is filed.

(ii) If a petition for rehearing or rehearing en banc is granted, the court of appeals shall hear and render a final determination of the appeal not later than 120 days after the date on which the order granting rehearing or rehearing en banc is entered.

(2)   The time limitations under paragraph (1) shall apply to—

(A)   an initial application for a writ of habeas corpus;

(B)   any second or successive application for a writ of habeas corpus; and

(C)   any redetermination of an application for a writ of habeas corpus or related appeal following a remand by the court of appeals en banc or the Supreme Court for further proceedings, in which case the limitation period shall run from the date the remand is ordered.

(3)   The time limitations under this section shall not be construed to entitle an applicant to a stay of execution, to which the applicant would otherwise not be entitled, for the purpose of litigating any application or appeal.

---

[*]   The enacting legislation states that new sections 2261–2266 "shall apply to cases pending on or after the date of enactment of this Act."

(4)(A)   The failure of a court to meet or comply with a time limitation under this section shall not be a ground for granting relief from a judgment of conviction or sentence.

(B)   The State may enforce a time limitation under this section by applying for a writ of mandamus to the Supreme Court.

(5)   The Administrative Office of the United States Courts shall submit to Congress an annual report on the compliance by the courts of appeals with the time limitations under this section.*

PRIVACY PROTECTION ACT OF 1980

(42 U.S.C. §§ 2000aa–2000aa–12); Guidelines (28 C.F.R. § 59.4).

§ 2000aa.   Searches and seizures by government officers and employees in connection with investigation or prosecution of criminal offenses

(a)   Work product materials

Notwithstanding any other law, it shall be unlawful for a government officer or employee, in connection with the investigation or prosecution of a criminal offense, to search for or seize any work product materials possessed by a person reasonably believed to have a purpose to disseminate to the public a newspaper, book, broadcast, or other similar form of public communication, in or affecting interstate or foreign commerce; but this provision shall not impair or affect the ability of any government officer or employee, pursuant to otherwise applicable law, to search for or seize such materials, if—

(1)   there is probable cause to believe that the person possessing such materials has committed or is committing the criminal offense to which the materials relate: *Provided, however,* That a government officer or employee may not search for or seize such materials under the provisions of this paragraph if the offense to which the materials relate consists of the receipt, possession, communication, or withholding of such materials or the information contained therein (but such a search or seizure may be conducted under the provisions of this paragraph if the offense consists of the receipt, possession, or communication of information relating to the national defense, classified information, or restricted data under the provisions of section 793, 794, 797, or 798 of Title 18, or section 2274, 2275 or 2277 of this title, or section 783 of Title 50, or if the offense involves the production, possession, receipt, mailing, sale, distribution, shipment, or transportation of child pornography, the sexual exploitation of children, or the sale or purchase of children under section 2251, 2251A, 2252, or 2252A of Title 18); or

(2)   there is reason to believe that the immediate seizure of such materials is necessary to prevent the death of, or serious bodily injury to, a human being.

(b)   Other documents

Notwithstanding any other law, it shall be unlawful for a government officer or employee, in connection with the investigation or prosecution of a criminal offense, to search for or seize documentary materials, other than work product materials, possessed by a person in connection with a purpose to disseminate to the public a newspaper, book, broadcast, or other similar form of public communication, in or affecting interstate or foreign commerce; but this provision shall not impair or affect the ability of any government officer or employee, pursuant to otherwise applicable law, to search for or seize such materials, if—

---

*   The enacting legislation states that the new §§ 2216–2266 "shall apply to cases pending on or after the date of enactment of this Act."

(1)   there is probable cause to believe that the person possessing such materials has committed or is committing the criminal offense to which the materials relate: *Provided, however,* That a government officer or employee may not search for or seize such materials under the provisions of this paragraph if the offense to which the materials relate consists of the receipt, possession, communication, or withholding of such materials or the information contained therein (but such a search or seizure may be conducted under the provisions of this paragraph if the offense consists of the receipt, possession, or communication of information relating to the national defense, classified information, or restricted data under the provisions of section 793, 794, 797, or 798 of Title 18, or section 2274, 2275, or 2277 of this title, or section 783 of Title 50, or if the offense involves the production, possession, receipt, mailing, sale, distribution, shipment, or transportation of child pornography, the sexual exploitation of children, or the sale or purchase of children under section 2251, 2251A, 2252, or 2252A of Title 18);

(2)   there is reason to believe that the immediate seizure of such materials is necessary to prevent the death of, or serious bodily injury to, a human being;

(3)   there is reason to believe that the giving of notice pursuant to a subpena duces tecum would result in the destruction, alteration, or concealment of such materials; or

(4)   such materials have not been produced in response to a court order directing compliance with a subpena duces tecum, and—

(A)   all appellate remedies have been exhausted; or

(B)   there is reason to believe that the delay in an investigation or trial occasioned by further proceedings relating to the subpena would threaten the interests of justice.

(c)   Objections to court ordered subpoenas; affidavits

In the event a search warrant is sought pursuant to paragraph (4)(B) of subsection (b) of this section, the person possessing the materials shall be afforded adequate opportunity to submit an affidavit setting forth the basis for any contention that the materials sought are not subject to seizure.

§ 2000aa–5.   Border and customs searches

This chapter shall not impair or affect the ability of a government officer or employee, pursuant to otherwise applicable law, to conduct searches and seizures at the borders of, or at international points of, entry into the United States in order to enforce the customs laws of the United States.

§ 2000aa–6.   Civil actions by aggrieved persons

(a)   Right of action

A person aggrieved by a search for or seizure of materials in violation of this chapter shall have a civil cause of action for damages for such search or seizure—

(1)   against the United States, against a State which has waived its sovereign immunity under the Constitution to a claim for damages resulting from a violation of this chapter, or against any other governmental unit, all of which shall be liable for violations of this chapter by their officers or employees while acting within the scope or under color of their office or employment; and

(2)   against an officer or employee of a State who has violated this chapter while acting within the scope or under color of his office or employment, if such State has not waived its sovereign immunity as provided in paragraph (1).

(b)   Good faith defense

It shall be a complete defense to a civil action brought under paragraph (2) of subsection (a) of this section that the officer or employee had a reasonable good faith belief in the lawfulness of his conduct.

(c)   Official immunity

The United States, a State, or any other governmental unit liable for violations of this chapter under subsection (a)(1) of this section, may not assert as a defense to a claim arising under this chapter the immunity of the officer or employee whose violation is complained of or his reasonable good faith belief in the lawfulness of his conduct, except that such a defense may be asserted if the violation complained of is that of a judicial officer.

(d)   Exclusive nature of remedy

The remedy provided by subsection (a)(1) of this section against the United States, a State, or any other governmental unit is exclusive of any other civil action or proceeding for conduct constituting a violation of this chapter, against the officer or employee whose violation gave rise to the claim, or against the estate of such officer or employee.

(e)   Admissibility of evidence

Evidence otherwise admissible in a proceeding shall not be excluded on the basis of a violation of this chapter.

(f)   Damages; costs and attorneys' fees

A person having a cause of action under this section shall be entitled to recover actual damages but not less than liquidated damages of $1,000, and such reasonable attorneys' fees and other litigation costs reasonably incurred as the court, in its discretion, may award: *Provided, however*, That the United States, a State, or any other governmental unit shall not be liable for interest prior to judgment.

(g)   Attorney General; claims settlement; regulations

The Attorney General may settle a claim for damages brought against the United States under this section, and shall promulgate regulations to provide for the commencement of an administrative inquiry following a determination of a violation of this chapter by an officer or employee of the United States and for the imposition of administrative sanctions against such officer or employee, if warranted.

(h)   Jurisdiction

The district courts shall have original jurisdiction of all civil actions arising under this section.

§ 2000aa–7.   Definitions

(a)   "Documentary materials", as used in this chapter, means materials upon which information is recorded, and includes, but is not limited to, written or printed materials, photographs, motion picture films, negatives, video tapes, audio tapes, and other mechanically,[1] magentically or electronically recorded cards, tapes, or discs, but does not include contraband or the fruits of a crime or things otherwise criminally possessed, or property designed or intended for use, or which is or has been used as, the means of committing a criminal offense.

(b)   "Work product materials", as used in this chapter, means materials, other than contraband or the fruits of a crime or things otherwise criminally possessed, or property designed

---

[1]   So in original. Probably should be "magnetically".

or intended for use, or which is or has been used, as the means of committing a criminal offense, and—

    (1) in anticipation of communicating such materials to the public, are prepared, produced, authored, or created, whether by the person in possession of the materials or by any other person;

    (2) are possessed for the purposes of communicating such materials to the public; and

    (3) include mental impressions, conclusions, opinions, or theories of the person who prepared, produced, authored, or created such material.

(c) "Any other governmental unit", as used in this chapter, includes the District of Columbia, the Commonwealth of Puerto Rico, any territory or possession of the United States, and any local government, unit of local government, or any unit of State government.

§ 2000aa–11. Guidelines for Federal officers and employees

(a) Procedures to obtain documentary evidence; protection of certain privacy interests

The Attorney General shall, within six months of October 13, 1980, issue guidelines for the procedures to be employed by any Federal officer or employee, in connection with the investigation or prosecution of an offense, to obtain documentary materials in the private possession of a person when the person is not reasonably believed to be a suspect in such offense or related by blood or marriage to such a suspect, and when the materials sought are not contraband or the fruits or instrumentalities of an offense. The Attorney General shall incorporate in such guidelines—

    (1) a recognition of the personal privacy interests of the person in possession of such documentary materials;

    (2) a requirement that the least intrusive method or means of obtaining such materials be used which do not substantially jeopardize the availability or usefulness of the materials sought to be obtained;

    (3) a recognition of special concern for privacy interests in cases in which a search or seizure for such documents would intrude upon a known confidential relationship such as that which may exist between clergyman and parishioner; lawyer and client; or doctor and patient; and

    (4) a requirement that an application for a warrant to conduct a search governed by this subchapter be approved by an attorney for the government, except that in an emergency situation the application may be approved by another appropriate supervisory official if within 24 hours of such emergency the appropriate United States Attorney is notified.

(b) Use of search warrants; reports to Congress

The Attorney General shall collect and compile information on, and report annually to the Committees on the Judiciary of the Senate and the House of Representatives on the use of search warrants by Federal officers and employees for documentary materials described in subsection (a)(3) of this section.

§ 2000aa–12. Binding nature of guidelines; disciplinary actions for violations; legal proceedings for non-compliance prohibited

Guidelines issued by the Attorney General under this subchapter shall have the full force and effect of Department of Justice regulations and any violation of these guidelines shall make the employee or officer involved subject to appropriate administrative disciplinary action. However, an issue relating to the compliance, or the failure to comply, with guidelines issued pursuant to this subchapter may not be litigated, and a court may not entertain such an issue as the basis for the suppression or exclusion of evidence.

[EDITOR'S NOTE: These guidelines appear in 28 C.F.R. Pt. 59. The procedural provisions are set out below.]

GUIDELINES

(28 C.F.R. § 59.4).

§ 59.4   Procedures.[1]

(a)   Provisions governing the use of search warrants generally.

(1) A search warrant should not be used to obtain documentary materials believed to be in the private possession of a disinterested third party unless it appears that the use of a subpoena, summons, request, or other less intrusive alternative means of obtaining the materials would substantially jeopardize the availability or usefulness of the materials sought, and the application for the warrant has been authorized as provided in paragraph (a)(2) of this section.

(2)   No federal officer or employee shall apply for a warrant to search for and seize documentary materials believed to be in the private possession of a disinterested third party unless the application for the warrant has been authorized by an attorney for the government. Provided, however, that in an emergency situation in which the immediacy of the need to seize the materials does not permit an opportunity to secure the authorization of an attorney for the government, the application may be authorized by a supervisory law enforcement officer in the applicant's department or agency, if the appropriate U.S. Attorney (or where the case is not being handled by a U.S. Attorney's Office, the appropriate supervisory official of the Department of Justice) is notified of the authorization and the basis for justifying such authorization under this part within 24 hours of the authorization.

(b)   Provisions governing the use of search warrants which may intrude upon professional, confidential relationships.

(1)   A search warrant should not be used to obtain documentary materials believed to be in the private possession of a disinterested third party physician,[2] lawyer, or clergyman, under circumstances in which the materials sought, or other materials likely to be reviewed during the execution of the warrant, contain confidential information on patients, clients, or parishioners which was furnished or developed for the purposes of professional counseling or treatment, unless—

(i)   It appears that the use of a subpoena, summons, request or other less intrusive alternative means of obtaining the materials would substantially jeopardize the availability or usefulness of the materials sought;

(ii)   Access to the documentary materials appears to be of substantial importance to the investigation or prosecution for which they are sought; and

(iii)   The application for the warrant has been approved as provided in paragraph (b)(2) of this section.

(2)   No federal officer or employee shall apply for a warrant to search for and seize documentary materials believed to be in the private possession of a disinterested third party physician, lawyer, or clergyman under the circumstances described in paragraph (b)(1) of this

---

[1]   Notwithstanding the provisions of this section, any application for a warrant to search for evidence of a criminal tax offense under the jurisdiction of the Tax Division must be specifically approved in advance by the Tax Division pursuant to section 6–2.330 of the U.S. Attorneys' Manual.

[2]   Documentary materials created or compiled by a physician, but retained by the physician as a matter of practice at a hospital or clinic shall be deemed to be in the private possession of the physician, unless the clinic or hospital is a suspect in the offense.

section, unless, upon the recommendation of the U.S. Attorney (or where a case is not being handled by a U.S. Attorney's Office, upon the recommendation of the appropriate supervisory official of the Department of Justice), an appropriate Deputy Assistant Attorney General has authorized the application for the warrant. Provided, however, that in an emergency situation in which the immediacy of the need to seize the materials does not permit an opportunity to secure the authorization of a Deputy Assistant Attorney General, the application may be authorized by the U.S. Attorney (or where the case is not being handled by a U.S. Attorney's Office, by the appropriate supervisory official of the Department of Justice) if an appropriate Deputy Assistant Attorney General is notified of the authorization and the basis for justifying such authorization under this part within 72 hours of the authorization.

(3)   Whenever possible, a request for authorization by an appropriate Deputy Assistant Attorney General of a search warrant application pursuant to paragraph (b)(2) of this section shall be made in writing and shall include:

(i)   The application for the warrant; and

(ii)   A brief description of the facts and circumstances advanced as the basis for recommending authorization of the application under this part.

If a request for authorization of the application is made orally or if, in an emergency situation, the application is authorized by the U.S. Attorney or a supervisory official of the Department of Justice as provided in paragraph (b)(2) of this section, a written record of the request including the materials specified in paragraphs (b)(3)(i) and (ii) of this section shall be transmitted to an appropriate Deputy Assistant Attorney General within 7 days. The Deputy Assistant Attorneys General shall keep a record of the disposition of all requests for authorizations of search warrant applications made under paragraph (b) of this section.

(4)   A search warrant authorized under paragraph (b)(2) of this section shall be executed in such a manner as to minimize, to the greatest extent practicable, scrutiny of confidential materials.

(5)   Although it is impossible to define the full range of additional doctor-like therapeutic relationships which involve the furnishing or development of private information, the U.S. Attorney (or where a case is not being handled by a U.S. Attorney's Office, the appropriate supervisory official of the Department of Justice) should determine whether a search for documentary materials held by other disinterested third party professionals involved in such relationships (e.g. psychologists or psychiatric social workers or nurses) would implicate the special privacy concerns which are addressed in paragraph (b) of this section. If the U.S. Attorney (or other supervisory official of the Department of Justice) determines that such a search would require review of extremely confidential information furnished or developed for the purposes of professional counseling or treatment, the provisions of this subsection should be applied. Otherwise, at a minimum, the requirements of paragraph (a) of this section must be met.

(c)   Considerations bearing on choice of methods. In determining whether, as an alternative to the use of a search warrant, the use of a subpoena or other less intrusive means of obtaining documentary materials would substantially jeopardize the availability or usefulness of the materials sought, the following factors, among others, should be considered:

(1)   Whether it appears that the use of a subpoena or other alternative which gives advance notice of the government's interest in obtaining the materials would be likely to result in the destruction, alteration, concealment, or transfer of the materials sought; considerations, among others, bearing on this issue may include:

(i)   Whether a suspect has access to the materials sought;

(ii)   Whether there is a close relationship of friendship, loyalty, or sympathy between the possessor of the materials and a suspect;

(iii)   Whether the possessor of the materials is under the domination or control of a suspect;

(iv)   Whether the possessor of the materials has an interest in preventing the disclosure of the materials to the government;

(v)   Whether the possessor's willingness to comply with a subpoena or request by the government would be likely to subject him to intimidation or threats of reprisal;

(vi)   Whether the possessor of the materials has previously acted to obstruct a criminal investigation or judicial proceeding or refused to comply with or acted in defiance of court orders; or

(vii)   Whether the possessor has expressed an intent to destroy, conceal, alter, or transfer the materials;

(2)   The immediacy of the government's need to obtain the materials; considerations, among others, bearing on this issue may include:

(i)   Whether the immediate seizure of the materials is necessary to prevent injury to persons or property;

(ii)   Whether the prompt seizure of the materials is necessary to preserve their evidentiary value;

(iii)   Whether delay in obtaining the materials would significantly jeopardize an ongoing investigation or prosecution; or

(iv)   Whether a legally enforceable form of process, other than a search warrant, is reasonably available as a means of obtaining the materials.

The fact that the disinterested third party possessing the materials may have grounds to challenge a subpoena or other legal process is not in itself a legitimate basis for the use of a search warrant.

FOREIGN INTELLIGENCE SURVEILLANCE ACT

(50 U.S.C. § 1861).

§ 1861.   Access to certain business records for foreign intelligence and international terrorism investigations

(a)   Application for order; conduct of investigation generally

(1)   Subject to paragraph (3), the Director of the Federal Bureau of Investigation or a designee of the Director (whose rank shall be no lower than Assistant Special Agent in Charge) may make an application for an order requiring the production of any tangible things (including books, records, papers, documents, and other items) for an investigation to obtain foreign intelligence information not concerning a United States person or to protect against international terrorism or clandestine intelligence activities, provided that such investigation of a United States person is not conducted solely upon the basis of activities protected by the first amendment to the Constitution.

(2)   An investigation conducted under this section shall

(A)   be conducted under guidelines approved by the Attorney General under Executive Order 12333 (or a successor order); and

(B)   not be conducted of a United States person solely upon the basis of activities protected by the first amendment to the Constitution of the United States.

(3) In the case of an application for an order requiring the production of library circulation records, library patron lists, book sales records, book customer lists, firearms sales records, tax return records, educational records, or medical records containing information that would identify a person, the Director of the Federal Bureau of Investigation may delegate the authority to make such application to either the Deputy Director of the Federal Bureau of Investigation or the Executive Assistant Director for National Security (or any successor position). The Deputy Director or the Executive Assistant Director may not further delegate such authority.

(b) Recipient and contents of application

Each application under this section

(1) shall be made to—

(A) a judge of the court established by section 1803(a) of this title; or

(B) a United States Magistrate Judge under chapter 43 of Title 28, who is publicly designated by the Chief Justice of the United States to have the power to hear applications and grant orders for the production of tangible things under this section on behalf of a judge of that court; and

(2) shall include—

(A) a specific selection term to be used as the basis for the production of the tangible things sought;

(B) in the case of an application other than an application described in subparagraph (C) (including an application for the production of call detail records other than in the manner described in subparagraph (C)), a statement of facts showing that there are reasonable grounds to believe that the tangible things sought are relevant to an authorized investigation (other than a threat assessment) conducted in accordance with subsection (a)(2) to obtain foreign intelligence information not concerning a United States person or to protect against international terrorism or clandestine intelligence activities, such things being presumptively relevant to an authorized investigation if the applicant shows in the statement of the facts that they pertain to—

(i) a foreign power or an agent of a foreign power;

(ii) the activities of a suspected agent of a foreign power who is the subject of such authorized investigation; or

(iii) an individual in contact with, or known to, a suspected agent of a foreign power who is the subject of such authorized investigation;

(C) in the case of an application for the production on an ongoing basis of call detail records created before, on, or after the date of the application relating to an authorized investigation (other than a threat assessment) conducted in accordance with subsection (a)(2) to protect against international terrorism, a statement of facts showing that—

(i) there are reasonable grounds to believe that the call detail records sought to be produced based on the specific selection term required under subparagraph (A) are relevant to such investigation; and

(ii) there is a reasonable, articulable suspicion that such specific selection term is associated with a foreign power engaged in international terrorism or activities in preparation therefor, or an agent of a foreign power engaged in international terrorism or activities in preparation therefor; and

(D) an enumeration of the minimization procedures adopted by the Attorney General under subsection (g) that are applicable to the retention and dissemination by the Federal Bureau of Investigation of any tangible things to be made available to the Federal Bureau of Investigation based on the order requested in such application.

(c)   Ex parte judicial order of approval

(1)   Upon an application made pursuant to this section, if the judge finds that the application meets the requirements of subsections (a) and (b) and that the minimization procedures submitted in accordance with subsection (b)(2)(D) meet the definition of minimization procedures under subsection (g), the judge shall enter an ex parte order as requested, or as modified, approving the release of tangible things. Such order shall direct that minimization procedures adopted pursuant to subsection (g) be followed.

(2)   An order under this subsection—

(A)   shall describe the tangible things that are ordered to be produced with sufficient particularity to permit them to be fairly identified, including each specific selection term to be used as the basis for the production;

(B)   shall include the date on which the tangible things must be provided, which shall allow a reasonable period of time within which the tangible things can be assembled and made available;

(C)   shall provide clear and conspicuous notice of the principles and procedures described in subsection (d);

(D)   may only require the production of a tangible thing if such thing can be obtained with a subpoena duces tecum issued by a court of the United States in aid of a grand jury investigation or with any other order issued by a court of the United States directing the production of records or tangible things;

(E)   shall not disclose that such order is issued for purposes of an investigation described in subsection (a); and

(F)   in the case of an application described in subsection (b)(2)(C), shall—

(i)   authorize the production on a daily basis of call detail records for a period not to exceed 180 days;

(ii)   provide that an order for such production may be extended upon application under subsection (b) and the judicial finding under paragraph (1) of this subsection;

(iii)   provide that the Government may require the prompt production of a first set of call detail records using the specific selection term that satisfies the standard required under subsection (b)(2)(C)(ii);

(iv)   provide that the Government may require the prompt production of a second set of call detail records using session-identifying information or a telephone calling card number identified by the specific selection term used to produce call detail records under clause (iii);

(v)   provide that, when produced, such records be in a form that will be useful to the Government;

(vi)   direct each person the Government directs to produce call detail records under the order to furnish the Government forthwith all information, facilities, or technical assistance necessary to accomplish the production in such a manner as will protect the secrecy of the production and produce a minimum of interference with the services that such person is providing to each subject of the production; and

(vii) direct the Government to—

(I)   adopt minimization procedures that require the prompt destruction of all call detail records produced under the order that the Government determines are not foreign intelligence information; and

(II) destroy all call detail records produced under the order as prescribed by such procedures.

(3)   No order issued under this subsection may authorize the collection of tangible things without the use of a specific selection term that meets the requirements of subsection (b)(2).

(4)   A denial of the application made under this subsection may be reviewed as provided in section 103.

(d)   Nondisclosure

(1)   No person shall disclose to any other person that the Federal Bureau of Investigation has sought or obtained tangible things pursuant to an order issued or an emergency production required under this section, other than to

(A)   those persons to whom disclosure is necessary to comply with such order or such emergency production;

(B)   an attorney to obtain legal advice or assistance with respect to the production of things in response to the order or the emergency production; or

(C)   other persons as permitted by the Director of the Federal Bureau of Investigation or the designee of the Director.

(2)(A)   A person to whom disclosure is made pursuant to paragraph (1) shall be subject to the nondisclosure requirements applicable to a person to whom an order or emergency production is directed under this section in the same manner as such person.

(B)   Any person who discloses to a person described in subparagraph (A), (B), or (C) of paragraph (1) that the Federal Bureau of Investigation has sought or obtained tangible things pursuant to an order or emergency production under this section shall notify such person of the nondisclosure requirements of this subsection.

(C)   At the request of the Director of the Federal Bureau of Investigation or the designee of the Director, any person making or intending to make a disclosure under subparagraph (A) or (C) of paragraph (1) shall identify to the Director or such designee the person to whom such disclosure will be made or to whom such disclosure was made prior to the request.

(e)   Liability for good faith disclosure; waiver

(1)   No cause of action shall lie in any court against a person who—

(A)   produces tangible things or provides information, facilities, or technical assistance in accordance with an order issued or an emergency production required under this section; or

(B)   otherwise provides technical assistance to the Government under this section or to implement the amendments made to this section by the USA FREEDOM Act of 2015.

(2)   A production or provision of information, facilities, or technical assistance described in paragraph (1) shall not be deemed to constitute a waiver of any privilege in any other proceeding or context.

(f)   Judicial review of FISA orders

(1)   In this subsection—

(A)   the term "production order" means an order to produce any tangible thing under this section; and

(B)   the term "nondisclosure order" means an order imposed under subsection (d).

(2)(A)(i)   A person receiving a production order may challenge the legality of the production order or any nondisclosure order imposed in connection with the production order by filing a petition with the pool established by section 1803(e)(1) of this title.

(ii)   The presiding judge shall immediately assign a petition under clause (i) to 1 of the judges serving in the pool established by section 1803(e)(1) of this title. Not later than 72 hours after the assignment of such petition, the assigned judge shall conduct an initial review of the petition. If the assigned judge determines that the petition is frivolous, the assigned judge shall immediately deny the petition and affirm the production order or nondisclosure order. If the assigned judge determines the petition is not frivolous, the assigned judge shall promptly consider the petition in accordance with the procedures established under section 1803(e)(2) of this title.

(iii)   The assigned judge shall promptly provide a written statement for the record of the reasons for any determination under this subsection. Upon the request of the Government, any order setting aside a nondisclosure order shall be stayed pending review pursuant to paragraph (3).

(B)   A judge considering a petition to modify or set aside a production order may grant such petition only if the judge finds that such order does not meet the requirements of this section or is otherwise unlawful. If the judge does not modify or set aside the production order, the judge shall immediately affirm such order, and order the recipient to comply therewith.

(C)(i)   A judge considering a petition to modify or set aside a nondisclosure order may grant such petition only if the judge finds that there is no reason to believe that disclosure may endanger the national security of the United States, interfere with a criminal, counterterrorism, or counterintelligence investigation, interfere with diplomatic relations, or endanger the life or physical safety of any person.

(ii)   If the judge denies a petition to modify or set aside a nondisclosure order, the recipient of such order shall be precluded for a period of 1 year from filing another such petition with respect to such nondisclosure order.

(iii)   Redesignated (ii)

(D)   Any production or nondisclosure order not explicitly modified or set aside consistent with this subsection shall remain in full effect.

(3)   A petition for review of a decision under paragraph (2) to affirm, modify, or set aside an order by the Government or any person receiving such order shall be made to the court of review established under section 1803(b) of this title, which shall have jurisdiction to consider such petitions. The court of review shall provide for the record a written statement of the reasons for its decision and, on petition by the Government or any person receiving such order

for writ of certiorari, the record shall be transmitted under seal to the Supreme Court of the United States, which shall have jurisdiction to review such decision.

(4)   Judicial proceedings under this subsection shall be concluded as expeditiously as possible. The record of proceedings, including petitions filed, orders granted, and statements of reasons for decision, shall be maintained under security measures established by the Chief Justice of the United States, in consultation with the Attorney General and the Director of National Intelligence.

(5)   All petitions under this subsection shall be filed under seal. In any proceedings under this subsection, the court shall, upon request of the Government, review ex parte and in camera any Government submission, or portions thereof, which may include classified information.

(g)   Minimization procedures

(1)   In general

The Attorney General shall adopt, and update as appropriate, specific minimization procedures governing the retention and dissemination by the Federal Bureau of Investigation of any tangible things, or information therein, received by the Federal Bureau of Investigation in response to an order under this subchapter.

(2)   Defined

In this section, the term "minimization procedures" means—

(A)   specific procedures that are reasonably designed in light of the purpose and technique of an order for the production of tangible things, to minimize the retention, and prohibit the dissemination, of nonpublicly available information concerning unconsenting United States persons consistent with the need of the United States to obtain, produce, and disseminate foreign intelligence information;

(B)   procedures that require that nonpublicly available information, which is not foreign intelligence information, as defined in section 1801(e)(1) of this title, shall not be disseminated in a manner that identifies any United States person, without such person's consent, unless such person's identity is necessary to understand foreign intelligence information or assess its importance; and

(C)   notwithstanding subparagraphs (A) and (B), procedures that allow for the retention and dissemination of information that is evidence of a crime which has been, is being, or is about to be committed and that is to be retained or disseminated for law enforcement purposes.

(3)   Rule of construction

Nothing in this subsection shall limit the authority of the court established under section 1803(a) of this title to impose additional, particularized minimization procedures with regard to the production, retention, or dissemination of nonpublicly available information concerning unconsenting United States persons, including additional, particularized procedures related to the destruction of information within a reasonable time period.

(h)   Use of information

Information acquired from tangible things received by the Federal Bureau of Investigation in response to an order under this subchapter concerning any United States person may be used and disclosed by Federal officers and employees without the consent of the United States person only in accordance with the minimization procedures adopted pursuant to subsection (g). No otherwise privileged information acquired from tangible things received by the Federal Bureau of

Investigation in accordance with the provisions of this subchapter shall lose its privileged character. No information acquired from tangible things received by the Federal Bureau of Investigation in response to an order under this subchapter may be used or disclosed by Federal officers or employees except for lawful purposes.

(i) Emergency authority for production of tangible things

(1) Notwithstanding any other provision of this section, the Attorney General may require the emergency production of tangible things if the Attorney General—

(A) reasonably determines that an emergency situation requires the production of tangible things before an order authorizing such production can with due diligence be obtained;

(B) reasonably determines that the factual basis for the issuance of an order under this section to approve such production of tangible things exists;

(C) informs, either personally or through a designee, a judge having jurisdiction under this section at the time the Attorney General requires the emergency production of tangible things that the decision has been made to employ the authority under this subsection; and

(D) makes an application in accordance with this section to a judge having jurisdiction under this section as soon as practicable, but not later than 7 days after the Attorney General requires the emergency production of tangible things under this subsection.

(2) If the Attorney General requires the emergency production of tangible things under paragraph (1), the Attorney General shall require that the minimization procedures required by this section for the issuance of a judicial order be followed.

(3) In the absence of a judicial order approving the production of tangible things under this subsection, the production shall terminate when the information sought is obtained, when the application for the order is denied, or after the expiration of 7 days from the time the Attorney General begins requiring the emergency production of such tangible things, whichever is earliest.

(4) A denial of the application made under this subsection may be reviewed as provided in section 1803 of this title.

(5) If such application for approval is denied, or in any other case where the production of tangible things is terminated and no order is issued approving the production, no information obtained or evidence derived from such production shall be received in evidence or otherwise disclosed in any trial, hearing, or other proceeding in or before any court, grand jury, department, office, agency, regulatory body, legislative committee, or other authority of the United States, a State, or a political subdivision thereof, and no information concerning any United States person acquired from such production shall subsequently be used or disclosed in any other manner by Federal officers or employees without the consent of such person, except with the approval of the Attorney General if the information indicates a threat of death or serious bodily harm to any person.

(6) The Attorney General shall assess compliance with the requirements of paragraph (5).

(j) Compensation

The Government shall compensate a person for reasonable expenses incurred for—

(1) producing tangible things or providing information, facilities, or assistance in accordance with an order issued with respect to an application described in subsection (b)(2)(C) or an emergency production under subsection (i) that, to comply with subsection (i)(1)(D), requires an application described in subsection (b)(2)(C); or

(2) otherwise providing technical assistance to the Government under this section or to implement the amendments made to this section by the USA FREEDOM Act of 2015.

(k)   Definitions

In this section:

(1)   In general

The terms "foreign power", "agent of a foreign power", "international terrorism", "foreign intelligence information", "Attorney General", "United States person", "United States", "person", and "State" have the meanings provided those terms in section 1801 of this title.

(2)   Address

The term "address" means a physical address or electronic address, such as an electronic mail address or temporarily assigned network address (including an Internet protocol address).

(3)   Call detail record

The term "call detail record"—

(A) means session-identifying information (including an originating or terminating telephone number, an International Mobile Subscriber Identity number, or an International Mobile Station Equipment Identity number), a telephone calling card number, or the time or duration of a call; and

(B)   does not include—

(i)   the contents (as defined in section 2510(8) of Title 18) of any communication;

(ii)   the name, address, or financial information of a subscriber or customer; or

(iii)   cell site location or global positioning system information.

(4)   Specific selection term

(A)   Tangible things

(i)   In general

Except as provided in subparagraph (B), a "specific selection term"—

(I)   is a term that specifically identifies a person, account, address, or personal device, or any other specific identifier; and

(II)   is used to limit, to the greatest extent reasonably practicable, the scope of tangible things sought consistent with the purpose for seeking the tangible things.

(ii)   Limitation

A specific selection term under clause (i) does not include an identifier that does not limit, to the greatest extent reasonably practicable, the scope of tangible things sought consistent with the purpose for seeking the tangible things, such as an identifier that—

(I)   identifies an electronic communication service provider (as that term is defined in section 1881 of this title) or a provider of remote computing service (as that term is defined in section 2711 of Title 18), when not used as part of a specific identifier as described in clause (i), unless the provider is itself a subject of an authorized investigation for which the specific selection term is used as the basis for the production; or

(II)   identifies a broad geographic region, including the United States, a city, a county, a State, a zip code, or an area code, when not used as part of a specific identifier as described in clause (i).

(iii) Rule of construction

Nothing in this paragraph shall be construed to preclude the use of multiple terms or identifiers to meet the requirements of clause (i).

(B) Call detail record applications

For purposes of an application submitted under subsection (b)(2)(C), the term "specific selection term" means a term that specifically identifies an individual, account, or personal device.

APPENDIX C

FEDERAL RULES OF CRIMINAL PROCEDURE FOR THE UNITED STATES DISTRICT COURTS

■ ■ ■

TITLE I. APPLICABILITY
  Rule 1. Scope; Definitions
  Rule 2. Interpretation
TITLE II. PRELIMINARY PROCEEDINGS
  Rule 3. The Complaint
  Rule 4. Arrest Warrant or Summons on a Complaint
  Rule 4.1. Complaint, Warrant, or Summons by Telephone or Other Reliable Electronic Means
  Rule 5. Initial Appearance
  Rule 5.1. Preliminary Hearing
TITLE III. THE GRAND JURY, THE INDICTMENT, AND THE INFORMATION
  Rule 6. The Grand Jury
  Rule 7. The Indictment and the Information
  Rule 8. Joinder of Offenses or Defendants
  Rule 9. Arrest Warrant or Summons on an Indictment or Information
TITLE IV. ARRAIGNMENT AND PREPARATION FOR TRIAL
  Rule 10. Arraignment
  Rule 11. Pleas
  Rule 12. Pleadings and Pretrial Motions
  Rule 12.1. Notice of an Alibi Defense
  Rule 12.2. Notice of an Insanity Defense; Mental Examination
  Rule 12.3. Notice of a Public-Authority Defense
  Rule 12.4. Disclosure Statement
  Rule 13. Joint Trial of Separate Cases
  Rule 14. Relief from Prejudicial Joinder
  Rule 15. Depositions
  Rule 16. Discovery and Inspection
  Rule 17. Subpoena
  Rule 17.1. Pretrial Conference
TITLE V. VENUE
  Rule 18. Place of Prosecution and Trial
  Rule 19. (Reserved)
  Rule 20. Transfer for Plea and Sentence
  Rule 21. Transfer for Trial
  Rule 22. (Transferred)
TITLE VI. TRIAL
  Rule 23. Jury or Nonjury Trial
  Rule 24. Trial Jurors
  Rule 25. Judge's Disability
  Rule 26. Taking Testimony
  Rule 26.1. Foreign Law Determination
  Rule 26.2. Producing a Witness's Statement
  Rule 26.3. Mistrial
  Rule 27. Proving an Official Record

Rule 28. Interpreters
Rule 29. Motion for a Judgment of Acquittal
Rule 29.1. Closing Argument
Rule 30. Jury Instructions
Rule 31. Jury Verdict
TITLE VII. POST-CONVICTION PROCEDURES
  Rule 32. Sentencing and Judgment
  Rule 32.1. Revoking or Modifying Probation or Supervised Release
  Rule 32.2. Criminal Forfeiture
  Rule 33. New Trial
  Rule 34. Arresting Judgment
  Rule 35. Correcting or Reducing a Sentence
  Rule 36. Clerical Error
  Rule 37. Ruling on a Motion for Relief That is Barred by a Pending Appeal
  Rule 38. Staying a Sentence or a Disability
  Rule 39. (Reserved)
TITLE VIII. SUPPLEMENTARY AND SPECIAL PROCEEDINGS
  Rule 40. Arrest for Failing to Appear in Another District or for Violating Conditions of Release Set in Another District
  Rule 41. Search and Seizure
  Rule 42. Criminal Contempt
TITLE IX. GENERAL PROVISIONS
  Rule 43. Defendant's Presence
  Rule 44. Right to and Appointment of Counsel
  Rule 45. Computing and Extending Time
  Rule 46. Release from Custody; Supervising Detention
  Rule 47. Motions and Supporting Affidavits
  Rule 48. Dismissal
  Rule 49. Serving and Filing Papers
  Rule 49.1. Privacy Protection for Filings Made With the Court
  Rule 50. Prompt Disposition
  Rule 51. Preserving Claimed Error
  Rule 52. Harmless and Plain Error
  Rule 53. Courtroom Photographing and Broadcasting Prohibited
  Rule 54. (Transferred)
  Rule 55. Records
  Rule 56. When Court Is Open
  Rule 57. District Court Rules
  Rule 58. Petty Offenses and Other Misdemeanors
  Rule 59. Matters Before a Magistrate Judge
  Rule 60. Victim's Rights
  Rule 61. Title

I.   SCOPE, PURPOSE AND CONSTRUCTION

Rule 1.   Scope; Definitions

(a) Scope.

(1) In General. These rules govern the procedure in all criminal proceedings in the United States district courts, the United States courts of appeals, and the Supreme Court of the United States.

(2) State or Local Judicial Officer. When a rule so states, it applies to a proceeding before a state or local judicial officer.

(3) Territorial Courts. These rules also govern the procedure in all criminal proceedings in the following courts:

(A) the district court of Guam;

(B) the district court for the Northern Mariana Islands, except as otherwise provided by law; and

(C) the district court of the Virgin Islands, except that the prosecution of offenses in that court must be by indictment or information as otherwise provided by law.

(4) Removed Proceedings. Although these rules govern all proceedings after removal from a state court, state law governs a dismissal by the prosecution.

(5) Excluded Proceedings. Proceedings not governed by these rules include:

(A) the extradition and rendition of a fugitive;

(B) a civil property forfeiture for violating a federal statute;

(C) the collection of a fine or penalty;

(D) a proceeding under a statute governing juvenile delinquency to the extent the procedure is inconsistent with the statute, unless Rule 20(d) provides otherwise;

(E) a dispute between seamen under 22 U.S.C. §§ 256–258; and

(F) a proceeding against a witness in a foreign country under 28 U.S.C. § 1784.

(b) Definitions. The following definitions apply to these rules:

(1) "Attorney for the government" means:

(A) the Attorney General or an authorized assistant;

(B) a United States attorney or an authorized assistant;

(C) when applicable to cases arising under Guam law, the Guam Attorney General or other person whom Guam law authorizes to act in the matter; and

(D) any other attorney authorized by law to conduct proceedings under these rules as a prosecutor.

(2) "Court" means a federal judge performing functions authorized by law.

(3) "Federal judge" means:

(A) a justice or judge of the United States as these terms are defined in 28 U.S.C. § 451;

(B) a magistrate judge; and

(C) a judge confirmed by the United States Senate and empowered by statute in any commonwealth, territory, or possession to perform a function to which a particular rule relates.

(4) "Judge" means a federal judge or a state or local judicial officer.

(5) "Magistrate judge" means a United States magistrate judge as defined in 28 U.S.C. §§ 631–639.

(6) "Oath" includes an affirmation.

(7) "Organization" is defined in 18 U.S.C. § 18.

(8) "Petty offense" is defined in 18 U.S.C. § 19.

(9) "State" includes the District of Columbia, and any commonwealth, territory, or possession of the United States.

(10) "State or local judicial officer" means:

    (A) a state or local officer authorized to act under 18 U.S.C. § 3041; and

    (B) a judicial officer empowered by statute in the District of Columbia or in any commonwealth, territory, or possession to perform a function to which a particular rule relates.

(11) "Telephone" means any technology for transmitting live electronic voice communication.

(12) "Victim" means a "crime victim" as defined in 18 U.S.C. § 3771(e).

(c) **Authority of a Justice or Judge of the United States.** When these rules authorize a magistrate judge to act, any other federal judge may also act.

Rule 2.   Interpretation

These rules are to be interpreted to provide for the just determination of every criminal proceeding, to secure simplicity in procedure and fairness in administration, and to eliminate unjustifiable expense and delay.

Rule 3.   The Complaint

The complaint is a written statement of the essential facts constituting the offense charged. Except as provided in Rule 4.1, it must be made under oath before a magistrate judge or, if none is reasonably available, before a state or local judicial officer.

Rule 4.   Arrest Warrant or Summons on a Complaint

(a) **Issuance.** If the complaint or one or more affidavits filed with the complaint establish probable cause to believe that an offense has been committed and that the defendant committed it, the judge must issue an arrest warrant to an officer authorized to execute it. At the request of an attorney for the government, the judge must issue a summons, instead of a warrant, to a person authorized to serve it. A judge may issue more than one warrant or summons on the same complaint. If an individual defendant fails to appear in response to a summons, a judge may, and upon request of an attorney for the government must, issue a warrant. If an organizational defendant fails to appear in response to a summons, a judge may take any action authorized by United States law.

(b) Form.

(1) Warrant. A warrant must:

(A) contain the defendant's name or, if it is unknown, a name or description by which the defendant can be identified with reasonable certainty;

(B) describe the offense charged in the complaint;

(C) command that the defendant be arrested and brought without unnecessary delay before a magistrate judge or, if none is reasonably available, before a state or local judicial officer; and

(D) be signed by a judge.

(2) Summons. A summons must be in the same form as a warrant except that it must require the defendant to appear before a magistrate judge at a stated time and place.

(c) Execution or Service, and Return.

(1) By Whom. Only a marshal or other authorized officer may execute a warrant. Any person authorized to serve a summons in a federal civil action may serve a summons.

(2) Location. A warrant may be executed, or a summons served, within the jurisdiction of the United States or anywhere else a federal statute authorizes an arrest. A summons to an organization under Rule 4(c)(3)(D) may also be served at a place not within a judicial district of the United States.

(3) Manner.

(A) A warrant is executed by arresting the defendant. Upon arrest, an officer possessing the original or a duplicate original warrant must show it to the defendant. If the officer does not possess the warrant, the officer must inform the defendant of the warrant's existence and of the offense charged and, at the defendant's request, must show the original or a duplicate original warrant to the defendant as soon as possible.

(B) A summons is served on an individual defendant:

(i) by delivering a copy to the defendant personally; or

(ii) by leaving a copy at the defendant's residence or usual place of abode with a person of suitable age and discretion residing at that location and by mailing a copy to the defendant's last known address.

(C) A summons is served on an organization in a judicial district of the United States by delivering a copy to an officer, to a managing or general agent, or to another agent appointed or legally authorized to receive service of process. If the agent is one authorized by statute and the statute so requires, a copy must also be mailed to the organization.

(D) A summons is served on an organization not within a judicial district of the United States:

(i) by delivering a copy, in a manner authorized by the foreign jurisdiction's law, to an officer, to a managing or general agent, or to an agent appointed or legally authorized to receive service of process; or

(ii) by any other means that gives notice, including one that is:

(a) stipulated by the parties;

(b) undertaken by a foreign authority in response to a letter rogatory, a letter of request, or a request submitted under an applicable international agreement; or

(c) permitted by an applicable international agreement.

(4) Return.

(A) After executing a warrant, the officer must return it to the judge before whom the defendant is brought in accordance with Rule 5. The officer may do so by reliable electronic means. At the request of an attorney for the government, an unexecuted warrant must be brought back to and canceled by a magistrate judge or, if none is reasonably available, by a state or local judicial officer.

(B) The person to whom a summons was delivered for service must return it on or before the return day.

(C) At the request of an attorney for the government, a judge may deliver an unexecuted warrant, an unserved summons, or a copy of the warrant or summons to the marshal or other authorized person for execution or service.

(d) Warrant by Telephone or Other Reliable Electronic Means. In accordance with Rule 4.1, a magistrate judge may issue a warrant or summons based on information communicated by telephone or other reliable electronic means.

Rule 4.1. Complaint, Warrant, or Summons by Telephone or Other Reliable Electronic Means

(a) In General. A magistrate judge may consider information communicated by telephone or other reliable electronic means when deciding whether to approve a complaint or to issue a warrant or summons.

(b) Procedures. If a magistrate judge decides to proceed under this rule, the following procedures apply:

(1) Taking Testimony Under Oath. The judge must place under oath—and may examine—the applicant and any person on whose testimony the application is based.

(2) Creating a Record of the Testimony and Exhibits.

(A) Testimony Limited to Attestation. If the applicant does no more than attest to the contents of a written affidavit submitted by reliable electronic means, the judge must acknowledge the attestation in writing on the affidavit.

(B) Additional Testimony or Exhibits. If the judge considers additional testimony or exhibits, the judge must:

(i) have the testimony recorded verbatim by an electronic recording device, by a court reporter, or in writing;

(ii) have any recording or reporter's notes transcribed, have the transcription certified as accurate, and file it;

(iii) sign any other written record, certify its accuracy, and file it; and

(iv) make sure that the exhibits are filed.

(3) Preparing a Proposed Duplicate Original of a Complaint, Warrant, or Summons. The applicant must prepare a proposed duplicate original of a complaint, warrant, or summons, and must read or otherwise transmit its contents verbatim to the judge.

(4) Preparing an Original Complaint, Warrant, or Summons. If the applicant reads the contents of the proposed duplicate original, the judge must enter those contents into an original complaint, warrant, or summons. If the applicant transmits the contents by reliable electronic means, the transmission received by the judge may serve as the original.

(5) Modification. The judge may modify the complaint, warrant, or summons. The judge must then:

(A) transmit the modified version to the applicant by reliable electronic means; or

(B) file the modified original and direct the applicant to modify the proposed duplicate original accordingly.

(6) Issuance. To issue the warrant or summons, the judge must:

(A) sign the original documents;

(B) enter the date and time of issuance on the warrant or summons; and

(C) transmit the warrant or summons by reliable electronic means to the applicant or direct the applicant to sign the judge's name and enter the date and time on the duplicate original.

(c) Suppression Limited. Absent a finding of bad faith, evidence obtained from a warrant issued under this rule is not subject to suppression on the ground that issuing the warrant in this manner was unreasonable under the circumstances.

Rule 5.   Initial Appearance

(a) In General.

(1) Appearance Upon an Arrest.

(A) A person making an arrest within the United States must take the defendant without unnecessary delay before a magistrate judge, or before a state or local judicial officer as Rule 5(c) provides, unless a statute provides otherwise.

(B) A person making an arrest outside the United States must take the defendant without unnecessary delay before a magistrate judge, unless a statute provides otherwise.

(2) Exceptions.

(A) An officer making an arrest under a warrant issued upon a complaint charging solely a violation of 18 U.S.C. § 1073 need not comply with this rule if:

(i) the person arrested is transferred without unnecessary delay to the custody of appropriate state or local authorities in the district of arrest; and

(ii) an attorney for the government moves promptly, in the district where the warrant was issued, to dismiss the complaint.

(B) If a defendant is arrested for violating probation or supervised release, Rule 32.1 applies.

(C) If a defendant is arrested for failing to appear in another district, Rule 40 applies.

(3) Appearance Upon a Summons. When a defendant appears in response to a summons under Rule 4, a magistrate judge must proceed under Rule 5(d) or (e), as applicable.

(b) Arrest Without a Warrant. If a defendant is arrested without a warrant, a complaint meeting Rule 4(a)'s requirement of probable cause must be promptly filed in the district where the offense was allegedly committed.

(c) Place of Initial Appearance; Transfer to Another District.

(1) Arrest in the District Where the Offense Was Allegedly Committed. If the defendant is arrested in the district where the offense was allegedly committed:

(A) the initial appearance must be in that district; and

(B) if a magistrate judge is not reasonably available, the initial appearance may be before a state or local judicial officer.

(2) Arrest in a District Other Than Where the Offense Was Allegedly Committed. If the defendant was arrested in a district other than where the offense was allegedly committed, the initial appearance must be:

(A) in the district of arrest; or

(B) in an adjacent district if:

(i) the appearance can occur more promptly there; or

(ii) the offense was allegedly committed there and the initial appearance will occur on the day of arrest.

(3) Procedures in a District Other Than Where the Offense Was Allegedly Committed. If the initial appearance occurs in a district other than where the offense was allegedly committed, the following procedures apply:

(A) the magistrate judge must inform the defendant about the provisions of Rule 20;

(B) if the defendant was arrested without a warrant, the district court where the offense was allegedly committed must first issue a warrant before the magistrate judge transfers the defendant to that district;

(C) the magistrate judge must conduct a preliminary hearing if required by Rule 5.1;

(D) the magistrate judge must transfer the defendant to the district where the offense was allegedly committed if:

(i) the government produces the warrant, a certified copy of the warrant, reliable electronic form of either; and

(ii) the judge finds that the defendant is the same person named in the indictment, information, or warrant; and

(E) when a defendant is transferred and discharged, the clerk must promptly transmit the papers and any bail to the clerk in the district where the offense was allegedly committed.

(4) Procedure for Persons Extradited to the United States. If the defendant is surrendered to the United States in accordance with a request for the defendant's extradition, the initial appearance must be in the district (or one of the districts) where the offense is charged.

(d) Procedure in a Felony Case.

(1) Advice. If the defendant is charged with a felony, the judge must inform the defendant of the following:

(A) the complaint against the defendant, and any affidavit filed with it;

(B) the defendant's right to retain counsel or to request that counsel be appointed if the defendant cannot obtain counsel;

(C) the circumstances, if any, under which the defendant may secure pretrial release;

(D) any right to a preliminary hearing; and

(E) the defendant's right not to make a statement, and that any statement made may be used against the defendant; and

(F) that a defendant who is not a United States citizen may request that an attorney for the government or a federal law enforcement official notify a consular office from the defendant's country of nationality that the defendant has been arrested—but that even without the defendant's request, a treaty or other international agreement may require consular notification.

(2) Consulting with Counsel. The judge must allow the defendant reasonable opportunity to consult with counsel.

(3) Detention or Release. The judge must detain or release the defendant as provided by statute or these rules.

(4) Plea. A defendant may be asked to plead only under Rule 10.

(e) Procedure in a Misdemeanor Case. If the defendant is charged with a misdemeanor only, the judge must inform the defendant in accordance with Rule 58(b)(2).

(f) Video Teleconferencing. Video teleconferencing may be used to conduct an appearance under this rule if the defendant consents.

Rule 5.1. Preliminary Hearing

(a) In General. If a defendant is charged with an offense other than a petty offense, a magistrate judge must conduct a preliminary hearing unless:

(1) the defendant waives the hearing;

(2) the defendant is indicted;

(3) the government files an information under Rule 7(b) charging the defendant with a felony;

(4) the government files an information charging the defendant with a misdemeanor; or

(5) the defendant is charged with a misdemeanor and consents to trial before a magistrate judge.

(b) Selecting a District. A defendant arrested in a district other than where the offense was allegedly committed may elect to have the preliminary hearing conducted in the district where the prosecution is pending.

(c) Scheduling. The magistrate judge must hold the preliminary hearing within a reasonable time, but no later than 14 days after the initial appearance if the defendant is in custody and no later than 21 days if not in custody.

(d) Extending the Time. With the defendant's consent and upon a showing of good cause—taking into account the public interest in the prompt disposition of criminal cases—a magistrate judge may extend the time limits in Rule 5.1(c) one or more times. If the defendant does not consent, the magistrate judge may extend the time limits only on a showing that extraordinary circumstances exist and justice requires the delay.

(e) Hearing and Finding. At the preliminary hearing, the defendant may cross-examine adverse witnesses and may introduce evidence but may not object to evidence on the ground that it was unlawfully acquired. If the magistrate judge finds probable cause to believe an offense has been committed and the defendant committed it, the magistrate judge must promptly require the defendant to appear for further proceedings.

(f) Discharging the Defendant. If the magistrate judge finds no probable cause to believe an offense has been committed or the defendant committed it, the magistrate judge must dismiss the complaint and discharge the defendant. A discharge does not preclude the government from later prosecuting the defendant for the same offense.

(g) Recording the Proceedings. The preliminary hearing must be recorded by a court reporter or by a suitable recording device. A recording of the proceeding may be made available to any party upon request. A copy of the recording and a transcript may be provided to any party upon request and upon any payment required by applicable Judicial Conference regulations.

(h) Producing a Statement.

(1) In General. Rule 26.2(a)–(d) and (f) applies at any hearing under this rule, unless the magistrate judge for good cause rules otherwise in a particular case.

(2) Sanctions for Not Producing a Statement. If a party disobeys a Rule 26.2 order to deliver a statement to the moving party, the magistrate judge must not consider the testimony of a witness whose statement is withheld.

Rule 6. The Grand Jury

(a) Summoning a Grand Jury.

(1) In General. When the public interest so requires, the court must order that one or more grand juries be summoned. A grand jury must have 16 to 23 members, and the court must order that enough legally qualified persons be summoned to meet this requirement.

(2) Alternate Jurors. When a grand jury is selected, the court may also select alternate jurors. Alternate jurors must have the same qualifications and be selected in the same manner as any other juror. Alternate jurors replace jurors in the same sequence in which the alternates were selected. An alternate juror who replaces a juror is subject to the same challenges, takes the same oath, and has the same authority as the other jurors.

(b) Objection to the Grand Jury or to a Grand Juror.

(1) Challenges. Either the government or a defendant may challenge the grand jury on the ground that it was not lawfully drawn, summoned, or selected, and may challenge an individual juror on the ground that the juror is not legally qualified.

(2) Motion to Dismiss an Indictment. A party may move to dismiss the indictment based on an objection to the grand jury or on an individual juror's lack of legal qualification, unless the court has previously ruled on the same objection under Rule 6(b)(1). The motion to dismiss is governed by 28 U.S.C. § 1867(e). The court must not dismiss the indictment on the ground that a grand juror was not legally qualified if the record shows that at least 12 qualified jurors concurred in the indictment.

(c) Foreperson and Deputy Foreperson. The court will appoint one juror as the foreperson and another as the deputy foreperson. In the foreperson's absence, the deputy foreperson will act as the foreperson. The foreperson may administer oaths and affirmations and will sign all indictments. The foreperson—or another juror designated by the foreperson—will record the number of jurors concurring in every indictment and will file the record with the clerk, but the record may not be made public unless the court so orders.

(d) Who May Be Present.

(1) While the Grand Jury Is in Session. The following persons may be present while the grand jury is in session: attorneys for the government, the witness being questioned, interpreters when needed, and a court reporter or an operator of a recording device.

(2) During Deliberations and Voting. No person other than the jurors, and any interpreter needed to assist a hearing-impaired or speech-impaired juror, may be present while the grand jury is deliberating or voting.

(e) Recording and Disclosing the Proceedings.

(1) Recording the Proceedings. Except while the grand jury is deliberating or voting, all proceedings must be recorded by a court reporter or by a suitable recording device. But the validity of a prosecution is not affected by the unintentional failure to make a recording. Unless the court orders otherwise, an attorney for the government will retain control of the recording, the reporter's notes, and any transcript prepared from those notes.

(2) Secrecy.

(A) No obligation of secrecy may be imposed on any person except in accordance with Rule 6(e)(2)(B).

(B) Unless these rules provide otherwise, the following persons must not disclose a matter occurring before the grand jury:

(i) a grand juror;

(ii) an interpreter;

(iii) a court reporter;

(iv) an operator of a recording device;

(v) a person who transcribes recorded testimony;

(vi) an attorney for the government; or

(vii) a person to whom disclosure is made under Rule 6(e)(3)(A)(ii) or (iii).

(3) Exceptions.

(A) Disclosure of a grand-jury matter—other than the grand jury's deliberations or any grand juror's vote—may be made to:

(i) an attorney for the government for use in performing that attorney's duty;

(ii) any government personnel—including those of a state, state subdivision, Indian tribe, or foreign government—that an attorney for the government considers necessary to assist in performing that attorney's duty to enforce federal criminal law; or

(iii) a person authorized by 18 U.S.C. § 3322.

(B) A person to whom information is disclosed under Rule 6(e)(3)(A)(ii) may use that information only to assist an attorney for the government in performing that attorney's duty to enforce federal criminal law. An attorney for the government must promptly provide the court that impaneled the grand jury with the names of all persons to whom a disclosure has been made, and must certify that the attorney has advised those persons of their obligation of secrecy under this rule.

(C) An attorney for the government may disclose any grand-jury matter to another federal grand jury.

(D) An attorney for the government may disclose any grand-jury matter involving foreign intelligence, counterintelligence (as defined in 50 U.S.C. § 3003), or foreign intelligence information (as defined in Rule 16(e)(3)(D)(iii)) to any federal law enforcement, intelligence, protective, immigration, national defense, or national security official to assist the official receiving the information in the performance of that official's duties. An attorney for the government may also disclose any grand jury matter involving, within the United States or elsewhere, a threat of attack or other grave hostile acts of a foreign power or its agent, a threat of domestic or international sabotage or terrorism, or clandestine intelligence gathering activities by an intelligence service or network of a foreign power or by its agent, to any appropriate federal, state, state subdivision, Indian tribal, or foreign government official, for the purpose of preventing or responding to such threat or activities.

(i) Any official who receives information under Rule 6(e)(3)(D) may use the information only as necessary in the conduct of that person's official duties subject to any limitations on the unauthorized disclosure of such information. Any state, state subdivision, Indian tribal, or foreign government official who receives information under Rule 6(e)(3)(D) may use the information only in a manner consistent with any guidelines issued by the Attorney General and the Director of National Intelligence.

(ii) Within a reasonable time after disclosure is made under Rule 6(e)(3)(D), an attorney for the government must file, under seal, a notice with the court in the district where the grand jury convened stating that such information was disclosed and the departments, agencies, or entities to which the disclosure was made.

(iii) As used in Rule 6(e)(3)(D), the term "foreign intelligence information" means:

(a) information, whether or not it concerns a United States person, that relates to the ability of the United States to protect against—

• actual or potential attack or other grave hostile acts of a foreign power or its agent;

• sabotage or international terrorism by a foreign power or its agent; or

• clandestine intelligence activities by an intelligence service or network of a foreign power or by its agent; or

(b) information, whether or not it concerns a United States person, with respect to a foreign power or foreign territory that relates to—

• the national defense or the security of the United States; or

• the conduct of the foreign affairs of the United States.

(E) The court may authorize disclosure—at a time, in a manner, and subject to any other conditions that it directs—of a grand-jury matter:

    (i) preliminarily to or in connection with a judicial proceeding;

    (ii) at the request of a defendant who shows that a ground may exist to dismiss the indictment because of a matter that occurred before the grand jury;

    (iii) at the request of the government, when sought by a foreign court or prosecutor for use in an official criminal investigation;

    (iv) at the request of the government if it shows that the matter may disclose a violation of State, Indian tribal, or foreign criminal law, as long as the disclosure is to an appropriate state, state-subdivision, Indian tribal, or foreign government official for the purpose of enforcing that law; or

    (v) at the request of the government if it shows that the matter may disclose a violation of military criminal law under the Uniform Code of Military Justice, as long as the disclosure is to an appropriate military official for the purpose of enforcing that law.

(F) A petition to disclose a grand-jury matter under Rule 6(e)(3)(E)(i) must be filed in the district where the grand jury convened. Unless the hearing is ex parte—as it may be when the government is the petitioner—the petitioner must serve the petition on, and the court must afford a reasonable opportunity to appear and be heard to:

    (i) an attorney for the government;

    (ii) the parties to the judicial proceeding; and

    (iii) any other person whom the court may designate.

(G) If the petition to disclose arises out of a judicial proceeding in another district, the petitioned court must transfer the petition to the other court unless the petitioned court can reasonably determine whether disclosure is proper. If the petitioned court decides to transfer, it must send to the transferee court the material sought to be disclosed, if feasible, and a written evaluation of the need for continued grand-jury secrecy. The transferee court must afford those persons identified in Rule 6(e)(3)(F) a reasonable opportunity to appear and be heard.

(4) Sealed Indictment. The magistrate judge to whom an indictment is returned may direct that the indictment be kept secret until the defendant is in custody or has been released pending trial. The clerk must then seal the indictment, and no person may disclose the indictment's existence except as necessary to issue or execute a warrant or summons.

(5) Closed Hearing. Subject to any right to an open hearing in a contempt proceeding, the court must close any hearing to the extent necessary to prevent disclosure of a matter occurring before a grand jury.

(6) Sealed Records. Records, orders, and subpoenas relating to grand-jury proceedings must be kept under seal to the extent and as long as necessary to prevent the unauthorized disclosure of a matter occurring before a grand jury.

(7) Contempt. A knowing violation of Rule 6, or of guidelines jointly issued by the Attorney General and the Director of National Intelligence pursuant to Rule 6, may be punished as a contempt of court.

(f) Indictment and Return. A grand jury may indict only if at least 12 jurors concur. The grand jury—or its foreperson or deputy foreperson—must return the indictment to a magistrate judge in open court. To avoid unnecessary cost or delay, the magistrate judge may take the return by video teleconference from the court where the grand jury sits. If a complaint or information is pending against the defendant and 12 jurors do not concur in the indictment, the foreperson must promptly and in writing report the lack of concurrence to the magistrate judge.

(g) Discharging the Grand Jury. A grand jury must serve until the court discharges it, but it may serve more than 18 months only if the court, having determined that an extension is in the public interest, extends the grand jury's service. An extension may be granted for no more than 6 months, except as otherwise provided by statute.

(h) Excusing a Juror. At any time, for good cause, the court may excuse a juror either temporarily or permanently, and if permanently, the court may impanel an alternate juror in place of the excused juror.

(i) "Indian Tribe" Defined. "Indian tribe" means an Indian tribe recognized by the Secretary of the Interior on a list published in the Federal Register under 25 U.S.C. § 479a–1.

Rule 7.   The Indictment and the Information

(a) When Used.

(1) Felony. An offense (other than criminal contempt) must be prosecuted by an indictment if it is punishable:

(A) by death; or

(B) by imprisonment for more than one year.

(2) Misdemeanor. An offense punishable by imprisonment for one year or less may be prosecuted in accordance with Rule 58(b)(1).

(b) Waiving Indictment. An offense punishable by imprisonment for more than one year may be prosecuted by information if the defendant—in open court and after being advised of the nature of the charge and of the defendant's rights—waives prosecution by indictment.

(c) Nature and Contents.

(1) In General. The indictment or information must be a plain, concise, and definite written statement of the essential facts constituting the offense charged and must be signed by an attorney for the government. It need not contain a formal introduction or conclusion. A count may incorporate by reference an allegation made in another count. A count may allege that the means by which the defendant committed the offense are unknown or that the defendant committed it by one or more specified means. For each count, the indictment or information must give the official or customary citation of the statute, rule, regulation, or other provision of law that the defendant is alleged to have violated. For purposes of an indictment referred to in section 3282 of title 18, United States Code, for which the identity of the defendant is unknown, it shall be sufficient for the indictment to describe the defendant as an individual whose name is unknown, but who has a particular DNA profile, as that term is defined in that section 3282.

(2) Citation Error. Unless the defendant was misled and thereby prejudiced, neither an error in a citation nor a citation's omission is a ground to dismiss the indictment or information or to reverse a conviction.

(d) Surplusage. Upon the defendant's motion, the court may strike surplusage from the indictment or information.

(e) Amending an Information. Unless an additional or different offense is charged or a substantial right of the defendant is prejudiced, the court may permit an information to be amended at any time before the verdict or finding.

(f)   **Bill of Particulars.** The court may direct the government to file a bill of particulars. The defendant may move for a bill of particulars before or within 14 days after arraignment or at a later time if the court permits. The government may amend a bill of particulars subject to such conditions as justice requires.

Rule 8.   Joinder of Offenses or Defendants

(a)   **Joinder of Offenses.** The indictment or information may charge a defendant in separate counts with 2 or more offenses if the offenses charged—whether felonies or misdemeanors or both—are of the same or similar character, or are based on the same act or transaction, or are connected with or constitute parts of a common scheme or plan.

(b)   **Joinder of Defendants.** The indictment or information may charge 2 or more defendants if they are alleged to have participated in the same act or transaction, or in the same series of acts or transactions, constituting an offense or offenses. The defendants may be charged in one or more counts together or separately. All defendants need not be charged in each count.

Rule 9.   Arrest Warrant or Summons on an Indictment or Information

(a)   **Issuance.** The court must issue a warrant—or at the government's request, a summons—for each defendant named in an indictment or named in an information if one or more affidavits accompanying the information establish probable cause to believe that an offense has been committed and that the defendant committed it. The court may issue more than one warrant or summons for the same defendant. If a defendant fails to appear in response to a summons, the court may, and upon request of an attorney for the government must, issue a warrant. The court must issue the arrest warrant to an officer authorized to execute it or the summons to a person authorized to serve it.

(b)   **Form.**

    (1)   **Warrant.** The warrant must conform to Rule 4(b)(1) except that it must be signed by the clerk and must describe the offense charged in the indictment or information.

    (2)   **Summons**. The summons must be in the same form as a warrant except that it must require the defendant to appear before the court at a stated time and place.

(c)   **Execution or Service; Return; Initial Appearance.**

    (1)   **Execution or Service.**

        (A)   The warrant must be executed or the summons served as provided in Rule 4(c)(1), (2), and (3).

        (B)   The officer executing the warrant must proceed in accordance with Rule 5(a)(1).

    (2)   **Return.** A warrant or summons must be returned in accordance with Rule 4(c)(4).

    (3)   Initial Appearance. When an arrested or summoned defendant first appears before the court, the judge must proceed under Rule 5.

(d)   **Warrant by Telephone or Other Means.** In accordance with Rule 4.1, a magistrate judge may issue an arrest warrant or summons based on information communicated by telephone or other reliable electronic means.

Rule 10. Arraignment

(a)   **In General.** An arraignment must be conducted in open court and must consist of:

    (1)   ensuring that the defendant has a copy of the indictment or information;

(2) reading the indictment or information to the defendant or stating to the defendant the substance of the charge; and then

(3) asking the defendant to plead to the indictment or information.

(b) Waiving Appearance. A defendant need not be present for the arraignment if:

(1) the defendant has been charged by indictment or misdemeanor information;

(2) the defendant, in a written waiver signed by both the defendant and defense counsel, has waived appearance and has affirmed that the defendant received a copy of the indictment or information and that the plea is not guilty; and

(3) the court accepts the waiver.

(c) Video Teleconferencing. Video teleconferencing may be used to arraign a defendant if the defendant consents.

Rule 11. Pleas

(a) Entering a Plea.

(1) In General. A defendant may plead not guilty, guilty, or (with the court's consent) nolo contendere.

(2) Conditional Plea. With the consent of the court and the government, a defendant may enter a conditional plea of guilty or nolo contendere, reserving in writing the right to have an appellate court review an adverse determination of a specified pretrial motion. A defendant who prevails on appeal may then withdraw the plea.

(3) Nolo Contendere Plea. Before accepting a plea of nolo contendere, the court must consider the parties' views and the public interest in the effective administration of justice.

(4) Failure to Enter a Plea. If a defendant refuses to enter a plea or if a defendant organization fails to appear, the court must enter a plea of not guilty.

(b) Considering and Accepting a Guilty or Nolo Contendere Plea.

(1) Advising and Questioning the Defendant. Before the court accepts a plea of guilty or nolo contendere, the defendant may be placed under oath, and the court must address the defendant personally in open court. During this address, the court must inform the defendant of, and determine that the defendant understands, the following:

(A) the government's right, in a prosecution for perjury or false statement, to use against the defendant any statement that the defendant gives under oath;

(B) the right to plead not guilty, or having already so pleaded, to persist in that plea;

(C) the right to a jury trial;

(D) the right to be represented by counsel—and if necessary have the court appoint counsel—at trial and at every other stage of the proceeding;

(E) the right at trial to confront and cross-examine adverse witnesses, to be protected from compelled self-incrimination, to testify and present evidence, and to compel the attendance of witnesses;

(F) the defendant's waiver of these trial rights if the court accepts a plea of guilty or nolo contendere;

(G) the nature of each charge to which the defendant is pleading;

(H) any maximum possible penalty, including imprisonment, fine, and term of supervised release;

(I) any mandatory minimum penalty;

(J) any applicable forfeiture;

(K) the court's authority to order restitution;

(L) the court's obligation to impose a special assessment;

(M) in determining a sentence, the court's obligation to calculate the applicable sentencing-guideline range and to consider that range, possible departures under the Sentencing Guidelines, and other sentencing factors under 18 U.S.C. § 3553(a);

(N) the terms of any plea-agreement provision waiving the right to appeal or to collaterally attack the sentence; and

(O) that, if convicted, a defendant who is not a United States citizen may be removed from the United States, denied citizenship, and denied admission to the United States in the future.

(2) Ensuring That a Plea Is Voluntary. Before accepting a plea of guilty or nolo contendere, the court must address the defendant personally in open court and determine that the plea is voluntary and did not result from force, threats, or promises (other than promises in a plea agreement).

(3) Determining the Factual Basis for a Plea. Before entering judgment on a guilty plea, the court must determine that there is a factual basis for the plea.

(c) Plea Agreement Procedure.

(1) In General. An attorney for the government and the defendant's attorney, or the defendant when proceeding pro se, may discuss and reach a plea agreement. The court must not participate in these discussions. If the defendant pleads guilty or nolo contendere to either a charged offense or a lesser or related offense, the plea agreement may specify that an attorney for the government will:

(A) not bring, or will move to dismiss, other charges;

(B) recommend, or agree not to oppose the defendant's request, that a particular sentence or sentencing range is appropriate or that a particular provision of the Sentencing Guidelines, or policy statement, or sentencing factor does or does not apply (such a recommendation or request does not bind the court); or

(C) agree that a specific sentence or sentencing range is the appropriate disposition of the case, or that a particular provision of the Sentencing Guidelines, or policy statement, or sentencing factor does or does not apply (such a recommendation or request binds the court once the court accepts the plea agreement).

(2) Disclosing a Plea Agreement. The parties must disclose the plea agreement in open court when the plea is offered, unless the court for good cause allows the parties to disclose the plea agreement in camera.

(3) Judicial Consideration of a Plea Agreement.

(A) To the extent the plea agreement is of the type specified in Rule 11(c)(1)(A) or (C), the court may accept the agreement, reject it, or defer a decision until the court has reviewed the presentence report.

(B) To the extent the plea agreement is of the type specified in Rule 11(c)(1)(B), the court must advise the defendant that the defendant has no right to withdraw the plea if the court does not follow the recommendation or request.

(4) Accepting a Plea Agreement. If the court accepts the plea agreement, it must inform the defendant that to the extent the plea agreement is of the type specified in Rule 11(c)(1)(A) or (C), the agreed disposition will be included in the judgment.

(5) Rejecting a Plea Agreement. If the court rejects a plea agreement containing provisions of the type specified in Rule 11(c)(1)(A) or (C), the court must do the following on the record and in open court (or, for good cause, in camera):

(A) inform the parties that the court rejects the plea agreement;

(B) advise the defendant personally that the court is not required to follow the plea agreement and give the defendant an opportunity to withdraw the plea; and

(C) advise the defendant personally that if the plea is not withdrawn, the court may dispose of the case less favorably toward the defendant than the plea agreement contemplated.

(d) Withdrawing a Guilty or Nolo Contendere Plea. A defendant may withdraw a plea of guilty or nolo contendere:

(1) before the court accepts the plea, for any reason or no reason; or

(2) after the court accepts the plea, but before it imposes sentence if:

(A) the court rejects a plea agreement under Rule 11(c)(5); or

(B) the defendant can show a fair and just reason for requesting the withdrawal.

(e) Finality of a Guilty or Nolo Contendere Plea. After the court imposes sentence, the defendant may not withdraw a plea of guilty or nolo contendere, and the plea may be set aside only on direct appeal or collateral attack.

(f) Admissibility or Inadmissibility of a Plea, Plea Discussions, and Related Statements. The admissibility or inadmissibility of a plea, a plea discussion, and any related statement is governed by Federal Rule of Evidence 410.

(g) Recording the Proceedings. The proceedings during which the defendant enters a plea must be recorded by a court reporter or by a suitable recording device. If there is a guilty plea or a nolo contendere plea, the record must include the inquiries and advice to the defendant required under Rule 11(b) and (c).

(h) Harmless Error. A variance from the requirements of this rule is harmless error if it does not affect substantial rights.

Rule 12. Pleadings and Pretrial Motions

(a) Pleadings. The pleadings in a criminal proceeding are the indictment, the information, and the pleas of not guilty, guilty, and nolo contendere.

(b) Pretrial Motions.

(1) In General. A party may raise by pretrial motion any defense, objection, or request that the court can determine without a trial on the merits. Rule 47 applies to a pretrial motion.

(2) Motions That May Be Made at Any Time. A motion that the court lacks jurisdiction may be made at any time while the case is pending.

(3) Motions That May Be Made Before Trial. The following defenses, objections, and requests must be raised by pretrial motion if the basis for the motion is then reasonably available and the motion can be determined without a trial on the merits:

    (A) a defect in instituting the prosecution, including:

        (i) improper venue;

        (ii) preindictment delay;

        (iii) a violation of the constitutional right to a speedy trial;

        (iv) selective or vindictive prosecution; and

        (v) an error in the grand-jury proceeding or preliminary hearing;

    (B) a defect in the indictment or information, including:

        (i) joining two or more offenses in the same count (duplicity);

        (ii) charging the same offense in more than one count (multiplicity);

        (iii) lack of specificity;

        (iv) improper joinder; and

        (v) failure to state an offense;

    (C) suppression of evidence;

    (D) severance of charges or defendants under Rule 14; and

    (E) discovery under Rule 16.

(4) Notice of the Government's Intent to Use Evidence.

    (A) At the Government's Discretion. At the arraignment or as soon afterward as practicable, the government may notify the defendant of its intent to use specified evidence at trial in order to afford the defendant an opportunity to object before trial under Rule 12(b)(3)(C).

    (B) At the Defendant's Request. At the arraignment or as soon afterward as practicable, the defendant may, in order to have an opportunity to move to suppress evidence under Rule 12(b)(3)(C), request notice of the government's intent to use (in its evidence-in-chief at trial) any evidence that the defendant may be entitled to discover under Rule 16.

(c) Deadline for a Pretrial Motion; Consequences of Not Making a Timely Motion.

    (1) Setting the Deadline. The court may, at the arraignment or as soon afterward as practicable, set a deadline for the parties to make pretrial motions and may also schedule a motion hearing. If the court does not set one, the deadline is the start of trial.

    (2) Extending or Resetting the Deadline. At any time before trial, the court may extend or reset the deadline for pretrial motions.

    (3) Consequences of Not Making a Timely Motion Under Rule 12(b)(3). If a party does not meet the deadline for making a Rule 12(b)(3) motion, the motion is untimely. But a court may consider the defense, objection, or request if the party shows good cause.

(d) Ruling on a Motion. The court must decide every pretrial motion before trial unless it finds good cause to defer a ruling. The court must not defer ruling on a pretrial motion if the deferral will adversely affect a party's right to appeal. When factual issues are involved in deciding a motion, the court must state its essential findings on the record.

(e) **[Reserved]**

(f) **Recording the Proceedings.** All proceedings at a motion hearing, including any findings of fact and conclusions of law made orally by the court, must be recorded by a court reporter or a suitable recording device.

(g) **Defendant's Continued Custody or Release Status.** If the court grants a motion to dismiss based on a defect in instituting the prosecution, in the indictment, or in the information, it may order the defendant to be released or detained under 18 U.S.C. § 3142 for a specified time until a new indictment or information is filed. This rule does not affect any federal statutory period of limitations.

(h) **Producing Statements at a Suppression Hearing.** Rule 26.2 applies at a suppression hearing under Rule 12(b)(3)(C). At a suppression hearing, a law enforcement officer is considered a government witness.

Rule 12.1. Notice of an Alibi Defense

(a) **Government's Request for Notice and Defendant's Response.**

(1) **Government's Request.** An attorney for the government may request in writing that the defendant notify an attorney for the government of any intended alibi defense. The request must state the time, date, and place of the alleged offense.

(2) **Defendant's Response.** Within 14 days after the request, or at some other time the court sets, the defendant must serve written notice on an attorney for the government of any intended alibi defense. The defendant's notice must state:

(A) each specific place where the defendant claims to have been at the time of the alleged offense; and

(B) the name, address, and telephone number of each alibi witness on whom the defendant intends to rely.

(b) **Disclosing Government Witnesses.**

(1) **Disclosure.**

(A) **In General.** If the defendant serves a Rule 12.1(a)(2) notice, an attorney for the government must disclose in writing to the defendant or the defendant's attorney:

(i) the name of each witness—and the address and telephone number of each witness other than a victim—that the government intends to rely on to establish that the defendant was present at the scene of the alleged offense; and

(ii) each government rebuttal witness to the defendant's alibi defense.

(B) **Victim's Address and Telephone Number.** If the government intends to rely on a victim's testimony to establish that the defendant was present at the scene of the alleged offense and the defendant establishes a need for the victim's address and telephone number, the court may:

(i) order the government to provide the information in writing to the defendant or the defendant's attorney; or

(ii) fashion a reasonable procedure that allows preparation of the defense and also protects the victim's interests.

(2) **Time to Disclose.** Unless the court directs otherwise, an attorney for the government must give its Rule 12.1(b)(1) disclosure within 14 days after the defendant serves notice of an intended alibi defense under Rule 12.1(a)(2), but no later than 14 days before trial.

(c) Continuing Duty to Disclose.

(1) In General. Both an attorney for the government and the defendant must promptly disclose in writing to the other party the name of each additional witness—and the address and telephone number of each additional witness other than a victim—if:

(A) the disclosing party learns of the witness before or during trial; and

(B) the witness should have been disclosed under Rule 12.1(a) or (b) if the disclosing party had known of the witness earlier.

(2) Address and Telephone Number of an Additional Victim Witness. The address and telephone number of an additional victim witness must not be disclosed except as provided in Rule 12.1 (b)(1)(B).

(d) Exceptions. For good cause, the court may grant an exception to any requirement of Rule 12.1(a)–(c).

(e) Failure to Comply. If a party fails to comply with this rule, the court may exclude the testimony of any undisclosed witness regarding the defendant's alibi. This rule does not limit the defendant's right to testify.

(f) Inadmissibility of Withdrawn Intention. Evidence of an intention to rely on an alibi defense, later withdrawn, or of a statement made in connection with that intention, is not, in any civil or criminal proceeding, admissible against the person who gave notice of the intention.

Rule 12.2. Notice of an Insanity Defense; Mental Examination

(a) Notice of an Insanity Defense. A defendant who intends to assert a defense of insanity at the time of the alleged offense must so notify an attorney for the government in writing within the time provided for filing a pretrial motion, or at any later time the court sets, and file a copy of the notice with the clerk. A defendant who fails to do so cannot rely on an insanity defense. The court may, for good cause, allow the defendant to file the notice late, grant additional trial-preparation time, or make other appropriate orders.

(b) Notice of Expert Evidence of a Mental Condition. If a defendant intends to introduce expert evidence relating to a mental disease or defect or any other mental condition of the defendant bearing on either (1) the issue of guilt or (2) the issue of punishment in a capital case, the defendant must—within the time provided for filing a pretrial motion or at any later time the court sets—notify an attorney for the government in writing of this intention and file a copy of the notice with the clerk. The court may, for good cause, allow the defendant to file the notice late, grant the parties additional trial-preparation time, or make other appropriate orders.

(c) Mental Examination.

(1) Authority to Order an Examination; Procedures.

(A) The court may order the defendant to submit to a competency examination under 18 U.S.C. § 4241.

(B) If the defendant provides notice under Rule 12.2(a), the court must, upon the government's motion, order the defendant to be examined under 18 U.S.C. § 4242. If the defendant provides notice under Rule 12.2(b) the court may, upon the government's motion, order the defendant to be examined under procedures ordered by the court.

(2) Disclosing Results and Reports of Capital Sentencing Examination. The results and reports of any examination conducted solely under Rule 12.2(c)(1) after notice under Rule 12.2(b)(2) must be sealed and must not be disclosed to any attorney for the government or the defendant unless the defendant is found guilty of one or more capital crimes and the defendant confirms an intent to offer during sentencing proceedings expert evidence on mental condition.

(3) Disclosing Results and Reports of the Defendant's Expert Examination. After disclosure under Rule 12.2(c)(2) of the results and reports of the government's examination, the defendant must disclose to the government the results and reports of any examination on mental condition conducted by the defendant's expert about which the defendant intends to introduce expert evidence.

(4) Inadmissibility of a Defendant's Statements. No statement made by a defendant in the course of any examination conducted under this rule (whether conducted with or without the defendant's consent), no testimony by the expert based on the statement, and no other fruits of the statement may be admitted into evidence against the defendant in any criminal proceeding except on an issue regarding mental condition on which the defendant:

(A) has introduced evidence of incompetency or evidence requiring notice under Rule 12.2(a) or (b)(1), or

(B) has introduced expert evidence in a capital sentencing proceeding requiring notice under Rule 12.2(b)(2).

(d) Failure to Comply.

(1) Failure to Give Notice or to Submit to Examination. The court may exclude any expert evidence from the defendant on the issue of the defendant's mental disease, mental defect, or any other mental condition bearing on the defendant's guilt or the issue of punishment in a capital case if the defendant fails to:

(A) give notice under Rule 12.2(b); or

(B) submit to an examination when ordered under Rule 12.2(c).

(2) Failure to Disclose. The court may exclude any expert evidence for which the defendant has failed to comply with the disclosure requirement of Rule 12.2(c)(3).

(e) Inadmissibility of Withdrawn Intention. Evidence of an intention as to which notice was given under Rule 12.2(a) or (b), later withdrawn, is not, in any civil or criminal proceeding, admissible against the person who gave notice of the intention.

Rule 12.3. Notice of a Public-Authority Defense

(a) Notice of the Defense and Disclosure of Witnesses.

(1) Notice in General. If a defendant intends to assert a defense of actual or believed exercise of public authority on behalf of a law enforcement agency or federal intelligence agency at the time of the alleged offense, the defendant must so notify an attorney for the government in writing and must file a copy of the notice with the clerk within the time provided for filing a pretrial motion, or at any later time the court sets. The notice filed with the clerk must be under seal if the notice identifies a federal intelligence agency as the source of public authority.

(2) Contents of Notice. The notice must contain the following information:

(A) the law enforcement agency or federal intelligence agency involved;

(B) the agency member on whose behalf the defendant claims to have acted; and

(C) the time during which the defendant claims to have acted with public authority.

(3) Response to the Notice. An attorney for the government must serve a written response on the defendant or the defendant's attorney within 14 days after receiving the defendant's notice, but no later than 21 days before trial. The response must admit or deny that the defendant exercised the public authority identified in the defendant's notice.

(4) Disclosing Witnesses.

(A) Government's Request. An attorney for the government may request in writing that the defendant disclose the name, address, and telephone number of each witness the defendant intends to rely on to establish a public-authority defense. An attorney for the government may serve the request when the government serves its response to the defendant's notice under Rule 12.3(a)(3), or later, but must serve the request no later than 21 days before trial.

(B) Defendant's Response. Within 14 days after receiving the government's request, the defendant must serve on an attorney for the government a written statement of the name, address, and telephone number of each witness.

(C) Government's Reply. Within 14 days after receiving the defendant's statement, an attorney for the government must serve on the defendant or the defendant's attorney a written statement of the name of each witness—and the address and telephone number of each witness other than a victim—that the government intends to rely on to oppose the defendant's public-authority defense.

(D) Victim's Address and Telephone Number. If the government intends to rely on a victim's testimony to oppose the defendant's public-authority defense and the defendant establishes a need for the victim's address and telephone number, the court may:

(i) order the government to provide the information in writing to the defendant or the defendant's attorney; or

(ii) fashion a reasonable procedure that allows for preparing the defense and also protects the victim's interests.

(5) Additional Time. The court may, for good cause, allow a party additional time to comply with this rule.

(b) Continuing Duty to Disclose.

(1) In General. Both an attorney for the government and the defendant must promptly disclose in writing to the other party the name of any additional witness—and the address, and telephone number of any additional witness other than a victim—if:

(A) the disclosing party learns of the witness before or during trial; and

(B) the witness should have been disclosed under Rule 12.3(a)(4) if the disclosing party had known of the witness earlier.

(2) Address and Telephone Number of an Additional Victim-Witness. The address and telephone number of an additional victim-witness must not be disclosed except as provided in Rule 12.3(a)(4)(D).

(c) Failure to Comply. If a party fails to comply with this rule, the court may exclude the testimony of any undisclosed witness regarding the public-authority defense. This rule does not limit the defendant's right to testify.

(d) Protective Procedures Unaffected. This rule does not limit the court's authority to issue appropriate protective orders or to order that any filings be under seal.

(e) Inadmissibility of Withdrawn Intention. Evidence of an intention as to which notice was given under Rule 12.3(a), later withdrawn, is not, in any civil or criminal proceeding, admissible against the person who gave notice of the intention.

Rule 12.4. Disclosure Statement

(a) Who Must File.

(1) Nongovernmental Corporate Party. Any nongovernmental corporate party to a proceeding in a district court must file a statement that identifies any parent corporation and any publicly held corporation that owns 10% or more of its stock or states that there is no such corporation.

(2) Organizational Victim. If an organization is a victim of the alleged criminal activity, the government must file a statement identifying the victim. If the organizational victim is a corporation, the statement must also disclose the information required by Rule 12.4(a)(1) to the extent it can be obtained through due diligence.

(b) Time for Filing; Supplemental Filing. A party must:

(1) file the Rule 12.4(a) statement upon the defendant's initial appearance; and

(2) promptly file a supplemental statement upon any change in the information that the statement requires.

Rule 13. Joint Trial of Separate Cases

The court may order that separate cases be tried together as though brought in a single indictment or information if all offenses and all defendants could have been joined in a single indictment or information.

Rule 14. Relief from Prejudicial Joinder

(a) Relief. If the joinder of offenses or defendants in an indictment, an information, or a consolidation for trial appears to prejudice a defendant or the government, the court may order separate trials of counts, sever the defendants' trials, or provide any other relief that justice requires.

(b) Defendant's Statements. Before ruling on a defendant's motion to sever, the court may order an attorney for the government to deliver to the court for in camera inspection any defendant's statement that the government intends to use as evidence.

Rule 15. Depositions

(a) When Taken.

(1) In General. A party may move that a prospective witness be deposed in order to preserve testimony for trial. The court may grant the motion because of exceptional circumstances and in the interest of justice. If the court orders the deposition to be taken, it may also require the deponent to produce at the deposition any designated material that is not privileged, including any book, paper, document, record, recording, or data.

(2) Detained Material Witness. A witness who is detained under 18 U.S.C. § 3144 may request to be deposed by filing a written motion and giving notice to the parties. The court may then order that the deposition be taken and may discharge the witness after the witness has signed under oath the deposition transcript.

(b) Notice.

(1) In General. A party seeking to take a deposition must give every other party reasonable written notice of the deposition's date and location. The notice must state the name and address of each deponent. If requested by a party receiving the notice, the court may, for good cause, change the deposition's date or location.

(2) To the Custodial Officer. A party seeking to take the deposition must also notify the officer who has custody of the defendant of the scheduled date and location.

(c) Defendant's Presence.

(1) Defendant in Custody. Except as authorized by Rule 15(c)(3), the officer who has custody of the defendant must produce the defendant at the deposition and keep the defendant in the witness's presence during the examination, unless the defendant:

> **(A)** waives in writing the right to be present; or

> **(B)** persists in disruptive conduct justifying exclusion after being warned by the court that disruptive conduct will result in the defendant's exclusion.

(2) Defendant Not in Custody. Except as authorized by Rule 15(c)(3), a defendant who is not in custody has the right upon request to be present at the deposition, subject to any conditions imposed by the court. If the government tenders the defendant's expenses as provided in Rule 15(d) but the defendant still fails to appear, the defendant—absent good cause—waives both the right to appear and any objection to the taking and use of the deposition based on that right.

(3) Taking Depositions Outside the United States Without the Defendant's Presence. The deposition of a witness who is outside the United States may be taken without the defendant's presence if the court makes case-specific findings of all the following:

> **(A)** the witness's testimony could provide substantial proof of a material fact in a felony prosecution;

> **(B)** there is a substantial likelihood that the witness's attendance at trial cannot be obtained;

> **(C)** the witness's presence for a deposition in the United States cannot be obtained;

> **(D)** the defendant cannot be present because:

>> **(i)** the country where the witness is located will not permit the defendant to attend the deposition;

>> **(ii)** for an in-custody defendant, secure transportation and continuing custody cannot be assured at the witness's location; or

>> **(iii)** for an out-of-custody defendant, no reasonable conditions will assure an appearance at the deposition or at trial or sentencing; and

> **(E)** the defendant can meaningfully participate in the deposition through reasonable means.

(d) Expenses. If the deposition was requested by the government, the court may—or if the defendant is unable to bear the deposition expenses, the court must—order the government to pay:

(1) any reasonable travel and subsistence expenses of the defendant and the defendant's attorney to attend the deposition; and

(2) the costs of the deposition transcript.

(e) Manner of Taking. Unless these rules or a court order provides otherwise, a deposition must be taken and filed in the same manner as a deposition in a civil action, except that:

(1) A defendant may not be deposed without that defendant's consent.

(2) The scope and manner of the deposition examination and cross-examination must be the same as would be allowed during trial.

(3) The government must provide to the defendant or the defendant's attorney, for use at the deposition, any statement of the deponent in the government's possession to which the defendant would be entitled at trial.

(f) Admissibility and Use as Evidence. An order authorizing a deposition to be taken under this rule does not determine its admissibility. A party may use all or part of a deposition as provided by the Federal Rules of Evidence.

(g) Objections. A party objecting to deposition testimony or evidence must state the grounds for the objection during the deposition.

(h) Depositions by Agreement Permitted. The parties may by agreement take and use a deposition with the court's consent.

Rule 16. Discovery and Inspection

(a) Government's Disclosure.

(1) Information Subject to Disclosure.

(A) Defendant's Oral Statement. Upon a defendant's request, the government must disclose to the defendant the substance of any relevant oral statement made by the defendant, before or after arrest, in response to interrogation by a person the defendant knew was a government agent if the government intends to use the statement at trial.

(B) Defendant's Written or Recorded Statement. Upon a defendant's request, the government must disclose to the defendant, and make available for inspection, copying, or photographing, all of the following:

(i) any relevant written or recorded statement by the defendant if:

• the statement is within the government's possession, custody, or control; and

• the attorney for the government knows—or through due diligence could know—that the statement exists;

(ii) the portion of any written record containing the substance of any relevant oral statement made before or after arrest if the defendant made the statement in response to interrogation by a person the defendant knew was a government agent; and

(iii) the defendant's recorded testimony before a grand jury relating to the charged offense.

(C) Organizational Defendant. Upon a defendant's request, if the defendant is an organization, the government must disclose to the defendant any statement described in Rule 16(a)(1)(A) and (B) if the government contends that the person making the statement:

(i) was legally able to bind the defendant regarding the subject of the statement because of that person's position as the defendant's director, officer, employee, or agent; or

(ii) was personally involved in the alleged conduct constituting the offense and was legally able to bind the defendant regarding that conduct because of that person's position as the defendant's director, officer, employee, or agent.

(D) Defendant's Prior Record. Upon a defendant's request, the government must furnish the defendant with a copy of the defendant's prior criminal record that is within the government's possession, custody, or control if the attorney for the government knows—or through due diligence could know—that the record exists.

(E) Documents and Objects. Upon a defendant's request, the government must permit the defendant to inspect and to copy or photograph books, papers, documents, data, photographs, tangible objects, buildings or places, or copies or portions of any of these items, if the item is within the government's possession, custody, or control and:

(i) the item is material to preparing the defense;

(ii) the government intends to use the item in its case-in-chief at trial; or

(iii) the item was obtained from or belongs to the defendant.

(F) Reports of Examinations and Tests. Upon a defendant's request, the government must permit a defendant to inspect and to copy or photograph the results or reports of any physical or mental examination and of any scientific test or experiment if:

(i) the item is within the government's possession, custody, or control;

(ii) the attorney for the government knows—or through due diligence could know—that the item exists; and

(iii) the item is material to preparing the defense or the government intends to use the item in its case-in-chief at trial.

(G) Expert witnesses. At the defendant's request, the government must give to the defendant a written summary of any testimony that the government intends to use under Rules 702, 703, or 705 of the Federal Rules of Evidence during its case-in-chief at trial. If the government requests discovery under subdivision (b)(1)(C)(ii) and the defendant complies, the government must, at the defendant's request, give to the defendant a written summary of testimony that the government intends to use under Rules 702, 703, or 705 of the Federal Rules of Evidence as evidence at trial on the issue of the defendant's mental condition. The summary provided under this subparagraph must describe the witness's opinions, the bases and reasons for those opinions, and the witness's qualifications.

(2) Information Not Subject to Disclosure. Except as permitted by Rule 16(a)(1)(A)–(D), (F), and (G), this rule does not authorize the discovery or inspection of reports, memoranda, or other internal government documents made by an attorney for the government or other government agent in connection with investigating or prosecuting the case. Nor does this rule authorize the discovery or inspection of statements made by prospective government witnesses except as provided in 18 U.S.C. 3 § 3500.*

(3) Grand Jury Transcripts. This rule does not apply to the discovery or inspection of a grand jury's recorded proceedings, except as provided in Rules 6, 12(h), 16(a)(1), and 26.2.

(b) Defendant's Disclosure.

(1) Information Subject to Disclosure.

(A) Documents and Objects. If a defendant requests disclosure under Rule 16(a)(1)(E) and the government complies, then the defendant must permit the government, upon request, to inspect and to copy or photograph books, papers, documents, data, photographs, tangible objects, buildings or places, or copies or portions of any of these items if:

(i) the item is within the defendant's possession, custody, or control; and

(ii) the defendant intends to use the item in the defendant's case-in-chief at trial.

(B) Reports of Examinations and Tests. If a defendant requests disclosure under Rule 16(a)(1)(F) and the government complies, the defendant must permit the government, upon request, to inspect and to copy or photograph the results or reports of any physical or mental examination and of any scientific test or experiment if:

(i) the item is within the defendant's possession, custody, or control; and

(ii) the defendant intends to use the item in the defendant's case-in-chief at trial, or intends to call the witness who prepared the report and the report relates to the witness's testimony.

(C) Expert witnesses. The defendant must, at the government's request, give to the government a written summary of any testimony that the defendant intends to use under Rules 702, 703, or 705 of the Federal Rules of Evidence as evidence at trial, if—

(i) the defendant requests disclosure under subdivision (a)(1)(G) and the government complies; or

(ii) the defendant has given notice under Rule 12.2(b) of an intent to present expert testimony on the defendant's mental condition.

This summary must describe the witness's opinions, the bases and reasons for those opinions, and the witness's qualifications.

(2) Information Not Subject to Disclosure. Except for scientific or medical reports, Rule 16(b)(1) does not authorize discovery or inspection of:

(A) reports, memoranda, or other documents made by the defendant, or the defendant's attorney or agent, during the case's investigation or defense; or

(B) a statement made to the defendant, or the defendant's attorney or agent, by:

(i) the defendant;

(ii) a government or defense witness; or

(iii) a prospective government or defense witness.

---

*   This provision is set out in Appendix B.

(c) Continuing Duty to Disclose. A party who discovers additional evidence or material before or during trial must promptly disclose its existence to the other party or the court if:

>   **(1)** the evidence or material is subject to discovery or inspection under this rule; and

>   **(2)** the other party previously requested, or the court ordered, its production.

(d) Regulating Discovery.

>   **(1) Protective and Modifying Orders.** At any time the court may, for good cause, deny, restrict, or defer discovery or inspection, or grant other appropriate relief. The court may permit a party to show good cause by a written statement that the court will inspect ex parte. If relief is granted, the court must preserve the entire text of the party's statement under seal.

>   **(2) Failure to Comply.** If a party fails to comply with this rule, the court may:

>>   **(A)** order that party to permit the discovery or inspection; specify its time, place, and manner; and prescribe other just terms and conditions;

>>   **(B)** grant a continuance;

>>   **(C)** prohibit that party from introducing the undisclosed evidence; or

>>   **(D)** enter any other order that is just under the circumstances.

Rule 17. Subpoena

(a) Content. A subpoena must state the court's name and the title of the proceeding, include the seal of the court, and command the witness to attend and testify at the time and place the subpoena specifies. The clerk must issue a blank subpoena—signed and sealed—to the party requesting it, and that party must fill in the blanks before the subpoena is served.

(b) Defendant Unable to Pay. Upon a defendant's ex parte application, the court must order that a subpoena be issued for a named witness if the defendant shows an inability to pay the witness's fees and the necessity of the witness's presence for an adequate defense. If the court orders a subpoena to be issued, the process costs and witness fees will be paid in the same manner as those paid for witnesses the government subpoenas.

(c) Producing Documents and Objects.

>   **(1) In General.** A subpoena may order the witness to produce any books, papers, documents, data, or other objects the subpoena designates. The court may direct the witness to produce the designated items in court before trial or before they are to be offered in evidence. When the items arrive, the court may permit the parties and their attorneys to inspect all or part of them.

>   **(2) Quashing or Modifying the Subpoena.** On motion made promptly, the court may quash or modify the subpoena if compliance would be unreasonable or oppressive.

>   **(3) Subpoena for Personal or Confidential Information About a Victim.** After a complaint, indictment, or information is filed, a subpoena requiring the production of personal or confidential information about a victim may be served on a third party only by court order. Before entering the order and unless there are exceptional circumstances, the court must require giving notice to the victim so that the victim can move to quash or modify the subpoena or otherwise object.

(d) Service. A marshal, a deputy marshal, or any nonparty who is at least 18 years old may serve a subpoena. The server must deliver a copy of the subpoena to the witness and must tender to the witness one day's witness-attendance fee and the legal mileage allowance. The server need not tender the attendance fee or mileage allowance when the United States, a federal officer, or a federal agency has requested the subpoena.

(e) Place of Service.

(1) In the United States. A subpoena requiring a witness to attend a hearing or trial may be served at any place within the United States.

(2) In a Foreign Country. If the witness is in a foreign country, 28 U.S.C. § 1783 governs the subpoena's service.

(f) Issuing a Deposition Subpoena.

(1) Issuance. A court order to take a deposition authorizes the clerk in the district where the deposition is to be taken to issue a subpoena for any witness named or described in the order.

(2) Place. After considering the convenience of the witness and the parties, the court may order—and the subpoena may require—the witness to appear anywhere the court designates.

(g) Contempt. The court (other than a magistrate judge) may hold in contempt a witness who, without adequate excuse, disobeys a subpoena issued by a federal court in that district. A magistrate judge may hold in contempt a witness who, without adequate excuse, disobeys a subpoena issued by that magistrate judge as provided in 28 U.S.C. § 636(e).

(h) Information Not Subject to a Subpoena. No party may subpoena a statement of a witness or of a prospective witness under this rule. Rule 26.2 governs the production of the statement.

Rule 17.1. Pretrial Conference

On its own, or on a party's motion, the court may hold one or more pretrial conferences to promote a fair and expeditious trial. When a conference ends, the court must prepare and file a memorandum of any matters agreed to during the conference. The government may not use any statement made during the conference by the defendant or the defendant's attorney unless it is in writing and is signed by the defendant and the defendant's attorney.

Rule 18. Place of Prosecution and Trial

Unless a statute or these rules permit otherwise, the government must prosecute an offense in a district where the offense was committed. The court must set the place of trial within the district with due regard for the convenience of the defendant, any victim, and the witnesses, and the prompt administration of justice.

Rule 19. [Reserved]

Rule 20. Transfer for Plea and Sentence

(a) Consent to Transfer. A prosecution may be transferred from the district where the indictment or information is pending, or from which a warrant on a complaint has been issued, to the district where the defendant is arrested, held, or present if:

(1) the defendant states in writing a wish to plead guilty or nolo contendere and to waive trial in the district where the indictment, information, or complaint is pending, consents in writing to the court's disposing of the case in the transferee district, and files the statement in the transferee district; and

(2) the United States attorneys in both districts approve the transfer in writing.

(b) Clerk's Duties. After receiving the defendant's statement and the required approvals, the clerk where the indictment, information, or complaint is pending must send the file, or a certified copy, to the clerk in the transferee district.

(c) Effect of a Not Guilty Plea. If the defendant pleads not guilty after the case has been transferred under Rule 20(a), the clerk must return the papers to the court where the prosecution began, and that court must restore the proceeding to its docket. The defendant's statement that the defendant wished to plead guilty or nolo contendere is not, in any civil or criminal proceeding, admissible against the defendant.

(d) Juveniles.

    (1) Consent to Transfer. A juvenile, as defined in 18 U.S.C. § 5031, may be proceeded against as a juvenile delinquent in the district where the juvenile is arrested, held, or present if:

        (A) the alleged offense that occurred in the other district is not punishable by death or life imprisonment;

        (B) an attorney has advised the juvenile;

        (C) the court has informed the juvenile of the juvenile's rights—including the right to be returned to the district where the offense allegedly occurred—and the consequences of waiving those rights;

        (D) the juvenile, after receiving the court's information about rights, consents in writing to be proceeded against in the transferee district, and files the consent in the transferee district;

        (E) the United States attorneys for both districts approve the transfer in writing; and

        (F) the transferee court approves the transfer.

    (2) Clerk's Duties. After receiving the juvenile's written consent and the required approvals, the clerk where the indictment, information, or complaint is pending or where the alleged offense occurred must send the file, or a certified copy, to the clerk in the transferee district.

Rule 21. Transfer for Trial

(a) For Prejudice. Upon the defendant's motion, the court must transfer the proceeding against that defendant to another district if the court is satisfied that so great a prejudice against the defendant exists in the transferring district that the defendant cannot obtain a fair and impartial trial there.

(b) For Convenience. Upon the defendant's motion, the court may transfer the proceeding, or one or more counts, against that defendant to another district for the convenience of the parties, any victim, and the witnesses, and in the interest of justice.

(c) Proceedings on Transfer. When the court orders a transfer, the clerk must send to the transferee district the file, or a certified copy, and any bail taken. The prosecution will then continue in the transferee district.

(d) Time to File a Motion to Transfer. A motion to transfer may be made at or before arraignment or at any other time the court or these rules prescribe.

Rule 22. [Transferred]

Rule 23. Jury or Nonjury Trial

(a) Jury Trial. If the defendant is entitled to a jury trial, the trial must be by jury unless:

> **(1)**   the defendant waives a jury trial in writing;

> **(2)**   the government consents; and

> **(3)**   the court approves.

(b) Jury Size.

> **(1) In General.** A jury consists of 12 persons unless this rule provides otherwise.

> **(2) Stipulation for a Smaller Jury.** At any time before the verdict, the parties may, with the court's approval, stipulate in writing that:

>> **(A)**   the jury may consist of fewer than 12 persons; or

>> **(B)**   a jury of fewer than 12 persons may return a verdict if the court finds it necessary to excuse a juror for good cause after the trial begins.

> **(3) Court Order for a Jury of 11.** After the jury has retired to deliberate, the court may permit a jury of 11 persons to return a verdict, even without a stipulation by the parties, if the court finds good cause to excuse a juror.

(c) Nonjury Trial. In a case tried without a jury, the court must find the defendant guilty or not guilty. If a party requests before the finding of guilty or not guilty, the court must state its specific findings of fact in open court or in a written decision or opinion.

Rule 24. Trial Jurors

(a) Examination.

> **(1) In General.** The court may examine prospective jurors or may permit the attorneys for the parties to do so.

> **(2) Court Examination.** If the court examines the jurors, it must permit the attorneys for the parties to:

>> **(A)**   ask further questions that the court considers proper; or

>> **(B)**   submit further questions that the court may ask if it considers them proper.

(b) Peremptory Challenges. Each side is entitled to the number of peremptory challenges to prospective jurors specified below. The court may allow additional peremptory challenges to multiple defendants, and may allow the defendants to exercise those challenges separately or jointly.

> **(1) Capital Case.** Each side has 20 peremptory challenges when the government seeks the death penalty.

> **(2) Other Felony Case.** The government has 6 peremptory challenges and the defendant or defendants jointly have 10 peremptory challenges when the defendant is charged with a crime punishable by imprisonment of more than one year.

> **(3) Misdemeanor Case.** Each side has 3 peremptory challenges when the defendant is charged with a crime punishable by fine, imprisonment of one year or less, or both.

(c) Alternate Jurors.

> **(1) In General.** The court may impanel up to 6 alternate jurors to replace any jurors who are unable to perform or who are disqualified from performing their duties.

(2) Procedure.

(A) Alternate jurors must have the same qualifications and be selected and sworn in the same manner as any other juror.

(B) Alternate jurors replace jurors in the same sequence in which the alternates were selected. An alternate juror who replaces a juror has the same authority as the other jurors.

(3) Retaining Alternate Jurors. The court may retain alternate jurors after the jury retires to deliberate. The court must ensure that a retained alternate does not discuss the case with anyone until that alternate replaces a juror or is discharged. If an alternate replaces a juror after deliberations have begun, the court must instruct the jury to begin its deliberations anew.

(4) Peremptory Challenges. Each side is entitled to the number of additional peremptory challenges to prospective alternate jurors specified below. These additional challenges may be used only to remove alternate jurors.

(A) One or Two Alternates. One additional peremptory challenge is permitted when one or two alternates are impaneled.

(B) Three or Four Alternates. Two additional peremptory challenges are permitted when three or four alternates are impaneled.

(C) Five or Six Alternates. Three additional peremptory challenges are permitted when five or six alternates are impaneled.

Rule 25. Judge's Disability

(a) During Trial. Any judge regularly sitting in or assigned to the court may complete a jury trial if:

(1) the judge before whom the trial began cannot proceed because of death, sickness, or other disability; and

(2) the judge completing the trial certifies familiarity with the trial record.

(b) After a Verdict or Finding of Guilty.

(1) In General. After a verdict or finding of guilty, any judge regularly sitting in or assigned to a court may complete the court's duties if the judge who presided at trial cannot perform those duties because of absence, death, sickness, or other disability.

(2) Granting a New Trial. The successor judge may grant a new trial if satisfied that:

(A) a judge other than the one who presided at the trial cannot perform the post-trial duties; or

(B) a new trial is necessary for some other reason.

Rule 26. Taking Testimony

In every trial the testimony of witnesses must be taken in open court, unless otherwise provided by a statute or by rules adopted under 28 U.S.C. §§ 2072–2077.

Rule 26.1. Foreign Law Determination

A party intending to raise an issue of foreign law must provide the court and all parties with reasonable written notice. Issues of foreign law are questions of law, but in deciding such issues a court may consider any relevant material or source—including testimony—without regard to the Federal Rules of Evidence.

Rule 26.2. Producing a Witness's Statement

(a) Motion to Produce. After a witness other than the defendant has testified on direct examination, the court, on motion of a party who did not call the witness, must order an attorney for the government or the defendant and the defendant's attorney to produce, for the examination and use of the moving party, any statement of the witness that is in their possession and that relates to the subject matter of the witness's testimony.

(b) Producing the Entire Statement. If the entire statement relates to the subject matter of the witness's testimony, the court must order that the statement be delivered to the moving party.

(c) Producing a Redacted Statement. If the party who called the witness claims that the statement contains information that is privileged or does not relate to the subject matter of the witness's testimony, the court must inspect the statement in camera. After excising any privileged or unrelated portions, the court must order delivery of the redacted statement to the moving party. If the defendant objects to an excision, the court must preserve the entire statement with the excised portion indicated, under seal, as part of the record.

(d) Recess to Examine a Statement. The court may recess the proceedings to allow time for a party to examine the statement and prepare for its use.

(e) Sanction for Failure to Produce or Deliver a Statement. If the party who called the witness disobeys an order to produce or deliver a statement, the court must strike the witness's testimony from the record. If an attorney for the government disobeys the order, the court must declare a mistrial if justice so requires.

(f) "Statement" Defined. As used in this rule, a witness's "statement" means:

(1) a written statement that the witness makes and signs, or otherwise adopts or approves;

(2) a substantially verbatim, contemporaneously recorded recital of the witness's oral statement that is contained in any recording or any transcription of a recording; or

(3) the witness's statement to a grand jury, however taken or recorded, or a transcription of such a statement.

(g) Scope. This rule applies at trial, at a suppression hearing under Rule 12, and to the extent specified in the following rules:

(1) Rule 5.1(h) (preliminary hearing);

(2) Rule 32(i)(2) (sentencing);

(3) Rule 32.1(e) (hearing to revoke or modify probation or supervised release);

(4) Rule 46(j) (detention hearing); and

(5) Rule 8 of the Rules Governing Proceedings under 28 U.S.C. § 2255.

Rule 26.3. Mistrial

Before ordering a mistrial, the court must give each defendant and the government an opportunity to comment on the propriety of the order, to state whether that party consents or objects, and to suggest alternatives.

Rule 27. Proving an Official Record

A party may prove an official record, an entry in such a record, or the lack of a record or entry in the same manner as in a civil action.

Rule 28. Interpreters

The court may select, appoint, and set the reasonable compensation for an interpreter. The compensation must be paid from funds provided by law or by the government, as the court may direct.

Rule 29. Motion for a Judgment of Acquittal

(a) Before Submission to the Jury. After the government closes its evidence or after the close of all the evidence, the court on the defendant's motion must enter a judgment of acquittal of any offense for which the evidence is insufficient to sustain a conviction. The court may on its own consider whether the evidence is insufficient to sustain a conviction. If the court denies a motion for a judgment of acquittal at the close of the government's evidence, the defendant may offer evidence without having reserved the right to do so.

(b) Reserving Decision. The court may reserve decision on the motion, proceed with the trial (where the motion is made before the close of all the evidence), submit the case to the jury, and decide the motion either before the jury returns a verdict or after it returns a verdict of guilty or is discharged without having returned a verdict. If the court reserves decision, it must decide the motion on the basis of the evidence at the time the ruling was reserved.

(c) After Jury Verdict or Discharge.

    (1) Time for a Motion. A defendant may move for a judgment of acquittal, or renew such a motion, within 14 days after a guilty verdict or after the court discharges the jury, whichever is later.

    (2) Ruling on the Motion. If the jury has returned a guilty verdict, the court may set aside the verdict and enter an acquittal. If the jury has failed to return a verdict, the court may enter a judgment of acquittal.

    (3) No Prior Motion Required. A defendant is not required to move for a judgment of acquittal before the court submits the case to the jury as a prerequisite for making such a motion after jury discharge.

(d) Conditional Ruling on a Motion for a New Trial.

    (1) Motion for a New Trial. If the court enters a judgment of acquittal after a guilty verdict, the court must also conditionally determine whether any motion for a new trial should be granted if the judgment of acquittal is later vacated or reversed. The court must specify the reasons for that determination.

    (2) Finality. The court's order conditionally granting a motion for a new trial does not affect the finality of the judgment of acquittal.

    (3) Appeal.

       (A) Grant of a Motion for a New Trial. If the court conditionally grants a motion for a new trial and an appellate court later reverses the judgment of acquittal, the trial court must proceed with the new trial unless the appellate court orders otherwise.

       (B) Denial of a Motion for a New Trial. If the court conditionally denies a motion for a new trial, an appellee may assert that the denial was erroneous. If the appellate court later reverses the judgment of acquittal, the trial court must proceed as the appellate court directs.

Rule 29.1. Closing Argument

Closing arguments proceed in the following order:

(a) the government argues;

(b) the defense argues; and

(c) the government rebuts.

Rule 30. Jury Instructions

(a) In General. Any party may request in writing that the court instruct the jury on the law as specified in the request. The request must be made at the close of the evidence or at any earlier time that the court reasonably sets. When the request is made, the requesting party must furnish a copy to every other party.

(b) Ruling on a Request. The court must inform the parties before closing arguments how it intends to rule on the requested instructions.

(c) Time for Giving Instructions. The court may instruct the jury before or after the arguments are completed, or at both times.

(d) Objections to Instructions. A party who objects to any portion of the instructions or to a failure to give a requested instruction must inform the court of the specific objection and the grounds for the objection before the jury retires to deliberate. An opportunity must be given to object out of the jury's hearing and, on request, out of the jury's presence. Failure to object in accordance with this rule precludes appellate review, except as permitted under Rule 52(b).

Rule 31. Jury Verdict

(a) Return. The jury must return its verdict to a judge in open court. The verdict must be unanimous.

(b) Partial Verdicts, Mistrial, and Retrial.

(1) Multiple Defendants. If there are multiple defendants, the jury may return a verdict at any time during its deliberations as to any defendant about whom it has agreed.

(2) Multiple Counts. If the jury cannot agree on all counts as to any defendant, the jury may return a verdict on those counts on which it has agreed.

(3) Mistrial and Retrial. If the jury cannot agree on a verdict on one or more counts, the court may declare a mistrial on those counts. The government may retry any defendant on any count on which the jury could not agree.

(c) Lesser Offense or Attempt. A defendant may be found guilty of any of the following:

(1) an offense necessarily included in the offense charged;

(2) an attempt to commit the offense charged; or

(3) an attempt to commit an offense necessarily included in the offense charged, if the attempt is an offense in its own right.

(d) Jury Poll. After a verdict is returned but before the jury is discharged, the court must on a party's request, or may on its own, poll the jurors individually. If the poll reveals a lack of unanimity, the court may direct the jury to deliberate further or may declare a mistrial and discharge the jury.

Rule 32. Sentencing and Judgment

(a) [Reserved.]

(b) Time of Sentencing.

(1) In General. The court must impose sentence without unnecessary delay.

(2) Changing Time Limits. The court may, for good cause, change any time limits prescribed in this rule.

(c) Presentence Investigation.

(1) Required Investigation.

(A) In General. The probation officer must conduct a presentence investigation and submit a report to the court before it imposes sentence unless:

(i) 18 U.S.C. § 3593(c) or another statute requires otherwise; or

(ii) the court finds that the information in the record enables it to meaningfully exercise its sentencing authority under 18 U.S.C. § 3553, and the court explains its finding on the record.

(B) Restitution. If the law permits restitution, the probation officer must conduct an investigation and submit a report that contains sufficient information for the court to order restitution.

(2) Interviewing the Defendant. The probation officer who interviews a defendant as part of a presentence investigation must, on request, give the defendant's attorney notice and a reasonable opportunity to attend the interview.

(d) Presentence Report.

(1) Applying the Sentencing Guidelines. The presentence report must:

(A) identify all applicable guidelines and policy statements of the Sentencing Commission;

(B) calculate the defendant's offense level and criminal history category;

(C) state the resulting sentencing range and kinds of sentences available;

(D) identify any factor relevant to:

(i) the appropriate kind of sentence, or

(ii) the appropriate sentence within the applicable sentencing range; and

(E) identify any basis for departing from the applicable sentencing range.

(2) Additional Information. The presentence report must also contain the following:

(A) the defendant's history and characteristics, including:

(i) any prior criminal record;

(ii) the defendant's financial condition; and

(iii) any circumstances affecting the defendant's behavior that maybe helpful in imposing sentence or in correctional treatment;

(B) information that assesses any financial, social, psychological, and medical impact on any victim;

(C) when appropriate, the nature and extent of nonprison programs and resources available to the defendant;

(D) when the law provides for restitution, information sufficient for a restitution order;

(E) if the court orders a study under 18 U.S.C. § 3552(b), any resulting report and recommendation;

(F) a statement of whether the government seeks forfeiture under Rule 32.2 and any other law; and

(G) any other information that the court requires, including information relevant to the factors under 18 U.S.C. § 3553(a).

(3) Exclusions. The presentence report must exclude the following:

(A) any diagnoses that, if disclosed, might seriously disrupt a rehabilitation program;

(B) any sources of information obtained upon a promise of confidentiality; and

(C) any other information that, if disclosed, might result in physical or other harm to the defendant or others.

(e) Disclosing the Report and Recommendation.

(1) Time to Disclose. Unless the defendant has consented in writing, the probation officer must not submit a presentence report to the court or disclose its contents to anyone until the defendant has pleaded guilty or nolo contendere, or has been found guilty.

(2) Minimum Required Notice. The probation officer must give the presentence report to the defendant, the defendant's attorney, and an attorney for the government at least 35 days before sentencing unless the defendant waives this minimum period.

(3) Sentence Recommendation. By local rule or by order in a case, the court may direct the probation officer not to disclose to anyone other than the court the officer's recommendation on the sentence.

(f) Objecting to the Report.

(1) Time to Object. Within 14 days after receiving the presentence report, the parties must state in writing any objections, including objections to material information, sentencing guideline ranges, and policy statements contained in or omitted from the report.

(2) Serving Objections. An objecting party must provide a copy of its objections to the opposing party and to the probation officer.

(3) Action on Objections. After receiving objections, the probation officer may meet with the parties to discuss the objections. The probation officer may then investigate further and revise the presentence report as appropriate.

(g) Submitting the Report. At least 7 days before sentencing, the probation officer must submit to the court and to the parties the presentence report and an addendum containing any unresolved objections, the grounds for those objections, and the probation officer's comments on them.

(h) Notice of Possible Departure from Sentencing Guidelines. Before the court may depart from the applicable sentencing range on a ground not identified for departure either in the presentence report or in a party's prehearing submission, the court must give the parties reasonable notice that it is contemplating such a departure. The notice must specify any ground on which the court is contemplating a departure.

(i) Sentencing.

(1) In General. At sentencing, the court:

(A) must verify that the defendant and the defendant's attorney have read and discussed the presentence report and any addendum to the report;

(B) must give to the defendant and an attorney for the government a written summary of—or summarize in camera—any information excluded from the presentence report under Rule 32(d)(3) on which the court will rely in sentencing, and give them a reasonable opportunity to comment on that information;

(C) must allow the parties' attorneys to comment on the probation officer's determinations and other matters relating to an appropriate sentence; and

(D) may, for good cause, allow a party to make a new objection at any time before sentence is imposed.

(2) Introducing Evidence; Producing a Statement. The court may permit the parties to introduce evidence on the objections. If a witness testifies at sentencing, Rule 26.2(a)–(d) and (f) applies. If a party fails to comply with a Rule 26.2 order to produce a witness's statement, the court must not consider that witness's testimony.

(3) Court Determinations. At sentencing, the court:

(A) may accept any undisputed portion of the presentence report as a finding of fact;

(B) must—for any disputed portion of the presentence report or other controverted matter—rule on the dispute or determine that a ruling is unnecessary either because the matter will not affect sentencing, or because the court will not consider the matter in sentencing; and

(C) must append a copy of the court's determinations under this rule to any copy of the presentence report made available to the Bureau of Prisons.

(4) Opportunity to Speak.

(A) By a Party. Before imposing sentence, the court must:

(i) provide the defendant's attorney an opportunity to speak on the defendant's behalf;

(ii) address the defendant personally in order to permit the defendant to speak or present any information to mitigate the sentence; and

(iii) provide an attorney for the government an opportunity to speak equivalent to that of the defendant's attorney.

(B) By a Victim. Before imposing sentence, the court must address any victim of the crime who is present at sentencing and must permit the victim to be reasonably heard.

(C) In Camera Proceedings. Upon a party's motion and for good cause, the court may hear in camera any statement made under Rule 32(i)(4).

(j) Defendant's Right to Appeal.

(1) Advice of a Right to Appeal.

(A) Appealing a Conviction. If the defendant pleaded not guilty and was convicted, after sentencing the court must advise the defendant of the right to appeal the conviction.

(B) Appealing a Sentence. After sentencing—regardless of the defendant's plea—the court must advise the defendant of any right to appeal the sentence.

(C) Appeal Costs. The court must advise a defendant who is unable to pay appeal costs of the right to ask for permission to appeal in forma pauperis.

(2) **Clerk's Filing of Notice.** If the defendant so requests, the clerk must immediately prepare and file a notice of appeal on the defendant's behalf.

(k) **Judgment.**

(1) **In General.** In the judgment of conviction, the court must set forth the plea, the jury verdict or the court's findings, the adjudication, and the sentence. If the defendant is found not guilty or is otherwise entitled to be discharged, the court must so order. The judge must sign the judgment, and the clerk must enter it.

(2) **Criminal Forfeiture.** Forfeiture procedures are governed by Rule 32.2.

Rule 32.1. Revoking or Modifying Probation or Supervised Release

(a) **Initial Appearance.**

(1) **Person In Custody.** A person held in custody for violating probation or supervised release must be taken without unnecessary delay before a magistrate judge.

(A) If the person is held in custody in the district where an alleged violation occurred, the initial appearance must be in that district.

(B) If the person is held in custody in a district other than where an alleged violation occurred, the initial appearance must be in that district, or in an adjacent district if the appearance can occur more promptly there.

(2) **Upon a Summons.** When a person appears in response to a summons for violating probation or supervised release, a magistrate judge must proceed under this rule.

(3) **Advice.** The judge must inform the person of the following:

(A) the alleged violation of probation or supervised release;

(B) the person's right to retain counsel or to request that counsel be appointed if the person cannot obtain counsel; and

(C) the person's right, if held in custody, to a preliminary hearing under Rule 32.1(b)(1).

(4) **Appearance in the District With Jurisdiction.** If the person is arrested or appears in the district that has jurisdiction to conduct a revocation hearing—either originally or by transfer of jurisdiction—the court must proceed under Rule 32.1(b)–(e).

(5) **Appearance in a District Lacking Jurisdiction.** If the person is arrested or appears in a district that does not have jurisdiction to conduct a revocation hearing, the magistrate judge must:

(A) if the alleged violation occurred in the district of arrest, conduct a preliminary hearing under Rule 32.1(b) and either:

(i) transfer the person to the district that has jurisdiction, if the judge finds probable cause to believe that a violation occurred; or

(ii) dismiss the proceedings and so notify the court that has jurisdiction, if the judge finds no probable cause to believe that a violation occurred; or

(B) if the alleged violation did not occur in the district of arrest, transfer the person to the district that has jurisdiction if:

(i) the government produces certified copies of the judgment, warrant, and warrant application or produces copies of those certified documents by reliable electronic means; and

(ii) the judge finds that the person is the same person named in the warrant.

(6)   Release or Detention. The magistrate judge may release or detain the person under 18 U.S.C. § 3143(a)(1) pending further proceedings. The burden of establishing by clear and convincing evidence that the person will not flee or pose a danger to any other person or to the community rests with the person.

(b)   Revocation.

(1)   Preliminary Hearing.

(A)   In General. If a person is in custody for violating a condition of probation or supervised release, a magistrate judge must promptly conduct a hearing to determine whether there is probable cause to believe that a violation occurred. The person may waive the hearing.

(B)   Requirements. The hearing must be recorded by a court reporter or by a suitable recording device. The judge must give the person:

(i)   notice of the hearing and its purpose, the alleged violation, and the person's right to retain counsel or to request that counsel be appointed if the person cannot obtain counsel;

(ii)   an opportunity to appear at the hearing and present evidence; and

(iii) upon request, an opportunity to question any adverse witness, unless the judge determines that the interest of justice does not require the witness to appear.

(C)   Referral. If the judge finds probable cause, the judge must conduct a revocation hearing. If the judge does not find probable cause, the judge must dismiss the proceeding.

(2)   Revocation Hearing. Unless waived by the person, the court must hold the revocation hearing within a reasonable time in the district having jurisdiction. The person is entitled to:

(A)   written notice of the alleged violation;

(B)   disclosure of the evidence against the person;

(C)   an opportunity to appear, present evidence, and question any adverse witness unless the court determines that the interest of justice does not require the witness to appear;

(D)   notice of the person's right to retain counsel or to request that counsel be appointed if the person cannot obtain counsel; and

(E)   an opportunity to make a statement and present any information in mitigation.

(c)   Modification.

(1)   In General. Before modifying the conditions of probation or supervised release, the court must hold a hearing, at which the person has the right to counsel and an opportunity to make a statement and present any information in mitigation.

(2)   Exceptions. A hearing is not required if:

(A)   the person waives the hearing; or

(B)   the relief sought is favorable to the person and does not extend the term of probation or of supervised release; and

(C) an attorney for the government has received notice of the relief sought, has had a reasonable opportunity to object, and has not done so.

(d) Disposition of the Case. The court's disposition of the case is governed by 18 U.S.C. § 3563 and § 3565 (probation) and § 3583 (supervised release).

(e) Producing a Statement. Rule 26.2(a)–(d) and (f) applies at a hearing under this rule. If a party fails to comply with a Rule 26.2 order to produce a witness's statement, the court must not consider that witness's testimony.

Rule 32.2. Criminal Forfeiture

(a) Notice to the Defendant. A court must not enter a judgment of forfeiture in a criminal proceeding unless the indictment or information contains notice to the defendant that the government will seek the forfeiture of property as part of any sentence in accordance with the applicable statute. The notice should not be designated as a count of the indictment or information. The indictment or information need not identify the property subject to forfeiture or specify the amount of any forfeiture money judgment that the government seeks.

(b) Entering a Preliminary Order of Forfeiture.

(1) Forfeiture Phase of the Trial.

(A) Forfeiture Determinations. As soon as practical after a verdict or finding of guilty, or after a plea of guilty or nolo contendere is accepted, on any count in an indictment or information regarding which criminal forfeiture is sought, the court must determine what property is subject to forfeiture under the applicable statute. If the government seeks forfeiture of specific property, the court must determine whether the government has established the requisite nexus between the property and the offense. If the government seeks a personal money judgment, the court must determine the amount of money that the defendant will be ordered to pay.

(B) Evidence and Hearing. The court's determination may be based on evidence already in the record, including any written plea agreement, and on any additional evidence or information submitted by the parties and accepted by the court as relevant and reliable. If the forfeiture is contested, on either party's request the court must conduct a hearing after the verdict or finding of guilty.

(2) Preliminary Order.

(A) Contents of a Specific Order. If the court finds that property is subject to forfeiture, it must promptly enter a preliminary order of forfeiture setting forth the amount of any money judgment, directing the forfeiture of specific property, and directing the forfeiture of any substitute property if the government has met the statutory criteria. The court must enter the order without regard to any third party's interest in the property. Determining whether a third party has such an interest must be deferred until any third party files a claim in an ancillary proceeding under Rule 32.2(c).

(B) Timing. Unless doing so is impractical, the court must enter the preliminary order sufficiently in advance of sentencing to allow the parties to suggest revisions or modifications before the order becomes final as to the defendant under Rule 32.2(b)(4).

(C) General Order. If, before sentencing, the court cannot identify all the specific property subject to forfeiture or calculate the total amount of the money judgment, the court may enter a forfeiture order that:

(i) lists any identified property;

(ii) describes other property in general terms; and

(iii) states that the order will be amended under Rule 32.2(e)(1) when additional specific property is identified or the amount of the money judgment has been calculated.

(3) Seizing Property. The entry of a preliminary order of forfeiture authorizes the Attorney General (or a designee) to seize the specific property subject to forfeiture; to conduct any discovery the court considers proper in identifying, locating, or disposing of the property; and to commence proceedings that comply with any statutes governing third-party rights. The court may include in the order of forfeiture conditions reasonably necessary to preserve the property's value pending any appeal.

(4) Sentence and Judgment.

(A) When Final. At sentencing—or at any time before sentencing if the defendant consents—the preliminary forfeiture order becomes final as to the defendant. If the order directs the defendant to forfeit specific property, it remains preliminary as to third parties until the ancillary proceeding is concluded under Rule 32.2(c).

(B) Notice and Inclusion in the Judgment. The court must include the forfeiture when orally announcing the sentence or must otherwise ensure that the defendant knows of the forfeiture at sentencing. The court must also include the forfeiture order, directly or by reference, in the judgment, but the court's failure to do so may be corrected at any time under Rule 36.

(C) Time to Appeal. The time for the defendant or the government to file an appeal from the forfeiture order, or from the court's failure to enter an order, begins to run when judgment is entered. If the court later amends or declines to amend a forfeiture order to include additional property under Rule 32.2(e), the defendant or the government may file an appeal regarding that property under Federal Rule of Appellate Procedure 4(b). The time for that appeal runs from the date when the order granting or denying the amendment becomes final.

(5) Jury Determination.

(A) Retaining the Jury. In any case tried before a jury, if the indictment or information states that the government is seeking forfeiture, the court must determine before the jury begins deliberating whether either party requests that the jury be retained to determine the forfeitability of specific property if it returns a guilty verdict.

(B) Special Verdict Form. If a party timely requests to have the jury determine forfeiture, the government must submit a proposed Special Verdict Form listing each property subject to forfeiture and asking the jury to determine whether the government has established the requisite nexus between the property and the offense committed by the defendant.

(6) Notice of the Forfeiture Order.

(A) Publishing and Sending Notice. If the court orders the forfeiture of specific property, the government must publish notice of the order and send notice to any person who reasonably appears to be a potential claimant with standing to contest the forfeiture in the ancillary proceeding.

(B) Content of the Notice. The notice must describe the forfeited property, state the times under the applicable statute when a petition contesting the forfeiture must be filed, and state the name and contact information for the government attorney to be served with the petition.

(C) Means of Publication; Exceptions to Publication Requirement. Publication must take place as described in Supplemental Rule G(4)(a)(iii) of the Federal Rules of Civil Procedure, and may be by any means described in Supplemental Rule G(4)(a)(iv). Publication is unnecessary if any exception in Supplemental Rule G(4)(a)(i) applies.

(D) Means of Sending the Notice. The notice may be sent in accordance with Supplemental Rules G(4)(b)(iii)–(v) of the Federal Rules of Civil Procedure.

(7) Interlocutory Sale. At any time before entry of a final forfeiture order, the court, in accordance with Supplemental Rule G(7) of the Federal Rules of Civil Procedure, may order the interlocutory sale of property alleged to be forfeitable.

(c) Ancillary Proceeding; Entering a Final Order of Forfeiture.

(1) In General. If, as prescribed by statute, a third party files a petition asserting an interest in the property to be forfeited, the court must conduct an ancillary proceeding, but no ancillary proceeding is required to the extent that the forfeiture consists of a money judgment.

(A) In the ancillary proceeding, the court may, on motion, dismiss the petition for lack of standing, for failure to state a claim, or for any other lawful reason. For purposes of the motion, the facts set forth in the petition are assumed to be true.

(B) After disposing of any motion filed under Rule 32.2(c)(1)(A) and before conducting a hearing on the petition, the court may permit the parties to conduct discovery in accordance with the Federal Rules of Civil Procedure if the court determines that discovery is necessary or desirable to resolve factual issues. When discovery ends, a party may move for summary judgment under Federal Rule of Civil Procedure 56.

(2) Entering a Final Order. When the ancillary proceeding ends, the court must enter a final order of forfeiture by amending the preliminary order as necessary to account for any third-party rights. If no third party files a timely petition, the preliminary order becomes the final order of forfeiture if the court finds that the defendant (or any combination of defendants convicted in the case) had an interest in the property that is forfeitable under the applicable statute. The defendant may not object to the entry of the final order on the ground that the property belongs, in whole or in part, to a codefendant or third party; nor may a third party object to the final order on the ground that the third party had an interest in the property.

(3) Multiple Petitions. If multiple third-party petitions are filed in the same case, an order dismissing or granting one petition is not appealable until rulings are made on all the petitions, unless the court determines that there is no just reason for delay.

(4) Ancillary Proceeding Not Part of Sentencing. An ancillary proceeding is not part of sentencing.

(d) Stay Pending Appeal. If a defendant appeals from a conviction or an order of forfeiture, the court may stay the order of forfeiture on terms appropriate to ensure that the property remains available pending appellate review. A stay does not delay the ancillary proceeding or the determination of a third party's rights or interests. If the court rules in favor of any third party while an appeal is pending, the court may amend the order of forfeiture but must not transfer any property interest to a third party until the decision on appeal becomes final, unless the defendant consents in writing or on the record.

(e) **Subsequently Located Property; Substitute Property.**

(1) **In General.** On the government's motion, the court may at any time enter an order of forfeiture or amend an existing order of forfeiture to include property that:

(A) is subject to forfeiture under an existing order of forfeiture but was located and identified after that order was entered; or

(B) is substitute property that qualifies for forfeiture under an applicable statute.

(2) **Procedure.** If the government shows that the property is subject to forfeiture under Rule 32.2(e)(1), the court must:

(A) enter an order forfeiting that property, or amend an existing preliminary or final order to include it; and

(B) if a third party files a petition claiming an interest in the property, conduct an ancillary proceeding under Rule 32.2(c).

(3) **Jury Trial Limited.** There is no right to a jury trial under Rule 32.2(e).

Rule 33. New Trial

(a) **Defendant's Motion.** Upon the defendant's motion, the court may vacate any judgment and grant a new trial if the interest of justice so requires. If the case was tried without a jury, the court may take additional testimony and enter a new judgment.

(b) **Time to File.**

(1) **Newly Discovered Evidence.** Any motion for a new trial grounded on newly discovered evidence must be filed within 3 years after the verdict or finding of guilty. If an appeal is pending, the court may not grant a motion for a new trial until the appellate court remands the case.

(2) **Other Grounds.** Any motion for a new trial grounded on any reason other than newly discovered evidence must be filed within 14 days after the verdict or finding of guilty.

Rule 34. Arresting Judgment

(a) **In General.** Upon the defendant's motion or on its own, the court must arrest judgment if the court does not have jurisdiction of the charged offense.

(b) **Time to File.** The defendant must move to arrest judgment within 14 days after the court accepts a verdict or finding of guilty, or after a plea of guilty or nolo contendere.

Rule 35. Correcting or Reducing a Sentence

(a) **Correcting Clear Error.** Within 14 days after sentencing, the court may correct a sentence that resulted from arithmetical, technical, or other clear error.

(b) **Reducing a Sentence for Substantial Assistance.**

(1) **In General.** Upon the government's motion made within one year of sentencing, the court may reduce a sentence if the defendant, after sentencing, provided substantial assistance in investigating or prosecuting another person.

(2) **Later Motion.** Upon the government's motion made more than one year after sentencing, the court may reduce a sentence if the defendant's substantial assistance involved:

(A) information not known to the defendant until one year or more after sentencing;

(B) information provided by the defendant to the government within one year of sentencing, but which did not become useful to the government until more than one year after sentencing; or

(C) information the usefulness of which could not reasonably have been anticipated by the defendant until more than one year after sentencing and which was promptly provided to the government after its usefulness was reasonably apparent to the defendant.

(3) Evaluating Substantial Assistance. In evaluating whether the defendant has provided substantial assistance, the court may consider the defendant's presentence assistance.

(4) Below Statutory Minimum. When acting under Rule 35(b), the court may reduce the sentence to a level below the minimum sentence established by statute.

(c) "Sentencing" Defined. As used in this rule, "sentencing" means the oral announcement of the sentence.

Rule 36. Clerical Error

After giving any notice it considers appropriate, the court may at any time correct a clerical error in a judgment, order, or other part of the record, or correct an error in the record arising from oversight or omission.

Rule 37. Ruling on a Motion for Relief That Is Barred by a Pending Appeal

(a) Relief Pending Appeal. If a timely motion is made for relief that the court lacks authority to grant because of an appeal that has been docketed and is pending, the court may:

(1) defer considering the motion;

(2) deny the motion; or

(3) state either that it would grant the motion if the court of appeals remands for that purpose or that the motion raises a substantial issue.

(b) Notice to the Court of Appeals. The movant must promptly notify the circuit clerk under Federal Rule of Appellate Procedure 12.1 if the district court states that it would grant the motion or that the motion raises a substantial issue.

(c) Remand. The district court may decide the motion if the court of appeals remands for that purpose.

Rule 38. Staying a Sentence or a Disability

(a) Death Sentence. The court must stay a death sentence if the defendant appeals the conviction or sentence.

(b) Imprisonment.

(1) Stay Granted. If the defendant is released pending appeal, the court must stay a sentence of imprisonment.

(2) Stay Denied; Place of Confinement. If the defendant is not released pending appeal, the court may recommend to the Attorney General that the defendant be confined near the place of the trial or appeal for a period reasonably necessary to permit the defendant to assist in preparing the appeal.

(c) Fine. If the defendant appeals, the district court, or the court of appeals under Federal Rule of Appellate Procedure 8, may stay a sentence to pay a fine or a fine and costs. The court may stay the sentence on any terms considered appropriate and may require the defendant to:

(1) deposit all or part of the fine and costs into the district court's registry pending appeal;

(2) post a bond to pay the fine and costs; or

(3) submit to an examination concerning the defendant's assets and, if appropriate, order the defendant to refrain from dissipating assets.

(d) Probation. If the defendant appeals, the court may stay a sentence of probation. The court must set the terms of any stay.

(e) Restitution and Notice to Victims.

(1) In General. If the defendant appeals, the district court, or the court of appeals under Federal Rule of Appellate Procedure 8, may stay—on any terms considered appropriate—any sentence providing for restitution under 18 U.S.C. § 3556 or notice under 18 U.S.C. § 3555.

(2) Ensuring Compliance. The court may issue any order reasonably necessary to ensure compliance with a restitution order or a notice order after disposition of an appeal, including:

(A) a restraining order;

(B) an injunction;

(C) an order requiring the defendant to deposit all or part of any monetary restitution into the district court's registry; or

(D) an order requiring the defendant to post a bond.

(f) Forfeiture. A stay of a forfeiture order is governed by Rule 32.2(d).

(g) Disability. If the defendant's conviction or sentence creates a civil or employment disability under federal law, the district court, or the court of appeals under Federal Rule of Appellate Procedure 8, may stay the disability pending appeal on any terms considered appropriate. The court may issue any order reasonably necessary to protect the interest represented by the disability pending appeal, including a restraining order or an injunction.

Rule 39. [Reserved]

Rule 40. Arrest for Failing to Appear in Another District

(a) In General. A person must be taken without unnecessary delay before a magistrate judge in the district of arrest if the person has been arrested under a warrant issued in another district for:

(i) failing to appear as required by the terms of that person's release under 18 U.S.C. §§ 3141–3156 or by a subpoena; or

(ii) violating conditions of release set in another district.

(b) Proceedings. The judge must proceed under Rule 5(c)(3) as applicable.

(c) Release or Detention Order. The judge may modify any previous release or detention order issued in another district, but must state in writing the reasons for doing so.

(d) Video Teleconferencing. Video teleconferencing may be used to conduct an appearance under this rule if the defendant consents.

Rule 41. Search and Seizure

(a) Scope and Definitions.

(1) Scope. This rule does not modify any statute regulating search or seizure, or the issuance and execution of a search warrant in special circumstances.

(2) Definitions. The following definitions apply under this rule:

(A) "Property" includes documents, books, papers, any other tangible objects, and information.

(B) "Daytime" means the hours between 6:00 a.m. and 10:00 p.m. according to local time.

(C) "Federal law enforcement officer" means a government agent (other than an attorney for the government) who is engaged in enforcing the criminal laws and is within any category of officers authorized by the Attorney General to request a search warrant.

(D) "Domestic terrorism" and "international terrorism" have the meanings set out in 18 U.S.C. § 2331.

(E) "Tracking device" has the meaning set out in 18 U.S.C. § 3117(b).

(b) Venue for a Warrant Application. At the request of a federal law enforcement officer or an attorney for the government:

(1) a magistrate judge with authority in the district—or if none is reasonably available, a judge of a state court of record in the district—has authority to issue a warrant to search for and seize a person or property located within the district;

(2) a magistrate judge with authority in the district has authority to issue a warrant for a person or property outside the district if the person or property is located within the district when the warrant is issued but might move or be moved outside the district before the warrant is executed; and

(3) a magistrate judge—in an investigation of domestic terrorism or international terrorism—with authority in any district in which activities related to the terrorism may have occurred has authority to issue a warrant for a person or property within or outside that district;

(4) a magistrate judge with authority in the district has authority to issue a warrant to install within the district a tracking device; the warrant may authorize use of the device to track the movement of a person or property located within the district, outside the district, or both; and

(5) a magistrate judge having authority in any district where activities related to the crime may have occurred, or in the District of Columbia, may issue a warrant for property that is located outside the jurisdiction of any state or district, but within any of the following:

(A) a United States territory, possession, or commonwealth;

(B) the premises—no matter who owns them—of a United States diplomatic or consular mission in a foreign state, including any appurtenant building, part of a building, or land used for the mission's purposes; or

(C) a residence and any appurtenant land owned or leased by the United States and used by United States personnel assigned to a United States diplomatic or consular mission in a foreign state.

(6) a magistrate judge with authority in any district where activities related to a crime may have occurred has authority to issue a warrant to use remote access to search electronic storage media and to seize or copy electronically stored information located within or outside that district if:

(A) the district where the media or information is located has been concealed through technological means; or

(B) in an investigation of a violation of 18 U.S.C. § 1030(a)(5), the media are protected computers that have been damaged without authorization and are located in five or more districts.

(c) Persons or Property Subject to Search or Seizure. A warrant may be issued for any of the following:

(1) evidence of a crime;

(2) contraband, fruits of crime, or other items illegally possessed;

(3) property designed for use, intended for use, or used in committing a crime; or

(4) a person to be arrested or a person who is unlawfully restrained.

(d) Obtaining a Warrant.

(1) In General. After receiving an affidavit or other information, a magistrate judge—or if authorized by Rule 41(b), a judge of a state court of record—must issue the warrant if there is probable cause to search for and seize a person or property or to install and use a tracking device.

(2) Requesting a Warrant in the Presence of a Judge.

(A) Warrant on an Affidavit. When a federal law enforcement officer or an attorney for the government presents an affidavit in support of a warrant, the judge may require the affiant to appear personally and may examine under oath the affiant and any witness the affiant produces.

(B) Warrant on Sworn Testimony. The judge may wholly or partially dispense with a written affidavit and base a warrant on sworn testimony if doing so is reasonable under the circumstances.

(C) Recording Testimony. Testimony taken in support of a warrant must be recorded by a court reporter or by a suitable recording device, and the judge must file the transcript or recording with the clerk, along with any affidavit.

(3) Requesting a Warrant by Telephonic or Other Reliable Electronic Means. In accordance with Rule 4.1, a magistrate judge may issue a warrant based on information communicated by telephone or other reliable electronic means.

(e) Issuing the Warrant.

(1) In General. The magistrate judge or a judge of a state court of record must issue the warrant to an officer authorized to execute it.

(2) Contents of the Warrant.

(A) Warrant to Search for and Seize a Person or Property. Except for a tracking-device warrant, the warrant must identify the person or property to be searched, identify any person or property to be seized, and designate the magistrate judge to whom it must be returned. The warrant must command the officer to:

(i) execute the warrant within a specified time no longer than 14 days;

(ii) execute the warrant during the daytime, unless the judge for good cause expressly authorizes execution at another time; and

(iii) return the warrant to the magistrate judge designated in the warrant.

(B) Warrant Seeking Electronically Stored Information. A warrant under Rule 41(e)(2)(A) may authorize the seizure of electronic storage media or the seizure or copying of electronically stored information. Unless otherwise specified, the warrant authorizes a later review of the media or information consistent with the warrant. The time for executing the warrant in Rule 41(e)(2)(A) and (f)(1)(A) refers to the seizure or on-site copying of the media or information, and not to any later off-site copying or review.

(C) Warrant for a Tracking Device. A tracking-device warrant must identify the person or property to be tracked, designate the magistrate judge to whom it must be returned, and specify a reasonable length of time that the device may be used. The time must not exceed 45 days from the date the warrant was issued. The court may, for good cause, grant one or more extensions for a reasonable period not to exceed 45 days each. The warrant must command the officer to:

(i) complete any installation authorized by the warrant within a specified time no longer than 10 days;

(ii) perform any installation authorized by the warrant during the daytime, unless the judge for good cause expressly authorizes installation at another time; and

(iii) return the warrant to the judge designated in the warrant.

(f) Executing and Returning the Warrant.

(1) Warrant to Search for and Seize a Person or Property.

(A) Noting the Time. The officer executing the warrant must enter on it the exact date and time it was executed.

(B) Inventory. An officer present during the execution of the warrant must prepare and verify an inventory of any property seized. The officer must do so in the presence of another officer and the person from whom, or from whose premises, the property was taken. If either one is not present, the officer must prepare and verify the inventory in the presence of at least one other credible person. In a case involving the seizure of electronic storage media or the seizure or copying of electronically stored information, the inventory may be limited to describing the physical storage media that were seized or copied. The officer may retain a copy of the electronically stored information that was seized or copied.

(C) Receipt. The officer executing the warrant must give a copy of the warrant and a receipt for the property taken to the person from whom, or from whose premises, the property was taken or leave a copy of the warrant and receipt at the place where the officer took the property. For a warrant to use remote access to search electronic storage media and seize or copy electronically stored information, the officer must make reasonable efforts to serve a copy of the warrant and receipt on the person whose property was searched or who possessed the information that was seized or copied. Service may be accomplished by any means, including electronic means, reasonably calculated to reach that person.

(D) Return. The officer executing the warrant must promptly return it—together with a copy of the inventory—to the magistrate judge designated on the warrant. The officer may do so by reliable electronic means. The judge must, on request, give a copy of the inventory to the person from whom, or from whose premises, the property was taken and to the applicant for the warrant.

(2) Warrant for a Tracking Device.

(A) Noting the Time. The officer executing a tracking-device warrant must enter on it the exact date and time the device was installed and the period during which it was used.

(B) Return. Within 10 days after the use of the tracking device has ended, the officer executing the warrant must return it to the judge designated in the warrant. The officer may do so by reliable electronic means.

(C) Service. Within 10 days after the use of the tracking device has ended, the officer executing a tracking-device warrant must serve a copy of the warrant on the person who was tracked or whose property was tracked. Service may be accomplished by delivering a copy to the person who, or whose property, was tracked; or by leaving a copy at the person's residence or usual place of abode with an individual of suitable age and discretion who resides at that location and by mailing a copy to the person's last known address. Upon request of the government, the judge may delay notice as provided in Rule 41(f)(3).

(3) Delayed Notice. Upon the government's request, a magistrate judge—or if authorized by Rule 41(b), a judge of a state court of record—may delay any notice required by this rule if the delay is authorized by statute.

(g) Motion to Return Property. A person aggrieved by an unlawful search and seizure of property or by the deprivation of property may move for the property's return. The motion must be filed in the district where the property was seized. The court must receive evidence on any factual issue necessary to decide the motion. If it grants the motion, the court must return the property to the movant, but may impose reasonable conditions to protect access to the property and its use in later proceedings.

(h) Motion to Suppress. A defendant may move to suppress evidence in the court where the trial will occur, as Rule 12 provides.

(i) Forwarding Papers to the Clerk. The magistrate judge to whom the warrant is returned must attach to the warrant a copy of the return, of the inventory, and of all other related papers and must deliver them to the clerk in the district where the property was seized.

Rule 42. Criminal Contempt

(a) Disposition After Notice. Any person who commits criminal contempt may be punished for that contempt after prosecution on notice.

(1) Notice. The court must give the person notice in open court, in an order to show cause, or in an arrest order. The notice must:

(A) state the time and place of the trial;

(B) allow the defendant a reasonable time to prepare a defense; and

(C) state the essential facts constituting the charged criminal contempt and describe it as such.

(2) Appointing a Prosecutor. The court must request that the contempt be prosecuted by an attorney for the government, unless the interest of justice requires the appointment of another attorney. If the government declines the request, the court must appoint another attorney to prosecute the contempt.

(3) Trial and Disposition. A person being prosecuted for criminal contempt is entitled to a jury trial in any case in which federal law so provides and must be released or detained as Rule 46 provides. If the criminal contempt involves disrespect toward or criticism of a judge, that judge is disqualified from presiding at the contempt trial or hearing unless the defendant consents. Upon a finding or verdict of guilty, the court must impose the punishment.

(b) Summary Disposition. Notwithstanding any other provision of these rules, the court (other than a magistrate judge) may summarily punish a person who commits criminal contempt in its presence if the judge saw or heard the contemptuous conduct and so certifies; a magistrate judge may summarily punish a person as provided in 28 U.S.C. § 636(e). The contempt order must recite the facts, be signed by the judge, and be filed with the clerk.

Rule 43. Defendant's Presence

(a) When Required. Unless this rule, Rule 5, or Rule 10 provides otherwise, the defendant must be present at:

(1) the initial appearance, the initial arraignment, and the plea;

(2) every trial stage, including jury impanelment and the return of the verdict; and

(3) sentencing.

(b) When Not Required. A defendant need not be present under any of the following circumstances:

(1) Organizational Defendant. The defendant is an organization represented by counsel who is present.

(2) Misdemeanor Offense. The offense is punishable by fine or by imprisonment for not more than one year, or both, and with the defendant's written consent, the court permits arraignment, plea, trial, and sentencing to occur by video teleconferencing or in the defendant's absence.

(3) Conference or Hearing on a Legal Question. The proceeding involves only a conference or hearing on a question of law.

(4) Sentence Correction. The proceeding involves the correction or reduction of sentence under Rule 35 or 18 U.S.C. § 3582(c).

(c) Waiving Continued Presence.

(1) In General. A defendant who was initially present at trial, or who had pleaded guilty or nolo contendere, waives the right to be present under the following circumstances:

(A) when the defendant is voluntarily absent after the trial has begun, regardless of whether the court informed the defendant of an obligation to remain during trial;

(B) in a noncapital case, when the defendant is voluntarily absent during sentencing; or

(C) when the court warns the defendant that it will remove the defendant from the courtroom for disruptive behavior, but the defendant persists in conduct that justifies removal from the courtroom.

(2) Waiver's Effect. If the defendant waives the right to be present, the trial may proceed to completion, including the verdict's return and sentencing, during the defendant's absence.

Rule 44. Right to and Appointment of Counsel

(a) Right to Appointed Counsel. A defendant who is unable to obtain counsel is entitled to have counsel appointed to represent the defendant at every stage of the proceeding from initial appearance through appeal, unless the defendant waives this right.

(b) Appointment Procedure. Federal law and local court rules govern the procedure for implementing the right to counsel.

(c) Inquiry Into Joint Representation.

    (1) Joint Representation. Joint representation occurs when:

        (A) two or more defendants have been charged jointly under Rule 8(b) or have been joined for trial under Rule 13; and

        (B) the defendants are represented by the same counsel, or counsel who are associated in law practice.

    (2) Court's Responsibilities in Cases of Joint Representation. The court must promptly inquire about the propriety of joint representation and must personally advise each defendant of the right to the effective assistance of counsel, including separate representation. Unless there is good cause to believe that no conflict of interest is likely to arise, the court must take appropriate measures to protect each defendant's right to counsel.

Rule 45. Computing and Extending Time

(a) Computing Time. The following rules apply in computing any time period specified in these rules, in any local rule or court order, or in any statute that does not specify a method of computing time.

    (1) Period Stated in Days or a Longer Unit. When the period is stated in days or a longer unit of time:

        (A) exclude the day of the event that triggers the period;

        (B) count every day, including intermediate Saturdays, Sundays, and legal holidays; and

        (C) include the last day of the period, but if the last day is a Saturday, Sunday, or legal holiday, the period continues to run until the end of the next day that is not a Saturday, Sunday, or legal holiday.

    (2) Period Stated in Hours. When the period is stated in hours:

        (A) begin counting immediately on the occurrence of the event that triggers the period;

        (B) count every hour, including hours during intermediate Saturdays, Sundays, and legal holidays; and

        (C) if the period would end on a Saturday, Sunday, or legal holiday, the period continues to run until the same time on the next day that is not a Saturday, Sunday, or legal holiday.

    (3) Inaccessibility of the Clerk's Office. Unless the court orders otherwise, if the clerk's office is inaccessible:

        (A) on the last day for filing under Rule 45(a)(1), then the time for filing is extended to the first accessible day that is not a Saturday, Sunday, or legal holiday; or

(B) during the last hour for filing under Rule 45(a)(2), then the time for filing is extended to the same time on the first accessible day that is not a Saturday, Sunday, or legal holiday.

(4) **"Last Day" Defined.** Unless a different time is set by a statute, local rule, or court order, the last day ends:

(A) for electronic filing, at midnight in the court's time zone; and

(B) for filing by other means, when the clerk's office is scheduled to close.

(5) **"Next Day" Defined.** The "next day" is determined by continuing to count forward when the period is measured after an event and backward when measured before an event.

(6) **"Legal Holiday" Defined.** "Legal holiday" means:

(A) the day set aside by statute for observing New Year's Day, Martin Luther King Jr.'s Birthday, Washington's Birthday, Memorial Day, Independence Day, Labor Day, Columbus Day, Veterans' Day, Thanksgiving Day, or Christmas Day;

(B) any day declared a holiday by the President or Congress; and

(C) for periods that are measured after an event, any other day declared a holiday by the state where the district court is located.

(b) **Extending Time.**

(1) **In General.** When an act must or may be done within a specified period, the court on its own may extend the time, or for good cause may do so on a party's motion made:

(A) before the originally prescribed or previously extended time expires; or

(B) after the time expires if the party failed to act because of excusable neglect.

(2) **Exception.** The court may not extend the time to take any action under Rule 35, except as stated in that rule.

(c) **Additional Time After Certain Kinds of Service.** Whenever a party must or may act within a specified time after being served and service is made under Federal Rule of Civil Procedure 5(b)(2)(C) (mailing), (D) (leaving with the clerk), or (F) (other means consented to), 3 days are added after the period would otherwise expire under subdivision (a).

Rule 46. Release from Custody; Supervising Detention

(a) **Before Trial.** The provisions of 18 U.S.C. §§ 3142 and 3144 govern pretrial release.

(b) **During Trial.** A person released before trial continues on release during trial under the same terms and conditions. But the court may order different terms and conditions or terminate the release if necessary to ensure that the person will be present during trial or that the person's conduct will not obstruct the orderly and expeditious progress of the trial.

(c) **Pending Sentencing or Appeal.** The provisions of 18 U.S.C. § 3143 govern release pending sentencing or appeal. The burden of establishing that the defendant will not flee or pose a danger to any other person or to the community rests with the defendant.

(d) **Pending Hearing on a Violation of Probation or Supervised Release.** Rule 32.1(a)(6) governs release pending a hearing on a violation of probation or supervised release.

(e) **Surety.** The court must not approve a bond unless any surety appears to be qualified. Every surety, except a legally approved corporate surety, must demonstrate by affidavit that its assets are adequate. The court may require the affidavit to describe the following:

(1) the property that the surety proposes to use as security;

(2) any encumbrance on that property;

(3) the number and amount of any other undischarged bonds and bail undertakings the surety has issued; and

(4) any other liability of the surety.

(f) **Bail Forfeiture.**

(1) **Declaration.** The court must declare the bail forfeited if a condition of the bond is breached.

(2) **Setting Aside.** The court may set aside in whole or in part a bail forfeiture upon any condition the court may impose if:

(A) the surety later surrenders into custody the person released on the surety's appearance bond; or

(B) it appears that justice does not require bail forfeiture.

(3) **Enforcement.**

(A) **Default Judgment and Execution.** If it does not set aside a bail forfeiture, the court must, upon the government's motion, enter a default judgment.

(B) **Jurisdiction and Service.** By entering into a bond, each surety submits to the district court's jurisdiction and irrevocably appoints the district clerk as its agent to receive service of any filings affecting its liability.

(C) **Motion to Enforce.** The court may, upon the government's motion, enforce the surety's liability without an independent action. The government must serve any motion, and notice as the court prescribes, on the district clerk. If so served, the clerk must promptly mail a copy to the surety at its last known address.

(4) **Remission.** After entering a judgment under Rule 46(f)(3), the court may remit in whole or in part the judgment under the same conditions specified in Rule 46(f)(2).

(g) **Exoneration.** The court must exonerate the surety and release any bail when a bond condition has been satisfied or when the court has set aside or remitted the forfeiture. The court must exonerate a surety who deposits cash in the amount of the bond or timely surrenders the defendant into custody.

(h) **Supervising Detention Pending Trial.**

(1) **In General.** To eliminate unnecessary detention, the court must supervise the detention within the district of any defendants awaiting trial and of any persons held as material witnesses.

(2) **Reports.** An attorney for the government must report biweekly to the court, listing each material witness held in custody for more than 10 days pending indictment, arraignment, or trial. For each material witness listed in the report, an attorney for the government must state why the witness should not be released with or without a deposition being taken under Rule 15(a).

(i) **Forfeiture of Property.** The court may dispose of a charged offense by ordering the forfeiture of 18 U.S.C. § 3142(c)(1)(B)(xi) property under 18 U.S.C. § 3146(d), if a fine in the amount of the property's value would be an appropriate sentence for the charged offense.

(j) **Producing a Statement.**

(1) **In General.** Rule 26.2(a)–(d) and (f) applies at a detention hearing under 18 U.S.C. § 3142, unless the court for good cause rules otherwise.

(2)   Sanctions for Not Producing a Statement. If a party disobeys a Rule 26.2 order to produce a witness's statement, the court must not consider that witness's testimony at the detention hearing.

Rule 47. Motions and Supporting Affidavits

(a)   In General. A party applying to the court for an order must do so by motion.

(b)   Form and Content of a Motion. A motion—except when made during a trial or hearing—must be in writing, unless the court permits the party to make the motion by other means. A motion must state the grounds on which it is based and the relief or order sought. A motion may be supported by affidavit.

(c)   Timing of a Motion. A party must serve a written motion—other than one that the court may hear ex parte—and any hearing notice at least 7 days before the hearing date, unless a rule or court order sets a different period. For good cause, the court may set a different period upon ex parte application.

(d)   Affidavit Supporting a Motion. The moving party must serve any supporting affidavit with the motion. A responding party must serve any opposing affidavit at least one day before the hearing, unless the court permits later service.

Rule 48. Dismissal

(a)   By the Government. The government may, with leave of court, dismiss an indictment, information, or complaint. The government may not dismiss the prosecution during trial without the defendant's consent.

(b)   By the Court. The court may dismiss an indictment, information, or complaint if unnecessary delay occurs in:

(1)   presenting a charge to a grand jury;

(2)   filing an information against a defendant; or

(3)   bringing a defendant to trial.

Rule 49. Serving and Filing Papers

(a)   When Required. A party must serve on every other party any written motion (other than one to be heard ex parte), written notice, designation of the record on appeal, or similar paper.

(b)   How Made. Service must be made in the manner provided for a civil action. When these rules or a court order requires or permits service on a party represented by an attorney, service must be made on the attorney instead of the party, unless the court orders otherwise.

(c)   Notice of a Court Order. When the court issues an order on any post-arraignment motion, the clerk must provide notice in a manner provided for in a civil action. Except as Federal Rule of Appellate Procedure 4(b) provides otherwise, the clerk's failure to give notice does not affect the time to appeal, or relieve—or authorize the court to relieve—a party's failure to appeal within the allowed time.

(d)   Filing. A party must file with the court a copy of any paper the party is required to serve. A paper must be filed in a manner provided for in a civil action.

(e)   Electronic Service and Filing. A court may, by local rule, allow papers to be filed, signed, or verified by electronic means that are consistent with any technical standards established by the Judicial Conference of the United States. A local rule may require electronic filing only if reasonable exceptions are allowed. A paper filed electronically in compliance with a local rule is written or in writing under these rules.

Rule 49.1. Privacy Protection for Filings Made with the Court

(a) Redacted Filings. Unless the court orders otherwise, in an electronic or paper filing with the court that contains an individual's social-security number, taxpayer-identification number, or birth date, the name of an individual known to be a minor, a financial-account number, or the home address of an individual, a party or nonparty making the filing may include only:

    (1) the last four digits of the social-security number and taxpayer-identification number;

    (2) the year of the individual's birth;

    (3) the minor's initials;

    (4) the last four digits of the financial-account number; and

    (5) the city and state of the home address.

(b) Exemptions from the Redaction Requirement. The redaction requirement does not apply to the following:

    (1) a financial-account number or real property address that identifies the property allegedly subject to forfeiture in a forfeiture proceeding;

    (2) the record of an administrative or agency proceeding;

    (3) the official record of a state-court proceeding;

    (4) the record of a court or tribunal, if that record was not subject to the redaction requirement when originally filed;

    (5) a filing covered by Rule 49.1(d);

    (6) a pro se filing in an action brought under 28 U.S.C. §§ 2241, 2254, or 2255;

    (7) a court filing that is related to a criminal matter or investigation and that is prepared before the filing of a criminal charge or is not filed as part of any docketed criminal case;

    (8) an arrest or search warrant; and

    (9) a charging document and an affidavit filed in support of any charging document.

(c) Immigration Cases. A filing in an action brought under 28 U.S.C. § 2241 that relates to the petitioner's immigration rights is governed by Federal Rule of Civil Procedure 5.2.

(d) Filings Made Under Seal. The court may order that a filing be made under seal without redaction. The court may later unseal the filing or order the person who made the filing to file a redacted version for the public record.

(e) Protective Orders. For good cause, the court may by order in a case:

    (1) require redaction of additional information; or

    (2) limit or prohibit a nonparty's remote electronic access to a document filed with the court.

(f) Option for Additional Unredacted Filing Under Seal. A person making a redacted filing may also file an unredacted copy under seal. The court must retain the unredacted copy as part of the record.

(g) Option for Filing a Reference List. A filing that contains redacted information may be filed together with a reference list that identifies each item of redacted information and specifies an appropriate identifier that uniquely corresponds to each item listed. The list must be filed under seal and may be amended as of right. Any reference in the case to a listed identifier will be construed to refer to the corresponding item of information.

(h) Waiver of Protection of Identifiers. A person waives the protection of Rule 49.1(a) as to the person's own information by filing it without redaction and not under seal.

Rule 50. Prompt Disposition

Scheduling preference must be given to criminal proceedings as far as practicable.

Rule 51. Preserving Claimed Error

(a) Exceptions Unnecessary. Exceptions to rulings or orders of the court are unnecessary.

(b) Preserving a Claim of Error. A party may preserve a claim of error by informing the court—when the court ruling or order is made or sought—of the action the party wishes the court to take, or the party's objection to the court's action and the grounds for that objection. If a party does not have an opportunity to object to a ruling or order, the absence of an objection does not later prejudice that party. A ruling or order that admits or excludes evidence is governed by Federal Rule of Evidence 103.

Rule 52. Harmless and Plain Error

(a) Harmless Error. Any error, defect, irregularity, or variance that does not affect substantial rights must be disregarded.

(b) Plain Error. A plain error that affects substantial rights may be considered even though it was not brought to the court's attention.

Rule 53. Courtroom Photographing and Broadcasting Prohibited

Except as otherwise provided by a statute or these rules, the court must not permit the taking of photographs in the courtroom during judicial proceedings or the broadcasting of judicial proceedings from the courtroom.

Rule 54. [Transferred[1]]

Rule 55. Records

The clerk of the district court must keep records of criminal proceedings in the form prescribed by the Director of the Administrative Office of the United States courts. The clerk must enter in the records every court order or judgment and the date of entry.

Rule 56. When Court Is Open

(a) In General. A district court is considered always open for any filing, and for issuing and returning process, making a motion, or entering an order.

(b) Office Hours. The clerk's office—with the clerk or a deputy in attendance—must be open during business hours on all days except Saturdays, Sundays, and legal holidays.

(c) Special Hours. A court may provide by local rule or order that its clerk's office will be open for specified hours on Saturdays or legal holidays other than those set aside by statute for observing New Year's Day, Martin Luther King, Jr.'s Birthday, Washington's Birthday, Memorial Day, Independence Day, Labor Day, Columbus Day, Veterans' Day, Thanksgiving Day, and Christmas Day.

---

[1]   All of Rule 54 was moved to Rule 1.

Rule 57. District Court Rules

(a) In General.

(1) Adopting Local Rules. Each district court acting by a majority of its district judges may, after giving appropriate public notice and an opportunity to comment, make and amend rules governing its practice. A local rule must be consistent with—but not duplicative of—federal statutes and rules adopted under 28 U.S.C. § 2072 and must conform to any uniform numbering system prescribed by the Judicial Conference of the United States.

(2) Limiting Enforcement. A local rule imposing a requirement of form must not be enforced in a manner that causes a party to lose rights because of an unintentional failure to comply with the requirement.

(b) Procedure When There Is No Controlling Law. A judge may regulate practice in any manner consistent with federal law, these rules, and the local rules of the district. No sanction or other disadvantage may be imposed for noncompliance with any requirement not in federal law, federal rules, or the local district rules unless the alleged violator was furnished with actual notice of the requirement before the noncompliance.

(c) Effective Date and Notice. A local rule adopted under this rule takes effect on the date specified by the district court and remains in effect unless amended by the district court or abrogated by the judicial council of the circuit in which the district is located. Copies of local rules and their amendments, when promulgated, must be furnished to the judicial council and the Administrative Office of the United States Courts and must be made available to the public.

Rule 58. Petty Offenses and Other Misdemeanors

(a) Scope.

(1) In General. These rules apply in petty offense and other misdemeanor cases and on appeal to a district judge in a case tried by a magistrate judge, unless this rule provides otherwise.

(2) Petty Offense Case Without Imprisonment. In a case involving a petty offense for which no sentence of imprisonment will be imposed, the court may follow any provision of these rules that is not inconsistent with this rule and that the court considers appropriate.

(3) Definition. As used in this rule, the term "petty offense for which no sentence of imprisonment will be imposed" means a petty offense for which the court determines that, in the event of conviction, no sentence of imprisonment will be imposed.

(b) Pretrial Procedure.

(1) Charging Document. The trial of a misdemeanor may proceed on an indictment, information, or complaint. The trial of a petty offense may also proceed on a citation or violation notice.

(2) Initial Appearance. At the defendant's initial appearance on a petty offense or other misdemeanor charge, the magistrate judge must inform the defendant of the following:

(A) the charge, and the minimum and maximum penalties, including imprisonment, fines, any special assessment under 18 U.S.C. § 3013, and restitution under 18 U.S.C. § 3556;

(B) the right to retain counsel;

(C) the right to request the appointment of counsel if the defendant is unable to retain counsel—unless the charge is a petty offense for which the appointment of counsel is not required;

(D) the defendant's right not to make a statement, and that any statement made may be used against the defendant;

(E) the right to trial, judgment, and sentencing before a district judge—unless:

> **(i)** the charge is a petty offense; or

> **(ii)** the defendant consents to trial, judgment, and sentencing before a magistrate judge;

(F) the right to a jury trial before either a magistrate judge or a district judge—unless the charge is a petty offense;

(G) any right to a preliminary hearing under Rule 5.1, and the general circumstances, if any, under which the defendant may secure pretrial release; and

(H) that a defendant who is not a United States citizen may request that an attorney for the government or a federal law enforcement official notify a consular officer from the defendant's country of nationality that the defendant has been arrested—but that even without the defendant's request, a treaty or other international agreement may require consular notification.

(3) Arraignment.

(A) Plea Before a Magistrate Judge. A magistrate judge may take the defendant's plea in a petty offense case. In every other misdemeanor case, a magistrate judge may take the plea only if the defendant consents either in writing or on the record to be tried before a magistrate judge and specifically waives trial before a district judge. The defendant may plead not guilty, guilty, or (with the consent of the magistrate judge) nolo contendere.

(B) Failure to Consent. Except in a petty offense case, the magistrate judge must order a defendant who does not consent to trial before a magistrate judge to appear before a district judge for further proceedings.

(c) Additional Procedures in Certain Petty Offense Cases. The following procedures also apply in a case involving a petty offense for which no sentence of imprisonment will be imposed:

(1) Guilty or Nolo Contendere Plea. The court must not accept a guilty or nolo contendere plea unless satisfied that the defendant understands the nature of the charge and the maximum possible penalty.

(2) Waiving Venue.

(A) Conditions of Waiving Venue. If a defendant is arrested, held, or present in a district different from the one where the indictment, information, complaint, citation, or violation notice is pending, the defendant may state in writing a desire to plead guilty or nolo contendere; to waive venue and trial in the district where the proceeding is pending; and to consent to the court's disposing of the case in the district where the defendant was arrested, is held, or is present.

(B) Effect of Waiving Venue. Unless the defendant later pleads not guilty, the prosecution will proceed in the district where the defendant was arrested, is held, or is present. The district clerk must notify the clerk in the original district of the defendant's waiver of venue. The defendant's statement of a desire to plead guilty or nolo contendere is not admissible against the defendant.

(3) Sentencing. The court must give the defendant an opportunity to be heard in mitigation and then proceed immediately to sentencing. The court may, however, postpone sentencing to allow the probation service to investigate or to permit either party to submit additional information.

(4)   Notice of a Right to Appeal. After imposing sentence in a case tried on a not-guilty plea, the court must advise the defendant of a right to appeal the conviction and of any right to appeal the sentence. If the defendant was convicted on a plea of guilty or nolo contendere, the court must advise the defendant of any right to appeal the sentence.

(d)   Paying a Fixed Sum in Lieu of Appearance.

(1)   In General. If the court has a local rule governing forfeiture of collateral, the court may accept a fixed-sum payment in lieu of the defendant's appearance and end the case, but the fixed sum may not exceed the maximum fine allowed by law.

(2)   Notice to Appear. If the defendant fails to pay a fixed sum, request a hearing, or appear in response to a citation or violation notice, the district clerk or a magistrate judge may issue a notice for the defendant to appear before the court on a date certain. The notice may give the defendant an additional opportunity to pay a fixed sum in lieu of appearance. The district clerk must serve the notice on the defendant by mailing a copy to the defendant's last known address.

(3)   Summons or Warrant. Upon an indictment, or upon a showing by one of the other charging documents specified in Rule 58(b)(1) of probable cause to believe that an offense has been committed and that the defendant has committed it, the court may issue an arrest warrant or, if no warrant is requested by an attorney for the government, a summons. The showing of probable cause must be made under oath or under penalty of perjury, but the affiant need not appear before the court. If the defendant fails to appear before the court in response to a summons, the court may summarily issue a warrant for the defendant's arrest.

(e)   Recording the Proceedings. The court must record any proceedings under this rule by using a court reporter or a suitable recording device.

(f)   New Trial. Rule 33 applies to a motion for a new trial.

(g)   Appeal.

(1)   From a District Judge's Order or Judgment. The Federal Rules of Appellate Procedure govern an appeal from a district judge's order or a judgment of conviction or sentence.

(2)   From a Magistrate Judge's Order or Judgment.

(A)   Interlocutory Appeal. Either party may appeal an order of a magistrate judge to a district judge within 14 days of its entry if a district judge's order could similarly be appealed. The party appealing must file a notice with the clerk specifying the order being appealed and must serve a copy on the adverse party.

(B)   Appeal from a Conviction or Sentence. A defendant may appeal a magistrate judge's judgment of conviction or sentence to a district judge within 14 days of its entry. To appeal, the defendant must file a notice with the clerk specifying the judgment being appealed and must serve a copy on an attorney for the government.

(C)   Record. The record consists of the original papers and exhibits in the case; any transcript, tape, or other recording of the proceedings; and a certified copy of the docket entries. For purposes of the appeal, a copy of the record of the proceedings must be made available to a defendant who establishes by affidavit an inability to pay or give security for the record. The Director of the Administrative Office of the United States Courts must pay for those copies.

(D) Scope of Appeal. The defendant is not entitled to a trial de novo by a district judge. The scope of the appeal is the same as in an appeal to the court of appeals from a judgment entered by a district judge.

(3) Stay of Execution and Release Pending Appeal. Rule 38 applies to a stay of a judgment of conviction or sentence. The court may release the defendant pending appeal under the law relating to release pending appeal from a district court to a court of appeals.

Rule 59. Matters Before a Magistrate Judge

(a) Nondispositive Matters. A district judge may refer to a magistrate judge for determination any matter that does not dispose of a charge or defense. The magistrate judge must promptly conduct the required proceedings and, when appropriate, enter on the record an oral or written order stating the determination. A party may serve and file objections to the order within 14 days after being served with a copy of a written order or after the oral order is stated on the record, or at some other time the court sets. The district judge must consider timely objections and modify or set aside any part of the order that is contrary to law or clearly erroneous. Failure to object in accordance with this rule waives a party's right to review.

(b) Dispositive Matters.

(1) Referral to Magistrate Judge. A district judge may refer to a magistrate judge for recommendation a defendant's motion to dismiss or quash an indictment or information, a motion to suppress evidence, or any matter that may dispose of a charge or defense. The magistrate judge must promptly conduct the required proceedings. A record must be made of any evidentiary proceeding and of any other proceeding if the magistrate judge considers it necessary. The magistrate judge must enter on the record a recommendation for disposing of the matter, including any proposed findings of fact. The clerk must immediately serve copies on all parties.

(2) Objections to Findings and Recommendations. Within 14 days after being served with a copy of the recommended disposition, or at some other time the court sets, a party may serve and file specific written objections to the proposed findings and recommendations. Unless the district judge directs otherwise, the objecting party must promptly arrange for transcribing the record, or whatever portions of it the parties agree to or the magistrate judge considers sufficient. Failure to object in accordance with this rule waives a party's right to review.

(3) De Novo Review of Recommendations. The district judge must consider de novo any objection to the magistrate judge's recommendation. The district judge may accept, reject, or modify the recommendation, receive further evidence, or resubmit the matter to the magistrate judge with instructions.

Rule 60. Victim's Rights

(a) In General.

(1) Notice of a Proceeding. The government must use its best efforts to give the victim reasonable, accurate, and timely notice of any public court proceeding involving the crime.

(2) Attending the Proceeding. The court must not exclude a victim from a public court proceeding involving the crime, unless the court determines by clear and convincing evidence that the victim's testimony would be materially altered if the victim heard other testimony at that proceeding. In determining whether to exclude a victim, the court must make every effort to permit the fullest attendance possible by the victim and must consider reasonable alternatives to exclusion. The reasons for any exclusion must be clearly stated on the record.

(3) Right to Be Heard on Release, a Plea, or Sentencing. The court must permit a victim to be reasonably heard at any public proceeding in the district court concerning release, plea, or sentencing involving the crime.

(b) Enforcement and Limitations.

(1) Time for Deciding a Motion. The court must promptly decide any motion asserting a victim's rights described in these rules.

(2) Who May Assert the Rights. A victim's rights described in these rules may be asserted by the victim, the victim's lawful representative, the attorney for the government, or any other person as authorized by 18 U.S.C. § 3771(d) and (e).

(3) Multiple Victims. If the court finds that the number of victims makes it impracticable to accord all of them their rights described in these rules, the court must fashion a reasonable procedure that gives effect to these rights without unduly complicating or prolonging the proceedings.

(4) Where Rights May Be Asserted. A victim's rights described in these rules must be asserted in the district where a defendant is being prosecuted for the crime.

(5) Limitations on Relief. A victim may move to reopen a plea or sentence only if:

(A) the victim asked to be heard before or during the proceeding at issue, and the request was denied;

(B) the victim petitions the court of appeals for a writ of mandamus within 10 days after the denial, and the writ is granted; and

(C) in the case of a plea, the accused has not pleaded to the highest offense charged.

(6) No New Trial. A failure to afford a victim any right described in these rules is not grounds for a new trial.

Rule 61. Title

These rules may be known and cited as the Federal Rules of Criminal Procedure.

APPENDIX D

PENDING AMENDMENTS TO THE FEDERAL RULES OF CRIMINAL PROCEDURE

■ ■ ■

[These amendments to Rules 12.4, 45 and 49 were approved by the Supreme Court on April 26, 2018, and were forwarded to Congress. They will take effect December 1, 2018, unless Congress enacts legislation to reject, modify or defer them.]

Rule 12.4. Disclosure Statement

(a) Who Must File.

(1) Nongovernmental Corporate Party. Any nongovernmental corporate party to a proceeding in a district court must file a statement that identifies any parent corporation and any publicly held corporation that owns 10% or more of its stock or states that there is no such corporation.

(2) Organizational Victim. Unless the government shows good cause, it must file a statement identifying any organizational victim of the alleged criminal activity. If the organizational victim is a corporation, the statement must also disclose the information required by Rule 12.4(a)(1) to the extent it can be obtained through due diligence.

(b) Time to File; Later Filing. A party must:

(1) file the Rule 12.4(a) statement within 28 days after the defendant's initial appearance; and

(2) promptly file a later statement if any required information changes.

Rule 45. Computing and Extending Time

* * * * *

(c) Additional Time After Certain Kinds of Service. Whenever a party must or may act within a specified time after being served and service is made under Rule 49(a)(4)(C), (D), and (E), 3 days are added after the period would otherwise expire under subdivision (a).

Rule 49. Serving and Filing Papers

(a) Service on a Party.

(1) What is Required. Each of the following must be served on every party: any written motion (other than one to be heard ex parte), written notice, designation of the record on appeal, or similar paper.

(2) Serving a Party's Attorney. Unless the court orders otherwise, when these rules or a court order requires or permits service on a party represented by an attorney, service must be made on the attorney instead of the party.

(3) Service by Electronic Means.

(A) Using the Court's Electronic-Filing System. A party represented by an attorney may serve a paper on a registered user by filing it with the court's electronic-filing system. A party not represented by an attorney may do so only if allowed by court order or local rule. Service is complete upon filing, but is not effective if the serving party learns that it did not reach the person to be served.

(B) Using Other Electronic Means. A paper may be served by any other electronic means that the person consented to in writing. Service is complete upon transmission, but is not effective if the serving party learns that it did not reach the person to be served.

(4) Service by Nonelectronic Means. A paper may be served by:

(A) handing it to the person;

(B) leaving it:

(i) at the person's office with a clerk or other person in charge or, if no one is in charge, in a conspicuous place in the office; or

(ii) if the person has no office or the office is closed, at the person's dwelling or usual place of abode with someone of suitable age and discretion who resides there;

(C) mailing it to the person's last known address—in which event service is complete upon mailing;

(D) leaving it with the court clerk if the person has no known address; or

(E) delivering it by any other means that the person consented to in writing—in which event service is complete when the person making service delivers it to the agency designated to make delivery.

(b) Filing.

(1) When Required; Certificate of Service. Any paper that is required to be served must be filed no later than a reasonable time after service. No certificate of service is required when a paper is served by filing it with the court's electronic filing system. When a paper is served by other means, a certificate of service must be filed with it or within a reasonable time after service or filing.

(2) Means of Filing.

(A) Electronically. A paper is filed electronically by filing it with the court's electronic-filing system. A filing made through a person's electronic-filing account and authorized by that person, together with the person's name on a signature block, constitutes the person's signature. A paper filed electronically is written or in writing under these rules.

(B) Nonelectronically. A paper not filed electronically is filed by delivering it:

(i) to the clerk; or

(ii) to a judge who agrees to accept it for filing, and who must then note the filing date on the paper and promptly send it to the clerk.

(3) Means Used by Represented and Unrepresented Parties.

(A) Represented Party. A party represented by an attorney must file electronically, unless nonelectronic filing is allowed by the court for good cause or is allowed or required by local rule.

(B) Unrepresented Party. A party not represented by an attorney must file nonelectronically, unless allowed to file electronically by court order or local rule.

(4) Signature. Every written motion and other paper must be signed by at least one attorney of record in the attorney's name—or by a person filing a paper if the person is not represented by an attorney. The paper must state the signer's address, e-mail address, and telephone number. Unless a rule or statute specifically states otherwise, a pleading need not be verified or accompanied by an affidavit. The court must strike an unsigned paper unless the omission is promptly corrected after being called to the attorney's or person's attention.

(5) Acceptance by the Clerk. The clerk must not refuse to file a paper solely because it is not in the form prescribed by these rules or by a local rule or practice.

(c) Service and Filing by Nonparties. A nonparty may serve and file a paper only if doing so is required or permitted by law. A nonparty must serve every party as required by Rule 49(a), but may use the court's electronic-filing system only if allowed by court order or local rule.

(d) Notice of a Court Order. When the court issues an order on any post-arraignment motion, the clerk must serve notice of the entry on each party as required by Rule 49(a). A party also may serve notice of the entry by the same means. Except as Federal Rule of Appellate Procedure 4(b) provides otherwise, the clerk's failure to give notice does not affect the time to appeal, or relieve—or authorize the court to relieve—a party's failure to appeal within the allowed time.